GIAMBATTISTA DELLA PORTA
DRAMATIST

Giambattista Della Porta
Dramatist

By LOUISE GEORGE CLUBB

PRINCETON UNIVERSITY PRESS
PRINCETON, NEW JERSEY
1965

The portrait of Della Porta on the title-page is from *Jo. Bapt. Portae Neapolitani Magiae naturalis libri XX . . .* , Naples, 1589.

Publication of this book has been aided by
the Ford Foundation program to support publication,
through university presses, of works in the
humanities and social sciences

Printed in the United States of America
by H. Wolff Book Mfg. Co.

To My Parents

Acknowledgments

I WISH to thank the Columbia University Department of English and Comparative Literature and the American Association of University Women for enabling me to incur the obligations here acknowledged:

In Naples to Fausto Nicolini, to Alfredo Simari and Antonio Laurino of the Biblioteca Nazionale, to Dora Marra Beth of the Istituto Italiano per gli Studi Storici, and to Rodolfo Permutti and his colleagues in the Mathematics Department of the University.

In Rome to the staff of the Biblioteca dell'Accademia dei Lincei, and to the staff of the Biblioteca del Vaticano.

In Florence to Messrs. Baglioni, Cotogni, and Manzuino of the Biblioteca Nazionale, to Anna Maria Crinò of the University, and to Vasco Ronchi of the Istituto Nazionale di Ottica at Arcetri.

In London to Dennis Rhodes of the British Museum, and in Cambridge to the librarians of St. John's College, Trinity College, and the University Library.

In Washington, D.C., to Louis B. Wright of the Folger Library for the richness of its collection and the innumerable services done me by its staff and visiting scholars.

Especially I thank the late Fred S. Tupper of The George Washington University for helping me to begin this project, Benjamin Hunningher of Columbia University and James G. McManaway of the Folger Library for helping me to end it, Edward D. Sullivan of Princeton University for naming it, and Harriet Anderson of the Princeton University Press for steering it into print.

My greatest and most deeply felt debts are to Marjorie Hope Nicolson, Professor Emeritus of Columbia University and presently member of the Institute for Advanced Study at Princeton and Maurice Valency of Columbia University for guiding me along the way with enormous learning, taste, and patience, and to my husband for doing the same and immeasurably more.

Contents

Contents

Introduction

THE two greatest tourist attractions of Naples about the year 1600 were, according to contemporary report, the baths at Pozzuoli and Giambattista Della Porta.[1] Certainly Della Porta was one of the most famous men in Italy. The Emperor Rudolph and the Duke of Florence sent embassies, and the Duke of Mantua came in person to see the Neapolitan wonder-worker who had penetrated the secrets of nature and was expected at any moment to discover the philosopher's stone. He could count as friends, admirers, or detractors the most learned men of his time—Kepler, for example, and Sarpi, Bodin, Campanella, Peiresc, and Galileo. The literate world knew the results of Della Porta's investigations, experiments, and speculations through his heterogeneous publications, from the earliest edition of his *Magiae naturalis* (Neapoli, 1558) to *De aëris transmutationibus* (Romae, 1610), the last of his scientific works printed in his lifetime. He wrote on cryptography, horticulture, optics, mnemonics, meteorology, physics, astrology, physiognomy, mathematics, and fortification, and when he died at eighty, he was preparing a treatise in support of his claim to the invention of the telescope. In his spare time, Della Porta wrote plays.

Seventeen of them have survived: a tragicomedy, a sacred tragedy, a secular tragedy, and fourteen comedies. This hobby was more important than he could have foreseen, for while modern historians of science consider Della Porta an interesting curiosity, historians of the drama regard him as the foremost Italian comic playwright of his time. Despite the condescending interest of the former and the admiration of the latter, however, Della Porta has been neglected by scholars. Although the *Magiae naturalis* and *De humana phys-*

---

[1] Bartolomeo Chioccarelli, *De illustribus scriptoribus qui in civitate et regno Neapolis ab orbe condito ad annum usque MDCXXXXVI, floruerunt* (Neapoli, 1780), 314.

iognomonia went into many editions and translations, and individual comedies were reprinted in Italy, adapted abroad in the seventeenth century, and are still occasionally included in modern anthologies of Italian drama, there has never been a complete edition of Della Porta's works, scientific or dramatic. Moreover, although for more than three centuries he has been the subject of paragraphs or chapters in encyclopedias, histories of science, literature, or drama, as well as of articles and pamphlets, there exists no definitive biography, no detailed analysis of the plays, no itemized account of their fortunes abroad. Instead, a great mass of fragmentary information and misinformation has waited to be sifted. The present study is an attempt to weld the sound pieces into a coherent synopsis of Della Porta's life, dramatic works, and influence, to indicate valuable sources and to suggest areas—and reasons—for further investigation.

Scraps of biographical material about Della Porta are to be found in the dedications and prologues to some of his works, in the many poems and epigrams addressed to him by such admirers as Bernardino Rota, the Cavalier Marino, and Giambattista Basile, in contemporary memoirs, compilations of witty sayings, collections of emblems, and above all in the two extant batches of Della Porta's correspondence: the first with Cardinal Luigi d'Este between 1579 and 1586, the second with his fellow members of the Accademia dei Lincei from 1603 until his death twelve years later. The first account of Della Porta's life was the deliberately misleading *précis* designed by the Lincei to give his memory an odor of orthodoxy, then left unpublished till the twentieth century. The Linceo manuscripts and the Este correspondence were not available to Giovanni Imperiali, Bartolomeo Chioccarelli, or Lorenzo Crasso, compilers of seventeenth-century biographical dictionaries in which brief biographies of Della Porta were first published. Pompeo Sarnelli appended to his translation of Della Porta's unpublished *Chirofisonomia* a biographical chapter based on documents furnished by Della

Introduction

Porta's descendants, Domenico and Niccolò di Costanzo. These four accounts, together with the general Neapolitan chronicles of Giovanni Antonio Summonte and Antonio Bulifon became the standard sources of information about Della Porta for historians of the next century.

In the early nineteenth century an increase of interest in Della Porta was reflected by the pamphlets of Henri Duchesne, Francesco Colangelo, Giovanni Palmieri, and Giuseppe Rossi, none of which, however, produced any important results. Later in the century, new discoveries were made, and articles written which remain valuable today. Francesco Fiorentino, the author of one of the best, attributed the resurgence of interest in Della Porta to Luigi Settembrini's urging his younger colleagues to study the neglected figures of the late Renaissance.[2] Fiorentino's research was facilitated by Giuseppe Campori's discovery of the Della Porta - Luigi d'Este correspondence and by Camillo Minieri-Riccio's publication of Della Porta's will.

At the beginning of our century new details about Della Porta's family were discovered by Gaetano Parascandalo and by Vincenzo Spampanato. Perhaps the largest contribution to knowledge of Della Porta's life was made by the archivists of the Accademia dei Lincei, especially Giuseppe Gabrieli, who between 1925 and 1940 compiled the best Della Porta bibliography to date, regularly published new fragments of knowledge, and ended by discovering the missing manuscript of *De telescopio*. In recent years one or another aspect of Della Porta's scientific career has attracted the attention of such historians of science as Gioacchino Paparelli, Mario Gliozzi, Vasco Ronchi, Lynn Thorndike, and George Sarton.

Della Porta's striking reputation as a scientist for so long

---

[2] "Del teatro di Giovan Battista de la Porta," *Giornale napoletano di filosofia e lettere, scienze morali e politiche*, Nuova serie, Anno II, Vol. III, fasc. 7 (marzo 1880), reprinted in *Studi e ritratti della Rinascenza* (Bari, 1911), 294.

obscured his greater significance as a dramatist that his early biographers were usually content merely to list his plays without comment. Even after Gennaro Muzio published the only complete edition of the comedies in 1726, eighteenth-century historians of literature like Girolamo Tiraboschi paid more attention to the scientific works. But Tiraboschi also praised the plays and helped to spread the mistaken notion that Della Porta wrote them in his last years. Subsequently, Pietro Napoli-Signorelli repeated the error, warmly praising Della Porta as one of the few good playwrights of the seventeenth century. Napoli-Signorelli's high opinion is the more valuable for being based on acquaintance not only with the comedies but with the three verse plays as well—an acquaintance shared by few other scholars in any century. No new observations on Della Porta the dramatist were made until the middle of the nineteenth century, when Julius Leopold Klein devoted some fifty pages of his voluminous history to an analysis of three Della Portean comedies, concluding that their author had improved the Seicento *imbroglio* by means of his well-organized scientific mind and understanding of psychology and political intrigue.

The renewal of interest in Della Porta's life in the late nineteenth century was extended to his plays. Eugenio Camerini hailed him as the worthiest of Goldoni's precursors, especially admiring Della Porta's adaptation of *commedia dell'arte* figures to learned comedy. Fiorentino added to his biographical summary two short but very valuable articles on the drama. Having obtained the sole known copy of *Penelope*, one of the two extant copies of *Ulisse*, and the manuscript of *Georgio*, Fiorentino described these three verse dramas, attempted to date the comedies, and succeeded at least in proving that many of them were not seventeenth- but sixteenth-century works. A few years later, Benedetto Croce discovered a printed copy of *Georgio*, and in the course of general research on Neapolitan literature and history, Croce turned up and published other useful items about Della Porta's theater, and also took part in the flurry of controversy about his relation to the *commedia dell'arte*.[3] To the north, interest in Della Porta was growing as a result of Arthur Ludwig Stiefel's and Joseph Vianey's investigations of his influence on Rotrou and Tristan L'Hermite. In our time further information about adaptations of Della Porta's comedies abroad has been supplied by Joseph Bolton, D. J. Gordon, and Hugh G. Dick.

Della Porta studies were launched in the twentieth century by Francesco Milano's long article, which attempted a classification of the comedies and established many of their Latin and earlier Italian sources. In the following decade Vincenzo Spampanato undertook a modern edition of the comedies, but issued only eight, without notes or prefaces. Abridgements of two of them appeared in a theatrical journal, following Anton Giulio Bragaglia's production of *La Cintia* at the Teatro delle Arti in 1940.

Some of the best work on Della Porta's theater is to be found in general histories of Italian literature or drama. Luigi Tonelli has emphasized Della Porta's sense of theater, Mario Apollonio and Marvin Herrick his blending of *commedia erudita* with *commedia dell'arte*. Attilio Momigliano likens Della Porta's florid imagination to Shakespeare's and classifies him with Bruno, Tasso, and Guarini as representative of the pre-baroque style, adding that these four transitional figures are more important to Italian literature than those whose way they prepared. Perhaps the most useful discussion of Della Porta's comedy is that of Ireneo Sanesi in his history of the genre in Italy. Recently, articles by Giorgio Pullini and Antonio Corsano have offered analyses, respectively, of Della Porta's prose style and of his intellectual characteristics revealed in both the scientific works and the comedies. Although no one has yet undertaken a

[3] See Appendix B for an account of this controversy.

complete study of Della Porta's comedy, various scholars have prepared the way for one. The non-comic dramas, however, have been generally ignored.

The characteristics invariably pointed out by admirers of the comedies are their expert construction and rich mixtures of learned with popular elements, and of sentiment with hilarity. The language is praised lavishly by some scholars, criticized by others, and has caused many to overestimate the baroque element in Della Porta's dramas. Whatever individual disagreements there may be, however, the scholarly consensus is that if the single masterpieces of Machiavelli and Bruno are excepted, Della Porta's are the best Italian comedies before Goldoni's.

On the periphery of Della Porta scholarship are the enthusiasts who have from time to time associated him with their doomed or dubious causes. Certain portions of the *Magiae naturalis* have caused his name to be invoked by spiritualists. A somewhat more respectable association was the department of Lombrosian criminal anthropology christened Gabinetto-Scuola di Antropologia Criminale "Giambattista della Porta," established at the University of Naples in 1917. Because of his *De humana physiognomonia* and *Chirofisonomia* Della Porta was regarded by the director and his colleagues as the Italian grandfather of their science and was extensively eulogized in the departmental journal, *Anomalo*. The department is no more, but the bust of Della Porta commissioned for its inauguration still ornaments the university. A decade later Della Porta became the patron saint of Neapolitan photographers when his claim to the invention of the camera obscura was defended against an attack in the Vicentine *Rivista fotografica italiana*. But however such manifestations may have spread Della Porta's fame, they added nothing to the miscellany of facts from which the following biographical sketch is constructed.

GIAMBATTISTA DELLA PORTA DRAMATIST

Della Porta's Life

Giovanni Battista was the third of Nardo Antonio Della Porta's four sons, and the second of the three who survived childhood. The boys' mother was a Neapolitan patrician, sister to Adriano Guglielmo Spadafora (or Spatafora), learned *conservator quinternionum* of the Naples archives from 1536.[1] The Della Portas claimed a family tree planted in the time of Hannibal. It flourished later in the person of the Lombard prince Adalferio, whose descendants held important positions in Salerno, Vico Equense, and Naples.[2] The main branch of the family, established in Salerno, was considered noble from the beginning of Angevine rule in the thirteenth century, but the subsidiary line from which Nardo's father, Ferdinando, sprang seems to have been less exalted.[3] Father and son are referred to in various documents, however, as *magnifici*,[4] a

[1] Francesco Fiorentino, *Studi e ritratti della Rinascenza* (Bari, 1911), 238, a reprinting of "Della vita e delle opere di Giovan Battista de la Porta," *Nuova Antologia*, Serie II, XXI (Roma, maggio 1880), 251–284. Della Porta's eldest brother, Francesco, who died in childhood, is mentioned only by Luigi Amabile, *Fra Tommaso Campanella, la sua congiura, i suoi processi e la sua pazzia* (Napoli, 1882), 33. Spadafora's fame as an antiquarian and collector is mentioned by Carlo Celano, *Notizie del bello, dell'antico e del curioso della città di Napoli . . .* (Napoli, 1692), I, 110.

[2] Giuseppe Gabrieli, "Giovan Battista Della Porta Linceo," *Giornale critico de filosofia italiana*, VIII, fasc. 1 (1927), 423; and Vincenzo Spampanato, "I Della Porta ne' *Duoi fratelli rivali*," *Anomalo* (Napoli, 1918), 199.

[3] Amabile noted that an established noble family would not have needed the privileges bestowed by Charles on the Neapolitan Della Portas (*. . . Campanella . . . congiura . . .*, 33, note b).

[4] Gaetano Parascandolo, *Notizie autentiche sulla famiglia e sulla patria di Giovanni Battista della Porta* (Napoli, 1903), 14.

term often used to denote untitled property owners of good birth.

Nardo Antonio's considerable wealth comprised land and ships. He once leased three vessels to Charles V, and together with his father and three uncles, received from the emperor in 1548 the formal status of familiar or court domestic, exemption from all tribunals but the *Collaterale,* and the right to maintain armed followers. From 1541 Nardo Antonio held the office of *Scrivano di Mandamento* or royal secretary for civil appeals to the vicariate, in which he was succeeded by his eldest surviving son, Gian Vincenzo.[5] Like many other petty nobles of the time, some of the Della Portas lost their fortunes in 1551 by supporting the unsuccessful anti-Spanish rebellion of Ferrante Sanseverino, prince of Salerno,[6] but Nardo Antonio must have cherished more profitable sympathies, for the Spanish viceroy never revoked his privileges nor deprived the family of the office which Gian Vincenzo held for many years.

The Neapolitan branch of the Della Portas had three domiciles: a town house in Via Toledo near the Piazza Carità, in that aromatic hive known today as Napoli vecchia but forming then the most elegant central section of the city; a villa in Due Porte, a tiny hamlet in the hills immediately to the northwest of Naples; and another, more magnificent, villa at Vico Equense. This little paradise on the sea, twelve miles south of the city, had been from the time of the Angevine kings a favored summer resort of aristocratic Neapolitans, who followed the example of Charles II by spending lavishly on local improvements. In the sixteenth century it became the site of the printing presses of Giovanni Cacchio, Carlino e Pace, and Orazio Salviani, from which issued learned texts in some of the most beautiful editions of the period. The Villa delle Pradelle at Vico Equense may well have been the actual birthplace of Giambattista and his brothers, for although he

[5] Gabrieli, "G. B. Della Porta . . . ," 423–24.
[6] Spampanato, "I Della Porta . . . ," 200.

always signed himself "napoletano" it appears that all his life Della Porta exercised rights in Vico Equense's church politics permitted only to native-born landowners.[7]

For many years the date of Della Porta's birth was, owing to his own mis-statements, a controversial subject, providing material for numerous little scholarly notes and articles and resulting in the playwright-scientist's being considered in some quarters a monster of unscientific inaccuracy, and in others a congenital liar. The preface to the first edition of *Magiae naturalis* gives an impression of experience and wisdom, but in the preface to the second edition of 1589, Della Porta stated that he was then fifty and that he had first published the book at fifteen. The earliest known edition, however, is that of 1558. In 1612 he wrote to Cardinal Borromeo that his *Taumatologia* contained the labors of seventy-seven years.[8] Della Porta was, in fact, seventy-seven at this time, but since even Hercules could hardly have begun such intellectual labors in the cradle, some scholars have been misled by his statement to think that he was eighty-five when he died in 1615, a misconception carelessly launched by Prince

[7] Parascandolo, *op.cit.*, 11ff. This neglected study of church records by the pastor of the parish church of SS. Cino e Giovanni in Vico Equense notes that citizens of towns tributary to Naples customarily had their children baptized in the capital so as to secure for them certain municipal privileges granted by Charles V. The most popular church for the ceremony was San Giovanni Maggiore, accounting for the great number of Neapolitan Christian names prefixed by "Giovanni" or "Gian," as in the case of the Della Porta brothers. Since Giambattista's heirs were excluded from the right of nominating rectors and chaplains in Vico Equense on grounds of Neapolitan birth, it might be concluded that Giambattista's simultaneous exercise of these rights in Vico Equense and of those of citizenship in Naples resulted from his birth in the former and baptism in the latter. The conclusion seems valid, even though it contradicts Carlo Celano's statement that Della Porta was born in Via Toledo, (*op.cit.*, I, 7), where there is a plaque bearing the same information, perhaps on Celano's authority.

[8] Gabrieli, "Bibliografia Lincea. I. Giambattista Della Porta. Notizia bibliografica dei suoi mss. e libri, edizioni, ecc., con documenti inediti," *Rendiconti della R. Accademia Nazionale dei Lincei. Classe di scienze morali, storiche, e filologiche*, Serie 6, VIII (Roma, 1932), 268.

Cesi in 1625.[9] Even the date of his death was temporarily cast
in doubt by a stonecutter's error in lettering the family tomb.
Such discrepancies and the equivocation in Della Porta's own
account are responsible for Gabrieli's and Duchesne's dating
his birth 1538 and 1545, respectively, and for Guiscardi's
dating his death 1610.[10] Now that Gioacchino Paparelli has
persuasively marshaled the arguments for dating Della
Porta's birth between October 3 and November 15, 1535,[11]
there remains in question only the reason for the mystery. It
is likely that Della Porta's conflicting statements about his
age were dictated less by forgetfulness or sheer inability to
tell the truth than by his instinct for showmanship in presenting an image of himself to the world, and in part by the necessity of self-defense. He loved secrets and ceremony, enjoyed mystifying the public, and cultivated a remarkable
variety of interests, some of which were frowned on by the
Inquisition. Had the Holy Office not threatened, or had he
not felt the Renaissance urge to be, or at least seem to be,
simultaneously as many things as possible, he might have
spared himself his unsynchronized attempts to appear now
more precocious, now more mature than he actually was.

Circumstances more than half determined Della Porta's
choice of a many-faceted *persona* for himself, by providing
him with a wonderfully broad education. Nardo Antonio
had a taste for learning, and so delighted in the company of
philosophers, mathematicians, poets, and musicians that his
house in Naples became a veritable academy.[12] In hot weather
the erudite society was probably transported down the coast

[9] Gabrieli, "G. B. Della Porta . . . ," 428.

[10] Gabrieli, "Bibliografia . . . Della Porta," 227; [Henri Gabriel
Duchesne], *Notice historique sur la vie et les ouvrages de J. B. Porta,
gentilhomme napolitain* (Paris, An. IX 1800–1801), 5; and Roberto
Guiscardi, . . . *MDCXV(?)* (n.p., 1885?).

[11] "La data di nascita di Giambattista Della Porta," *Vita italiana*, IV
(Buenos Aires, 1955), 14–15.

[12] Gabrieli, "G. B. Della Porta . . . ," 424.

to the Villa delle Pradelle, as Giambattista's learned circle of friends was to be in later years. In this intellectual ambience Gian Vincenzo, Giambattista, and Gian Ferrante were reared, stimulated by celebrated visitors and tutored by permanent members of the group. Giambattista's lifelong devotion to his maternal uncle, and the similarity between their minds and methods observed by Bernardino Rota [13] suggest that Spadafora supervised his nephew's education, which included the usual humanistic curriculum but emphasized mathematics and medicine. Della Porta's first biographer, Pompeo Sarnelli, skims over the early years of schooling by remarking that in boyhood the future playwright and scientist shone in literary studies, composing admirable orations in Latin and the vernacular after he had mastered rhetoric and poetics, and excelled in "natural philosophy," substituting his own speculations wherever the opinions of his masters struck him as commonplace.[14] Among these masters were Domenico Pizzimenti, classicist and alchemist, Donato Antonio Altomare and Giovanni Antonio Pisano, philosophers and doctors active in Naples during Della Porta's youth. The last of these, who was also public lecturer in applied medicine from 1557 to 1585 and attracted capacity crowds,[15] is praised by Della Porta in the dedication of *De refractione* (1593) to Pisano's son, Ottavio. Possibly Della Porta also attended lectures by the adventurous physician Girolamo Cardano, who roamed the peninsula, expounding his wild and brilliant theories at every university which received him. Although the University of Naples was not officially established until 1581, there were *scuole pubbliche* fostering science, to which

[13] *Delle poesie . . . colle annotazioni di Scipione Ammirato sopra alcuni sonetti* (Napoli, 1737), 206. First edition 1572.

[14] "Vita di Gio: Battista Della Porta," in *Della Chirofisonomia*, trans. . . . (Napoli, 1677), A7verso.

[15] Gabrieli, "Spigolature Dellaportiane," *Rendiconti . . .*, Serie 6, XI (Roma, 1936), 492; and Amabile, . . . *Campanella . . . congiura . . .*, 35, note a.

the young experimenter progressed when his private instruction ended, and where he could have heard Cardano.[16] But while *Magiae naturalis* XVII, 15, indicates that Della Porta knew and disagreed with some of Cardano's teachings, there is no proof of personal acquaintance between them.

Gian Vincenzo, Giambattista, and Gian Ferrante were all deeply interested in music, and refused to allow a total lack of talent for it to impede their progress in theory at the Scuola di Pitagora, an exclusive academy of musicians,[17] who were apparently sufficiently impressed by sheer intellectual power to receive into their midst the trio of tone-deaf young mathematicians.

Had Nardo Antonio intended to rear his sons as professional scholars, applied music would not have been introduced into their curriculum. But the Della Portas were too much aware of social position to think in terms of professions or specialization; Giambattista and his brothers struggled vainly to carry a tune because singing was a courtly accomplishment, and they were being trained as courtiers, i.e., as learned gentlemen with the emphasis on GENTLEMEN. To this end they were taught to dress well, to dance, to ride, and to take part in tournaments and other games. Such training inculcated in Della Porta a lasting taste for public finery and noble company, despite the natural inclination which later led him in his private life to play the part of the other-worldly scholar, unathletic and carelessly dressed.

The only one of his youthful recreations which left a mark on his career was the drama. Spurred on by Ferrante Sanseverino's patronage of private theatricals as well as of professional troupes,[18] wealthy Neapolitans of Nardo Antonio's

[16] Lorenzo Crasso, *Elogii di huomini letterati* (Venetia, 1666), I, 170. Crasso said Della Porta followed in the footsteps of Arnaldo di Villanuova and Cardano, but he may have referred only to the undoubted influence of their works.

[17] Gabrieli, "G. B. Della Porta . . . ," 424.

[18] Giovanni Antonio Summonte, *Historia della città e regno di Napoli*, 2ª ed. (Napoli, 1675), IV, 235.

generation delighted in dressing up and reciting comedies for each other. The incomplete records of Neapolitan academies offer only hints about the literary milieu in which Giambattista grew up. The scientific brotherhood of the Segreti is the only sixteenth-century academy with which the Della Portas have been linked by historians of these societies. But on the fragmentary membership lists of mid-century academies, the names of Neapolitan literary lions are frequently mingled with those of Della Porta's teachers and of families to whom he was bound by friendship or marriage. Before its dissolution in 1543, the Accademia Pontaniana included Bernardino Rota,[19] the leading Neapolitan poet of his generation, who later addressed a poem jointly to Della Porta and his uncle, A. G. Spadafora.[20] Probably Rota was one of the early *distinti letterati* in Spadafora's own academy, of which little is known save that it still existed in 1589.[21] Until 1580 the poet Giovanni Battista Rinaldi presided over a club which held summer meetings at the Carafa villa in Vico Equense.[22] Proof of Giambattista's later association with the Carafas and the proximity of their estates suggests that the Della Portas were among Rinaldi's acquaintance. Through Rota and G. A. Pisano, they may also have been connected with the poet Angelo di Costanzo and with the Sereni, the Eubolei, and the Ardenti, three of the many academies suppressed by the viceroy in 1547 and 1548, in retribution for Neapolitan objections to the Spanish Inquisition.[23]

Rota and di Costanzo both wrote comedies,[24] and one of the latter's fellow members in the Accademia degl'Incogniti,

[19] Camillo Minieri-Riccio, "Cenno storico delle accademie fiorite in Napoli," *Archivio storico per le province napoletane* v, fasc. II (Napoli, 1880), 364.

[20] See page 7, note 13.

[21] Minieri-Riccio, *op.cit.*, v, fasc. III, 603.

[22] *Ibid.*, v, fasc. II, 370.

[23] *Ibid.*, v, fasc. III, 590; IV, fasc. I, 172–174; and IV, fasc. III, 520.

[24] Benedetto Croce, *I teatri di Napoli. Secolo XV–XVIII* (Napoli, 1891), 47–8, 49. Croce's source was Minturno's *Arte poetica* (Venetia, 1564), Lib. II, 66, 114.

Giovanni Domenico di Lega,[25] was the author of a very early sacred tragedy.[26] Possibly these were among the first examples of drama set before the young Della Porta. In spite of the difficulty of dating the composition of most of his dramatic works, it is safe to suppose that he first tried his hand at playwriting in boyhood, and that some of his published comedies were revisions of scripts he originally produced for the amateur players among his family and friends, a conclusion supported by several of his contemporaries' later references to Della Porta's literary precocity. The first of his comedies, *L'Olimpia*, was published in 1589 but composed in "i suoi primi anni," according to Pompeo Barbarito. Regrettably, the editor did not specify which years he meant. The earliest possible date for the play is 1550.

In that year Della Porta was fifteen, the age at which he claims to have published the first edition of the *Magia*. In the absence of an edition to substantiate the claim, however, and despite the twisting and turning of his words and dates by scholars who wish to avoid impugning his veracity, it seems necessary either to agree with Edward Rosen that Della Porta was quite willing to lie in order to pass himself off on the public as a *wunderkind*,[27] or to assume that he hoped to excuse as youthful errors certain magic formulae in the book which first attracted the Inquisition's attention to him. But although the *Magiae* was not printed until Della Porta was twenty-three, it is very probable that at fifteen he was already experimenting with chemicals, herbs, and magnets, and collecting the occult rumors which make up the first version of this remarkable work. His classics master, Pizzimenti, later privately claimed to be the author of the original *Magiae*.[28] But whatever aid he may have received, Della Porta was uni-

[25] Minieri-Riccio, *op.cit.*, IV, fasc. III, 528.

[26] Lione Allacci, *Drammaturgia . . . accrescuita e continuata fino all'anno MDCCLV* (Venezia, 1755), 539.

[27] *The Naming of the Telescope* (New York, 1947), 15 *passim*.

[28] Nicolas Guibert, *De interitu alchymiae metallorum transmutatoriae tractatus aliquot . . .* (Tulli, 1614), 134.

versally credited with the work. The years of his young manhood, of which even less is known than of other parts of his long, poorly documented life, were probably the most untroubled he was ever to enjoy, for the clouds that were to settle permanently over him later had not appeared and could not appear until they had been set in motion by the disquieting reputation he was now in the process of acquiring.

In this pleasant period perhaps occurred the youthful love affair recorded by Giulio Cesare Capaccio. Once involved, Della Porta felt that he had been incautious and determined to fall out of love. Either his will power was strong or his love weak, for he succeeded, then celebrated his release by inventing an *impresa:* a butterfly breaking out of a cocoon, with the motto, *Et feci et fregi.*[29] His own man once more, Giambattista could return to the laboratory.

He was not working alone. Gian Vincenzo followed the example of their uncle in building a collection of books, statues, and ancient marbles. His interest lay more in the library than the laboratory, and he put his classical learning at the disposal of his experimenting younger brother.[30] The elder was more proficient in the art of astrology, which fascinated them both, and it has been suggested that he taught Giambattista much of what he knew, especially about the classical methods of prognostication. There was great love between the two, and the marked taste Giambattista displayed all his life for working in fellowship was undoubtedly fostered not only by the atmosphere of his father's circle, but also by the long and fruitful association with his quiet, learned elder brother. The youngest, Gian Ferrante, shared the others' interests, but before fame touched the family he died, leaving behind an excellent collection of crystals and geological specimens as a monument to his scholarly pursuits.

[29] *Delle imprese trattato . . . in tre libri diviso* (Napoli, 1592), I, 39verso–40.
[30] Crasso, *op.cit.*, 171.

About the time of his death the Della Porta fortunes dwindled a bit, necessitating the sale of Gian Ferrante's collection.[31]

The financial crisis may have been precipitated by expenditures in the name of learning. The mysterious and undoubtedly costly academy of the Segreti was formed probably before Della Porta's first travels, during the period when he was collecting material and preparing his first published work. Each aspirant to the academy, which met in its founder's home, was required to discover a secret of nature unknown to the rest of mankind.[32] To judge by some of the harebrained fictions Della Porta published as scientific revelations, the emphasis was on *meraviglia* rather than on empirical proof. Nevertheless, the founder's pride in his academy was justified, for the joint experiments of its members produced many of the valid observations of phenomena in physics, optics, and botany which appear in the greatly augmented second edition of the *Magiae*. It is not known whether or not the Segreti were organized before 1558, in time to contribute to the first edition, that shorter and less scientific potpourri of magic.[33]

While his experiments proceeded apace, Della Porta turned another part of his mercurial mind to an interest that lay out-

[31] Gabrieli, "G. B. Della Porta . . . ," 429.

[32] *Magiae naturalis libri viginti* (Neapoli, 1589), preface. The 1558 edition in four books and the augmented 1589 edition in twenty will henceforth be distinguished as *Magiae*$_1$ and *Magiae*$_2$, respectively.

[33] Derek Price, in his introduction to the facsimile edition of the anonymous English translation, *Natural Magick* (London, 1658), facsimile (New York, 1957), v; and Martha Ornstein in *The Role of Scientific Societies in the Seventeenth Century*, 3d ed. (Chicago, 1938), 74, state that the Segreti and the Oziosi were one and the same group. George Sarton in *Six Wings: Men of Science in the Renaissance* (Bloomington, 1957), 87, declared that the Segreti were organized in 1560 and the Oziosi somewhat earlier. Actually, there is no proof of when the Segreti began, and the Oziosi, which was not a scientific but a literary academy, was organized in 1611. See Antonio Bulifon, *Giornali di Napoli dal MDXLVII al MDCCVI, Vol. I, 1547-1691* (Napoli, 1932), 91.

side the laboratory. The art of cryptography appealed to his love of mystery, and since its use in diplomatic dispatches provided a practical demand for a work on the subject, he found it worth his while to make a compilation of cipher systems. Published in 1563, *De furtivis literarum* added greatly to his growing fame. By 1564 he was so well-known as to be included among the celebrities whose witty sayings were being collected by Lodovico Domenichi for the sixth edition of his *Facetie*.[34]

About this time Della Porta began to travel. In Spain he presented Philip II with his book on ciphers. If the gift was in printed form, it may be assumed that Della Porta traveled out of Italy in 1563 or 1564. But as he took with him also the third edition of the *Magiae* (Antwerp, 1561), with a three-line dedication to King Philip added as a politic after-thought,[35] the trip may have begun in 1561, when *De furtivis literarum* was still in manuscript. His preface to the *Magiae* recalls that wherever he went in France and Spain he sought out learned men and libraries, buying books as his means permitted and gathering new "secrets." Known by reputation as a promising mathematician, doctor, and philosopher, he was well received by the Spanish king, a fact which added to his prestige at home in Spanish-ruled Naples, and which may have helped him through later difficulties with the authorities. Like the date, the itinerary of this journey is unknown. Della Porta also traveled extensively in Italy; his *Villae* reveals the author's familiarity with Calabria, Puglia, and Sicily, while at least one of his sojourns in the north is illuminated by a little batch of letters from, to, and about Della Porta in the Este family archives.[36]

By 1566, to judge from the publication in Naples that year

[34] *Della scelta de motti, burle facetie di diversi signori, et d'altre persone private*. Libri sei. 6ª ed. (Fiorenza, 1566), 88. Domenichi died in 1564, leaving material to be added to the sixth edition.

[35] Gabrieli, "G. B. Della Porta . . . ," 425.

[36] Giuseppe Campori, ed., *Giovan Battista della Porta e il cardinale Luigi d'Este, notizie e documenti* (Modena, 1872).

of his *Arte del ricordare*, he was at home again. The breadth of Della Porta's interests and the number of subjects which he had staked out for conquest explain his personal concern with cultivation of the memory. He wrote the treatise either in order to organize methods for his own improvement, or to increase his fame by sharing the means which had already proved successful with him. He was, of course, not unaware that the subject was currently in vogue. Della Porta clearly did not have a photographic memory, but his talent for categorizing and organizing enabled him to use mnemonic devices with high efficiency. The book was written in Latin but was not published in its original version until 1602. The first edition was in the translation of Dorandino Falcone da Gioia, obviously a pseudonym, perhaps of the author himself.

L'arte del ricordare testifies to Della Porta's continued interest in the drama, by its references to the importance of good memory to players, and its lists of mnemonic ways to remember the difficult names of Plautus's characters. Della Porta was composing plays during the 1560's and 1570's but he sent only his non-dramatic works to the printer. *La turca* contains a reference to "quest' anno del settantadue" (II, 3); there is every possibility that Della Porta wrote this comedy in 1572 and that he was producing other works of this genre, for in 1578 Giovanni Matteo Toscanò hailed him as a flower of Italian literature.[37] Evidently his three published works were not the only bids for fame he had made so far; he could hardly have gained a name for literary talent with his books on natural magic, cryptology, and mnemonic devices.

It is possible that Toscanò chose to praise Della Porta with the poets rather than with the investigators of hidden truth, out of fear of seeming to approve studies which had become

[37] *Peplus Italiae . . . In quo illustres viri grammatici, oratores, historici, poëtae, mathematici, philosophi, medici, iurisconsulti (quotquot trecentis ab hinc annis tota Italia floruerunt) eorumque patriae, professiones, & litterarum monumenta tum carmine tum soluta oratione recensentur* (Lutetiae), Lib. IV, 116.

suspect. For at this time occurred a hair-raising event in Della Porta's life, one that was to influence everything else in it, from his scientific aims to his daily habits. It inevitably caused suppression of facts and dissemination of lies by his family and friends, perhaps deliberate destruction of letters, and left to posterity as a record of his life only fragments of a colorful mosaic.

The cataclysm was a brush with the Inquisition. It was only that—nothing to compare with the horrors in store for Campanella, Bruno, and the other unfortunates who could not or would not abandon their research or alter their views to suit the censors. But it was enough to frighten Della Porta, to make him modify his investigations and conceal the incident as much as possible.

No one knows exactly when it happened. A record made by the notary Joele in 1580 of Inquisitional activities before that year notes "Item: le ripetitioni per Gio:battista dela porta," referring to the re-examination of testimony required by Rome in all inquisitional trials. Amabile declared that imprisonment in Rome ordinarily preceded such re-examination, and that if Giuseppe Valleta, in his study of the Holy Office in Naples, neglected to mention any incarceration in his brief account of Della Porta's sentence, it was because Valletta was less concerned with accuracy than with expounding his thesis that the Neapolitan Inquisition's function was primarily preventive, not punitive.[38] The trial and probable imprisonment must, in any case, have taken place before November 1579, for by that date Della Porta was in Naples, free to accept Cardinal Luigi d'Este's invitation to join him in Rome.[39] The immediate cause of Della Porta's being haled before the Inquisition was a denunciation by some fellow Neapolitans who were scandalized by his growing reputation

[38] *Il S. Officio della Inquisizione in Napoli* (Città di Castello, 1892), I, 326f. The work of Valletta referred to is in manuscript at the Biblioteca Nazionale of Naples, Codice x.

[39] Campori, *op.cit.*, 7.

for magic and by the titles of *Indovino* and *Mago* bestowed on him by the populace.[40] Both Giambattista and Gian Vincenzo were adept at casting horoscopes, and the former had, in addition, a pretty knack for prophecy. He neither took all comers nor charged fees, and he believed in his prophecies. When they proved true, as they quite often did, no one doubted that it was due to the occult knowledge he had acquired in his workroom. Magic was a passion with Della Porta. If it was later modified for a time by external pressures, the passion never left him, not even in the last years of his life.

The denunciation must have been made between 1558, when Della Porta's first work appeared, and 1578, when Toscanò praised his poetry. Apparently not wanting to omit so famous a name from his roster of celebrities, yet recognizing the imprudence of lauding the forbidden lore on which the fame was based, Toscanò compromised by praising Della Porta only for his literary hobby, though he had never published a line of poetry or drama. However uncertain the date, the watchdogs of the true faith surely snapped at him. Della Porta was summoned before the tribunals in Naples and Rome, perhaps briefly imprisoned, and charged by papal order to disband his academy and refrain from practicing illicit arts. As a parting shot, the Neapolitan tribunal commanded him to write a comedy.[41] Corsano suggests that the judges knew Della Porta's reputation as an amateur playwright and therefore advised him, half sardonically, half indulgently, to stick to his plays.[42] This sort of literary recommendation was not uncommonly issued from the inquisitional bench. Luigi Tansillo was once brought into court for mak-

---

[40] Bulifon, *op.cit.*, 98. Fiorentino's opinion (*op.cit.*, 258) that the trouble was sparked by Bodin's attack in 1581 is proved invalid by Amabile's discovery that the trial antedated 1580.

[41] Amabile, *Il S. Officio* . . . , 327, note 1.

[42] Antonio Corsano, "G. B. Della Porta," *Giornale critico della filosofia italiana*, Terza serie, Anno XXXVIII, fasc. 1, (gennaio-marzo 1959), 80.

ing offensive jokes in his *Vendemmiatore*, and was ordered to make reparation by writing a comedy and re-working his unfinished Christian epic, *Le lacrime di San Pietro*.

The papal order disbanding the Segreti has never come to light, but the academy did cease functioning, and in the *Magiae₂* preface is referred to as a thing long past. Sarnelli reported, without evidence, that when Della Porta was called to Rome to account for his writings, the inquisitors were vastly impressed by his learning, and when he had satisfactorily proved that his secrets were all "natural," he was given an official commendation and was feted by the leading local prelates.[43] Almost certainly this story is part of the whitewash posthumously spread on Della Porta's name by his family and associates. That he himself refers only obliquely to his clash with the Inquisition, and that his friends felt it necessary to publish pious lies about him at his death testify to the truth of Lorenzo Crasso's observation in 1666 that Della Porta had suffered anguish of soul when he was forced first to defend, then to recant his opinions.[44] The Inquisition had not finished with him entirely—this was never to be—but for the time being he was let off with a warning. Soon afterward, he joined the Jesuit lay congregation and began to distinguish himself by zealous performance of religious duties, spending one day a week on works of charity.[45]

Fear of imprisonment, torture, or death was not the only possible motive for Della Porta's immediate submission to the Inquisition. The temper of his mind must be considered. He was never much interested in theological or philosophical speculation. His own words prove his preference for studying sensible objects:

. . . nam disputationes de naturae principiis, de vacuo, de generatione, et corruptione, et eiusmodi talia, quia longe a nostro sensu remota sunt, maximisque ambagibus involuta, non ita animum

---

[43] *Op.cit.*, 29.
[44] *Op.cit.*, 172.
[45] Gabrieli, "G. B. Della Porta . . . ," 424.

oblectant, ut ad eorum indagationem curiosum virum contor-
queant.[46]

Always concerned with the immediate, the tangible, he often
even lost enthusiasm for his own discoveries and experiments
after observing the basic spectacular fact and completing the
concrete part of the investigation. Since it was precisely
speculation that the Inquisition considered most dangerous
to the faith, there was little likelihood of Della Porta's becoming at its hands a martyr to free thought. Moreover,
there was little honor attached to such martyrdom. Francesco
Fiorentino, a true child of the nineteenth century, barely hid
his disgust at Della Porta's failure to join the glorious ranks
of those who suffered for science, liberty of conscience, and
other noble concepts yet unhatched in the sixteenth century,[47] but the fact is that the ranks did not seem glorious
then. As Jefferson B. Fletcher observed of the Counter-
Reformation period, "orthodoxy was a pride of caste"[48] and
Della Porta, who dearly loved a lord, not to mention pomp,
circumstance, and ritual, and who was indeed a Catholic by
nature, may well have regarded heretics as many Anglicans
regarded Dissenters. There have always existed Catholics
who recognize that the church can be wrong, but agree that
it would be ill-bred to say so. In late sixteenth-century Italy,
under Spanish influence, the majority of educated people
shared this attitude. No wonder, then, that Della Porta submitted to the commands of the Inquisition and avoided pub-
licizing his encounter with the tribunal.

Between 1566 and 1583 he published nothing, but his experiments continued, and his fame grew fat on the reports of
those who visited the Academy of the Segreti in its heyday.

[46] *De aëris transmutationibus* (Romae, 1610), proemio. (. . . for debates about the first principles of nature, the void, generation, corrup-
tion, and such matters, because they are greatly confused obscurities
and far beyond our powers of perceiving, do not so delight the spirit
as to turn the inquisitive man to their investigation.)

[47] *Studi* . . . , 268.

[48] *Literature of the Italian Renaissance* (New York, 1934), 22.

The result was the offer of a connection very valuable to a scientist under the surveillance of the Inquisition and in need of financial backing for his experiments: Cardinal Luigi d'Este, who upheld the tradition of his family by patronizing learning, and who, because of the Estensi's battle with the papacy over Ferrara, was perhaps sympathetic toward scholars suspected by the Roman Inquisition, heard enthusiastic praise of Della Porta from his own doctor, Teodosio Panizza. He wrote to the Neapolitan marvel in November 1579, inviting him to join the Este household in Rome.[49] In addition to money and protection, the cardinal's invitation offered the possibility of angling at close quarters for the offices of Papal Engineer or Papal Secretary of Ciphers, either of which would have done much to rehabilitate Della Porta's reputation for orthodoxy. He accepted the offer with alacrity and arrived in Rome within two months. His Maecenas, sojourning at Tivoli, sent orders that the new dependent be lodged in Palazzo d'Este and supplied with money. The majordomo, Tolomeo, settled the learned newcomer in the apartments of Dr. Panizza, who had not accompanied his patron to Tivoli. This arrangement satisfied Della Porta well enough, but poor Panizza began to regret his earnest recommendation of the great wizard.

The discommoded doctor's letters to the cardinal provide rare details of one side of Della Porta's personality. Blaming the trouble on Tolomeo's bad managements, Panizza complained that his social life had been demolished by the habits of the southern genius, who insisted on going to bed immediately after dinner, rose very early and noisily to study before breakfast, and demanded that total silence be maintained whenever he was working or sleeping. This excessive and antisocial concentration on study does not match the picture others have drawn of Della Porta as a gregarious host and inspired conversationalist, but his moods were doubtless as

[49] All correspondence between members of the Este households referred to in the following six paragraphs is from Campori, *op.cit.*, 7–26.

varied as his interests, and though he preached moderation, he tended toward extremes. At one period in his life he was even taken with a notion for absolute solitude, and almost decided to retire permanently with his books to the Island of Ponza,[50] even today a wild, if lovely, retreat.

As he began his service with Luigi d'Este, Della Porta had better reasons than usual for working hard. He wanted a position at the papal court; another of Panizza's complaints was that Della Porta continually harped on the possibility of the cardinal's helping him to one of the desired offices. Utilizing every means to advancement, Della Porta sent his patron plays along with reports on his experiments. One of the cardinal's letters acknowledges receipt of a comedy and tragicomedy, and announces his intention of having the former staged. Such valuable bits of evidence about the dating of the plays are all too rare.

Life in Luigi d'Este's household had its drawbacks, especially when the master was away. Tolomeo was a scrupulous but unimaginative administrator, who could not understand why the resident inventor needed more than the daily twelve *baiocchi* allotted to ordinary dependents. The ill-treated but faithful Panizza had to write several times to the cardinal in Tivoli and Ferrara before Della Porta received the necessary increase in allowance. Any reluctance the prelate might have felt to disburse additional amounts to his protégé was overcome by Panizza's report that during a bout of tertian fever, Della Porta had refused 150 ducats offered by Cardinal Orsini, assuring the solicitous prince that excellent care was provided him in the Este establishment.

Della Porta's susceptibility to fever was only one of the physical weaknesses which plagued him all his long life. But he bore illness well and turned his suffering to profit when he could, by studying his symptoms and trying out his own medicines. His prescriptions were famous but not always successful; a remedy for the "stone," published in the *Magiae*[2],

[50] Gabrieli, "G. B. Della Porta . . . ," 425.

never cured the physician himself of that ailment. Fever kept him in Rome in August and September 1580, preventing him from obeying the cardinal's summons to join him in Venice. When Della Porta at last was strong enough to travel he left Rome on October 1, and reached Venice on December 1. Luigi d'Este wrote to Panizza that Della Porta had arrived in good health but that there had been no word from him on the road. Panizza could offer no explanation, and Della Porta never revealed where he had spent the two months. In all likelihood, he had done nothing more sinister than to travel slowly, stopping to visit scholars and libraries along the way. It was characteristic of the *Mago*, however, to make a mystery of his journey, by his reticence implying any number of occult commitments. Luigi d'Este, in the hope of profiting from Della Porta's astrological and alchemical lore, may have been impressed by his portentous silence. At any rate, the cardinal asked no questions.

Settled in Venice for the time being, Della Porta began work on a parabolic mirror and an "occhiale." The latter was probably a large magnifying or burning glass, or perhaps an experiment in eyeglasses. Campori believed that it was a telescope, hoping to connect the project at Venice with the widespread belief that Della Porta was the original inventor of the telescope. Cardinal d'Este returned alone to Rome, but Della Porta kept him informed of all progress. He was delighted to have at his disposal the skilled glassworkers in the environs of Venice, and reported on November 29, 1580, that with the help of Giacomo Contarini he had found an artisan of Murano capable of constructing the delicate mirror. But if the Venetian craftsmen pleased him, the *aria grossa* of the lagoons did not, and he blamed it for the new attack of fever which now forced him to bed. Again a Panizza came to the rescue, this time the brother of Teodosio, one Alessandro, who on learning of Della Porta's indisposition, awakened him at three A.M. to transfer him bag and baggage from rented lodgings to the Panizza home, where a proper cure might be effected. When the cardinal returned to Ferrara, he sent for Della Porta, but the eager lens-designer was loath to leave his Murano project. He used bad weather and his own illness to excuse the delay. Finally, with rather bad grace, he agreed to leave Venice, in December 1580, but his love of secrecy was outraged by having to reveal his plans to Contarini and to leave the lens-grinding under his supervision.

In February 1581, Della Porta was still with the cardinal in Ferrara. The Este court had for three generations boasted a brilliant literary circle. Della Porta could hardly have avoided meeting Tasso and Guarini; the prologue to *Penelope* suggests contact with the latter and all three of Della Porta's verse dramas reflect the influence of Tasso and of the earlier Ferrarese lion, G. B. Giraldi Cinthio.[51] But the only record of Della Porta's visit to the city is a business letter he wrote to Pietro Burghetti, ordering some property in Naples to be sold. Perhaps the sale was necessitated by Luigi d'Este's failure to finance Della Porta, but there was no lessening of cordiality between them, even after the Neapolitan at last went home in April 1581. Later the same year, when the cardinal made a triumphant entry into Rome, ending a temporary exile imposed on him and winning a round in the Este-Vatican battle, Della Porta sent his patron warm congratulations, accompanied by some carnation conserve, good for plague, falling sickness, vertigo, poison, and animal bites. This useful remedy was made from Della Porta's own recipe, tested in his laboratory and guaranteed efficient. The cardinal responded with an invitation to Tivoli.

In the following year the versatile experimenter perfected a process for extracting beechnut oil and created a sensation with his demonstration before the Reggente de Cancelleria, by order of the Spanish viceroy. He boasted to Teodosio Panizza in September 1582 that his discovery was the talk of the town and was unsurpassed in importance by any other in the world. Apparently he did not realize the commercial

[51] See Chapter v, p. 126ff.

value of his "secret" until he had already published it. Upon receiving belated bids from merchants, he admitted, with rarely revealed chagrin, "Sia maladetta la mia disgratia che dopo fatto lo matrimonio vengano mille mariti." [52] Advised of his protégé's latest success. Cardinal d'Este promised to help him obtain the equivalents of patents on his process in the various cities where it might be used.

The cardinal, however, like the Dukes of Mantua and Tuscany, the Holy Roman Emperor, and all the aristocratic angels who smiled on the famous *Mago* at one time or another, was more interested in distilled gold than in beechnut oil, and must have congratulated himself on his investment when he heard through Panizza that Della Porta was on the verge of discovering the *lapis philosophorum*. Della Porta's own excitement about it reduced him almost to babbling. His epistolary style was usually breezy and informal, sometimes to the point of rudeness, although the prose of his scientific and dramatic works is as fulsomely elegant as a well-performed sarabande, but when he thought himself on the verge of achieving the highest aim of alchemy, words temporarily failed him, and he repeated stupidly that "È la più bella cosa che sia in terra" and "spero essere il più felice che sia in terra." [53] His hopes were delayed by quarrels, domestic troubles, and a steady stream of visitors, Neapolitans and foreigners, who flocked to the informal academy in Della Porta's house, kept him from sleeping, drove him to desperation, and worst of all, prevented him from testing his new secret. Meanwhile he cherished the untried recipe, which he had learned from one Angelo Siciliano, who learned it from a friend, who learned it from a Spanish doctor, who learned it from a French monk. Della Porta's burst of interest in the subject was most timely, coinciding with the furor caused

[52] (Cursed be my misfortune that after the wedding a thousand suitors appear.)

[53] (It is the most beautiful thing on earth . . . I hope to be the happiest man on earth.)

all over Europe by the case of Sebastian Siebenfreund, murdered in Wittenberg for reputedly knowing the secret of the philosophers' stone.[54] Cardinal d'Este snapped at Della Porta's news and invited him to Rome posthaste, but apparently when the tests were made they yielded nothing, for the ecstatic alchemist dropped the matter and pleaded hot weather as an excuse for staying at home.

Although his attempts to find the philosophers' stone were abortive, his other projects were literally bearing fruit. At one or both of his villas, Della Porta planted orchards for experiments in grafting, cross-breeding, and other "secrets" of plant cultivation. In 1583 he published *Pomarium*, a treatise on fruit-growing, followed the next year by *Olivetum*, on tree culture. Both were later included in his larger treatment of agriculture, *Villae* (1592). It usually took at least two years after a manuscript's completion to license it for printing, so *Pomarium* and *Olivetum* must have been ready by 1581 and 1582, respectively. Unlike his elder brother, who took so long to write *De emendatione temporum* that Scaliger was able to publish the material first,[55] Giambattista composed rapidly, and by May of 1583 he had finished another book, parts of which, however, may have been ready as early as 1581. This was *De humana physiognomonia*, possibly his most famous and certainly one of his most curious works. He announced its completion to Cardinal d'Este, adding with some bitterness that the licensing would probably take longer than the writing.[56]

This book reflects Della Porta's passion for categorizing and his belief in a system of signs whereby the unity of creation is manifested. Supposedly originating with Orpheus and flourishing in innumerable Renaissance scientific and literary works, the Doctrine of Signatures, interpreting the virtues of plants by their outward characteristics, was essential to Della

[54] Fiorentino, *op.cit.*, 250.
[55] Amabile, . . . *Campanella . . . congiura . . .* , 34.
[56] Campori, *op.cit.*, 26.

Portean thought. His discussion in the *Magiae*$_2$ (I, II) has been cited as the definitive exposition of the doctrine as understood in his time and in the succeeding century.[57] In the *Physiognomonia* the principle is applied to sentient life in the thesis that physical traits shared by animals and men are indices to their characters. Comparing the faces of a sheep and a sheeplike man, Della Porta observes that the wide, strongly defined mouth common to both indicates stupidity and impiety (II, 16). He agrees with Aristotle that fleshy faces denote laziness, and illustrates the point with parallel figures of a man and a cow who look like brother and sister (II, 10).

In the course of expounding this ingenious and absurd system, Della Porta describes himself, adapting the facts to his classical ideal of the golden mean. He says he is of medium height and weight, his brow moderately high, his dark hair moderately curly, his face of medium sharpness, his eyebrows symmetrical, and his voice moderately loud. Only the admission that his eyes are deep and bright agrees with contemporary portraits which unanimously show him with a sharply thin face, long irregular nose, and unusually high forehead.

The *Physiognomonia* was finally published in 1586, with a dedication to Luigi d'Este. The censors' unusually long delay is not hard to explain. Since the additions of Pope Paul IV to the *Index* in 1559, all the arts of divination, physiognomy specifically included, had been under official fire.[58] The reasoning behind the church's attack may be deduced from Della Porta's defense, which denied fixed destiny and reaffirmed individual responsibility. Divining human character was not far removed from soothsaying, and to suppose that internal qualities depend on external features was tantamount to a denial of free will. Under the influence of classical lit-

[57] Hazel A. Stevenson, "The Major Elizabethan Poets and the Doctrine of Signatures," *Florida State University Studies*, No. 5 (1952), II, 15.

[58] Lynn Thorndike, *A History of Magic and Experimental Science*, VI (New York, 1941), 147.

erature in the Renaissance the idea of *fortuna* or Fate had gradually been separated from the Christian concept of divine providence. Simultaneously, the strangle hold exerted by judiciary astrology on the minds of peasant and scholar alike threatened to choke belief in free will. Alarmed, Counter-Reformation popes encouraged attack on astrology. The bulls of Sixtus V in 1585 and 1586 outlawed fortunetelling by means of chiromancy, physiognomy, or other arts.[59] The accusation of determinism was to plague Della Porta for some time to come. He tried to avoid it at this point, perhaps at the censors' command, by affixing to the *Physiognomonia* a preface declaring that human features indicate only *tendencies,* and that the choice of following or resisting one's natural bent always rests with the individual conscience.

Meanwhile, Della Porta's interest in finding the philosophers' stone had not died; he seems in 1586 to have made some progress in his search, for in a letter congratulating Cardinal d'Este on recovery from an illness, the indefatigable alchemist promised to visit his patron two months hence, in August, bringing with him the secret of the stone, if possible. Less than two weeks later, in another characteristically careless letter to the cardinal, dated June 27, Della Porta betrayed great depression. Obviously as busy as ever, he still planned to visit Rome and to deliver two new books to the licensers: the *Phytognomonica*, or physiognomy of plants, and *Magnalia naturae*, Della Porta's current title for his augmented edition of *Magiae naturalis.* He announced that the former contained over 2000 secrets, the fruit of research so extensive that the human mind could go no further.[60] The more famous *Magiae*$_2$ is an even stranger book, combining valuable observations of physical phenomena, including a detailed description of Della Porta's re-invention of the camera obscura, and chapters on magnetism, farming, and Empedoclean atomism with notes on compounding cosmetics, charms, love

[59] *Ibid.*, v (1941), 68, 245; VI, 147.
[60] Campori, *op.cit.*, 26–27.

philtres, and practical jokes. Even in those unspecialized times such a miscellany appeared frivolous to more serious scientists, for whom Giovanni Francesco Sagredo spoke in remarking to Galileo that Della Porta's place among scholars was like that of church bells among musical instruments.[61]

But while, on one hand, Della Porta was more content with himself than any man is entitled to be, on the other he was in poor spirits. He wrote, speaking of his secrets,

Avea deliberato non farli vedere ad huomo e per gelosia che altri non gli sapesse e per dubbio di qualche maleficio che insegna. Adesso che mi sono venuti in fastidio con la vita insieme, darò lo libro a V.S. Ill. ma.[62]

Explanations of Della Porta's depression at this time can be conjectural only, and none has more authority than another. Three years earlier he had mentioned domestic troubles; Della Porta must have married sometime before his fortieth year, for he had adult grandsons when he was in his seventies. These were the children of his daughter Cinzia, who married Alfonso di Costanzo of Pozzuoli and survived her father. Colangelo supposed on slim evidence that Cinzia had a brother and sister who died young.[63] That Della Porta had nephews and cousins is stated in his will. Considering the communal arrangements preferred even today by Italian clans, it is quite probable that a fairly large number of Della Portas, Spadaforas, de Gennaros and di Costanzos lived at least part of each year under the Della Porta roof in Via Toledo. If the 1580's were the years in which marriages had to be arranged for the younger generation of Della Portas,

---

[61] Galileo Galilei, *Le Opere . . . ristampa della Edizione Nazionale*, ed. Antonio Favaro, XI (Firenze, 1934), letter 765, 398.

[62] Campori, *op.cit.*, 28. (I had decided not to show them to anyone, both from desire for secrecy and from fear of their teaching evil. Now that they, together with my life, disgust me, I will give the book to Your Most Illustrious Lordship.)

[63] F.C.S.D.O. [Francesco Colangelo, Sacerdote dell'Oratorio], *Racconto istorico della vita di Giovanni Battista Della Porta filosofo napolitano con un'analisi della sue opere stampate* (Napoli, 1813), 21,

their conflicting claims may have made Giambattista's life a *fastidio*. Perhaps his own marriage was unhappy or perhaps his wife died during this period, leaving him to shoulder domestic responsibilities alone.

But the unhappiness expressed in 1586 may equally well have sprung from other causes. Della Porta was never physically strong; his whole constitution must have been affected by long sieges of the fever to which he was susceptible. Perhaps he had already begun to suffer from the kidney ailments which were to torment him in old age. He was wont to say cheerfully that in illness he was expiating his sins,[64] apparently preferring immediate pain to that in the hereafter.

More distressing than family trouble or sickness to one of Della Porta's intellectually heterodox but religiously orthodox mind, however, was pressure from the ecclesiastical authorities. The scholastically trained minds of the censors had quickly perceived the ultimate danger of Della Porta's investigations of forbidden knowledge, especially judiciary astrology. After his censure by the Inquisition, he had found it difficult to obtain licenses for his books. Jean Bodin had attacked him as a sorcerer in 1581.[65] The authorities had forced him to wait three years for the printing of *Physiognomonia*. The divining arts which fascinated him had been denounced by the pope. Now, with two works in manuscript, Della Porta could foresee the licensing delays, perhaps the eventual impossibility of printing. The preface to the *Magiae*$_2$ of 1589 is the work of a man embattled. A brief apologia of his studious life, it contains Della Porta's famous statement that the first edition was published when he was fifteen. He may have hoped thereby to excuse some of the magic recipes, significantly omitted in the second edition. He accused Bodin of being a Huguenot, and declared himself an investigator of nature, denying that his title of *Mago* connoted occult powers. These were obviously attempts to placate the

[64] Gabrieli, "G. B. Della Porta . . . ," 428.
[65] *De magorum demonomania* (Basileae, 1581), Lib. II, Cap. II.

Inquisition, and they took a spiritual toll of the author. Would not any man who had just been forced to defend the reputation which was once his boast feel "in fastidio con la vita insieme"?

Della Porta fulfilled his promise to visit the cardinal in Rome in October 1586.[66] By 1588, when the *Phytognomonica* was published, he was again in Naples. The second edition of *Magiae naturalis* was at last published in Naples in 1589, a milestone year which saw also the printing of *L'Olimpia*, the first of Della Porta's plays to reach the press. The author was apparently not much excited by the latter event; Pompeo Barbarito, editor of the comedy, recounts Della Porta's reluctance to make public this "trifle" which had, however, been acclaimed at private performances. The production Barbarito singles out was a magnificent one staged for the Count of Miranda, current viceroy of Naples, but there had undoubtedly been earlier performances in Della Porta's familiar circle. The "reluctance" referred to was probably no more than the traditional gentlemanly deprecation of vernacular compositions, but it is not to be questioned that Della Porta was prouder of the *Magia* than of *L'Olimpia* and expected his true fame to come from works like the former, despite the latter's immediate popularity.

According to Amabile's dating of events in Tommaso Campanella's life, 1589 was the year in which the brilliant young Dominican first visited Naples, where he was introduced into the intellectual circle surrounding the Della Porta brothers, including Colantonio Stigliola, Giovanni Paolo Vernalione, and Marthos Gorostiola.[67] Della Porta, ordinarily proud of his learned acquaintances, left no trace in his published works or correspondence of the connection with

[66] Campori, *op.cit.*, 28.

[67] Pierre Gassendi, *The Mirrour of True Nobility and Gentility. Being the Life of the Renowned Nicolaus Claudius Fabricius, Lord of Peiresk, Senator of the Parliament at Aix.* Englished by W. Rand (London, 1657), 37; and Amabile, . . . *Campanella* . . . *congiura* . . . , 34.

Campanella. His silence must be interpreted as caution, and indeed anyone whom the Inquisition had already distinguished with a reproof was well-advised for his health's sake to minimize his association with the unfortunate friar from Calabria, whose heretical, anti-Aristotelian philosophy and ill-fated conspiracy earned him twenty-seven years of intermittent imprisonment. Campanella himself, however, reveals that he knew Della Porta fairly well and was influenced by the older philosopher's theories. In his *De libris propriis.* Cap. 1, art. 1, Campanella states that in 1590 he wrote *De sensu rerum:*

Ad istorum vero librorum *De sensu rerum* compositionem, movit me praesertim disputatio habita in Comitiis publicis, et seorsum Joannes Baptista Porta, qui scripserat Phythognomoniam, ubi sympathiae et antipathiae rerum dicebat non posse reddi rationem, quando simul suum librum excusum examinabamus.[68]

Elsewhere Campanella declares himself indebted to Della Porta for medical care when he was suffering an ocular inflammation. In a semi-public demonstration of his skill, Della Porta applied to Campanella's eyes a collyrium of his own concoction which immediately cured the affliction.[69]

Despite a paucity of evidence, it is clear that this ac-

[68] Quoted by Francesco Fiorentino, *Bernardino Telesio, ossia studi storici sull'idea della natura nel Risorgimento italiano,* II (Firenze, 1874), 111. Misreading of this passage has given rise to the idea that Della Porta and Campanella held a public dispute. Fiorentino (*Studi . . . ,* 263) even suggested that it was held in San Domenico Maggiore under the auspices of the Oziosi. But though they were informal gatherings earlier, the academy was not officially inaugurated until 1611, at which time Campanella was in prison. In any case, the above passage distinctly refers to two separate events: a public dispute between parties un-named, and a conversation between himself and Della Porta. (I was moved to write this book, *De sensu rerum,* chiefly by a debate held in a public hall, and especially by Joannes Baptista Porta, who wrote Pythognomonia, in which he said that the sympathy and antipathy of things cannot be explained, when we examined his printed book together.)

[69] *Medicinalium juxta propria principia* (Lugduni, 1635), lib. 6, cap. 6, 395.

quaintance offered Campanella literary as well as scientific associations. The only poet mentioned in Amabile's sketch of the group around Della Porta is Giulio Cesare Cortese.[70] This friendship alone would suffice to connect Della Porta with the main current of Neapolitan literary life. Although academies formed and dissolved as fast as snowflakes, their raw material remained more or less the same, and the fragmentary records of their appearances and disappearances often reveal hereditary patterns. In 1586, for example, Cortese formed the Svegliati with members of G. B. Rinaldi's defunct academy, convoking them in Thomas Aquinas' erstwhile lecture hall in the cloister of San Domenico Maggiore.[71] Between 1593, when the Svegliati were suppressed, and 1615, when the four-year-old Accademia degli Oziosi took possession of it,[72] this room apparently remained an informal meeting-place for the intelligentsia. A character in Fabrizio Marotta's *Il ratto* (1603) jokingly says he has left his master "nel chiostro di S. Domenico disputando in cuius con alquanti Scolari, che beffandolo gli erano intorno" [73] (II, 4). Like Della Porta, Barbarito, and Campanella, Marotta later belonged to the Oziosi, and it is likely that among the "Scolari" alluded to in his private joke of 1603 were some future fellow academicians. Giovanni Battista Manso's inauguration of the Oziosi in 1611 gave a name to a literary circle which had probably flourished for years, unofficially or under other auspices. Since Della Porta was a charter member of the academy, there can be little doubt that he had long been part of the group which became its nucleus. Certainly it was for just such cultivated spectators as Manso, Francesco Zazzero, Giulio Cesare Capaccio, and the others

[70] . . . *Campanella . . . congiura . . .* , 37.

[71] Minieri-Riccio, *op.cit.*, V, fasc. III, 605.

[72] *Ibid.*, V, fasc. I, 153. The following information about the Oziosi is from this source, 148ff., which is also the source used by Michele Maylender, *Storia delle accademie d'Italia* (Bologna, 1930), IV, 184ff.

[73] (. . . in the cloister of S. Domenico arguing with several scholars who stood about making fun of him.)

whose names appear on the Oziosi Charter that Della Porta's comedies were privately performed before publication. And it was just such a literary milieu that Campanella entered when he visited Della Porta in 1589.

By 1590 the applause of his friends and the success of *L'Olimpia* had resolved whatever doubts Della Porta may have had about publishing his plays, and Barbarito easily prevailed upon him to seek a license for his tragicomedy, *Penelope*, which appeared in 1591. The editor's dedication names nine comedies, already known to audiences and destined for the press.

The death of Cardinal d'Este in 1587 had not ended Della Porta's travels. He was heard to say in later years that philosophers should travel in their youth and stay at home as they grew old.[74] But apparently the time of repose still seemed distant to him in his late fifties, for by 1592 he was again in Venice. There he renewed a cherished friendship with Fra Paolo Sarpi, to whom he had owned himself indebted in the preface to the *Magiae₂*, declaring that the famous Servite scholar must have been fathered by an encyclopedia. They had met in 1581, during Della Porta's first sojourn in Venice,[75] and the bond between them was strengthened when Sarpi was sent on Servite business to Naples between 1585 and 1588.[76] Sarpi combined the pursuit of learning with the duties of high office in his religious order and managed to stay out of prison and, eventually, to die of natural causes, but he was patriotically active in the long struggle of the Venetian Republic against the Vatican. For this, as well as for his independent intellectual excursions and his correspondence with Huguenots, he was regarded with marked disfavor by the Roman Inquisition. Even before the papal ban on Venice in 1606, communication between Sarpi and his

---

[74] Gabrieli, "G. B. Della Porta . . . ," 426.

[75] Gabrieli, "Spigolature . . . ," 493.

[76] Luigi Firpo, "Appunti campanelliana, xxv, Storia di un furto," *Giornale critica della filosofia italiana*, Anna xxxv, Vol. x, fasc. iv (1956), 546.

southern friend lapsed. In the interests of personal security, Della Porta made many such sacrifices.

The year 1592 was an especially dangerous one in Venice for those on whom the Holy Office frowned, for in May, Giordano Bruno was denounced as a heretic, tried, and extradited to Rome, to be seen no more until his execution in 1600. Della Porta's works and extant correspondence ignore Bruno as they do Campanella, undoubtedly for the same reason, but it is inconceivable that the two Neapolitan philosophers should not have been somehow known to each other. They held similar views on magic, on universal atomism, and on the unity of all created life. Both published works on the art of memory. They had in common a number of acquaintances. As visiting celebrities on the Venetian intellectual scene, they would have found it difficult to avoid contact with one another.[77] But if association with Bruno was risky before he was apprehended by the Inquisition, it became downright suicidal afterward, and no one can be surprised at Della Porta's reticence on the subject.

Since 1589 he had published nothing more than a pair of innocuous plays, but suddenly six weeks before the pressure against Bruno finally broke, Della Porta was served by the Venetian Inquisition with an order from Cardinal Sanseverino in Rome, forbidding him under pain of excommunication and a fine of 500 gold ducats, to publish anything at all without express permission from the Roman High Tribunal.[78] The local Inquisitors who signed the document were, with one exception, the same who presided subsequently at Bruno's trial.[79] This order made Della Porta a suspect of dis-

[77] Vincenzo Spampanato, "Somiglianze tra due commediografi napoletani," *Rassegna critica di letteratura italiana*, Anno XI (Napoli, 1906), 145–67. Spampanato would have had it that Bruno's *Candelaio* influenced several of Della Porta's comedies, but the arguments are unconvincing.

[78] Fiorentino, *Studi . . .* , 265. The Latin order discovered by Fiorentino in the Archivio de' Frari, Venice, is reprinted here.

[79] Spampanato, *Vita di Giordano Bruno con documenti editi e inediti* (Messina, 1921), 487.

tinction. Previously, licenses for his works had been issued by the censors in Naples, but after April 9, 1592, he was forced to submit every manuscript directly to Rome. The prohibition did not slow his immediate output, however; the comedy *La fantesca*, its dedication dated April 15, appeared shortly afterward in Venice, and *Villae* was published in Frankfort, also in 1592. Although translations of his earlier works had been printed abroad, he had never before published a first edition outside of Italy. The Frankfort printing may have been an attempt to circumvent the Inquisition, but the results must have been unsatisfactory, for he never used this ruse again.

Although he was careful not to publicize it, Della Porta's taste for philosophical and scientific investigation and the doubtful society of those who engaged in it was not at all dampened by proofs of the Inquisition's continued interest in him. The company of which he made one in Padua in the early months of 1593 might have provided enough unorthodoxy to occupy a regiment of Inquisitors. It was an illustrious trio, consisting of Della Porta, Sarpi, and the young, relatively unimportant Galileo, and it turned into a quartet when Campanella joined them later.[80] Unfortunately there is no record of their conversations. The letters which must have passed before and after between Della Porta and Sarpi have never come to light, and the frequent compliments and occasional insults which in later years were exchanged, for the most part indirectly, by Galileo and the old Neapolitan say nothing of earlier encounters. At the Padua meeting of 1593 there must have been some discussion of Della Porta's *De refractione*, published in Naples later that year, the trea-

[80] Firpo, *op.cit.*, 545. This information is owed to the conscientious methods of one Lalande, librarian at the Bibliothèque Royale, who sometime before 1848 summarized the contents of a letter Campanella wrote to Peiresc in 1636. The original letter subsequently disappeared during Guglielmo Libri's systematic looting of French libraries, and has never been recovered.

tise on optics which figured after 1611 in the controversy over the invention of the telescope.

The next eight years in Della Porta's life are unaccounted for. His only new publication during this period was *La trappolaria* in 1596. That the comedy was printed in Bergamo may indicate another northern journey. Meanwhile, vernacular translations of his earlier works were gaining international prestige.[81] The Italian version of *Physiognomonia*, with difficulty licensed and printed in 1598, was probably translated by the author himself, although it bears the name of Giovanni de Rosa, a friend who later was one of the executors of Della Porta's will.

The tireless old scientist may have been in Venice again in 1601, when two of his comedies, *I due fratelli rivali* and *La Cintia* were printed there, but in the spring he was at home to receive the complimentary visit of Nicolas Claude Fabri de Peiresc, then a neophyte scholar, later a champion of learning, protector of Gassendi and Campanella. The young French nobleman came recommended by Fra Paolo Sarpi and made an excellent impression on the Della Porta brothers. Through them Peiresc obtained entry into the studios of other learned Neapolitans, such as Ferrante Imperato, and was permitted by Gian Vincenzo and Giambattista Della Porta not only to examine their private museum but to observe their experiments as well. Peiresc was touched by the reverence which gray-haired Giambattista showed toward his elder brother, whom he treated like a father.[82] Not only at home but in Naples generally, Gian Vincenzo was a some-

---

[81] Della Porta says in the preface to *Magiae₂* that his works have already been translated into French, Spanish, and Arabic. All extant translations are listed in Gabrieli's "Bibliografia . . . Della Porta . . ."

[82] Gassendi, *op.cit.*, 36. The same passage reveals that a correspondence flourished between Peiresc and the Della Portas, but it is now lost, together with the results of Peiresc's research for a short biography of Giambattista, a project he described to Paolo Gualdo in a letter of January 25, 1617 published in *Lettere d'uomini illustri, che fiorirono nel principio del secolo decimosettimo, non più stampate* (Venezia, 1744), 280.

what more important person than his internationally famous brother. As the heir to his father's office he functioned with unparalleled honesty, and formed close personal bonds with the current viceroy and his powerful entourage. Gian Vincenzo's collections were celebrated, and the superiority of his classical learning gave rise to the rumor that he was responsible for large sections of his brother's books. He corresponded with Peiresc in 1602, but as he did not share in the connection Giambattista formed with Federigo Cesi in 1603, it is presumed that Gian Vincenzo died before or in that year.[83]

Since the Inquisitional order of 1592 Della Porta had published nothing new about the "illicit arts," but he was still actively investigating them and could not keep silence forever. In 1601 he published *Coelestis physiognomoniae*, which aimed at reconciling the art of prophecy based on a mysterious connection between earth and the stars with the orthodox church doctrine of free will and condemnation of judiciary astrology. It was a difficult feat of juggling, one he would never have attempted had he not been moved to it by the Inquisition's constant suspicion. His theory here was akin to that in *De humana physiognomonia:* man is directed not by astral influences but by the elements which compose his body and which also determine the various characters of planets and stars. Human beings and heavenly bodies are all part of a vast system of signatures. By reading the natural signs, an expert can foretell the future to which the indicated tendencies will lead, provided that they are not overruled by free will. Recanting his former belief in judiciary astrology and emphasizing the natural basis of his prophetic art, Della Porta sought to remove dangerous interpretations from the title of *Mago* which he had proudly claimed in *Magiae*₁ and

---

[83] Gassendi, *op.cit.*, 62–63. Without citing his authority, Amabile dated Gian Vincenzo's death 1606 (. . . *Campanella . . . congiura . . .*, 34).

provided with an elaborately and apologetically innocent definition in *Magiae₂*.

The next year saw the publication of *Ars reminiscendi*, an augmentation of the earlier treatise on memory, his only nondramatic work of which the Italian version appeared before the Latin. Simultaneously another press brought out *Pneumaticorum . . . cum duobus libris curvilineorum elementorum*, a relatively sober work on hydraulics and pure mathematics, testifying to Della Porta's awareness of the new objectivity in science. He always liked to have a finger in the latest pie. But his gullibility and hankering after the occult made him incapable of total objectivity; the index to his lost *Taumatologia* indicated that his penchant for demonology was even stronger in his last years than it had been formerly.

A new chapter in Della Porta's life began in 1603 with the introduction of Federigo Cesi, marchese di Monticelli, a grave scholar of eighteen. Apparently some correspondence had passed between the two before their first meeting in Naples.[84] At this time Cesi was struggling to save from dissolution a recently founded brotherhood which he hoped to build into a sort of institute for scientific research. He and the three other charter members had vowed dedication to learning and hoped eventually to spread like a religious order, establishing research centers all over the world. Their emblem was a lynx, inspired by Della Porta's *impresa* on the title-page of the 1589 *Magiae₂* and the words in the preface: ". . . lynceis oculis perpendens quae se sibi demonstrant, ut, re inspecta, sedulo operetur." [85]

No sooner had the newly christened Lincei agreed upon a code for their private communications and begun to outline

[84] "Il carteggio Linceo della vecchia accademia di Federico Cesi (1603–1630)," *Atti e memori dell'Accademia Nazionale dei Lincei, Classe di scienze morali, storiche e filologiche*, Serie 6, VII, fasc. 1 (Roma, 1938), 35.

[85] (. . . with lynx-like eyes, examining those things which manifest themselves, so that having observed them, he may zealously use them.)

their first projects than Cesi's father, the Duke of Acqua-sparta, forbade their association, regarding it as a cabal against his own authority and a plot to alienate his son's mind from family interests.[86] The Lincei were temporarily scattered and Cesi traveled to Naples, where he described his academy to Della Porta, who responded with a vociferous enthusiasm which contrasted amusingly with Cesi's calm determination. The only thing the old *Mago* liked more than hugging a secret to himself was sharing one with a handful of elite colleagues in an atmosphere of organized mystery. Remembering, perhaps, his own forcibly disbanded academy of the Segreti, Della Porta encouraged the young nobleman's project. His knack of foreseeing the future may have given him an inkling of the important part he was later to play in the history of the Lincei. His approval of Cesi's intention combined with a respect for high birth prompted him in 1604 to write a history of the Cesi family, tracing it in true humanistic fashion back to Hercules.[87] A brief version survives, together with many fulsome compliments, in the dedicatory letter to Cesi prefacing *De distillatione*, a treatise on chemistry and alchemy, finished in 1604 and printed four years later.

While Della Porta heaped admiration on Cesi, he was himself courted in the most gratifying manner with a request which proved the extent of his fame. The Holy Roman Emperor Rudolph II, an amateur astronomer and alchemist who understandably preferred conversation with Kepler to conference with ambassadors, sent an envoy to Naples to invite Della Porta or one of his trained disciples to Prague,[88] where the imperial castle housed a laboratory and an observatory. Unable to accept the invitation, Della Porta wished nonetheless to strengthen and to use the offered connection; there-

[86] Domenico Carutti, *Breve storia della Accademia dei Lincei* (Roma, 1883), 11; and Baldassare Odescalchi, *Memorie istorico-critiche dell'Accademia de' Lincei* . . . (Roma, 1806), 13ff.

[87] "Il carteggio Linceo . . . ," 42.

[88] Sarnelli reprinted the lost letter, *op.cit.*, 210.

fore, he responded by dedicating to the emperor his *Tau-matologia*, an encyclopedia of seventy-five secrets by which the old scientist set great store.[89] His intention was not so much to honor Rudolph as to enlist his aid, for the censors were highly unsympathetic to the *Taumatologia*. But the emperor could not or would not secure a license for the book, and there is no record of further communication between author and dedicatee.

Meanwhile, the Roman Tribunal seemed quite willing to license Della Porta's more straightforward writings and his comedies. *La sorella* was printed in 1604 and *L'astrologo, La turca*, and *La carbonaria* all appeared in 1606. An augmented edition of *Pneumaticorum* was also issued that year in an Italian translation by "Juan Escrivano." *De munitione*, a quite unoriginal work on fortification, was licensed at the same time, although its printing was delayed two years. Another comedy, *Il moro*, followed in 1607. This was the year in which Sarpi was stabbed by assassins, but survived, to the disappointment of the Roman Curia. Della Porta's reaction is not recorded, but the event could have done nothing to calm his fear of the religious authorities.

Nevertheless Della Porta could not give up fortune-telling, and in 1608 was still hoping for the censors' approval of a manuscript on palmreading which he had written in 1581. Despite his solicitations on its behalf, *Chirofisonomia* was not published for sixty-two years after his death. Of no scientific or literary value, this book nonetheless deserves some attention for its compact illustration of Della Porta's merits and failings as an investigator of nature. His study of hands and feet is based on an extension of the theory which underlies his entire philosophy of nature, the Doctrine of Signatures. He introduces his findings with this premise,

. . . determinai, che il Sommo Artefice e creator delle cose havesse sempre un'istesso ordine in tutte le sue opre serbato, indi

[89] The dedication is in the Archivio Linceo Codice IX with the manuscripts of Della Porta owned by the Academy.

mi rivolse alle medesime ragioni, le quali ho assegnate nella
Fisonomia humana, celeste, e delle piante . . .[90]

There follows a good deal of systematic nonsense: quotations
from the ancients, especially Aristotle (toward whom Della
Porta was not invariably respectful), charts of hands divided
into parts corresponding to the planets, lists of character
traits which may be deduced from lines in the palm, compari-
sons of human hands and animal paws falling in the same
planetary classification, and so on. Yet the methods Della
Porta employed in preparing this patchwork of superstition
are those of an empirical scientist with a Baconian determination to see for himself what others are content to accept on
classical authority. To test the theory that dire events and
evil character are visibly marked in hands and feet, he spared
no effort to procure criminals and other unfortunates for
examination, as his own words reveal:

Et acciò che havessi abbondanza de gli huomini sopra accennati,
convenni col Boja Napolitano, ch'era all'hora un certo nominato
Antonello Cocozza, che quando egli deponeva dalle forche gli
appiccati, e gli portava al Ponte Ricciardo (questo è un luogo
mille passi dalla Città di Napoli distante; dove i meschini stanno
pendenti, per terrore de' scelerati, che forse di là passano, fin
tanto che si marciscono, e dalle pioggie, e da' venti sono con-
sumati) avvisasse l'hora di quella trasportatione, et io andando
à quel luogo osservava le dispositioni delle mani, e de' piedi, e
quelle disegnava con uno stile nelle carte, à ciò destinate, ò pure
con il gesso ne formava il lor cavi, accioche buttandovi doppo
la cera ne havessi in casa i lineamenti, e da ciò havessi campo di
studiarvi la notte in casa, e di conferirli con gl'altri; e conferiti
insieme i segni ne cavassi la verità, faccendo sempre l'istesso, fin
à tanto, che trovassi tutti i segni, che dinotano tal'uno dover
esser sospeso; e così sodisfacessi à me stesso. In oltre acciòche io

[90] *Della Chirofisonomia,* trans. P. Sarnelli (Napoli, 1677), 21. (I decided that the Great Artificer and creator of things had always observed the same order in all His works, whereupon I returned to the
same explanations which I had adopted in [my works on] human,
celestial, and botanical physiognomy.)

sapessi gli estinti d'atroce morte, ed uccisi, convenni con i Diaconi della Chiesa Cathedrale Napolitana (de' quali è il pietoso ufficio sepellire nella Chiesa di S. Restituta Vergine, e Martire gli uccisi, ed i morti senza confession) che mi avvisassero, quando la morte d'alcuni di questi avveniva, acciò andando à quella venerabile Chiesa, guardate le costitutioni delle mani, piedi, e fronti, e delineati il numero, e la qualità delle ferite, similmente potessi conferirli con gli altri; onde conoscessi quali di quelle fossero più valide, e quali più deboli à dimostrare. Ne hebbi minor pensiero à visitare tutte le carceri publiche, dove sempre è racchiusa gran moltitudine de' facinorosi ladri, parricidi, assassini di strada, e d'altri huomini di simile fattezza, per vedere diligentemente le loro mani, doppo contemplando i piedi, e le mani de gli animali, conferii le loro figure con quelle de gli huomini, non senza naturali ragioni, e con l'istesso metodo, del quale mi sono servito nella Fisonomia.[91]

His scientific method was excellent thus far, but it went no further. Satisfied by personal observation that criminals' hands and feet bore the telltale signs he expected, he never

[91] *Ibid.*, 23–24. (And so that I might have enough such men I arranged for the Neapolitan executioner, Antonello Cocozza, to notify me whenever he took down hanged men and carried them to the Ricciardo bridge (a place 1000 steps from Naples, where the unfortunates are hung as an example to evil passers-by until the elements destroy them). Going there I observed their hands and feet and sketched them on paper or else took plaster casts of them, from which later to make wax figures; thus at night I could study them at home, comparing them with others, from the signs coming to the truth, until I had discovered all the signs indicating hanging; thus I satisfied myself. Moreover, in order to know more about those who are murdered or die violent deaths, I arranged with the deacons of the Neapolitan Cathedral (who have the pious duty of burying in the Church of St. Restituta Virgin and Martyr all those who are killed and those who die unshriven) to notify me when death occurred, and going to that venerable church, I observed the hands, feet and foreheads, sketched the number and position of the wounds to compare with the others, so as to know which were valid and which weak for demonstration. Nor was I less assiduous in visiting public jails where there were always many thieves, parricides, street assassins and similar men, so that I could study their hands and later observing the hands and feet of animals, I compared them with those of the men, not without natural explanations and by the same method I used in the *Physiognomy*.)

undertook any general examination of people in better circumstances, and therefore never discovered how many virtuous men have vicious hands.

Della Porta's advancing age, great fame, and obvious willingness to obey the Inquisition by now almost guaranteed him peace in his remaining years, but he was never to be in the censors' good graces, and was glad to have any help he could get in the continual struggle over licensing. Federigo Cesi undertook to influence his uncle, Cardinal Bartolomeo, in behalf of his controversial friend, who was soon calling on the young aristocrat for all his licenses. The letters which passed between Rome and Naples from 1608 until Della Porta's death in 1615 reveal [92] the strong mutual admiration and personal interest which existed between the young marquis and the old *Mago*, even before the latter joined the Lincei, and continued undiminished, despite occasional evidence of senility on Della Porta's part and superciliousness on Cesi's.

Although the torments of kidney stones forced the septuagenarian to retire to his favorite villa for a large part of 1608, enthusiasm for nature's marvels kept him as busy as ever, and in October he wrote excitedly to Cesi that he had learned several new secrets from a Signor Borelli, whose interest in science was so sincere that he had paid the extravagant sum of 100 *scudi* for a slave on whom to try a new recipe for poison.

In 1609 Della Porta published two comedies, *La furiosa* and *La Chiappinaria*, and finished *De aëris transmutationibus*, a work on meteorology, which was published the following year with a dedication to Cesi. In August an old acquaintance, Galileo, created a furor by demonstrating his *occhiale* to the Venetian Senate. Cesi immediately asked Della Porta's opinion of the talked-of instrument, and was answered with more irritation than accuracy, "Del secreto dell'occhiale l'ho

[92] Letters referred to in the following five paragraphs are from "Il carteggio Linceo . . . ," 112–24.

visto, et è una coglionaria et è presa dal mio Libro 9 De Refractione, e la scriverò. . . ." [93] As promised, a design of the telescope is crudely sketched in the margin. There is, in fact, no word about anything resembling a telescope in Book 9 of *De refractione*, nor even in Book 8, which deals with lenses. Della Porta was probably thinking of the passage in *Magiae*$_2$, XVII, 10, which mentions a combination of concave and convex lenses. But his light tone is more revealing than his vague memory, for, as Vasco Ronchi observes, if Della Porta had invented the instrument in question, he would not have joked about it at this juncture. Some months later he wryly expressed regret that Galileo and not he, had "accomidato mia inventione," but he did not insist much on his claim to priority.

Cesi's succession to the dukedom of Acquasparta had freed him by 1610 to develop his cherished academy, and after the publication that year of *De aëris* . . . , the Lincei invited Della Porta to join them. Charmed, as usual, by the prospect of cozy exchanges of secrets, passwords, codes, and all the ritual of a solemn fraternity, the old scientist was delighted to accept, and indeed was wise to do so, for the academy, supported by Cesi's wealth, planned to publish its members' research and could exert more pressure on the licensers than an individual could hope to do. Yet his membership was even more to the academy's advantage than to his own. For all his dodging of the Inquisition, the old Neapolitan had a name to conjure with. World-famous as a scientist, physician, philosopher, general scholar, dramatist, and wit, he could not but lend authority and prestige to any academy he joined, especially a brand-new, rather revolutionary one founded by very young men and dedicated, not to gentle arts or to abstract speculation, but to direct investigation of nature.

[93] (Concerning the secret of the telescope, I have seen it, and it is nonsense and it is taken from my Book 9 *De Refractione*, and I shall write it down. . . .)

Moreover, Della Porta owned a magnificent library, which Cesi hoped he would bequeath to the Lincei.

Often as he had undertaken it, travel had never been easy for the constitutionally weak Della Porta, and now it was out of the question, so Cesi made a second trip to Naples for the investiture which took place July 6, 1610. According to the entry he himself made in the Linceo register, Della Porta was then seventy-five years old.[94] Shortly afterward, proudly announcing himself "Linceo," he published and dedicated to Cesi a new edition of *Elementorum curvilineorum* with an added section on squaring the circle. It was a characteristic display of bravura to tackle in his old age this knottiest of mathematical problems. He did not solve it.

The following April Galileo was made a member of the Accademia dei Lincei during a visit to Rome, where he expounded his celestial discoveries to Pope Paul V. He seems to have concurred in the popular opinion, supported by the other Lincei and by Kepler,[95] that Della Porta was indeed the inventor of the telescope, for he later permitted these lines by Giovanni Faber, another Linceo, to appear in the preface to the *Saggiatore:*

> Porta tenet primas, habet Germane secundas,
> Sunt, Galilee, tuus tertia regna labor.
> Sidera sed quantum terris coelestia distant
> Ante alios tantum tu, Galilee, nites . . .[96]

But after the *Sidereus nuncius* revealed Galileo's findings to the literate public in 1610, and counter-claims broke out from

[94] Gabrieli, "Le ricerche e le carte di A. Statuti sulla storia dei primi Lincei (per gli anni 1603–1630)," *Memorie della Pontifica Accademia dei Nuovi Lincei,* Serie II, VIII (Roma, 1925), 448. The entire register of the early Lincei is reprinted in this article.

[95] Johannes Kepler, *Dissertatio cum nuncio sidereo,* April 19, 1610, in Galileo, *Le Opere* . . . , III (Firenze, 1930), 108.22–109.2.

[96] *Le opere* . . . , VI (Firenze, 1936), 205.
> (Porta holds the first, the German has the second.
> The third realm, Galileo, is your work.
> But the heavenly constellations are as far from earth
> As you, Galileo, shine before others.)

various would-be fathers of the telescope,[97] Della Porta felt that he had not been given his due. He complained in a long letter to an anonymous friend, perhaps Faber, that, like Galileo, he had suffered much from plagiarists and had not only been robbed of credit for the invention of the telescope, but had also seen his work on the magnet filched by a certain barbarous Englishman, who was, moreover, mad enough to believe that the earth moves.[98] He was justified in asking recognition for his explorations, but certainly he never constructed a telescope nor specifically described one, and though his study of the magnet [99] was undeniably valuable, it was too inconclusive to justify doubts of the "barbarous" Gilbert's originality. Perhaps because he realized the weakness of his claim to the telescope, Della Porta made no public charges, and busied himself instead with writing a treatise to be called *De telescopio*, lamenting the while that old age slowed his work.

His continued enthusiasm for the Lincei brotherhood, however, was vigorously youthful, and he was overjoyed when Cesi decided to open a branch of the academy in Naples.[100] Della Porta was to be the local chief, and his first duty was to suggest for membership a very few, highly qualified Neapolitans, while Cesi's assistant, Francesco Stelluti, was looking for

[97] Although Galileo's development and use of the telescope associated the instrument with his name in the public mind, he neither could nor did claim credit for the original invention. For bibliography on the origin and development of the telescope, see Marjorie Nicolson, "The Telescope and Imagination," *Modern Philology*, xxxii (1935), 241, note 18. Professor Nicolson emphasizes the importance of the Dutch and German claimants, cites various seventeenth century accounts, including those of Hieronymus Sirturus (1618) and Robert Hooke (1665), and recommends among modern accounts, C. Singer, "Steps leading to the invention of the first optical apparatus," *Studies in the history and method of science* (Oxford, 1921), ii, 385ff., and R. T. Gunther, *Early science in Oxford*, ii (1923), 288–331.

[98] "Il carteggio Linceo . . . ," 308–10.

[99] *Magia naturalis*, vii (1589), i.e., Magia₂.

[100] Information in this paragraph is from a letter in "Il carteggio Linceo . . . ," 125–31.

a palace or villa to serve as a headquarters. Della Porta submitted four names, three of scholars admirably suited to the august academy, the fourth of his eighteen-year-old grandson, Filesio di Costanzo, whose only qualifications for membership were that he was literate and devoted to his grandfather. Motivated in part, perhaps, by affection for Della Porta, but more certainly by a desire to secure his library for the Lincei, Cesi agreed to number Filesio among them, and instructed Stelluti to remind the old man, when next they discussed the final disposition of his books, that his grandson would share the benefit which inheritance of the library would confer upon the Lincei.

Della Porta meanwhile was dangling his books as bait in another pond. The previous year he had donated several volumes and promised the whole collection in the future to the Ambrosian Library of the Milanese Cardinal Federigo Borromeo. Following this generous gesture, Della Porta dropped a hint or two about his pet project, the *Taumatologia,* which the censors had so far refused to license, but all the cardinal sent in return were thanks, and a portrait, with relic, of Saint Carlo Borromeo.[101] After that Della Porta began promising his books to the Lincei, but in the end, whether by his design or carelessness, they passed with the bulk of his property to his daughter.[102]

That property, which he assessed in 1612, was considerable, although probably not as extensive as his father's had been. In addition to the town house and two villas which became entirely his after his brother's death, Della Porta had inherited 20,000 ducats from his father, had been given large sums by royalty and other patrons, and had earned 12,000

[101] Gabrieli, "Bibliografia . . . Della Porta," 267–68, contains four letters from Della Porta to Borromeo.

[102] Della Porta's will was published in Camillo Minieri-Riccio, *op.cit.,* v, fasc. 1, 137–41, note 5. A facsimile of the will was printed in Felice Genta, *Dopo la denigrazione di G. B. della Porta* (Napoli, 1928), 32–33.

ducats with his pen.[103] A large part of his wealth, however, was tied up in the collection of antiquities which Giambattista and Gian Vincenzo had amassed together, and great amounts had been poured into research and experiments. The "secrets" to be revealed in the *Taumatologia*, Della Porta estimated, had cost him, his colleagues, and Cardinal d'Este a total of 100,000 *scudi*.[104]

Still he lived well in these last years, as he had been accustomed to do all his life. His daughter and her four sons ministered to his domestic comfort, and though in one letter to Cesi he spoke distastefully of one nephew or grandson greedy for his inheritance,[105] on the whole he was content with his family. The wit that led him to concoct emblems for his friends in the midst of laboratory experimentation,[106] and the literary whimsy that prompted him to give his daughter and grandsons romantic names from his comedies were stimulated by a variety of literary associations. The preface to Cortese's *Vaiasseide* (1614) testifies to the existence of a contemporary academy devoted to Neapolitan dialect literature, called the *Schirchiate de lo Mandracchio e' Mprovesante de lo Cerriglio* (roughly, the Wits of the Mandracchio and Improvisers of the Cerriglio).[107] The Mandracchio was a waterfront district of Naples,[108] and the Cerriglio a popular local tavern. Although the club probably met in Cortese's house,[109] its spiritual home was the Cerriglio, which became both subject and setting of dialect poems. Cortese wrote a mock epic, *Lo Cerriglio 'ncantato*, recounting the Cerriglio kingdom's

---

[103] "Il carteggio Linceo . . . ," 214.

[104] Gabrieli, "Bibliografia . . . Della Porta," 268.

[105] "Il carteggio Linceo . . . ," 214. The reference is to an un-named "nipote."

[106] Gabrieli, "Spigolature . . . ," 505–18.

[107] Minieri-Riccio, *op.cit.*, v, fasc. III, 585. The other known members were Ferdinando Boccosi, Francesco Mezzacapo, and Lelio Flauto.

[108] Raffaele D'Ambra, *Vocabolario Napolitano-Toscano domestico di arti e mestieri* . . . (Napoli, 1873), 234.

[109] Minieri-Riccio, *op.cit.*, 585.

fall and transformation into a tavern.[110] The greatest of the dialect writers, G. B. Basile, who was probably in the Schirchiate and was certainly a friend of both Cortese and Della Porta, entitled the third of his nine Neapolitan eclogues *Talia o lo Cerriglio*, picturing the inn as a rollicking den of thieves.[111] Another favorite subject of the Schirchiate was *lo chiappo*, the hangman's noose, as indicated by the manuscript discovered by Minieri-Riccio of an anonymous member's *Discurzo Napolitano ncoppa l'accellenze de lo Chiappo*.[112] The title of Della Porta's *Chiappinaria* (1609) seems to allude to this joke. More significantly, he named the Cerriglio as headquarters for the criminal characters in *L'astrologo* (1606) and made it the central scene of action in *La tabernaria* (1616), a comedy written partly in Neapolitan dialect. On the wispy evidence of five references to the Schirchiate, Minieri-Riccio was unable to establish the date of its founding or to identify more than four of its members. But Della Porta's use of the club's special *topoi* suggests that he was either a member or an interested associate, and that the group was active before 1606, the year of *Astrologo's* publication.

A well-documented and more dignified literary society enjoyed by Della Porta in his last years was the Academy of the Oziosi, officially begun in 1611.[113] Perhaps remembering the Svegliati's disbanding by one Spanish viceroy and the earlier wholesale suppression of academies by another,[114] the chief Ozioso, Manso, protected his academy by extending membership to the current viceroy, Pedro Fernando de Castro, Count of Lemos. The count actually furnished for their entertainment a comedy of his own writing,[115] and the

[110] Napoli: per Camillo Cavallo, 1645.

[111] *Le muse napolitane. Egloghe di Gian Alesio Abbattutis* (Napoli, 1635). There was probably an earlier edition in Basile's lifetime.

[112] Minieri-Riccio, *op.cit.*, v, fasc. III, 585.

[113] Antonio Bulifon, *op.cit.*, 91.

[114] Minieri-Riccio, *op.cit.*, v, fasc. III, 605; IV, fasc. I, 172.

[115] Croce, *I teatri di Napoli* . . . , 782.

Oziosi flourished. Giambattista Marino's election as prince of the academy and his publication of an octave in praise of Della Porta [116] occurred after the old man's death, but in his lifetime also the Oziosi numbered many notable men of letters. Scipione Errico was a charter member, [117] and the versatile Gabriele Zinano was soon admitted, as was G. B. Basile, who wrote a complimentary ode on Della Porta's *Georgio* (1611). Drama seems especially to have been cultivated by the Oziosi, although no other playwright of Della Porta's stature emerged from their number. Zinano was admired for his tragedy *L'Almerigo*, Errico and Basile wrote plays, in addition to their works in other genres, and among the other dramatists in this first crop of Oziosi were Andrea Santa Maria, Francesco Zazzero; Ettore Pignatelli; Fabrizio Carafa; Filippo Caetani, duke of Sermoneta; and Fabrizio Marotta. [118] These early Oziosi formed a distinguished and stimulating circle, of which Milton may have seen traces some twenty-five years later, when he visited the aged Manso in Naples and wrote verses to Basile's niece, singing in Rome. [119]

But although Della Porta was an active member of the academy, he seems to have regarded it rather negligently, maintaining his *persona* of serious scientist who wrote comedies only as "scherzi de' suoi studi più gravi" (*Carbonaria*

[116] *La galeria del Cavalier Marino. Distinta in pitture, & sculture* (Napoli [1620]), 179.

[117] He is called Scipione Teodoro by historians of the Oziosi (see Minieri-Riccio, *op.cit.*, v, fasc. 1, 149), but is identified by means of his academic name "l'Incognito," with Scipione Errico. (See Allacci, *op.cit.*, 40.)

[118] All of these are represented in Allacci's bibliography of the drama, *op.cit.* Chiocarelli listed three additional comedies of Basile, now lost. See Croce, *Saggi sulla letteratura italiana del '600,* 3ª ed. riv. (Bari, 1948), 112.

[119] Basile's sister Adriana (or Andreana), herself a singer, married Muzio Baroni, a servitor of Luigi Carafa, charter member of the Oziosi. Of their union was born Leonora Baroni, to whom Milton addressed three Latin epigrams. Little known details of Adriana's career have recently been published by Anna Maria Crinò in "Virtuose di canto e poeti a Roma e a Firenze nella prima metà del seicento," *Studi secenteschi,* i (Firenze, 1960), 175-93.

prologue, A3). Unlike his fellow academicians, he never advertised his membership on a title-page. There is no record of his academic name, and he did not deign to contribute to the Oziosi's collection of memorial verse on the death of Queen Margaret of Austria.[120] In contrast, he often publicized his connection with the Accademia dei Lincei, and in his eagerness to augment the prestige of that exclusively scientific society, he proposed that Cesi admit to it several of the most aristocratic Oziosi.

A minor struggle now ensued between sober youth and giddy old age. Cesi, whose devotion to learning was so unswerving that he spent his honeymoon in Palestrina writing an archeological monograph on the nearby Temple of Fortune,[121] intended to make his academy a tight network of dedicated scholars. The liberal Della Porta, on the contrary, envisioned an organization something like the Order of Malta, with ceremonial trappings and honorary membership for nobly born dilettantes, among them the Spanish viceroy. Possibly Cesi felt that his own high rank, further adorned in 1613 with the title of Prince of Sant'Angelo e Polo, shed sufficient lustre of this sort on the academy. Eventually he admitted Tommaso Carafa at Della Porta's request, but suggested tactfully that Neapolitan membership be strictly limited until the academy possessed a local place for its meetings. Meanwhile he sent rings for the new members, and Della Porta answered with an account of the manner in which he bestowed them:

Ho ricevuto tre anelli, e l'ho cominciato a distribuire, ma non senza qualche cerimonie: L'ho fatti ingenocchiare, ci l'ho posti in dito con belle parole, e con molti ringratiamenti di V.S.Illma. Mi duole non haver le apparecchiate vesti, e se piace a Dio che habbiamo il palazzo, farò due vesti di seta d'oro, o di broccato,

120 Ottavio Caputi, *Relatione della pompa funerale che si celebrò in Napoli, nella morte della Serenissima Reina Margherita d'Austria . . .* (Napoli, 1612).

121 Information in the next five paragraphs is scattered throughout the letters in "Il carteggio Linceo . . . ," 140-487.

una per il vice Principe, e l'altra per il ricevuto Linceo. E bisogna fare un libretto sulle cerimonie, che senza questo, par che sia gioco di putti . . .[122]

The most famous of the Lincei was now very old and ill, but the pains of fever, catarrh, and kidney stones did not overwhelm him. In 1611 he published *Georgio*, a sacred tragedy followed by a comedy, *La tabernaria*, perhaps in 1612.[123] In that year one of his friends suggested that he write a verse tragedy about the death of Ulysses. Obligingly he did so, and together with a comedy, *I due fratelli simili*, *Ulisse* was printed in 1614, the last of his works to be published in his lifetime.

Though he sent no scientific books to the printer after 1610, Della Porta never abandoned his laboratory, and the Inquisition never abandoned its watch over him. He was experimenting with mercury in 1612 and still nursed some hope of discovering the philosophers' stone. That summer he informed Cesi that he was planning a book on the telescope in answer to Galileo's attackers, Sisi and the others who "parlano al sproposito, perchè non sanno di prospettiva." [124] He announced also that some Venetian merchants had approached him about publishing his complete works, but that he had no time to write all the necessary dedications. It is more than likely that the censors would have opposed the project. They steadily refused to license the *Taumatologia*,

[122] (I have received three rings and have begun to distribute them, but not without some ceremony. I made the recipients kneel and I put the rings on their fingers with fine words and with many thanks to Your Most Illustrious Lordship. I regret not having robes ready, and if God permits us to have the palace, I shall order two robes of gold silk or brocade, one for the Vice-Prince, and the other for the Linceo initiate. And we should write a handbook of the ceremonies, for without this, it would seem a childish game . . .)

[123] Fiorentino believed the 1616 Ronciglione edition to be the first, although Allacci attested to the existence of a 1612 Ronciglione edition (*op.cit.*, 747).

[124] (. . . talk nonsense, because they know nothing about perspective.)

even after Cesi gave it a less occult-sounding title, and they inspected Della Porta's mail, often forcing his correspondents to address their communications through intermediaries. Either as a proof of orthodox piety or as a preliminary to his approaching end, Della Porta constructed a chapel to St. John the Baptist near one of his villas and entreated the Vatican to attach an indulgence to it. The indulgence was granted, but the license for the *Taumatologia* was permanently withheld. The censors' mistrust seems to have been justified; the manuscript index through which the *Taumatologia* has survived reveals that Della Porta had returned more credulously than ever to belief in demonology.[125]

In 1613 the Lincei ordered a medal struck in honor of their illustrious eldest member, and hopefully discussed the possibility of publishing his complete works. The plan came to nothing, but Della Porta was gratified by the homage and continued working to deserve it. Cesi reported to Galileo in June that, although the old man's memory was somewhat weakened, he had a number of compositions in hand and daily received the admirers who visited him in droves. For every visitor bent on scientific enlightenment, there were four or five attracted by Della Porta's reputation as a wonderworker and seer. Although he claimed to be irritated by the crowds, he often obliged with a demonstration in fortunetelling, reiterating the while that he employed only natural means. Upon being shown a portrait of Henri IV, he dazzled the company by foretelling that monarch's violent death. Later, when history had borne him out, Della Porta explained to his friend, Stelluti, that he had based his prediction on the king's pouting lower lip, which made him look as though he were on the verge of tears.

In the summer of 1614 the venerable *Mago* was shaken by

---

125 Gioacchino Paparelli, "*La Taumatologia* di Giovanbattista della Porta," *Filologia Romanza*, Anno II, fasc. 4, No. 8 (Torino, 1955), 418–29. Comparing the Montpellier and Lincei Mss, Paparelli concludes that the *Taumatologia* was never more than an index (427).

the death of his youngest grandson, Attilio, and was bedridden by a nearly fatal concentration of kidney stones. But following a special blessing obtained from the pope by Cesi, Della Porta rallied, and in October, announced to Galileo that he was constructing a new kind of telescope which would penetrate the empyrean. This was his last project. A few days before his death, he told Nicantonio Stelliola, that the telescope was the most difficult thing he had ever undertaken and that it had killed him. He died on February 4, 1615, and after a magnificent funeral, was buried in the family vault in the Church of San Lorenzo. His will, notarized on February 1, is signed almost illegibly in the hand of a very ill and tired old man. With the exception of small bequests to a cousin, Urania "Spatafore," and a nephew or grandson, Trojano de Gennaro, and several religious charities, Della Porta's property was left to his daughter, Cinzia di Costanzo, and her three sons, Eugenio, Filesio, and Leandro.[126]

Some of his papers went into the Lincei collection, but many of them passed through Della Porta's heirs and Lorenzo Crasso to Pompeo Sarnelli and then disappeared, after Sarnelli had extracted material for a short biography, appended to his translation of *Chirofisonomia* in 1677. The other works which were unpublished in Della Porta's lifetime are known only by title, with the exception of *De telescopio*, discovered in manuscript in 1940 and published in 1962.[127]

It is most regrettable that Peiresc's plan in 1617 for a biographical sketch of Della Porta [128] never bore fruit; the French scholar might have issued a franker account than his Italian contemporaries dared to give. The Inquisition became more and more suspicious of the Lincei as time passed, until, weakened by Cesi's death in 1630 and Galileo's condemnation in 1633, the academy drifted into a long hibernation. The

[126] See page 46, note 102.

[127] Giovan Battista Della Porta, *De Telescopio*. Con introduzione di Vasco Ronchi e Maria Amalia Naldoni (Firenze).

[128] *Lettere d'uomini illustri* . . . , 280. (See page 35, note 82.)

Neapolitan branch could not survive Della Porta long and died even before Cesi, either from natural debility or by Spanish order.[129] The biographical notes made by Cesi or Faber and sent to Giovanni Ricchio in 1625 to be worked into the academy's official eulogy of Della Porta was, of necessity, an attempt to make the Lincei and their illustrious *Vice Principe* palatable to the Inquisition. Although the account contains certain useful facts, it completely ignores Della Porta's lifelong troubles with the Inquisition and concentrates on his piety, charitable works, and friendships with highly-placed churchmen. It even goes so far as to allege that he scrupulously avoided attending risqué plays, and wrote his own comedies solely for didactic purposes.[130] These and Della Porta's own attempts to whitewash his reputation are responsible for the scarcity of factual material about his life and for the enormous amount of misinformation that his would-be biographers must sift.

The historians of magic and of Renaissance science who refer to Della Porta agree that he lacked common sense. The breadth of his learning and the depth of his interest in natural phenomena are unquestioned. Like the best of his colleagues, he recognized the value of experimentation, but his methods were even faultier than most. A little-known letter written to Giovan Francesco Angelita provides one of the best examples of Della Porta's merits and shortcomings in this connection. In answer to Angelita's request for information about procreation in snails, Della Porta replies that he is not satisfied with the authority of the ancients, for he believes in his own eyes more than in Aristotle. He has noticed baby snails appearing in one of his flower boxes in which there are no adult snails, and deduces that these creatures are born of

---

[129] For Lincei history, see Carutti, *op.cit.*; Odescalchi, *op.cit.*; J. Plancus (Giovanni Bianchi), *Fabii Columnae Lyncei . . . vita* (Firenze, 1744); and Michele Maylender, *op.cit.*, III.
[130] Gabrieli, "G. B. Della Porta. . . ." 423–28.

putrefaction. He ends with a recommendation that Angelita cease wasting time on such trifles.[131]

The *Magiae₂* is essentially only a combination of medieval secret lore with fifteenth and sixteenth century discoveries in physics; even the sections on magnetism and the camera obscura, much respected in his time, were not new.[132] *De refractione* is recognized as a serious work but does not justify his being called the father of modern optics, for it adds nothing to the *Opticae thesaurus* of his predecessor Risner.[133]

Illustrating the Renaissance search for unity in nature, all his works take for granted a universal plan which expresses itself in analogies among all forms of existence: between men and animals in the *Physiognomonia* and *Chirofisonomia*, between animals, and plants in the *Phytognomonica*. But utility was always Della Porta's highest aim; every book of the *Magiae₂* emphasizes the practical application of the secrets of nature revealed therein.

At least in the fields of botany and natural history modern historians of science take Della Porta seriously. In his experimental orchards he achieved solid results in grafting and plant feeding, described with charmingly poetic embellishments in *Villae* and *Magiae₂* III. The greatest of Renaissance natural historians, Ulisse Aldovrandi, acknowledged his debt to Della Porta's observation of bird life.[134] And even his jumbled laboratory work benefited future scientists. Antonio Corsano observes that although Della Porta's desire to as-

---

[131] *I pomi d'oro . . . Dove si contengono due lettioni de' fichi l'una, e de' melloni l'altra. Nelle quali non solo si scorgano le lor lodi, e le loro eccellenze, ma si scoprono molti segreti per usarli, e per cultivarli. E si notavi molti errori di diversi grand'huomini intorno al loro sentimento. Aggiuntavi una lettione della lumaca dove si pruova, ch'ella sia maestra della vita humana. Opra non meno ripiena di dottrina, che di piacere* (Ricanato, 1607), 164.

[132] Mario Gliozzi, "L'invenzione della camera oscura," *Archeion*, XIV, fasc. I (Roma, 1932), 221–29.

[133] Sarton, *op.cit.*, 87.

[134] Thorndike, *op.cit.*, VI, 258.

tound his friends made him neglect to search for constant laws and vital connections, his work was so varied and unceasing that he could not avoid occasionally formulating sensible and careful criteria for research.[135]

Thorndike suggests an influence on Francis Bacon, specifically of Della Porta's plans in *Magiae*₂ xx, 5, for an instrument for long-distance hearing, to be constructed according to principles based on observation of sharp-eared animals.[136] Be that as it may, Della Porta was in many ways like the author of the *Advancement of Learning*. He had the same reverence for nature and concern with utility, the same lamentable impatience with details. And certainly, for all his credulity and carelessness, Della Porta's hope of treasuring up all the secrets of nature within the covers of a single book had a touching Baconian grandeur.

Both Bacon and Della Porta would be unpleasantly surprised to know that modern readers neglect their scientific works for the essays of one and the dramas of the other. Although Della Porta took pride in his plays, his deprecation of them was not mere convention. He considered them a hobby, a frivolous ornament to the results of his serious studies. This relative negligence has increased the difficulty of investigating his dramatic works. So vaguely and so rarely does his surviving correspondence mention the plays, that it has never been possible even to date these compositions accurately.

[135] *Op.cit.*, 88.
[136] *Op.cit.*, vi, 421.

Dating Della Porta's Plays

ALTHOUGH Della Porta began writing his plays in early youth,[1] he did not publish one until his life was two-thirds over. The certainty that there were time gaps between composition and printing and the probability that in old age Della Porta revised some of his youthful works make the chronology of *il Mago*'s theater a mystery which would have delighted him. Among the scholars who have investigated the plays, only Francesco Fiorentino has tried to date them.[2] Unfortunately, his conclusions are as fragmentary as the evidence on which they rest.

After dedicating *Olimpia* in 1589, Pompeo Barbarito arranged the publication of *Penelope* in 1591, together with a preface listing Della Porta's unpublished plays to date. In addition to a number of "Tragedie e martiri di Santi," there were nine comedies: "*La Fantesca, lo Spagnuolo, il Negromante, l'Astrologo, l'Alchimista, il Pedante, la Notte, la Cintia,* et *la Sregha* [*sic*] ch'è pur sua e va stampata sotto nome di Mario Carduino detta *la Santa. . . .*"[3] Barbarito also re-

---

[1] Pompeo Barbarito, Dedication to *Olimpia*, dated August 15, 1589 (2ª ed. Vinegia, 1597), 2verso.

[2] *Studi e ritratti della Rinascenza* (Bari, 1911), 294-340, a reprinting of "Del teatro di Giovan Battista de la Porta," *Giornale napoletano di filosofia e letteratura, scienze morali e politiche,* Nuova Serie, Anno ii, Vol. iii, fasc. 7 (marzo 1880, Napoli), 92-118, 329-43.

[3] Dedication to *Penelope* (Napoli, 1591), A2verso-A3. (Tragedies and [plays about] saints' martyrdoms . . . [and nine comedies] *The Maidservant, The Spaniard, The Necromancer, The Astrologer, The Alchemist, The Pedant, The Night, Cintia* and *The Witch* which is also his, though published under the title of *The Saint* by Carduino.)

vealed here that *Olimpia* was Della Porta's firstborn, as well as his first published, play, and that *Penelope* had been composed "molt'anni prima" and later revised.

A more precise list of Della Porta's plays was issued in 1610 by Bartolomeo Zannetti as an appendix to *Elementorum curvilineorum.*[4] With the twelve comedies and one tragicomedy already in print, Zannetti listed as unpublished: a treatise, "*Arte da Comporre Comedie*"; a translation of Plautus; three "Tragedie—*S. Giorgio, S. Dorotea, S. Eugenia*"; six comedies—"*I Simili, La Notte, Il Fallito, La Strega, L'Alchimista, La Bufalaria*"; and seven others without titles. Five of these employed the same plot and characters and were performed in sequence, the first containing the argument for all five, the second providing the protasis, followed by the general peripety, and the fifth concluding with the catastrophe proper to itself and to the other four. The other pair was written for performance in alternate acts, following a single plot as it unfolded simultaneously in town and in the country. Zannetti had various manuscripts, both those in Della Porta's own keeping and those which he had entrusted to his fellow Linceo, Anastasius de Filiis.

Before Della Porta's death in 1615, the printing of *I due fratelli simili, Georgio*, and *Ulisse* brought to sixteen the total of his published plays. In the following year *La tabernaria* went to press with a dedication by Antonio Rossetti stating that this play had "sedici sorelle" and was "forse in questo genere, suo ultimo parto."[5]

---

4 (Romae: per Bartholomeum Zannettum, 1610), 97–99. The Appendix, slightly augmented, was reprinted separately the following year (Romae, 1611).

5 (Ronciglione, 1616), A2verso. In his *Drammaturgia* (Venezia, 1755) Lione Allacci listed a 1612 Ronciglione edition of this comedy, as did Gennaro Muzio in his edition of Della Porta's comedies, *Delle commedie* (Napoli, 1726) and Giuseppe Gabrieli in "Bibliografia Lincea. Giambattista Della Porta," *Rendiconti dell'Accademia Nazionale dei Lincei. Classe di scienze morali* . . . , Ser. 6, VIII (Roma, 1932). Both apparently lean on Allacci's authority. Fiorentino, however, believed the 1616 edition to be the first one, and the evidence supports his con-

Dating Della Porta's Plays

The unpublished plays were never properly accounted for. In 1653, G. B. Filippo Ghirardelli referred to Della Porta's *Notte* as still in manuscript.[6] Lorenzo Crasso stated in 1666 that Della Porta was the author of nine dramatic works: *"Giorgio, Penelope, Fratelli rivali, Turca, Fantesca, Cintia, Furiosa, Intrighi, Sorella."*[7] Crasso's inclusion of *Intrighi*, never mentioned by anyone else[8] was probably a careless mistake, like his omission of Della Porta's nine other published plays. The name may have been an alternate title for one of the omitted comedies; it would fit almost any of them.

The seventeenth-century Della Porta bibliography that is most trustworthy was compiled about 1646 by Bartolomeo Chioccarelli, who had studied under Della Porta and was known for painstaking scholarship.[9] Chioccarelli named sixteen published plays, overlooking only *Ulisse*. He listed as unpublished: *"La Notte, Il Fallito, La Strega, L'Alchimista, S. Dorotheae, S. Eugeniae"*; the translation of Plautus; the critical treatise which he called *"De arte componendi"*; and the seven untitled comedies, which he described just as Zannetti had done. In numbering the plays Chioccarelli followed Zannetti's order with one or two exceptions, so that his list was in effect a revision of the one appended to the *Elementorum curvilineorum* in 1610.

---

jecture. No 1612 edition is known to exist today; Allacci was not always reliable, as is proved by his designating *Penelope* as a prose work; and Rossetti's dedication, dated January 29, 1616, claimed to be introducing *Tabernaria* to the world. (. . . sixteen sisters [and was] his last offspring of this sort [the drama]).

[6] *Difesa* published with his *Costantino* in 1653 (2d ed., Roma, 1660), Index, 15.

[7] *Elogi di huomini letterati* (Venetia, 1666), I, 174.

[8] Except by Pompeo Sarnelli, who simply copied Crasso's list in his "Vita di Gio: Battista della Porta," prefixed to the translation of *Della Chirofisonomia* (Napoli, 1677), A6verso–A7.

[9] See Pietro Giannone, *Istoria civile del regno di Napoli* (5ᵃ ed., Napoli, 1723), Cap. 3, 230. Chioccarelli's work was finally published, after more than a century, as *De illustribus scriptoribus qui in civitate et regno Neapolis ab orbe condito ad annum usque MDCXXXXXVI, floruerunt* (Neapoli, 1780). The account of Della Porta is in I, 313–17.

All of the above sources were available to Fiorentino in 1880, and although he did not milk them quite dry of evidence, he used them, together with a few hints in Della Porta's correspondence and in the plays themselves, to establish at least a few dates of composition. From Barbarito's list and the request at the end of *Astrologo* for as much applause as greeted its "altre tre sorelle" (v, 5), Fiorentino deduced that *Olimpia* was followed by *Fantesca*, and that *Cintia* came third, judging from its curtain line reference to an unspecified number of "*altre.*" [10] Fiorentino was very cautious about dating these plays however. He cited one of Cardinal d'Este's letters discovered by Campori [11] to prove that one comedy and the tragicomedy had been finished by 1580,[12] and he concluded from a reference in *La turca* to "Quest'anno del settantadue" (II, 3) that this comedy was at least begun by 1572, although Barbarito did not include it on his list nineteen years later.[13] With regard to the nine other comedies not mentioned by Barbarito, Fiorentino was even more reticent. Because in the prologue to *Carbonaria* Della Porta called his comedies "fruits of leisure time" instead of "childhood games," as he had done in the prologue to *Fratelli rivali*, Fiorentino classified *Carbonaria* among the late plays, along with the *Chiappinaria*, proved by a reference to Philip III of Spain (I, 1) to have been finished after Philip II's death in September, 1598.[14] Turning to Della Porta's tragedies, Fiorentino reasoned that if manuscripts of *Georgio, Sant' Eugenia,* and *Santa Dorotea* were sent to Anastasius de Filiis, and de Filiis died in 1608, then the three sacred tragedies must have been ready before that date.[15] As for *Ulisse*, it was

[10] *Op.cit.,* 327.
[11] Giuseppe Campori, ed., *Giovan Battista della Porta e il cardinale Luigi d'Este, notizie e documenti* (Modena, 1872), 10.
[12] *Op.cit.,* 332.
[13] *Ibid.,* 331.
[14] *Ibid.,* 332.
[15] *Ibid.,* 321.

unique in having been dated exactly by the author's own announcement early in 1612,[16] an announcement which Fiorentino cited together with the Imprimatur obtained for this tragedy a few months later.[17] Unable to discover anything further about the unpublished plays listed by Barbarito and Zannetti, Fiorentino noted Scipione Volpicella's unsuccessful attempt to find some trace of "la Santa," [18] and concluded that the critical treatise, the Plautus translation, two sacred tragedies, and fifteen comedies were lost.

Although later scholars have hazarded new guesses, none of them has added anything substantial to Fiorentino's dating of Della Porta's plays. Barbarito's vague phrase "i suoi primi anni," [19] combined with Sarnelli's observations on Della Porta's literary precocity,[20] may have determined Francecso Milano's opinion that *Fantesca* and *Cintia* were ready by 1550, and *Olimpia* even earlier.[21] Ireneo Sanesi accepts Milano's statement with a grain of salt,[22] and Gabrieli borrowed the date without acknowledgement.[23] Daniel Boughner, in *The Braggart in Renaissance Comedy*,[24] on page 31 dates *Fantesca* 1550 and on page 313 dates *Fantesca* and *Olimpia* ca. 1580 and *Cintia* ca. 1550, despite the certainty that *Olim-*

[16] "Il Carteggio Linceo della vecchia accademia di Federico Cesi (1603–1630)," *Atti e memori dell'Accademia Nazionale dei Lincei, Classe di scienze morali, storiche e filologiche*, Ser. 6, VII, fasc. 1 (Roma, 1938), 232.

[17] *Op.cit.*, 305.

[18] *Ibid.*, 328. The "Mario Carduino" under whose name, according to Barbarito, the play was published, may perhaps be identified with the Mario Cardoino living in Naples between 1537 and 1548, to whom Honorato Fascitello addressed letters. See Dionigi Atanagi (ed.), *Delle lettere facete, et piacevoli, di diversi grandi huomini . . . Libro Secondo* (Venetia, 1575), letters 41–46.

[19] Dedication to *Penelope*, 2verso.

[20] *Op.cit.*, A6verso.

[21] "Le commedie di Giovanbattista della Porta," *Studi di letteratura italiana* II, fasc. 2 (Napoli, 1900), 314.

[22] *La commedia*, 2ª ed. riv. ed acc. (Milano, 1954), I, 411.

[23] "Bibliografia Lincea . . . ," 254.

[24] (Minneapolis, 1954).

pia was the first comedy. Plausibly, but without explanation, Mary Augusta Scott dated *Cintia* and *Fantesca* 1567.[25]

The mystery cannot yet be dispelled, but it may be diminished. Fiorentino's search for internal evidence of dating stopped with historical allusions, and he overlooked some of these. When his conclusions are studied together with the neglected allusions and the more subtle internal evidence in the comedies, a sequence suggests itself which corresponds more or less to the order of publication. In some cases the imagery seems to connect certain plays with specific periods in Della Porta's scientific career. Tentative dating of the dissimilar non-comic works must depend on such minutiae. But the comedies lend themselves to broader speculation, and seem to fall into four groups. The semi-farces which are known to be Della Porta's first comedies reflect in common a perfunctory morality and a primary concern with structural complexity. The second group comprises only two comedies, which are marked by a bitter satirical tone and a new exuberance of language. There was a third period of serious romantic comedies, in which Della Porta, having learned to plot without effort, concentrated on enriching his love stories with deeper moral and sentimental sensibility and his comic episodes with more generous borrowings from the *commedia dell'arte*. Eventually he turned away from this nearly tragicomic genre. Just as his last tragedy is the most classical of his works, so his last comedies are a return to semi-farce, but they are distinguished from his earliest comedies by a flavor of moral sweetness mingled with *commedia dell'arte* spice.

The order of the three non-comic verse dramas is unquestioned. *Penelope* was ready by 1580 and *Ulisse* was begun and finished in 1612. *Georgio* and the lost *Santa Dorotea* and *Sant' Eugenia* came somewhere between the tragicomedy and the secular tragedy, before de Filiis' death in 1608. If it were known exactly when Della Porta wrote the section on

[25] *Elizabethan Translations from the Italian* (Boston, 1916), 211 and 218.

earthquakes in *De aëris transmutationibus,* dedicated 1609 and published 1610, it might be possible to assign at least the revision of *Georgio* to the same general period, for in this play alone he broke into a rash of images involving earthquakes (I, 2; I, 3; II, 7). Moreover, the frantic insistence in *Georgio* on the futility of astrology and of belief in fate suggests that it was one of Della Porta's nervous attempts to comply with the Inquisitional order, issued before 1580, that he abjure "illicit arts" such as fortune-telling.[26] Furthermore, the subject of *Georgio* seems to link the play with the period of Della Porta's employment by the Este family. As patron saint of Ferrara, St. George was regarded as almost an Este himself.

The four surviving comedies listed in 1591 were probably ready much earlier. Perhaps, as Milano believed, *Olimpia* was finished and *Fantesca* and *Cintia* were being written in 1550. If the ordinary adolescent is incapable of writing such plays, so is the ordinary adult; and it must be remembered that at fifteen, Della Porta was also compiling the *Magiae naturalis.* Still, 1550 is an arbitrary date for the first three comedies. There is proof only that *Olimpia* was ready by 1580, when Della Porta sent a comedy and a tragicomedy to Cardinal Luigi d'Este. Perhaps an early version of *Fantesca* was composed in 1550, but Pantaleone's reference to King Philip and the Conquest of Portugal (IV, 7) indicates revision in or after 1581. *Cintia,* generally considered to have been third in order simply because its last line alludes to "others," whereas *Astrologo*'s curtain speech mentions "three others," resembles *Olimpia* and *Fantesca* in the studied complexity of its intrigue and in the dubious chastity of its heroine. But there is no evidence for dating it in any one specific year before 1591. It opens with a denunciation of judiciary astrology which might have been written sometime in the late sixties

[26] *Georgio* is the only one of Della Porta's dramas extant in manuscript. It is at the Biblioteca Nazionale of Naples in Codice XIII, E. 8. It shows signs of revision after September 1611.

or early seventies after the Holy Office warned Della Porta. The moral and sentimental discussions in *Cintia*, which herald the serious comedies of a later period, might have been added at the same time to make the licentious action of the play less repugnant to the censors.

L'Astrologo, the fourth comedy, is clearly a result of Della Porta's encounter with the Inquisition; it was probably his response to the Inquisitors' ominously jesting suggestion that he write a comedy as penance for his forbidden practices. The villain of the piece is a charlatan versed in the jargon of astrology, but he sets out to perform feats of alchemy and general necromancy only. Della Porta's comedy was clearly inspired by Ariosto's *Negromante* and originally may have borne the same name; the title character is referred to indiscriminately throughout as *negromante* and *astrologo*. Influenced by the Church's growing disapproval of judiciary astrology and specific admonition against his own activities, Della Porta probably changed the name of his comedy and embellished it with attacks on astrology. Barbarito undoubtedly erred in listing *Negromante* and *Astrologo* as separate works, for Della Porta's later and more trustworthy bibliographers, Zannetti and Chioccarelli, omitted the former from their lists of unpublished comedies.

The new bitter tone of *Astrologo* characterizes the second and most limited category of Della Porta's comedies. The sexual rivalry and hatred between fathers and sons, and the satire on contemporary criminal life in *Astrologo* are echoed only in *La turca*. Fiorentino's assertion that at least a part of *Turca* belonged to 1572 is supported by this similarity. It seems more than likely, then, that a minimum of five of the extant comedies were ready by the early seventies. Moreover, it was at about this time that Della Porta was haunting prisons and hospitals and enlisting the local hangman's aid in his preparation of the *Chirofisonomia*, finished sometime before 1581. The underworld characters in *Astrologo* and *Turca* are clearly the results of this research.

Dating Della Porta's Plays

La trappolaria seems to have followed closely on the heels of this phase, by virtue of its florid language and its traces of Della Porta's studies of criminal physiognomy. The heroine's care for her virginity also indicates that *Trappolaria* was at least revised while Della Porta was approaching the period of his serious comedies, in which chastity was absolute. Because *Trappolaria* was published in 1596 and was not mentioned by Barbarito in 1591, it has been tacitly assumed that the comedy was written during the five-year interim. Essentially, however, *Trappolaria* is in the style of *Olimpia* and *Fantesca*, and it is very likely that it existed before 1591 in an early version and under another title. Among the six comedies later assumed lost, Barbarito mentioned *"lo Spagnuolo."* Significantly, this title never reappeared after 1596. The *innamorato*, technically the hero, of *Trappolaria* is a Neapolitan masquerading as a Spaniard. The *innamorata* is really Spanish and is even listed as such in the *dramatis personae*, as though for emphasis. The prologue identifies the comedy with this heroine and promises that it will be as quick and witty as ladies of Spain always are. The last scene ends with an announcement that "i trattamenti della Spagnuola son finiti" (v, 6). In the latter half of the sixteenth century some Italians began to follow the Spanish fashion of inserting the titles of plays in their own final lines.[27] Sometimes comedies had alternate titles before publication. Della Porta's lost *La notte* was known also as *La pietra*, because of the pebble that figured importantly in it,[28] and each of the other comedies may likewise have had more than one name. Pieced together, such scraps of evidence support the conjecture that *Trappolaria* and *"Spagnuolo"* were the same play. The clever

[27] See A. Restori, "Appunti teatrali spagnuoli," *Studj di filologia romanza*, vii, fasc. 20 (Roma, 1898), 426.

[28] Pietro Napoli-Signorelli, *Vicende della cultura nelle Due Sicilie*, 2ᵃ ed. napoletana (Napoli, 1811), v, 528. Napoli-Signorelli did not give his evidence for this assertion, but its validity was supported by Ghirardelli's reference to the way Della Porta used the pebble in *La notte* (*op.cit.*, 173).

servant Trappola dominates the action and, after a few performances, probably pushed his way into the title. The comedy may originally have been named for its disguised hero; more probably it was called *La Spagnuola*, like its heroine. Barbarito could easily have made a mistake in gender in noting down the title.

After 1591, without deserting his early forms and themes, Della Porta appears to have yielded, like Borghini and Oddi, to Spanish influence and to Counter-Reformation demands for increased didacticism. The result was his quartet of exceedingly romantic dramas savoring of tragicomedy while permeated by the extravagant blend of classical and *commedia dell'arte* humor peculiar to his ripe years. Neither *La sorella, I due fratelli rivali, Il moro, La furiosa*, nor any titles which might apply to them appeared on the 1591 list. *Sorella*, the least romantic and probably the earliest of the group, contains an allusion to trouble between Elizabeth of England and Philip II (III, 6), but as there was little else between those two in any year, the reference reveals only that *Sorella* must pre-date Philip's death in 1598.[29] To judge from the braggart's line, "Il Re Cattolico ha fatto pace con quel di Francia"[30] (I, 2), *Il moro* would seem to have been written in 1598, between the signing of the peace treaty of Vervins, May 2, by Henri IV and Philip II, and the death of the latter on September 13. *Furiosa* was ready before 1604, when Lucrezio Nucci declared that it had been circulating in bad copies for some time.[31] It is likely that all four of the plays in

29 Boughner, *op.cit.*, 313, and Giovanni Grazzini, *Enciclopedia dello spettacolo* (Roma, 1957), IV, 403, date it 1589. Neither indicates an authority for the date, and I have discovered none. Francesco Saverio Quadrio in *Della storia e della ragione d'ogni poesia* (Bologna e Milano, 1739–1749), III, 11, dated the first edition 1584. Croce corrected Quadrio's error, substituting the true date of 1604 (*I teatri di Napoli. Secolo XV–XVIII*, Napoli, 1891, 70, note 3.).

30 (The Catholic King has made peace with the King of France.)

31 ". . . mi forzarò ancora di stampare la Foriosa [*sic*] la Turca, e l'Astrologo, dell'istesso, che vanno à torno disperse, scorrette, e mal trattate." (Dedication to *La sorella*, Napoli, 1604.)

the serious vein were composed in the last decade of the sixteenth century.

Of the four remaining published comedies not mentioned
by Barbarito, one, *I due fratelli simili*, may be a leftover from
the period of *Olimpia*. Perhaps it was a superficial revision of
Il pedante, included by Barbarito; its *agent provocateur* is a
knavish Latin tutor. Though published only the year before
Della Porta's death, and spotted with passages typical of his
elaborate late style, *Fratelli simili* is poorly constructed, as if it
were a beginner's experiment. The only certainty about this
comedy, however, is that it was ready for the press in 1610,
when Zannetti listed it as *I simili* and that it was published
four years later under the longer title obviously calculated to
appeal to admirers of *Fratelli rivali*.

La tabernaria, which is known to have been Della Porta's
last play, proves that in old age he reverted to the classical
semi-farce, retaining, however, the full-blown language, the
commedia dell'arte variations, and the moral sensibility developed since his salad days. By virtue of Barbarito's omitting
them and of their general resemblance to *Tabernaria*, *Chiappinaria* and *Carbonaria* appear also to have issued from this
mellow last period. The almost perfect balance in *Carbonaria*
of the best elements from all of Della Porta's periods, make
it seem very late, perhaps next-to-last in order, but there is no
indication of exactly how long after 1591 or before 1606 it
was composed. If a braggart captain is acceptable as a wit-
ness, *Chiappinaria* may be dated by Dragoleone's unre-
strained boast that his help is sought by the emperor against
the Hungarian rebels, by the Great Turk against his mutinous
slaves and the Persians, by Philip III against Count Maurizio
in Flanders, and by the French king against the Huguenots
(1, 1). Perhaps Dragoleone refers to the year 1600, in which
Maurice of Nassau led an expedition against Philip III's
troops in Flanders, Mohammed III fought simultaneously
the Shah of Persia and the Jelali insurrectionists, and the Imperial army at last subdued the Transylvanians. On the other

hand, Della Porta may have aimed at a comic effect which depended on Dragoleone's boasts' being several years out-of-date.

It is usually assumed that *La tabernaria* was composed after 1610, because it was not included among the plays in manuscript on Zannetti's list. There is an alternative to this assumption. The title *La bufalaria* listed by Zannetti may have been an alias for *Tabernaria*. When Chioccarelli compiled the next Della Porta bibliography, *Bufalaria* was not numbered among the unpublished works. The original title may have been a tribute to Ariosto, whose *Scolastica* was the main source of *Tabernaria*. In *Il negromante*,[32] from which Della Porta had borrowed for his *Astrologo*, Ariosto refers to "l'osteria del Bufalo" (IV, 2) in Cremona. The inn that is the center of *Tabernaria*'s action might, in a pre-1610 version, have been called *Il Bufalo*. Many *commedie erudite* contain references to places and characters in other comedies; such allusions delighted the *cognoscenti*. Possibly Della Porta reworked the comedy before its publication, transferring the action to the famous Neapolitan hostelry, *Il Cerriglio*, in order to please a more limited group of *cognoscenti*, the members of Cortese's academy, the *Schirchiate de lo Mandracchio e' Mprovesante de lo Cerriglio*. Only if the two titles refer to one play is it understandable that *Tabernaria* should never have been mentioned until its publication, at which point *Bufalaria* was dropped from the list of Della Porta's unpublished comedies and disappeared. If this conjecture is valid, it follows that Della Porta had written all of his comedies before 1610.

There is no proof that the busy septuagenarian was concerned with the drama in the last three years of his life. Three acts of a Latin comedy dominated by a character called Theophila were discovered in 1940, appended to the manuscript of *De telescopio*,[33] which Della Porta was writing just

[32] Venezia, 1535.
[33] Gabrieli's discovery of *De telescopio* in Ms. XIV of the Accademia dei Lincei was announced by Maria Amalia Naldoni in "Un manoscritto

before he died, but the Latin fragments are not in his usual hand and cannot be identified with any of his missing works.

The identification of *Spagnuolo, Negromante, Pedante,* and *Bufalaria* as alternate titles for *Trappolaria, Astrologo, Fratelli simili,* and *Tabernaria,* respectively, would account for Chioccarelli's listing as unpublished plays only *La notte, Il fallito, La strega, L'alchimista, Santa Dorotea, Sant' Eugenia,* and the seven untitled experiments in multiple comic structure.[34] The theory of alternate titles may be recommended for its plausibility as well as for supporting Chioccarelli's accuracy without diminishing by more than four the number of manuscripts which future Della Porta scholars may hope to unearth.[35]

---

inedito di G. B. della Porta," *Atti della Fondazione Ronchi* (1946), Iⁿᵉ année, n. 1–2, 48. Gabrieli himself referred to the Latin fragment thus: "Frammento (d'altra mano? d'altro inchiostro) di tragedia latina, dove appare spesso un personaggio Theophila, car. 148–156." ("Bibliografia Lincea . . . ," 218). Nevertheless, the play is indisputably a comedy.

[34] Allacci listed a *Santa Dorotea Vergine e Martire* (Siena, 1555) in *ottava rima* (*op.cit.,* 265). Gabrieli ("Bibliografia Lincea . . . ," 258) misread the date as 1655 and identified this title as a posthumous edition of Della Porta's *S. Dorotea,* despite its being in the *ottava rima* of the *sacra rappresentazione* rather than in the *versi sciolti* of the Counter-Reformation *tragedia sacra.* On inquiring at the Biblioteca Comunale of Siena, Gabrieli was told that the library lacked a 1655 *Santa Dorotea* and that no Sienese bibliographer listed one, but that there was on hand a *Rappresentatione di Santa Dorotea Vergine e Martire* of 1610. Gabrieli's erroneous listing of a 1655 edition of Della Porta's *Dorotea* found its way recently into Grazzini's article on Della Porta in *Enciclopedia dello spettacolo* (IV, 403).

[35] See Appendix A for a chart of the information about the dating of the plays.

III

Theater Between 1550 and 1614

The half-dozen decades during which Della Porta wrote were a period prolific of drama, despite intermittent attacks by the reforming clergy and the intransigence of the censors. Playgoing was a favorite recreation, indoors for the upper class, and usually outdoors for the others. Though in time his comedies reached both, Della Porta wrote all his plays for the former.

The private theater flourished in several guises. School performances like those of the "nobili giovani dell'Alberto" [1] were encouraged by the *dilettanti* and those subtler members of the clergy who descried the drama's potential for propaganda. Cultivated noblemen also rigged up scenery in their homes and decked themselves out as kings, soldiers, slaves, shepherds, priests, pedants, and ladies. The prologue to *La furiosa* gives a backstage glimpse of Della Porta's aristocratic young friends so occupied.

Theatrical entertainments were a regular activity in some academies and the sole purpose of others, such as the Neapolitan Amorosi [2] or the Roman Nascosti.[3] Occasionally the amateurs tried to rival professional actors by improvising comedies,[4] but the bulk of the academic repertoires was drama in

[1] Beltrame Poggi, *La Cangenia. Tragicomedia* (Fiorenza, 1561), dedication, Aiiverso.

[2] Benedetto Croce, *I teatri di Napoli: secolo XV–XVIII* (Napoli, 1891), 80, note 1.

[3] Lione Allacci, *Drammaturgia*, 2ª ed. accr. (Venezia, 1755), 213.

[4] Andrea Perrucci, *Dell'arte rappresentativa premeditata, e all'improviso* (Napoli, 1699), 190.

the literary tradition, furnished largely by the members themselves or by their friends. It was a mark of caste and culture to publish a play under one's academic name.[5]

Naturally, the most elaborate private performances were sponsored by the courts, often with costly scenery. In Naples the Spanish viceroys, the local scions of great families, and the wealthiest private citizens frequently backed splendid productions of plays they had enjoyed in home or school performances. Della Porta's *Olimpia*, probably written first for his circle of learned intimates, was later played against a magnificent background for the viceregal court of Miranda's day.[6] *La sorella* was sumptuously produced by Don Francesco Blanco, a Maecenas whom Della Porta gratefully called "l'Alessandro Magno dei nostri tempi." [7]

The tradition of the private theater was hardly new. These literary amateurs of the drama were doing, on a larger scale, what their grandfathers had done before them. But there was a difference in the kind of plays they performed. By midcentury the first phase of experiments with classical forms had ended and to the accompanying crescendo of debate between Ancients and Moderns, playwrights had begun answering demands for new subjects, forms, and aims in the theater.

One of the forces determining the course of drama in the latter sixteenth century was the church. Directed by the Vatican, supported by the Spanish occupation, depending on the Society of Jesus and the Inquisition, the Counter-Reformation movement was attempting to repair the spiritual and temporal damage inflicted on the Church of Rome by Protestants and Turks. The new attitudes prescribed by the Council of Trent in its determination to recoup Catholic losses were not officially defined until 1565, but they had

[5] With characteristic mockery Bruno parodied this practice on the title-page of his *Candelaio*, "Comedia del Bruno Nolano achademico di nulla achademia; detto il fastidito. . . ."

[6] *L'Olimpia* (Napoli, 1589), prologue, A2.

[7] *La sorella* (Napoli, 1604), dedication.

already been at work in the theater for some years. The
Counter-Reformers' program for the laity was designed to
prevent heresy, to increase devotion, and to improve public
morals. Obviously the drama was a carrier of virulent immorality, heresy, and dangerously satirical opinions. Even
religious drama had become offensive to reformed taste. The
old *sacre rappresentazioni* were full of honest piety, but their
accretions of romantic fiction and juxtaposition of gross comedy with sacred history were unedifying. Moreover, the accompanying spectacle and the *intermedii* were often pagan
and lascivious: there were entirely too many lightly clad
nymphs in some of the tableaux. Secular tragedy, of course,
was even more pagan, with its pre-Christian characters
swearing by various gods, praying to Fate, and committing
suicide without a scruple.

Some Counter-Reformers thought that drama should be
abolished altogether. In 1558 Pope Sixtus V prohibited
women from acting in Rome.[8] Sixteen years later, Gregory
XIII outlawed comedies even in private homes.[9] He permitted the Last Judgment to be enacted by Jesuits that year,
but even sacred plays were often banned. The bans never
held for long. Saint Carlo Borromeo, bishop of Milan,
strained every nerve to oust players from his diocese and to
prevent all stage representations. In 1565 he declared theaters
of any sort to be off limits for the clergy.[10] In 1569, unable
to keep acting troupes out of Milan, he managed to obtain an
almost prohibitive censorship decree, re-issued in 1570.[11] His
campaign was considerably hindered, however, by amateurs
of drama like Don Alvaro de Sande, temporary governor of
Lombardy in 1572, who arranged private performances and

[8] Michele Scherillo, *La commedia dell'arte in Italia* (Torino, 1884),
138.
[9] Alessandro D'Ancona, *Origini del teatro italiano* (Torino, 1891),
II, 183.
[10] Scherillo, *op.cit.*, 139.
[11] D'Ancona, *op.cit.*, II, 179.

patronized players, as much to spite Borromeo as to please himself.[12]

The clergy also produced champions of the drama, and playwrights as well, who supported its cause against Borromeo.[13] In the end, the pro-theater party won, not because its arguments made any converts, but simply because the public, aristocratic and plebeian, demanded drama and, despite fulminations and interdictions, found a way to have it.

What the Counter-Reformers could not suppress, they influenced. By 1550 the drama had begun to reflect their care for morality and orthodoxy, a care that increased as the century progressed. The Jesuits, ever specialists in bending secular institutions to the service of religious authority, took the lead in theater reform and, operating as the avant-garde of the Counter-Reformation, set up standards and produced examples to be followed by playwrights of the laity and of other religious orders. The Quattrocento *sacre rappresentazioni* were still brought out on special occasions and were widely printed in forms suitable for performance in convents and monasteries, but they were generally considered quaint, and, as such, unworthy of serious imitation. The specifically Jesuit drama was inaugurated with the transformation of the dying *sacra rappresentazione* into *tragedia sacra* or *spirituale*, an application of neoclassical conventions to religious subjects.

The reformers hoped to preserve classical form and style, while purging drama of paganism and licentiousness, but their attempts were ultimately self-defeating. The insistence on didacticism even in secular works necessarily limited the content of drama, causing many playwrights to concentrate instead on form and to develop a remarkable technical proficiency in manipulating ever more complicated plots. Searching for safe subjects, many of them fell back on

[12] Scherillo, *op.cit.*, 143.
[13] D'Ancona, *op.cit.*, ii, 179.

Giraldi's sentimental feminine themes, on *romanzi, novelle,* pastoral poetry, and on the various sorts of "escape" drama, compact of romance and adventure, imported by the Spanish occupation. The result was a breeding-ground for opiate lyricism and a sensuality which was the more pernicious for being cloaked in moral rectitude. When these elements were mingled with familiar classical and religious material, new and strange forms appeared in the theater.

In describing the mixed bag of dramatic forms evident in this period, Italian scholars are given to quoting Shakespeare:

The best actors in the world, either for tragedy, comedy, history, pastoral, pastoral-comical, historical-pastoral, tragical-historical, tragical-comical-historical, pastoral, scene individable, or poem unlimited.[14]

If Polonius had, in fact, intended reference to the Italian theater of the Counter-Reformation, he would have had to include several other exotic terms, such as *Rappresentatione spirituale, Tragedia spirituale, Comedia spirituale, Tragicomedia, Tragicomedia pastorale, Tragedia pastorale, Tragicomedia boscareccia, Grottesca drammatica, Rappresentatione amorosa, Favola tragisatiricomica, Arcicomedia capriciosa morale, Hierotragedia* . . . ,[15] not to mention the various kinds of farces and the improvised comedies of the popular theater.

This was a period dominated by the peculiarly Italian con-

[14] *Works,* ed. G. L. Kittredge (Boston, 1936), *Hamlet,* II, 2.
[15] The above terms appear on the title-pages of the following works, respectively: Giovanni Stochmar, *La maravigliosa rappresentatione spirituale . . . nella quale si tratta della miseria, vita, & fine del genere humano* (Venezia, 1610); Pier Giovanni Brunetto, *David sconsolato* (Fiorenza, 1586); Ercolano Ercolani, *Eliodoro* (Siena, 1605); Beltrame Poggi, *La Cangenia* (Fiorenza, 1561); Pietro Benedetti, *Il magico legato* (Venezia, 1607); Strozzi Cicogna, *Delia* (Vicenza, 1593); Diomisso Guazzoni, *Andromeda* (Venezia, 1587); Lauro Settizonio [Pseud. for G. B. Leoni], *Florinda* (Venezia, 1607); Raffaele Gualterotti, *La Verginia* (Fiorenza, 1584); Giovanni Battista Leoni, *Roselmina* (Venetia, 1595); Bernardino Cenati, *La Silvia errante* (Venezia, 1608); Giovanni Battista Liviera, *Giustina* (Padova, 1593).

cept of *meraviglia*, which in the Renaissance had taken almost as many forms as there were literary genres. The marvelous sometimes consisted in situation or action, as it does in the *Decameron*, a collection of marvels: marvels of fortune, of wit, of absurdity, of love. It was used as a touchstone of critical theory in innumerable sixteenth-century analyses of catharsis. The marvelous also appeared as a structural principle, supporting the fantastically complex scaffolding of Ariosto's *tour de force*. In the Counter-Reformation period the marvelous was alternately interpreted as the admirable and ingenious, and was pursued in strange combinations of forms, in tortuous plots, in the extremes of sensibility encouraged by Jesuit devotionalism, and in excesses of language, until it became a *sine qua non* of Seicento style, expressed in Marino's "È del poeta il fin la meraviglia." [16]

Yet while practice tended to extremes, to hybrid forms, exaggerated sentimentality, freakish language, and above all, to the marvelous and the moral, dramatic theory remained neoclassical. The Moderns quarreled with the Ancients' interpretations of the *Poetics* but rarely disputed Aristotle's authority. Even the least conservative of the playwrights observed the unities of time and place and frequently paid lip service to Aristotle in prefaces or prologues which accorded ill with the plays which followed them.

Della Porta was both a conservative neoclassicist and a dabbler in the latest fashions. He wrote in the time-honored genres of comedy and tragedy; he also tried his hand at sacred tragedy and tragicomedy. His neglected non-comic works are significant as illustrations of Della Porta's approach to three flourishing and controversial forms of his day.

TRAGEDY

In the 1540's and 1550's, while the Council of Trent was reshaping the Church, Giraldi Cinthio was shaping the Italian tragedy for sixty years to come. Adducing Aristotle's author-

[16] (The aim of the poet is the marvelous.)

ity whenever possible, Giraldi departed from the strictest interpretations of the *Poetics* and from models like Trissino's in order to please his public. He advocated fictional subjects, complex double plots, and division into five acts of several scenes each. He used the chorus sparingly and permitted happy endings. He preferred heroines to heroes, *meraviglia* to moderation, and romantic love to other subjects. He was studiedly didactic and sententious. He established Seneca as the classical model for himself and for a host of his successors.

Emilio Bertana distinguished four kinds of tragedy after Giraldi: historical, "horrible," classical, and romanesque.[17] Such classification is purely external, resting on differences in source material, and leaves out of account a considerable overlapping of categories. The element of horror authorized by Seneca, for example, was everywhere in evidence, answering the native demand for *meraviglia*, a demand strengthened by reawakened Catholic fervor for miracles and martyrdom. Tragedies based on *novelle* were often "horrible," but they were not alone. Not even classic examples of the type, Luigi Groto's *Dalida* (1572), Antonio Decio's *Acripanda* (1592), and the like, are more gruesome than many romanesque tragedies, such as Gabriele Zinano's *Almerigo* (1590). Also unimpeded by categorical limits was the influence of the pastoral tragicomedy, spreading preciosity and erotic sentimentality everywhere.

As Professor Weinberg has demonstrated, Renaissance literary theory and practical criticism of tragedy was "invariably put in terms of Aristotle."[18] But in late sixteenth century practice, although all secular tragedies were neoclassical in form and procedure, few were so in content. Historical or classical incidents were often treated like romantic fiction. Francesco Bracciolini, a master of Gothic tragedy in the style of Tasso's *Re Torrismondo* (1587), borrowed the

[17] *La tragedia* (Milano, 1905), 71.
[18] *A History of Literary Criticism in the Italian Renaissance* (Chicago, 1961), II, 953.

protagonists of his *Pentesilea* (1614) from Homer and re-modeled them along the lines of Tancredi and Clorinda. Even tragedies copied from Greek models reflected the influence of Giraldi, the *romanzi*, or the pastoral tragicomedy: Giovanni Andrea dell'Anguillara's *Edippo* (1565) is a Counter-Reformation *Oedipus tyrannos*, tainted with pathos produced by emphasis on the female woes of Giocasta and her daughters; Bongianni Gratarolo's *Astianatte* (1589) or any of Lodovico Dolce's classical adaptations are more restrained emotionally but tend to Cinthian prolix *sententiae* rather than to Greek simplicity; Vincenzo Iacobilli's *Hippolito* (1601) combines the plot of *Phaedra* with a double love intrigue and begins with a defense of retired country life, both pastoral commonplaces. On the whole, the tragedy of Della Porta's time was more romantic than classical, more lyrical than heroic, more Latin than Greek, and behind a camouflage of neoclassical form, it was moving toward seventeenth century *melodramma* and *oratorio*.

The move was inevitable. It is hard to maintain moderation and balance in any age of *commitment*, and despite endless discussion and adaptation of classical principles, it was hard to keep a classical spirit alive in the era of Catholic Reaction. When dramatists were not constructing romantic or pastoral "escapes," they were proselytizing. Subjects and attitudes typical of the Counter-Reformation began appearing in tragedy. Moral lessons lurked in choral utterances. Christian didacticism governed even tragedies with pagan settings. Thus Groto's *Hadriana* (1578) ends with a preachment on filial obedience, and Dolce's *Marianna* illustrates "Come l'ira è cagione/ D'incomparabil mali." [19]

Protestant persecution of Catholics became a popular subject. A rash of Mary Stuart plays broke out after that queen's execution, among them a lost tragedy of Tommaso Campanella (1598); Carlo Ruggeri's *Reina di Scozia;* and Federigo Della Valle's *Reina di Scozia*, called *Maria la reina* in its first

[19] Vinegia, 1565, v, 3. (How wrath causes incomparable evils.)

version (1591); [20] according to Mario Apollonio, the latter reveals the temper of the times in its two allegorical levels: Mary is both a symbol of persecuted Catholicism and a figure of the Blessed Virgin Mary in her sorrowful aspect. Her other aspects were presented in *Giuditta* and *Ester,* which also belong on one level to Della Valle's trilogy in honor of the Mother of God. [21]

Some difficulty was created for writers of tragedy by the Church's condemnation of the concept of Fate. Belief in Fate or Fortune was associated not only with paganism but also with Machiavelli, of whom the Tridentine Council eloquently expressed its opinion by putting his entire works on the *Index* at its inception, and was in effect a denial of the doctrine of Divine Providence. Long before the papal bull of 1586 against the divining arts and the belief in Fate on which they depended, the Church's disapproval became apparent and increasingly dangerous to ignore. But for centuries the concept of a capricious Fortune had been intrinsic to tragedy, and dramatists bred in the tradition of classical imitation hardly knew how to do without it.

Some of them solved the dilemma by prefacing their pagan tragedies with apologies for using "Gentile" terms, such as *fato, destino, sorte, fortuna,* and *stelle nimiche,* begging the enlightened audience's forbearance toward the superstitions of the invincibly ignorant characters. Most dramatists, however, excused their references to Fate by equating it with Divine Providence. The Church had always taught that the phenomena attributed by pagans to Fortune or to astral influences were actually caused by the Prime Mover, and the doctrine had been mentioned occasionally in drama before the Counter-Reformation. [22] But in Della Porta's time it became a common dramatic formula. Not every playwright

[20] Croce, *Teatri di Napoli* . . . , 83.

[21] *Storia del teatro italiano,* 2ª ed. (Firenze, 1943–1951), III, 282.

[22] See Aretino's ironic statement of it in his comedy, *La Talanta,* v, 1 (written 1541, published Ferrara, 1553).

discussed God and Fortune at as great length as Francesco Bozza did in the prologue to his *Fedra* (1578), but it was a rare tragedy of the latter sixteenth century which lacked a line of homage to *il Gran Motor*.

The wave of didacticism which cast up lessons in morality and theology, also swept politics onto the stage in tragedies dealing with the "reason of state."[23] *Ragion di stato*, a catch-phrase borrowed from Guicciardini and connoting pragmatical statecraft, was the subject of numerous Counter-Reformation treatises. Among the earliest and the best-known was Giovanni Botero's semi-official expression of the Church's opposition to Machiavellian political theory, *Della ragion di stato* (1589). Using expediency as an argument, Botero preached reconciliation between politics and morality. But the argument for ethical politics implicitly recognizes a conflict of private with public morality, of the individual conscience with the "reason of state."

As sixteenth-century dramatists soon realized, it was a conflict tailor-made for tragedy. In *Merope* (1589), *Vittoria* (1603), *Polidoro* (1605), and *Tancredi* (1597), Pomponio Torelli used the theme to good effect, as did Ridolfo Campeggi in his *Tancredi* (1614). The conflict between the hero and his daughter in this last play is essentially the same as that in Giraldi's famous *Orbecche* (1541). But whereas the "heavy" father in the older play seems a sadistic madman, Tancredi is believably motivated. He desires his daughter's happiness, but when she contracts a marriage which threatens his Sicilian alliance and endangers his sovereignty (ii, 2), he is willing to commit murder. He prefers to sacrifice personal virtue to *ragion di stato*. The struggle of state and individual was a theme which mixed easily with other contemporary dramatic elements: with horror, romantic love, fiction or his-

---

[23] See Croce, *Storia delle età barocca in Italia . . .* 2ª ed. riv. (Bari, 1946), 76ff. for analysis of this concept, and *La letteratura italiana* (Bari, 1956), i, 443–46, and *Nuovi saggi sulla letteratura italiana del seicento* (Bari, 1931), 53, for examples of its use in tragedy.

tory, with religious propaganda in Della Porta's *Georgio*, or with pastoral preciosity in Prospero Bonarelli's *Solimano* (1619), a romanesque-historical study of tyranny based on the incident in Persian history which also inspired Fulke Greville's *Mustapha*. But this trend did not result in a tradition of political-historical tragedy to rival that of England. Indeed, Riccoboni declared that Italian tragedy worthy of the name had disappeared by 1620.[24] Allowing for exaggeration and for a few notable exceptions it is true that in the seventeenth century Italian dramatists turned from neoclassical concepts of tragedy to concentrate on the romantic, pastoral, and lyrical forms which were at last to evolve into opera.

SACRED TRAGEDY

The species of tragedy which survived longest was developed by the Counter-Reformation. In the decade or so before the Council of Trent adjourned, Christian substance and classical form were fused in a new genre, the *tragedia sacra*, which brought Italian religious drama closer to secular tragedy than it had been before.[25] The first religious tragedies were written by Jesuits for performance in their own colleges, and by 1591 the *Ratio studiorum* included drama in the curriculum, with stipulations amplified in the 1599 edition that the subject be sacred, the language Latin, and the characters male in fact and in dress.[26] But long before the 1590's, the fashion had spread beyond the seminary and all regulations had been relaxed. Translations multiplied, and though Latin drama was continued into the seventeenth century by clerics like Padre Stefoni, sacred tragedy in the ver-

[24] *Histoire du théâtre italien depuis la decadence de la comédie latine* . . . (Paris, 1728), 262f.

[25] Sacred comedy existed also, but as a separate and fairly rare genre. Its bizarre marriage of allegory with comic intrigue is represented by Ercolani's *Eliodoro, commedia spirituale* (1605), and Capelletti's *Clesebia, overo scorta alla religione, commedia spirituale* (1616).

[26] Apollonio, *op.cit.*, III, 267.

nacular soon became the rule.[27] The prohibition against female characters was speedily disregarded.

The kinship of the *tragedia sacra* to the old *sacra rappresentazione* is immediately apparent. Lottini's *Sacra rappresentazione di Sant'Agnesa* (1592) and many other sacred tragedies well into the seventeenth century bore the old designation but belonged unquestionably to the new genre. Both were based on Scripture or hagiographies, although sacred tragedy abode by the official Imprimatur and avoided the apocrypha dear to writers of *sacre rappresentazioni*.

In form, however, the old and new genres differed greatly. In the *tragedia sacra* all the conventions established for secular tragedy by a half century of neoclassical experimentation were put to work *ad majorem Dei gloriam*. Gone was the *ottava rima* of the *sacra rappresentazione*, replaced by Trissino's *versi sciolti*. The traditional scenes in which the saintly protagonist converted his oppressors to Christianity now bristled with stichomythy. The pains of hell, the joys of heaven, and the martyrdoms once so graphically presented (often to the distress of the actors) were now relegated to narratives. The plot was divided into five acts, each con-

[27] The anonymous *Saul* (1566) and *Il martirio di Santa Caterina* (ca. 1568), cited by Benedetto Soldati, *Il Collegio Mamertino e le origini del teatro gesuitico*, Torino, 1908, 17, are among the first examples of Italian *tragedia sacra*. Allacci (*op.cit.*, 539) mentioned *La morte di Cristo, tragedia*, of Giovanni Domenico di Lega (Napoli, 1549), which may be an earlier example. Giano Anisio's *Protogonos* (Neapoli, 1536), a Latin tragedy in five acts with chorus, on the subject of the Fall, is a precursor of Counter-Reformation sacred tragedy, but its mixture of a chorus of angels with a chorus of classical nymphs, its Greek substitutions for Old Testament names, and its complete identification of God the Father with Jupiter are distinctly pre-Tridentine. Giovanni Francesco Conti Stoa's *Tragedia de Passione Dōinii Jesu Christi: que Theoandrathanatos* (1508) is less like Counter-Reformation sacred tragedy than like the sixteenth-century Protestant *or* Catholic plays written in Latin on Christian subjects for a Hroswithan purpose, i.e., to provide schoolboys with something less profane than Terence as a textbook. The earliest certain date for Jesuit sacred tragedy in Latin is 1564, the year of Stefano Tuccio's *Juditha* (appended to Soldati, *op.cit.*).

cluded by a choral utterance in the Renaissance lyric forms common to secular tragedy. The unities of time and place took precedence over the facts of the story. In the preface to *Giustina* (composed in 1602) Bonaventura Morone explained that although in fact his heroine's history began in Antioch and ended sometime later in Nicomedia, he had departed from exact truth in order to avoid violating the sacrosanct unities.[28]

Most *tragedie sacre* were neoclassical only in form however. There were a few austere exceptions among the Old Testament dramatizations, but by their subject matter the martyr tragedies were usually denied real tragic action. Despite the playwrights' attempts to engage adventitious characters in sustained conflict, the succession of temptations usually withstood by an unwavering central figure was inevitably reminiscent of *sacra rappresentazione tableaux*. The national taste for marvels of horror was a great enemy to classical decorum. Used to the grisly spectacles provided by the *sacre rappresentazioni* and confirmed in bloodthirstiness by the secular tragedies of Giraldi and his successors, the public panted for the details of every martyrdom. Lottini described his hero's death twice in his tragedy of San Lorenzo (1592)[29] in order to provide the requisite number of chills. In this way the pent-up sensuality nourished by Counter-Reformation policy and Jesuit methods of meditation found an outlet, at the sacrifice of classical moderation.

The element of the supernatural also was tempting to authors in search of sensationalism, and although a few conservatives limited themselves to an angel in the prologue, abstractions and creatures from the other world grew more numerous and more terrifying until, by the early seventeenth century, the *dramatis personae* of more than one sacred tragedy would have served the most fullblown *sacra rappresentazione* of a hundred years earlier. Morone's *Mortorio di Cristo*

[28] Venezia, 1617, A3verso.
[29] IV, 7 and V, 2.

(1612) includes, in addition to the Blessed Virgin Mary, the Apostles, and other Gospel figures, the ghost of Adam, personifications of Death and Justice, one devil, several zombies, and a generous supply of angels. The same *tragedia spirituale* illustrates the ubiquity of pastoral elements in drama post-dating *Il pastor fido:* when Peter laments his betrayal of Christ, he is answered and advised by Echo, just as if he were a lovelorn shepherd, piping his woes to the woodland glade (III, 2).

These breaches of decorum were easily tolerated. Most playwrights regarded the sacred tragedy less as a classical improvement on the outmoded *sacra rappresentazione* than as a Christian improvement on the profane tragedy. Antonio Ongaro's sonnet congratulating Giovanni Andrea Ploti on having substituted Judith for Phaedra or Dido [30] defines the mission of sacred tragedy as understood by most literati of the Counter-Reformation. Edification replaced catharsis as the function of tragedy. Brunetto's *Davide sconsolato* (1586), concluding with the Hebrew king's statement that he (and, by implication, the audience too) is now purged of dangerous emotions, is a rare exception. The usual purpose of sacred tragedy was quite the opposite—to excite strong religious feeling.

Many *tragedie sacre*, like Lottini's *Sant'Agnesa*, were mere naïve and monotonous stimulations to piety. In Della Valle's *Giuditta* and *Ester*, however, didacticism was subordinated to art. Giovanni Maria Cecchi's religious plays, among the finest examples of the genre, were as theatrically effective as his famous comedies. Other sacred tragedies were intended for reading as well as for performance. Morone recommended *Il mortorio di Cristo* to his fellow Minorites as a systematized guide to meditation.[31] Theological discussion abounds in the most intellectual of these tragedies. The hero-saint is frequently pitted against an examining board of pagan

[30] *Giuditta* (Piacenza, 1589), Preface.
[31] Cremona, 1612, preface, t5verso.

philosophers. Challenged by one such inimical pack, Antonio Spezzani's S. Catherina effects a mass conversion.[32] Even when other points of doctrine were not introduced, the famous question of Fate and Divine Providence was almost sure to arise. The Church's pronouncement was hammered home again and again, sometimes by long expositions, like that in Della Porta's *Georgio*, or else by frequent references to the *Gran Motor eterno* who is the only Fate.

In Della Porta's time writers of sacred tragedy could be numbered in the hundreds. The genre lived on into mid-seventeenth century in the works of Padre Scamacca and others, but the decline of its popularity was ordained decades earlier by the addition of music to the poetic text. Religious dramas like Andreini's *Adamo* (1613) and *Maddalena lasciva e penitente* (1612), with their music, tableaux, and varied meters, reflect a changing taste, and are only one step removed from the *Oratorio sacro* which, cultivated by St. Filippo Neri, was to supersede the sort of sacred tragedy Della Porta wrote.

TRAGICOMEDY

In the prologue to *La Penelope* Della Porta heralded his work as the first tragicomedy since Plautus' *Amphytrion* (A2verso). The Neapolitan jack-of-all-learning always fancied himself in the role of a pioneer, and his magico-scientific career was punctuated by squabbles over priority. Sometimes his claims were justified. Undeniably he broke new ground in botany and, as his contemporaries believed, in optics as well. But the field of tragicomedy had obviously been ploughed before Della Porta came to it.

The term *tragicomedia* appeared as early as 1493, claiming descent from Plautus,[33] but for a long time thereafter no one was entirely sure what it meant. Used to cover a multitude of genres, the word was applied to: the Spanish dialogue novel *Celestina* (translated 1506); Marcantonio Epicuro's *Cecaria*

[32] *Rappresentatione di Santa Catherina* (Bologna, 1587), Act II, 7–8.
[33] Marvin T. Herrick, *Tragicomedy. Its Origin and Development in Italy, France, and England* (Urbana, 1955), 63.

(1535), a thoroughly undramatic discussion of Platonic love; Delle Valle's lyrical *Adelonda di Frigia* (performed 1595); Poggi's pseudo-historical *Cangenia* (1561); Guazzoni's tearful comedy *Quintilia* (1579); G. B. Leoni's morality play *La conversione del peccatore a Dio* (1591); and G. B. Ciotti's *Apollo favorevole*, "*Tragicomedia politicale*" (1597). Taken all together, these plays (*Celestina* excepted) seem to have nothing consistently in common but a happy ending, and even that is variable, sometimes general, but often restricted to the sympathetic characters.

From this apparent disorder, however, two dominant kinds of tragicomedy emerged in turn. First was the "happy tragedy" cultivated in mid-century by G. B. Giraldi Cinthio. He himself referred to it as *tragicomedia* because the term was current,[34] but he considered *tragedia di fin felice* or *fin lieto* a more accurate designation. *Selene, Altile, Arrenopia*, and his other *tragedie di fin lieto* contain no humor or satire. Their choruses intone *sententiae*. Their plots involve regal characters in desperately serious conflicts which end bloodily for the villains. Giraldi recommended the complexities of linked peripeties and agnitions for all kinds of tragedy, and thought that double plots with *nodi intricati*, considered inferior by Aristotle and commonly associated with comedy, were especially appropriate to *tragedia di fin lieto*.[35] He observed the formality of adducing Plautus as a classical authority for tragicomedy,[36] but his true reason and justification for mixing genres was that the mixtures were applauded. Imbued with Tridentine spirit, the public liked Giraldi's novellesque intrigue plots, which substituted the interest of action for the possibly dangerous stimulation of thought. It approved his romantic idealization of women, his love stories full of emotional movement but free of sexual immorality or illicit passion. Reformed audiences were reassured by

[34] *Altile*, prologue, in *Tragedie* (Venezia, 1583), II, 9. First published 1543.

[35] *Discorsi . . . intorno al comporre de i romanzi, delle comedie, e delle tragedie, e di altre maniere di poesie* (Vinegia, 1554), 224.

[36] *Ibid.*, 220.

Giraldi's orthodox didacticism and by the strict justice he always dispensed, rewarding virtue and punishing vice.

Tragicomedy was not defined and established as a genre, however, until Guarini took the pastoral themes made familiar in drama by Beccari and Tasso and fused them with the complex fictional plot and sententiousness inherited from Giraldi, to produce *Il pastor fido,* a pastoral tragicomedy which touched off a critical war, and set an international fashion. Guarini's mixture of genres was deliberate and the ingredients were measured exactly:

> . . . chi compone Tragicomedie . . . prende dall'una [tragedia] le persone grandi, non l'azione; la fauola verisimile ma non vera; gli affetti mossi, ma rintuzzati; il diletto non la mestizia; il pericolo non la morte. Dall'altra [comedia] il riso non dissoluto, le piaceuolezze modeste, il nodo finto, il riuolgimento felice, & sopra tutto l'ordine Comico.[37]

Tragicomedy aimed at purging melancholy by means of delight,[38] and had, therefore, to provide a universally happy ending. Guarini considered the conclusion an essential difference between his kind of tragicomedy and *tragedia di fin lieto*.[39]

The battles waged in academies and on paper over Giraldi's *tragedie di fin lieto* were mild compared to the disputes which arose as *Il pastor fido* was read in installments for several years before its publication in 1590.[40] Bound by the

[37] *Il verrato ovvero difesa di quanto ha scritto M. Giason Denores, Contra le tragicomedie, et le pastorali, in un suo discorso di poesia* (Ferrara, 1588), 19recto and verso. (. . . the writer of tragicomedies . . . from tragedy takes high-ranking characters, not high action; a plausible but not factual plot; moved but subdued passions; delight, not misery; danger, not death. From comedy he takes seemly laughter, modest pleasures, fictional complications, happy ending, and above all comic structure.)

[38] *Ibid.,* 26.

[39] *Compendio della poesia tragicomica, tratto dai duo verati . . .* (Venetia, 1601), 40–41.

[40] See Weinberg for a full account of this great literary quarrel, *op.cit.,* II, 1074–1105.

limits of a pastoral never-never land, Guarini's mixture of comic and tragic elements was far less free than that in contemporary English tragicomedies, rich jumbles of realism and romance, plebeians and nobles, low style and lofty. To conservative purists like Giason Denores, however, the intrigue of amorous shepherds, didactic priests, and farcical satyrs, seemed a monstrous infraction of classical rules. But though the controversy occupied not a few critics and produced numerous *Discorsi* and *Trattati*, the issue was decided by audiences and dramatists, who welcomed Guarini's genteel sensuality and sheer music, and were glad to escape into Arcady from the difficulties created for the drama by Counter-Reformation policy. The *Pastor fido* was imitated even before it was completed, and all Italian tragicomedy (as well as much tragedy and comedy) after Guarini owed something to him.

Even non-pastoral plays which bore the label *tragicomedia* were reminiscent of *Il pastor fido*. Leoni's *Antiloco* (1594), a romanesque adventure drama, is cinctured by a prologue and epilogue describing the disarming of Amor. Della Valle's *Adelonda* contains neither pastoral nor comic elements, but it meets the requirements of the new tragicomedy with its Golden Age setting, magical atmosphere, lyrical emotionalism, and its broad, soft moral reiterated by a chorus in flowing draperies—nature must govern love.

The Italian lachrymose comedy, which, by virtue of its mixture of very high with very low life and of romantic idealism with farce, might have aspired to the name of tragicomedy, was never so called after *Il pastor fido* was established as the generic archetype. Guazzoni's *Quintilia* was subtitled *tragicommedia* in 1579, but the tearful dramas of Oddi and his imitators and Della Porta's *Fratelli rivali, Moro,* and *Furiosa* were regarded without qualification as *commedie erudite*. Technically, therefore, *La Penelope* is Della Porta's only tragicomedy.

Della Porta's Verse Dramas

DELLA PORTA wrote *Penelope* before 1580,[1] borrowing his plot from the *Odyssey*. Though he hailed his work as the first Italian tragicomedy, it followed every rule laid down by Giraldi Cinthio for the *tragedia di fin lieto*. Indeed, Giraldi had cited the *Odyssey* as the classic example of "happy tragedy":

. . . le [tragedie] infelici sono piu simili alla Iliade, et le liete alla Odissea, si per lo argumento, come per la mescolanza delle persone, che parue c'Homero in quiste due compositioni ci uolesse cosi dare l'essempio dell'una et dell'altra Tragedia: . . . onde si vede quanto si siano ingannati coloro c'hanno detto che la Iliade ci da la forma della Tragedia, et l'Odissea quella della

[1] See Chapter III regarding the date of *Penelope's* composition. In 1591 it was printed in Naples by the heirs of Matteo Cancer with a preface by Pompeo Barbarito. Zannetti, Chioccarelli, and Brunet referred only to this edition. Allacci listed another, "Napoli, per Gio. Domenico Rocangliolo, 1628," and Gabrieli mentioned second and third editions "Roma, 1620, 1628" ("Bibliografia Lincea. I. Giambattista Della Porta.—Notizia bibliografica dei suoi mss. e libri, edizioni, ecc. con documenti inediti," *Rendiconti della R. Accademia Nazionale dei Lincei. Classe di scienze morali* . . . Serie 6, VIII, Roma, 1932, 255), minus printers, but no exemplars of any of these have been discovered. Allacci apparently never saw a copy of *Penelope* (despite his detailed listing of the doubtful second edition), for he referred to it as a prose work. Historians of the drama from Napoli-Signorelli on mention it by title, but the only discussion of the play is Francesco Fiorentino's brief description in "Del teatro di Giovan Battista de la Porta," *Studi e ritratti della Rinascenza* (Bari, 1911), 294-340, reprinted from *Giornale napoletano di filosofia e lettere, scienze morali e politiche* . . . , Nuova serie, III, fasc. 7 (marzo 1880). Fiorentino used the Vatican Library's copy of the 1591 edition. I have discovered no other copy.

Comedia, dandoci insieme amendue l'essempio della Tragedia: quella della Tragedia del fine infelice: questa di quella di fin felice. Ma incorsero costoro in simile errore, perche furono d'opinione che non si potesse far Tragedia, che finisce in allegrezza.[2]

The one noticeable difference between *Penelope* and "happy tragedies" like *Altile* and *Selene* is that instead of merely trimming the function of the chorus, as Giraldi had done, Della Porta dispensed with it altogether.

As a protégé of Luigi d'Este, Della Porta was admitted to Ferrarese literary circles of the generation after Giraldi's. His affinity for Cinthian precepts may have originated with this association, which also kept him abreast of the critical war set off in the 1580's by *Il pastor fido*. The latter was a *cause célèbre* of the sort with which Della Porta liked to be connected, and *Penelope* was the only thing he had on hand which might be used as a link.[3] Therefore he made haste to represent himself as the first since Plautus to concoct a tragicomedy. The claim necessitated ignoring earlier mixtures of tragedy and comedy, among them Giraldi's, and overlooking

---

[2] *Discorsi . . . intorno al comporre de i romanzi, delle comedie, e delle tragedie, e di altre maniere di poesie* (Venegia, 1554), 225. (. . . tragedies with unhappy endings are more like the *Iliad* and those with happy endings like the *Odyssey*, both in subject and in mixture of characters, as if in these two works, Homer wished to give us an example of each kind of tragedy . . . thus it is clear how mistaken are those who say the *Iliad* is the model of tragedy and the *Odyssey* of comedy, since both are models of tragedy: the former of tragedy with an unhappy end, the latter of tragedy with a happy end. But those people fell into such error because of the opinion that tragedy cannot end happily.

[3] It was not the last time he was to pull himself onto a bandwagon by questionable means. When he was experimenting with combinations of lenses, he must have known that other scientists had done and were doing the same thing. But later, when Galileo's discoveries made news, Della Porta claimed on doubtful evidence to be the inventor of the telescope. See his letter of August 28, 1609 to Cesi in "Il carteggio linceo della vecchia accademia di Federico Cesi (1603–1630)," *Rendiconti della R. Accademia Nazionale dei Lincei. Classe di scienze morali . . .* Serie 6, VII, fasc. 1 (Roma, 1938), 114.

the essential dissimilarity of *Penelope* to the pastoral genre which had assumed a monopoly of the label *tragicomedia*.

Della Porta revised his play before its publication in 1591 and probably added the prologue at the same time, in an after-the-fact attempt to place himself in the vanguard of the new controversial movement. After the opening observation that comedy deals with ordinary people and concludes joyously, whereas tragedy presents the downfall of the mighty, he states:

> L'autor di qsta hà scelto il bello, e'l buono,
> De l'vna e l'altra, e l'ha congionto in vna
> Tragicomedia sì, ch'in vn vedrete
> Di Dei, di Rè, d'Heroi sentenze graui
> E'n fin lieti, e festeuoli successi.[4]

But this description would fit any of Giraldi Cinthio's *tragedie di fin lieto*. Della Porta needed a brand new element to point to, something that would prove him more than a Cinthian imitator and would qualify *Penelope* as a forerunner of the *Pastor fido*. Remembering that the pastoral tragicomedy provides a single comic outcome for virtuous and vicious characters alike, in distinction to Giraldi's meting out of exact justice, Della Porta tried to associate *Penelope* with the new fashion thus:

> Ne per hauer Tragicomedia detto,
> Vna historia stimar deuete, mista
> Di successi tra lieti, e sanguinosi;
> Perch'ella è tutta d'allegrezza colma,[5]

---

[4] (The author of this has chosen the beautiful and the good of the one and of the other, and has joined them in a tragicomedy, so that you will see the serious pronouncements of gods, kings, and heroes, together with joyous events at the conclusion.) In this and in the succeeding chapter passages are quoted as they appear in the original editions. Confusing misprints and abbreviations are indicated by "[*sic*]," but all accents have been allowed to stand without comment.

[5] (Nor because I have said tragicomedy should you think this a story in which happy and bloody events are mixed, for this is crowned with complete joy,)

but, unable to ignore the bloody facts of his story, added
lamely,

> E su pur morti vi saranno alcuni,
> Sol raccontar l'vdrete, anzi voi stessi
> Per lor opre maluaggie, inique, e felle
> Degni di più ria morte gli farete,
> E ne haurete piacer, anzi che noia.[6]

The qualifying clause undermines his claim. Penelope's
suitors are no less dead for being massacred offstage. The
method of presenting their death is exactly that dictated by
Giraldi for the "happy tragedy":

Si fanno nondimeno queste morti in casa, perche non s'intro-
ducono per la commiseratione, ma per la giustizia. Et si fa che
gli spettatori ne sentono le uoci di fuori; ouero che lor sono
narrate, o da messo, o da altra persona, che scielga l'auttore atta
a far questo.[7]

Thus Della Porta's claims to originality cannot be admitted.
Penelope was not an innovation. It blazed no trail for the
pastoral tragicomedy, it mingles tragic and comic elements
hardly at all, and is essentially tragicomedy of the same type
as Giraldi's *tragedia di fin lieto*.[8]

---

[6] (and if a few people die, you will merely hear of it; moreover, because of their evil, wicked, and sinister acts, you yourselves will judge
them deserving of a harsher death, and you will be rather pleased than
distressed by it.)

[7] *Discorsi* . . . , 222. (Nevertheless these deaths must occur within
[i.e. offstage], because they are introduced for the sake of justice
rather than to arouse pity. And it must be handled so that the audience
hears the voices from outside or hears an account of them from a messenger or some other person whom the author chooses for the purpose.)

[8] Whether or not Della Porta knew it, he was not even the first to
dramatize the *Odyssey* as tragicomedy. An *Ulixe patiente, tragicommedia in terzine* was dedicated to Ippolito de'Medici by Giovanni
Falugi sometime before the cardinal's death in 1535. The manuscript
was never published and is preserved at the Biblioteca Nazionale of
Florence, Codice Maglibecchiano c. vi, 167. Like Della Porta, Falugi
adapted Books 16-23 of the *Odyssey*, but as his title indicates, his em-

Della Porta's Verse Dramas

Cardinal Luigi d'Este did not care much for *Penelope*.[9] But his opinion cannot be considered representative for his time. The Estensi were ever better patrons than critics. Luigi's great-uncle, Ippolito, had not been impressed by *Orlando Furioso*. *Penelope* is not a great play, but it is a well-constructed one. The plot observes the unities of time, place, and action prescribed for comedy and tragedy alike, and yet includes the entire account of Odysseus' wanderings. Five acts cover the events in Ithaca described in Books 16–23 of Homer's epic, allowing twenty-four hours for Ulisse to return, investigate his wife's plight, plan his strategy, effect his revenge, and reveal himself to his household. He and the other characters are not too busy, however, to deliver long soliloquies narrating all the occurrences of the past ten years, and a good many earlier ones as well. By Aristotelian definition [10] the plot is complex, depending on agnitions and a peripety leading to a double conclusion, Ulisse's revenge and Penelope's reward. But despite multiplicity of episode, character, and aim, unity is the final effect; the motives of all sixteen characters are developed and related to the twofold primary issue so as to achieve a close interaction, admirable for its balance.

Orderliness, however, is not enough; drama requires conflict. The basic situation in *Penelope* is alive with theatrical possibilities, but fidelity to the letter of the *Odyssey* hampers their development. Can Penelope hold out against remarriage in the face of persuasions and threats? Can Ulisse find a way to destroy the suitors, who greatly outnumber him? Della Porta's protagonists feel little doubt about the answers to these questions. Penelope is consistently firmer than Gibraltar, and at the outset, Ulisse receives Minerva's assurance of

---

phasis is on Ulysses, not Penelope. See Ferdinando Neri, *La tragedia italiana del '500* (Firenze, 1904), 16, note 3. Allacci listed no other dramatic versions of the material until the seventeenth century.

[9] Giuseppe Campori, ed., *Giovan Battista della Porta e il cardinale Luigi d'Este . . .* (Modena, 1872), 10.

[10] *Poetics* x, Loeb Classical Library (London, 1932).

victory. The heroine is left with very little to do. Her part in preparing the suitors' downfall is finished by the end of Act II, when she produces Ulisse's bow and proclaims that she will marry whoever is able to use it. From then on she has only to reiterate her yearning for her husband and her determination to die before belonging to anyone else. Ulisse fritters away four acts, spying on the household, gathering reasons for doing what he and Minerva have long ago agreed on. In the fifth he slaughters the suitors offstage. Eumeo's description of the scene to Icario (v, 2) is an excellent paraphrase of Homer, but neither the narration nor the hearer's reaction to it produces dramatic action or an effective substitute thereof. Ulisse occupies himself for the rest of the play with further testing of his wife's invincible chastity.

Sustained conflict is missing. If Della Porta had played more freely with his borrowed plot, if Ulisse's identity were temporarily concealed from the audience, if the *dea ex machina* Minerva were not introduced so early, too palpable and too articulate, if Penelope were momentarily susceptible to temptation or to fear, the play might be gripping. As it is, the dramatic effects result only from contrast of sentiments and from the pleasing irony of Ulisse's unsuspected presence in his own home, where his enemies hope for and Penelope laments his continued absence. The moments of theatrical vitality all depend on purely emotional tension. Fortunately, Della Porta exploits such moments to the fullest, in the nocturnal scene, for example, in which from her terrace Penelope worries aloud about Ulisse, who stands below and comforts her, unseen and unheard except by the audience (III, 9). Unlike Romeo and Juliet, the middle-aged Ithacan lovers do not end the scene in duet.

Despite Della Porta's deep sympathy with the classical spirit and his fidelity to Homer's story, the theme and purpose of *Penelope* are totally un-Homeric. However closely his plot follows the *Odyssey*, Della Porta gives it an unmistakably Counter-Reformation interpretation. The very title testifies to a shift of emphasis. Ulisse is actually the protagonist, but Penelope is the soul of the play. To be sure, the ancients had their Antigones and Medeas, but only a late Renaissance playwright, confirmed in the tradition of *Orbecche, Marianna,* and their sisters, would have adapted the *Odyssey* as a she-drama. Admittedly Plautus had dramatized the situation of two faithful, waiting wives in *Stichus,* which Della Porta undoubtedly remembered as he wrote *Penelope,* but the loyal creatures in the Latin comedy are barely given a nod of approval from their returning husbands before the aimless but amusing action takes another direction. Della Porta's heroine is not so casually treated.

Neither sentimental nor novellesque, *Penelope* belongs only in part to that harvest of semi-romantic tragedies and tragicomedies planted by Giraldi. But a Cinthian didacticism governs Della Porta's intentions. Obeying the Counter-Reformation moral strictures, he promises in the prologue to make justice prevail and to provide the female part of his audience with a model of wifely virtue suitable for universal imitation. Eumeo's adieu in the last lines of Act V charges the spectators to praise "Il viuer casto, e l'honorato nome/ Di Penelope . . ." (Scene 7). [11]

In order to increase Penelope's moral stature, Della Porta introduces several scenes which Homer authorizes by only a few words. On the basis of a reference in the *Odyssey* Book 19 to the desire of Penelope's parents for her remarriage, and

[11] (The chaste life and honored name of Penelope.) The sexual mores of literary heroines seem to have been as popular a subject of public discussion in the later Renaissance as the behavior of more substantial women is with the locker-room crowd today. The figures of Penelope and Dido received special attention. Prospero Bonarelli, in the preface to *Solimano* (Roma, 1632; first edition Venezia, 1619), declares himself on the side of the cynics. Barbarito dedicated *Penelope* to Gesualdo because the latter "has always been a supporter of Penelope's chastity" (A2). A character in Della Porta's *Tabernaria* (III, 9) comes almost to blows in defense of Dido's reputation. Della Porta himself chooses to ignore Pausanius' slur on Penelope's character (*Description of Greece,* Book VIII, xii, 5–7, trans. W. H. S. Jones, III, Loeb Classical Library, London, 1933, 407), and defends her good name by making her chastity a moral pivot for his tragicomedy.

with the Plautine authority of *Stichus* i, 2,[12] Della Porta creates an emotional dispute between the faithful wife and her father Icario (i, 4). The scene is an early version of the encounter between Oriana and Omone in Della Porta's serious comedy, *Il moro* (i, 4). The latter, formal yet turbulent with its conflicts of love with honor, honor with duty, duty with friendship, is strikingly Corneillian in tone. Penelope does not really feel pulled in two directions, but she is nonetheless Oriana's ancestor. Della Porta's mature concept of drama as moral conflict owes much to the less complicated Counter-Reformation emphasis on moral example which determines the character of Penelope.

The didactic intention separates *Penelope* in spirit from the *Odyssey*. The heroine who emerges in Della Porta's adaptation is not a Greek queen but a Renaissance lady. She must not wheedle jewels from her suitors to increase her husband's store, as Homer's shrewd housewife does (*Od.* Bk. 18). The latter-day Penelope takes the modern view of valuable gifts and proudly returns them to the senders rather than compromise her reputation. Her virtue is ornamented by physical and social graces. Like every true Renaissance lady, she inspires Petrarchan poetry. Eurymachus' brief complaint to Penelopeia in Book 18 of the *Odyssey* becomes, in Della Porta's hands, an extended contest of praise between Eurimaco and Antinoö. They are for all the world like a pair of sonneteering Renaissance lovers, and their vocabulary is straight out of a velvet-bound *petrarchino:*

> Mira la chioma d'or, che sciolta ondeggia
> Al'aura, e fa la fronte più serena,
> Hor qual cuor sia giamai, che non desij
> Morir, cosi sotto bei nodi auolto? [13]

---

[12] Plautus, *Works*, trans. Paul Nixon, v, Loeb Classical Library (London, 1938).

[13] (Behold the golden tress which waves, loosened, in the breeze and makes the brow more serene. Lives there a heart which would not wish to die bound by such lovely knots?)

Several other commonplaces of Renaissance literature turn up during the systematic demonstration of Penelope's perfections. The suitors choose as messenger an old woman of the Celestina stamp, cousin to the subtle-tongued panderesses of Aretine comedy. True to type, she delivers a plea in the overworked *carpe diem* vein, which Penelope rejects with sound moral arguments. There follows a gratuitous discussion of feminine honor, in which Penelope denies that secrecy is the best guardian of fair fame (III, 1). This has little to do with the immediate case; the suitors are proposing marriage, after all, and honor is not in question. But the scene proves that Penelope can handle the topics of conversation likely to arise in cultivated Renaissance circles, and that her opinions are irreproachable.

Some of the underlings also belong to the sixteenth century rather than to classical antiquity and, by their misdeeds, indirectly contribute to the general didactic effect. In the prologue stressing *Penelope*'s moral seriousness, Della Porta repudiates the stock characters of comedy, as Plautus had done in the prologue to *Captivi:* [14]

> Quì non di gloriosi Capitani
> Vedrete i vanti, ò vecchi auari, e sciocchi,
> Non isfacciate meretrici, ò ingordi
> Ruffiani, ò affamati Parasiti.
> Non serui astuti, fraudolenti, e iniqui,
> Non giouani otiosi, innamorati,
> . . . .[15]   (A4verso)

And yet, without admitting any specifically comic scenes, Della Porta introduces three subdued specimens of these stock types into his *tragicomedia*. In Book 18 of the *Odyssey* Iros, the beggar with whom Odysseus wrestles, is character-

---

[14] *Ibid.*, 1 (1937).

[15] (You will not see here the boasts of vainglorious captains, nor miserly and foolish old men, nor bold-faced prostitutes, nor greedy procurers, nor famished parasites. Nor shrewd, cheating, and wicked servants, nor idle, enamoured youths . . .)

ized as a simple coward who turns to jelly at the first suggestion of a fight. The equivalent character in *Penelope* wears the colors of a traditional braggart, eloquently boastful of his prowess until Ulisse actually lays hands on him (III, 5). Like the word-brave captains of Renaissance comedy and their prototypes in Plautus, he stops posing only in a crisis. Despite his promise to the contrary, Della Porta apparently could not resist the impulse to include a braggart, if only a sketchy one. In his comedies he is partial to the type, repeating it often and with increasing mastery.

Two other stock characters of comedy, the courtesan and the lover, are represented in the persons of Melantho and Eurimaco. Taking his cue from Homer's laconic reference to their illicit affair, Della Porta brings them together in love scenes typical of the *commedia erudita*. He endows Melantho with all the cloying charm exerted by those night-blooming beauties who undulate through Renaissance *novelle* and comedies, always ready for a romp, simultaneously lustful and literary. Without ceasing to be the malicious handmaid of the *Odyssey*, Melantho has become expert at exchanging overripe civilities with her lover. He urges in hyperbole; she acquiesces in epigram.

Eurimaco has more to say, as befits the languidly lamenting Petrarchan lover he is. The object of his worship is, of course, Penelope. To the Mercutian counselor who would stab him awake with cynical warnings that love is not a god, but a disease, Eurimaco gives an answer packed with oxymoron, war metaphors, and the rest of the conventional machinery necessary to all Romeos determined to love their Rosalines by the book:

> La possanza d'amor, ch'ognialtra vince
> Il ciel trapassa, el core, el petto impiaga
> Di Gioue istesso . . .
> . . . .
> E fa che in mezo l'acque, in mezo al gelo. [*sic*]
> Bruggi d'ardente foco . . .
> . . . .

E vinto son non da signore, e Dio,
Ma dal signore de' signori, e Dio
Di Dei, come posso io far resistenza?
. . . .
Come fuggir poss'io se meco viene
La fiamma? E se me stesso fuggir cerco
Seguo me stesso, io scaccio, io l'ho scacciato,
Et io son quel, che fuggo, e quel, che seguo? [16]   (III, 1)

But like many an *innamorato* of comedy, Eurimaco is not scrupulous about a bit of sport with Melantho, conducted in terms fully as Petrarchan:

Se voi sete il mio sol, voi la mia aurora;
Non sarà mai per me felice giorno,
Se non qnanto [*sic*] mi specchio ne vostri occhi,[17]   (II, 2)

Such figures, however, do not make of *Penelope* a true mingling of comic and tragic elements. In developing his Homeric originals, Della Porta merely reverted to the habit, acquired in writing comedy, of cutting characters to fit stock patterns. But as he uses them in *Penelope*, none of them, not even the braggart, produces a comic effect; through them, Della Porta teaches morality by contrast. They excite neither the laughter nor the sympathy associated with the same types in his comedies. The background is too dark, and they are marked for death.

The final scenes of *Penelope* are shaped by the concept of *meraviglia*, which flourished with unwonted vigor during the

[16] (The power of love, which surpasses all other, penetrates heaven and wounds the heart and breast of Jove himself . . .
And in the midst of water, in the midst of ice, makes me burn with fierce fire . . .
And I am conquered not by a lord and god, but by the lord of lords and god of gods, how can I resist?
How can I flee if the flame comes with me? And if in trying to flee myself, I follow myself, in driving away am driven away, and am both he who flees and he who follows?)
[17] (If you are my sun, you my dawn, it will never be a beautiful day for me except when I am mirrored in your eyes.)

Counter-Reformation and which governed Della Porta's mind with unusual force. In all its forms the marvelous demands exaggeration. It surpasses reality by replacing the probable with the barely possible. To the author of *Magiae naturalis* and *Taumatologia,* pursuit of *meraviglia* was a life's work. When he turned from the secrets of nature to write a play, he could not leave off hunting miracles. In *Penelope,* Della Porta's method of driving home his moral lesson is to make his heroine not merely chaste and constant, but a marvel of chastity and constancy.

In the first four acts of the play, Penelope goes through her paces, rejecting her father's expedient counsel, disdaining threats, ignoring Eurimaco's blandishments, making the most heroic answers to the searching questions of the unrecognized beggar. Early in Act V Ulisse ends the main action by slaughtering the suitors. He spends the remaining five scenes measuring how far Penelope's virtue can be pushed, and to this end orders Telemaco to swear that his father is dead and to command that his mother fulfill her promise to marry the user of Ulisse's bow. Like Boccaccio's Gualtiero, Ulisse is going too far. Della Porta is aware of this, and makes Telemaco object to his father's excessive suspicion with the just observation that Penelope has suffered enough already. The dictates of moderation and reason are expressed only to be overridden. Ulisse is, in fact, neither suspicious nor sadistic. For four acts he has been saddened by his wife's unhappiness, and he is convinced by his own observation and by Minerva's testimony that Penelope is true to him. But the purpose of this play is to make Penelope's constancy as marvelous as Griselda's patience, and his insistence on more proof is simply Della Porta's way of engineering the final demonstration.

Though reluctant, Telemaco plays his part well, offering Penelope opportunities for greater and greater heroism. When he describes his visit to Menelaus' court, Penelope underscores the contrast between herself and the fickle Helen by interrupting the narrative with:

O rovina, ò diluuio rio, che uscendo
D'Argo inondò l'Asia & l'Europa tutta,
Cagion di tanto sangue, e tanti morti.[18]   (IV, 4)

Reminded of her promise to marry the winner of the contest, Penelope answers like Bradamante (no gentleman, despite her armor) that she never meant to keep her word: she cares little for fair dealing but is prepared to suffer any torture rather than betray her conjugal ideals. At last she tries to goad the uncomfortable Telemaco into killing her. In preferring death to remarriage, Penelope raises her constancy to the highest possible power and qualifies as a full-fledged marvel.

Satisfied, Ulisse abruptly reveals himself. At this point, Della Porta's Penelope is as wary as Homer's, but for different reasons. The Greek queen is warned by her common sense that the man may be another fortune-hunting impostor. But her Counter-Reformation counterpart is so consistently aware of the virtue she represents and of the contrast it affords to Helen's vice, that she attributes her hesitation to deliberate avoidance of that easy credulity by which Helen fell. But when convincing proof is produced, "Lopa" and "Lisso" are reunited (V, 6). Apparently sixteenth-century notions of stage decorum were not opposed to the use of nicknames between royal consorts.[19]

Despite Cardinal Luigi's poor opinion of it, *Penelope* should have been a great success with the literary clergy and the public it influenced. Classical in structure and plot, more controlled than the Cinthian she-tragedies with happy endings, imbued with the elements of *meraviglia* delightful to audiences, yet providing a non-pagan moral example, Della Porta's tragicomedy strikes exactly that balance of neoclas-

[18] (Oh ruin, oh horrid flood, which, emerging from Argus inundated Asia and all Europe, cause of so much blood and so many deaths.)

[19] This embarrassingly intimate detail must have been theatrically successful, for Della Porta repeated it as a recognition device in *Il moro* (IV, 6), and *L'Ulisse* (V, 3).

sicism and Christian didacticism which was the current ideal of conservative critics and liberal censors.

IL GEORGIO

Il Georgio, Della Porta's only extant sacred drama, probably owes its survival to a performance in 1611 by or for the newborn Accademia degli Oziosi. The play was published that year, dedicated to one of the author's fellow academicians, Ferrante Rovito, and prefaced by two poems of another, G. B. Basile, implying a production witnessed by both. Della Porta may have written the play about the patron saint of Ferrara in the late seventies or the eighties, in order to please Cardinal d'Este. Although both the popular *sacra rappresentazione* about St. George and the account of his life in the *Legenda Aurea* include several miracles and end with the saint's death, Della Porta preferred to concentrate on a single incident. This decision was doubtless determined by his notions of classical unity, but the influence of the Estes is visible in his choice—St. George's rescue of a princess from a dragon, an incident which has a celebrated analogue in the rescue of Angelica by Ruggiero, legendary founder of the Este family.[20]

As the least classical genre of the day, sacred tragedy cannot have held much intrinsic attraction for Della Porta. But he undertook it at least three times, moved probably by pride in his versatility and by a desire to ingratiate himself with the religious authorities. *Georgio* is not much like either of the two most common types of *tragedia spirituale*, the Old Testament moralization and the *martirio* variety, depicting the sufferings of Christ or of some notable virgin-martyr. Della Porta may have produced standard examples of the latter

---

[20] *Orlando Furioso*, x, 92ff. Della Porta may also have known Feo Belcari's *sacra rappresentazione* about St. George and the dragon, of which only four stanzas are extant. See Paul Colomb de Batines, *Bibliografia delle antiche rappressentazioni italiane sacre e profane stampate nei secoli XV e XVI* (Firenze, 1852), 12.

type in his lost tragedies about St. Dorotea and St. Eugenia, two saints whose histories would lend themselves easily to the genre. St. George, as it happens, was also both virgin and martyr, but neither of these aspects of his life is of any importance in Della Porta's drama about him. His chastity is mentioned but not demonstrated, and he is happily alive at the end of the play. So are all of the other characters. Even the dragon escapes injury. In short, *Georgio* is neither just a stage adaptation of incidents culled from a hagiography, nor a tragedy, even in the widest sense of the word.

Della Porta seems to have taken his plot from Euripides' *Iphigenia in Aulis*, and from Jacopo de Voragine's *Legenda Aurea*, perhaps by way of Mantuan. Della Porta surely knew also the old *ottava rima* drama, *La Rappresentazione di Santo Giorgio*, reprinted at least nine times in the sixteenth and early seventeenth centuries.[21] It follows the account of Jacopo de Voragine, except in the spelling of the saint's name. Della Porta apparently went to the *Legenda Aurea* for the official version and came away with the Latinate spelling, "Georgio." From the Greek tragedy came the situation of the father who must sacrifice his child to the general welfare. This dilemma was dear to Renaissance dramatists, who presented it sometimes in a Greek setting, as Dolce did in *Ifigenia* (1566), sometimes in the Hebrew trappings of the Jephtha story, as Spezzani did in the long second *intermedio* of his *Rappresentazione di S. Catherina* (1587). The mediaeval source provided *Georgio*'s felicitous catastrophe in the most famous incident in the life of St. George, his conversion of a kingdom by rescuing its princess from a dragon.

So strong is the classical element in Della Porta's sacred tragedy that for the first three acts there is not a trace of Christianity, and except for the exotic Eastern setting and the unclassical dragon, both reminiscent of Ariosto, *Georgio* at first seems to be a typical late Renaissance dramatization of Greek myth. King Sileno confers with his secretary about

21 *Ibid.*, 51–52.

sacrificing the princess Alcinoë to a lake-dwelling dragon who threatens the city. To stave off a general disaster, Sileno has passed a law providing the monster with a daily ration of two citizens selected by lot. A local oracle has prophesied succour from "vn Cavalier istrano, e d'altra legge" (I, 10), but no immediate hope of deliverance is visible. Now that the lottery has designated his daughter as the dragon's repast, the king wishes to invoke royal prerogative, but is restrained by fear of popular rebellion. In the midst of these worries, he must also attend to affairs of state, among them the visit of the African King Mammolino, bidden by another oracle to search for a wife in this part of the world. In order to lure Alcinoë and Queen Deiopeia back to the palace from the distant garden where they are amusing themselves, Sileno sends word that Alcinoë's wedding to Mammolino is in preparation. The ruse works until Deiopeia accidentally meets Mammolino and learns that he knows nothing about the betrothal. Mammolino falls in love with Alcinoë at first sight and pleads with the Senate and people for her life, to no avail. Resigning herself, Alcinoë departs to face the dragon, leaving her parents and lover grief-stricken.

These events require three full acts, during which paganism prevails unchallenged. Faith in oracles, dreams, gods, and fate is expressed on all sides, and the chorus invokes Hercules and Bacchus with fervor. But between Acts III and IV a sudden change occurs. The chorus, or probably one-half of it (there are no indications in the text), curses fate, "gran tiranno del mondo" in the first part of a two-part ode, to which the other half of the chorus replies with a brusque contradiction:

> Pazzo sei se tu stimi
> Altro che'l destin sia,
> Larue sogno, e pazzia,
> L'huom troua questo nome,
> Che non fa pensar come
> Il suo poco saper, perche'l destino,

Altro non fù mai, ch'l voler diuino.
Non vengon dalla sorte
Puniti i nostri eccessi.
Noi siam fabri à noi stessi,
De nostri danni, in noi
Del mal sta la radice.
Libero è'l voler nostro, e non mai seruo,
Ma noi'l facciamo dal piacer proteruo.
Quell'mmobil Motore
Che'l Ciel muoue, e le Stelle,
Quanto versano quelle,
O di bene, ò di male,
Opra è de nostre mani,
Et dispensa la sorte hor chiara, hor bruna,
Perch'ei comanda il fato, e la fortuna.[22]

This illogical choral ode fulfills a dramatic purpose by modulating the tragedy into a Christian key, prior to Georgio's entrance in Act IV. The saint's tardiness indicates that his formal function will be less that of hero than of *deus ex machina*, and, therefore, his arrival ends the play's dramatic tension along with its pagan tone. From this moment on, the action atrophies in a series of narrations and descriptions. Georgio identifies himself as a knight-errant of Christ, hears of the local predicament, and departs to lend a hand (IV, 1). His servant delivers a eulogy of Georgio (IV, 2). Alcinoë's meeting with the dragon and her rescue by Georgio are described by a pair of messengers (IV, 3; V, 1). In the remaining scenes, Mammolino and Alcinoë are betrothed, Sileno and his subjects reconciled, and Georgio delivers sev-

[22] (You are mad if you think aught but that destiny is a spectre, a dream, and a madness. Man invents this name, which does not remind him how little he knows, for destiny was never anything but the divine will. Our excesses are not punished by chance. We make our own ills, the root of evil is in us. Our will is free, never a servant, but through pleasure we make it stubborn. That unmoved Mover who moves Heaven and the Stars, whatever they pour down of good or of evil is the work of our hands, and He dispenses fortune, now light, now dark, for He commands fate and fortune.)

eral lectures on Christian doctrine. Nothing occurs to break any rule of Senecan classicism, but the tenor of the last two acts and the resultant effect of the whole play are not only non-classical but anti-classical.

Like *Penelope*, *Georgio* is didactic, but with a difference. The tragicomedy uses a pagan situation to teach a general moral lesson in the uncontroversial virtue of chastity, much as Padre Scamacca's *Oreste* teaches the Fourth Commandment.[23] But *Georgio* has a more specific aim: to help stamp out a current error by promulgating the doctrines of divine providence and free will. Unfortunately, Della Porta never managed to be any more coherent on the subject than in the choral ode just quoted. Obviously he tried to assimilate the official Church pronouncement into his system of thought, but this scrambled expression leaves some doubt that he clearly understood the dogma. The scientist who prefaced his treatise on astrology with a denial of astrology is reflected in the playwright who denounced the workings of fate in a play full of pagan oracles and dreams, all of which prove true.[24] The characters themselves are not quite certain which of their old beliefs to discard and which can be reconciled with their newly acquired Christianity. Rejoicing at the happy conclusion, Mammolino exclaims:

> Fatal fu la venuta in questa Terra,
> E fatal fu l'amor, che m'arse, e'l foco,
> E voi foste ancor libera dal fato,
> E fatal fu l'oracolo . . .
> Hor conferendo i primi detti meco
> Dell'Oracolo santo, che nel seno
> Eran della sovrana eterna mente,
>
> . . . .

[23] See Emilio Bertana, *La tragedia* (Milano, 1905), 186, for analysis of this play.

[24] Cf. Della Valle, who showed how Counter-Reformation playwrights should treat pagan superstitions, by exposing the falsity of dreams in *Adelonda di Frigia* (III, 1), first performed in Torino, 1595.

... mi rallegro ...
Poiche i cieli di me prendono cura.[25]   (v, 4)

Mammolino may be forgiven for his confusion; after all, he has been a Christian for only twenty minutes. Della Porta might be excused on similar grounds—the concepts of fate and of divine providence had long existed in a comfortable contradictory dualism. The Church's full-scale campaign against the former was relatively recent when *Georgio* was composed.

The characterization does not compensate for the unbalanced structure and garbled doctrine. Georgio is a faceless abstraction. Deiopeia moves predictably and with dignity from suspicion to grief to joy. The dragon never appears, although his presence is continuously felt and contributes much *meraviglia*. One interesting reaction reported of him is his reluctance to eat anyone as beautiful as Alcinoë but he overcomes this un-monster-like weakness, and is thwarted of his meal only by Georgio's intervention. The princess behaves with the wordy highmindedness characteristic of royal maiden sacrifices from Dolce's Ifigenia to Dottori's Merope. But she has touches of individuality which she owes to the insight which Della Porta often manifested in dealing with love. Alcinoë makes an indignant scene with her father about his intention to sacrifice her (iii, 2), but no sooner does she meet Mammolino and hear his expressions of pity than she assumes an attitude of noble resignation, making a most favorable impression on the handsome young king (iii, 3). At the happy denouement, when everyone is declaiming in a highflown vein about the blessings of Christianity, Alcinoë says in answer to a proposal of marriage that although she

25 (Fated was my coming to this land, and fated was the love and the fire which burn me, and by fate you were still free, and fateful was the oracle . . .
Now considering within myself the first pronouncements of the blessed Oracle, which were in the bosom of the sovereign eternal mind . . .
I rejoice . . . that the heavens watch over me.)

had intended to vow her virginity to the new God, she will allow Mammolino to change her mind. This piece of coquetry is accompanied by a blush and seems very natural and refreshing in the midst of so many *sententiae* (v, 4).

In the character of King Sileno lies whatever justification Della Porta had for terming this play a tragedy. He was bound to name it after the saint among its characters, but there is nothing human or tragic about Georgio; protected by heaven from physical and spiritual danger, he is no more than a symbol of militant Christianity. Sileno, on the other hand, is involved in a conflict which, but for the grace of God, must inevitably result in tragedy. Seen from one approach, the clash is between love and duty. He must sacrifice his daughter or break the law which protects his kingdom. But from another point of view, the conflict is between private and public duty, i.e., private and public morality. This element connects *Georgio* with the fashion for the *ragion di stato* as a tragic subject. Della Porta complicated Sileno's choice by making him openly ambitious for power. The ambition had been satisfied once, but its cost is now apparent. When the dragon first battened on the kingdom, the Senate and populace wanted to disperse and to move away, but Sileno persuaded them to stay together under his rule and to stave off the dragon's threats with human sacrifice. Therefore he is not faultless. His responsibility is made quite clear in the Senator's description of the people's suffering and anxiety over the daily lottery (i, 1). To Sileno's suggestion that kings are above laws, the Senator answers that the regal responsibility is, in this case, greater than usual. The law which now claims the king's only child is *his* law, made originally to further his ambition. The duties of a ruler are cogently set forth by his secretary and the others who favor Alcinoë's death. In the first act, after much argument back and forth, Sileno decides to condemn his daughter, but is led many times thereafter by his wife's recriminations, Alcinoë's pleas, and his own love, to the brink of breaking the law.

What could have become tragedy, however, is cut short and diverted into channels of Christian didacticism and *meraviglia*. The besieged people take the matter out of Sileno's hands by sending their prefect with an armed guard to escort Alcinoë to the dragon. The king no longer has a choice, moral or otherwise, and he has no share of responsibility for the preservation and conversion of his kingdom, effected solely by Divine Providence working through Georgio. The moral abdication in Act III of what has seemed to be the tragic hero reinforces the impression of disunity in this play which technically observes the unities faithfully.

The political lesson is not consistent either. Della Porta begins by picturing the burdens and misery of oppressed people with real feeling, and ends by taking his stand on the other side. After the first few scenes the mob is always referred to as a dangerous animal which must be controlled and guided by superior beings. Obtaining Alcinoë by threats of rebellion, the facile mob regrets its insistence and would change, too late, when it beholds her beauty and pathetic bravery (IV, 3). When Georgio has put all to rights again, the people and Senate send a representative in chains to beg the king's pardon.

Although *Georgio* is among Della Porta's weakest plays, it has powerful moments, thanks to his sense for dramatic encounter and reluctance to let slip any opportunity of exploiting the emotional, ironic, or pathetic potentialities of a situation, conventional though its psychological results might be. Sileno's first meeting with his daughter after his painful decision, for example, is charged with irony and pathos. A tense dialogue, partly in stichomythy, emphasizes the contrast between Alcinoë's innocent doubt and Sileno's guilty knowledge. Puzzled by her father's ill-concealed grief, unaware that her own fate is the cause, the princess questions him sympathetically. His answers ring changes on her words and point mysteriously to the truth until her unfelicitous choice of image reminds Sileno of the dragon's habitat and wrings from him a bitter cry:

ALCINOË

. . . Di gratia non fate
Ch'l cuor vi roda vn così ascoso serpe.

SILENO

Veramente quel serpe è che mi rode.

ALCINOË

Ne vi molesti il duol più che noi altre.

SILENO

Anzi te più che gli altri annoia il duole.

ALCINOË

. . . .
Ma al fine il pianto vince, e sparger fuori,
Ne veggio un largo laco.

SILENO

Ahi laco, ahi laco.[26]   (II, 3)

There is nothing subtle or original about Sileno, Deiopeia, Mammolino, and Alcinoë; they are psychologically identical with similarly placed characters in other tragedies of the period. But if they are not unusual, they are articulate, and until Della Porta clogs the action with narration in Acts IV and V, he gives his characters as much breathing space as they can use and sets up for them situations so innately dramatic that simply by going through their expected paces, the characters acquire a certain vitality. Georgio, himself, of course, cannot be considered a failure in characterization, because he is not intended to be a character at all; he and the dragon are engaged in a religious miracle, the simplest manifestation of *meraviglia*.

---

[26] (ALCINOË. . . . please do not let your heart be gnawed by a serpent thus hidden.
SILENO. Truly it is that serpent which gnaws me.
ALCINOË. Nor let this grief trouble you more than it does us.
SILENO. Indeed this grief troubles you more than it does the others.
ALCINOË. . . . but at last the tears conquer and I see a great lake of them gush out.
SILENO. Alas, lake, lake.)

Fiorentino longed to interpret the kingdom of Sileno as Naples and the dragon as the Spanish viceregency and Inquisition, but decided that the political inference was unjustified, because of the Lincei's rules against mixing in politics.[27] Fiorentino was right, but for the wrong reason. Della Porta did not become a Linceo until 1610, long after the composition of *Georgio*. He was on good terms with the Spanish, belonging to the social circle of at least two of the viceroys, and he obviously wrote *Georgio* to placate the Inquisition and to prove himself orthodox on the subject of Divine Providence and free will. For these reasons, and not because of any Lincei rules, it is unwise to read attacks on Spain or the Inquisition into *Georgio*. It is not equally certain, however, that Della Porta did not get in a dig or two at the Jesuits. Scheming to save Alcinoë from the mob, Sileno decides to hide her in a tomb, so that he will be justified in swearing that she is among the dead. His secretary remonstrates that truth is more than an artful arrangement of words. Sileno maintains that lies are useful and can even be right. Replying that kings should not openly advance this opinion, the secretary reveals his own superior craftiness (1, 3). The target of this pointed scene may have been the general Machiavellian doctrine of ends justifying means, an axiom which the Jesuits attacked vigorously because they were themselves frequently accused of endorsing it. Courting the Inquisition's approval, Della Porta had joined a Jesuit lay congregation, and in his position, could not risk seriously offending the Society; his thrust at duplicity, therefore, was perhaps intended simply to support the sort of Jesuit anti-Machiavellian propaganda represented by Botero's *Della ragion di stato*. Still, the thrust was itself double and might have drawn blood from Machiavellian Jesuits.

Except for this doubtful instance, there are no hidden meanings in *Georgio*. Despite his penchant for secrets and codes, Della Porta was perfectly straightforward in dramatiz-

[27] *Op.cit.*, 322–23.

ing the story of St. George. What could have been alle-
gorized is presented as simple, if miraculous, fact. Georgio is
not a knight errant on one level of interpretation and a fisher
of souls on another. He combines both functions in the single
role of chivalrous missionary. The dragon is not a symbol but
a real fallen angel who, like Milton's, sometimes inhabits the
form of an earthly monster requiring pagan sacrifice (v, 3).
The symbolism in Georgio's binding of the dragon with
Alcinoë's girdle (v, 1) remains latent. Unlike Spenser, Della
Porta built no allegory of chastity on this action but merely
included it without comment as it came to him from the
Legenda aurea. Deiopeia decrees the erection of a bronze
arch depicting Georgio, Alcinoë, and the girdle-bound
dragon (v, 3), but although the grouping suggests an emblem, Della Porta provided no motto for it.

Georgio is a very uneven play, mixing without blending a
variety of ingredients: classical, romantic, religious, and
philosophical. It has no hero, and no consistent tone. It shifts
focus and method bumpily. It is, in one sense, the most
baroque of Della Porta's dramas. Its language contributes to
this effect by its unwonted complexity.[28]

That *Georgio* is a failure does not affect its use in a general examination of Della Porta. His other works in this
genre, if indeed the genre was the same, are lost, and only
Georgio affords any clue to Della Porta's approach to sacred
tragedy. But the faults of *Georgio* reveal more of the man
than of the artist. Its curious confusion of motives, beliefs,
images astronomical and medical, its stops and starts in
progress, the incongruous Christian conclusion abruptly imposed on a classical foundation—all are lapses which make
Georgio a unique reflection of the personal conflict of interests testified to by the fragmentary facts of Della Porta's
biography.

[28] See Chapter v for discussion of Della Porta's verse style.

L'ULISSE

After a brief survey of Counter-Reformation secular tragedy, the reader who takes up Della Porta's *Ulisse* for the first
time might reasonably expect it to be classical legend tricked
out in a double *intreccio*, with disguises, enamoured heroines,
ingenious metaphors, diabolic tortures, pastoral laments, and
paraphrases from the *Summa theologica*. But *Ulisse* satisfies
none of these expectations. Although Della Porta's use of theatrical techniques developed after Giraldi and his refusal to
endorse pagan ideas reflect the times in which he wrote, the
play is a rare example of conservative theory put into practice. It is neoclassical according to the most conservative
standards of the sixteenth century.

Ulisse may have been the only secular tragedy Della Porta
ever wrote. It is certainly the only one he published. He
began it in his seventy-eighth year, at the request of "un
signore," [29] possibly one of the highborn gentlemen whose
society the class-conscious old scholar so much enjoyed in
the Accademia degli Oziosi. Della Porta was very busy and
not very well in 1612, but he took up the commission with
his usual generosity of interest, complaining only that the
work was fatiguing because so little was known of Ulysses'
death.[30] Despite the perennial fascination exerted by the
figure of Ulysses on the Italian imagination, there were few
sixteenth-century plays about him.[31] Della Porta turned to
Pausanius and to the fragmentary account of the *Thelegony*
by the Cyrenian Eugamon for his plot, choosing only those
elements which could be worked into a tragic sequel to his

[29] Giuseppe Gabrieli, "Giovan Battista Della Porta Linceo," *Giornale
critico di filosofia italiana*, VIII, fasc. 1 (1927), 377.

[30] Gabrieli, "Bibliografia Lincea . . . ," 268.

[31] Falugi's *Ulixe patiente* (see page 91, note 8), an anonymous
Penelope, componimento per musica, 1597 (Allacci, *op.cit.,* 618), and
Della Porta's own *Penelope* are the only ones which come to mind. But
in the seventeenth and eighteenth centuries the characters of the
Odyssey appeared in numerous plays, the greater number of them
drammi per musica united to scores by Monteverdi, Alessandro Scar-
latti, and lesser fry.

Penelope, written some thirty years earlier. To leave no doubt of his intentions, he brought Neptune onstage in the first scene, as he had done in *Penelope*, making him echo his own lines from the past, "Mi vince Ulisse, Ulisse pur mi vince." [32]

Omitting pieces of the story as told in the epic cycle, adapting others to emphasize the continuity between *Penelope* and *Ulisse*, and adding still others to support the classically tragic effect he had decided upon, Della Porta begins his play on the day of Ulisse's death. Nettuno, the vengeful seagod, rejoices at the prospect and exhorts the ghosts of Penelope's suitors to continue troubling their old enemy's dreams. Returning from the oracle to which he was sent to learn the cause of the king's evil dreams, Eumeo is afraid to repeat the sybil's fearful pronouncement that Ulisse will be killed by his son at the instigation of the boy's mother. Hoping to cut the trouble in half, Eumeo tells his master only the first part of the prophecy. Telemaco returns from his successful wooing of King Alcinoö's daughter and Ulisse condemns him to death, despite Penelope's pleading. Later the king is persuaded to commute the sentence to exile. Penelope believes that Eumeo has invented the prophecy because of some resentment he harbors against Telemaco. To save himself from the death Penelope orders for him, Eumeo blurts out the rest of the oracle to Ulisse, who promptly claps the queen into prison. He commands that all newcomers to Ithaca be challenged, lest they be supporters of Telemaco. Consequently, when Ulisse's unknown son Teligono reaches Ithaca, sent by Circe to meet his father, he is inhospitably treated by the royal shore patrol, several of whom he kills. Foolishly fearing no one save Telemaco and Penelope, Ulisse upbraids the young stranger and is stabbed for his pains. The truth is revealed too late. Both are remorseful, the son for his parricide, the father for his suspicions of Telemaco and Penelope. Ulisse dies slowly, leaving time for reconciliation all round.

[32] (I am vanquished by Ulisse, Ulisse yet vanquishes me.)

The action is developed according to the five-act blueprint which had become standard for tragedy by the end of the sixteenth century and which Della Porta preferred for all his plays, comic and tragic. In the first act the exposition is accomplished gracefully and, mercifully, without point-blank recitals of the facts. The next two acts present the subsequent doubts, conflicts, and decisions, culminating in Telemaco's banishment, which constitutes a reversal of fortunes for all four of the main characters: Telemaco loses his status, Penelope her son, Eumeo Penelope's favor, and Ulisse his protection against the disaster he is trying to avoid. A chain reaction of reversals is set off, illustrating Della Porta's use in tragedy of a principle of construction which guided him in his comedies and which he describes as "peripety born of peripety" (*Carbonaria* prologue). From Eumeo's reversal arises Ulisse's suspicions of Penelope, resulting in her imprisonment. At the end of the fourth act, Ulisse has unwittingly completed all the preparations necessary to his own ruin. The catastrophe comes from outside in the first part of Act v, and the prophecy is fulfilled in the third scene, when Teligono stabs Ulisse. The catastrophe is immediately followed by agnition which reveals plain truth to the characters (v, 3). Two more scenes are devoted to the denouement which tapers the tragedy gently to the mood of subdued sadness expressed by Telemaco in the last lines (v, 5). All of the action, except for Teligono's arrival by ship, is presented onstage, but it is action which even the most rigidly neoclassical critic could not challenge. Thus Della Porta managed to combine dramatic movement with respect for decorum.

The unities of time and place are carefully observed, as they are in all of Della Porta's plays. But *Ulisse* has also a unity of action which its author had failed to achieve in *Georgio*. Not only are all the characters cast in the tragic mold, meeting Giraldi Cinthio's requirement of "una sola qualità di persona" [33] for tragedy with a sad ending, but also

[33] *Discorsi* . . . , 224.

the plot is single and therefore unique among Della Porta's plays. All the others contain at least a subsidiary love story, but in *Ulisse* the central conflict is the only one there is.[34] The tragedy is not without digressions however. A discreet number of narrations and soliloquies of past events is provided, but these are set-pieces intended to embellish the action, not to complicate it. *Ulisse* has its share of *sententiae* too, another testimony to Della Porta's respect for Giraldi's dramatic theory, although the digressions in *Ulisse* are not nearly as numerous nor as turgid as those in Cinthian tragedy.

The machinery of *Ulisse* is largely Cinthian, characterized by vengeful ghosts, act and scene divisions, and a restricted chorus. But in spirit Della Porta's tragedy belongs with the selected handful of restrained Greek imitations in the Trissino tradition and is strikingly different from contemporary chivalric tragedy like Bracciolini's and from the Jesuit tragedies which squeezed Christian doctrine out of pagan plots. Even more striking in a tragedy dated 1612 is the absence of pastoral elements. Eumeo seems to be on the verge of an Arcadian rhetorical commonplace when he begins his dispraise of court life (I, 3). But before a sheep-bell can clink, he takes a philosophical tone and makes it clear that there is more of the Stoic than of the Arcadian in him. His monologue is actually an extended *sententia* of the Senecan stamp, its function to give the drama moral weight, not decoration, Bembo's "gravità," not "piacevolezza." Perhaps because he had no lyrical gift, as the choruses in *Ulisse* suggest, Della

---

[34] Joseph Kennard refers briefly to *Ulisse* as similar to Dottori's *Aristodemo* in being *implessa* or complicated tragedy rather than *piana*, without disguise or entanglement (*The Italian Theatre from its Beginning to the Close of the Seventeenth Century*, New York, 1932, 227, note 7). This needs clarification. *Ulisse* is *implessa* by virtue of its peripety and agnition. But *Aristodemo* contains a love plot mixed with the central conflict of the protagonist, who in attempting to save his recognized daughter, causes her death and that of another daughter in disguise. In *Ulisse* there is no subplot to complicate the story and no disguise. Teligono never pretends to be anyone but himself. Ulisse is ignorant, not of his identity, but of his existence.

Porta was never touched by the contemporary craze for pastoralism.

His natural inclinations, however, cannot account for his ignoring the element of horror which filled a large number of tragedies from *Orbecche* to *Alvida* with blood, hacked limbs, and severed heads. The description of Ulisse's revenge in *Penelope* or of the dragon's foul lair in *Georgio* proves that Della Porta could chill spines when he wished. Always eager to astound scientists with monstrous secrets from his laboratory, why did he bar Cinthian horror from *Ulisse*? It can have been only because his taste for this kind of *meraviglia* was at war with the formative principle of his theater —respect for classical moderation.

One conspicuously modern touch in *Ulisse* is the introduction of the "reason of state" theme, albeit in a subordinate position. Public opinion and the burdens of kingship are admitted as serious considerations (III, 1); they do not, however, constitute one of the two poles of the tragic conflict, as they must do in the true political tragedy.

But if Della Porta took little notice of the purely theatrical fashions of his time, he was mindful of the new moral and theological standards set for the drama by the Council of Trent. Perhaps it was the Church's stand which for years restrained him from attempting secular tragedy. If he followed his natural preference for classical subjects, he would have to come to grips with the matter of Fate, the hinge on which Greek tragedy moves. But an endorsement of Fate would run him afoul of the Inquisition. His difficulty was increased by his own belief in Fate. He had done violence to it in deference to orthodoxy, but there are numerous hints that his private opinion never changed.[35] Given these complications,

[35] Despite the denial of judiciary astrology and divination in general in the proemium of *Coelestis physiognomoniae*, Della Porta continued his divining until the end of his life, as Stelluti recounts in a letter reproduced by Gabrieli in "Spigolature Dellaportiane," *Rendiconti della R. Accademia Nazionale dei Lincei. Classe di scienze morali . . . ,* Serie 6, XI, fasc. 7–10 (Roma, 1936), 512–14.

it would have been safer for Della Porta to limit himself to comedy or to sacred tragedy depending on Divine Providence.

But the versatile experimenter apparently hankered to try secular tragedy before he died and was probably easily persuaded by the "gentleman" who suggested *Ulisse* to him. But how could he write on a pre-Christian subject, maintain decorum, present a valid heroic conflict, and yet ignore the concept of Fate? It could not be done perfectly. But Della Porta contrived to minimize the dangers of the undertaking.

His first cautious step was to preface *Ulisse* with the following disclaimer:

La presente Tragedia è rappresentata da persone Gentili, e perciò se ui trovano dẽtro queste parole, Fato, Destino, sorte, fortuna, forza, e necessità di stelle, Dei, & altre simili, è stato fatto per conformarsi con gli antichi loro costumi, e riti: ma queste, conforme alla Religione Catolica, sono tutte vanità, perche si ha da attribuire à Dio benedetto, causa suprema, & uniuersale, ogni effetto, & euenimento.[36]   (A3)

Secondly, Della Porta emphasized the non-pagan corollaries of Fate. Although the oracle which begins the trouble is the voice of Fate, and despite the choral lament "Misero è ben quel' huomo/ Cui la perversa sorte/ Lo perseque e lo sforza/ . . . / Che vincon sempre le nemiche stelle" [37] (IV, 6), Telemaco's commentary draws this conclusion from the events:

[36] Cf. similar notices appended to *Aristodemo* (Padova, 1692, first edition Padova, 1657), Campeggi's *Tancredi* (Bologna, 1614), and the prologue to Bozza's *Fedra* (Vinegia, 1578). (This tragedy is enacted by Gentiles [*i.e.*, pagans] and therefore if it contains such words as fate, destiny, luck, fortune, force and necessity of stars, gods etc., that is done in order to conform with their ancient customs and rites: but these, according to the Catholic religion, are all false, because every effect and event must be ascribed to Our Blessed God, supreme and universal Cause of all.)

[37] (Certainly wretched is he whom bad luck pursues and forces . . . whom inimical stars always vanquish.)

Ahi vano, ahi cieco mōdo ecco i tuoi frutti
Quant' egli oprò mentre fra noi si uisse
E senno ed arte e forza in pace ò in guerra
Breu' ora inuola e'l tutto è poca terra.[38]   (v, 5)

It is not the malignancy of Fate or of inimical stars which Ulisse's death illustrates, but the vanity of human wishes. Such a reflection belongs as much to the Christian as to the pagan world-view. Della Porta avoided danger to himself and to the integrity of his play by neither endorsing Fate nor introducing an anachronistic idea of providence. His subdued statement of human impotence is at once classical and Christian.

Having diminished the active role of Fate in the tragic conflict, Della Porta needed a force which would reflect Fate's workings but remain autonomous. He turned therefore to *Oedipus tyrannos*, regarded as the "perfect tragedy" by conservative critics, who quoted Aristotle's opinion that, of all tragic figures, Oedipus, who unwittingly brings on his own ruin, is most worthy of compassion.[39]

Accordingly, Della Porta discovered his hero's opponent in the hero himself and produced a tragedy rooted in irony. If the result is not a tragedy of character, it at least takes a step in that direction. From the beginning it is clear that Ulisse must hound himself to death because of a flaw in his character. It is, fittingly, the flaw of a clever man. When Nettuno recognizes that ". . . di natio sospetto Vlisse è pieno" [40] (I, I), and urges Megera and the ghosts to aggravate Ulisse's suspicion, the seagod is only speeding his enemy along the course he would have taken naturally. Wily and

[38] (Ah, empty, ah blind world, here are your rewards. Whatever he accomplished while he lived among us—wisdom and art and strength in peace or war—is stolen away by an instant and all of it is now only a little dust.)

[39] We have Lucrezio Nucci's word for it that Della Porta agreed with this evaluation and imitated the structure of *Oedipus tyrannos* even in comedy (*La sorella*, Napoli, 1604, dedication).

[40] (Ulisse is full of innate suspicion.)

sophisticated, Ulisse is quick to believe ill of others; a simpler mind would hesitate to think Telemaco a potential parricide, but Ulisse immediately apprehends the political advantages to his son of such a crime. Heir to Ithaca and husband to the heir of Feacia, Telemaco could join both kingdoms under his sceptre, were his father out of the way. In his anger, Ulisse gives way to *hubris*: "Chi di frodi, e d'inganni Vlisse vince?" [41] (I, 5), and glorying in his pride of mind, dupes himself into scheming against his innocent son. Eavesdropping on Telemaco's soliloquy, Ulisse refuses to accept at face value the prince's filial utterances. (II, 1). Instead he imagines them to be loaded with menacing irony. The true irony, of course, lies in his misinterpretation. Too used to fraud to rely on the honesty of others, the past master of intrigues falls prey to his greatest danger: he outsmarts himself.

His mental inferiors understand his character more than he does himself. The old counselor sent by Penelope to influence Ulisse despairs before he begins of besting the king's eloquence or logic. At last the old man takes this line: "If you kill Telemaco, the people, who love him, will kill you, and he will have fulfilled the prophecy by causing your death" (III, 1). The counselor wins a commutation of the sentence, but only by using the sort of tricky reasoning which weighs most with Ulisse.

But if the character of Ulisse is well conceived, it is not equally well developed. His experience with the stock types of comedy had made Della Porta expert in creating vivacious characters on the basis of single exaggerated traits. But he was less successful at delineating a complicated tragic protagonist. Ulisse in the grip of his besetting sin is a compelling figure; Ulisse in other attitudes is grotesque. Called upon to express his love of life, he so much overstates it as to seem mad (IV, 6), which was certainly not Della Porta's intention. The alleged conflict in Ulisse's heart between paternal affection and self-preservation is likewise unconvincing. On hear-

[41] (Who can beat Ulisse at trickery and deceit?)

ing the oracle's pronouncement, Ulisse reacts totally like a man too clever for his own good. So he is; his behavior in the heat of the moment is an accurate index. Later, when he declares in a conventional soliloquy that he is being pulled two ways (II, 5), he is not believable. His fatherly feeling is as improbable as the mental exhaustion which determines his temporary decision to leave the government in Penelope's hands (IV, 1). He compels attention and belief only when he is caught in the complex machinery of his own mind. It is this tragic flaw which Della Porta intended to emphasize and from which he draws an explicit moral in the second choral ode, "Sospetto iniquo, e rio/ Di tanto mal cagione" [42] (II, 5). Ulisse himself realizes at the end that he has battled the wrong foe (V, 5).

The other characters are few and unremarkable. Penelope expresses, consecutively, wifely devotion, maternal ferocity, vindictiveness, and injured innocence, but these qualities are mechanically assumed, without ever cohering to form a living character. Eumeo is a more successful creation, trying earnestly to live up to the position given him in recompense for his fidelity. The guileless old man knows how ill-equipped he is to handle weighty matters, and as he sees the ill fruits of his good intentions, Eumeo longs for the humble life he once knew. His best scenes are full of dignified pathos. Telemaco and Teligono are colorless. The former is much in evidence, but in spite of his passionate denials of guilt, he arouses little interest or sympathy. Like his half-brother, he is a purely functional character. Fiorentino was of the opinion that Della Porta sketched Don Carlos, Don John of Austria, and Philip II of Spain in the figures of Telemaco, Teligono, and Ulisse.[43] The possibility is very unlikely. The classical situation came ready-made from Pausanius, and the suggested analogue in sixteenth-century history is really quite dissimilar.

[42] (Evil and horrid suspicion, cause of so much evil.)
[43] *Op.cit.*, 307.

Della Porta's Verse Dramas

Ulisse is the last of Della Porta's three extant noncomic plays. How well he was pleased with it and how it succeeded with audiences is not known. It was admired in the eighteenth century,[44] but not performed. Della Porta's neoclassicism was, of course, the reason for such latter-day approval. *Ulisse*, single in plot, unromantic, short on Renaissance themes, is the most classical of his works. It also illustrates the inhibitions caused by his classical inclination and training. Despite its admirable structure, irony, and dignity, *Ulisse*, like *Penelope*, is stiff. Della Porta's respect for decorum and reverence for epic tradition hampered his imagination. In comedy he felt freer. Plautus and Terence did not awe him. The comic setting, the city street, exuded an atmosphere propitious to Della Porta's talent. In such surroundings his ingenuity and flair for comic exaggeration could run riot, balanced and given shape by a fundamental classicism of structure.

His freedom in tragedy was limited also by the exigencies of the style he deemed appropriate. It is not the style of his comedies and his correspondence; that is fluent, witty, and eloquent, but not grand. For *Penelope*, *Georgio*, and *Ulisse*, Della Porta wanted heroic style. The kind he chose and the use he made of it deserve close scrutiny.

[44] Napoli-Signorelli, *Vicende della cultura nelle Due Sicile* 2ª napoletana (1810–1811), v, 525.

Della Porta's Verse Style

Dũque illustri miei Reggi à voi mi volgo,
E vi consiglio, ch'abbracciate quella
Infinita bellezza, che se stessa
Vagheggia sempre, e se n'infiamma, & arde
Dell'amor dell'amante, e quel che nasce
(Senza vscir da se stesso, ò scemar nulla)
Indicibile Amor dall'uno, all'altro,
Quel l'amato, e l'amante unito rende.
Onde son tre Persone in vn sol Nume.
A tal Motor eterno, immobil Dio
Somma potenza dell'eterno polo,
Sempiterna cagion ch'ordina, e crea
Quanto quà giù di grande, e bel si scorge:
(Che fiori, gemme, Stelle, Sole, e Lune
Tutte sembianze son torbide, e vili
Dell'eterna bellezza) à quella solo
Drizzati [*sic*] i vostri cuori, e i vostri prieghi.
Gli Altari, i Tempi, e i Sacrificij santi
A lui si dia l'ossequio, e'l vero culto.
Che dà nel Cielo eterno, eterna vita.
Lasciate i sassi, e i legni, sordi, e muti,
Gl'Idoli fatti dalle vostre mani,
Che di mortal velen v'enpino [*sic*] l'alme.
E quel mostro, che quì vedeste vinto,
E un Angiol dell'Inferno, l'vn di quelli
Dell'impura contage, che dal Cielo
Superbi, e rebelanti ne fur suelti.
Io v'inuito al Battesmo sacrosanto,
Che bagnadovi [*sic*] il capo con tal'acqua,
Rendero l'Alma immacolata, e bella,

Della Porta's Verse Style

Come dalle di Dio sacrate mani
Venne pura dal Cielo, e senza colpa.
E farò che godiate à pien per questa
Tesori immarcescibili del Cielo.[1]   (*Georgio* v, 3)

BARELY hinting at a metaphor, chaste in its adjectives, and innocent of the tiniest conceit, Georgio's sermon eschews the language which was beginning to dominate contemporary tragedies, providing their heroines with complexions of "animated snow" [2] and describing St. Lawrence on his grill as a "heavenly salamander." [3] Just as he treated his subjects with a classical moderation uncommon in actual contemporary practice, Della Porta wrote verse which seemed restrained in comparison with the baroque and lyrical outpourings of most Counter-Reformation dramatists.

Della Porta's three plays in *versi sciolti* were separated by long intervals totaling something more than thirty-two years,

[1] (Therefore, my illustrious rulers, to you I turn, and I advise you to embrace that infinite beauty that eternally contemplates and enamours itself and burns with the lover's love, and that which is born (without emerging from itself or diminishing anything), indescribable Love from one to the other, unites the loved one and the lover. Whence there are three persons in a single Divinity. To that eternal Mover, unmoved God, highest power of the eternal poles, eternal Cause which orders, and creates whatever of greatness or beauty can here be discerned: (for flowers, jewels, Stars, Sun, and Moon all are clouded and lowly images of the eternal beauty) to that [beauty] alone turn your hearts and your prayers. The Altars, Temples, and holy Sacrifices, the observances and true worship belong to him who in eternal Heaven gives eternal life. Leave the stones and pieces of wood, deaf and dumb, the Idols made by your hands, which fill souls with fatal poison. And that monster which you saw vanquished here, is an Angel of Hell, one of the sinful band who, proud and rebellious, were torn from Heaven. I invite you to most holy Baptism, for bathing your head with such water, I will make your soul again as immaculate and beautiful as when it came pure and blameless from Heaven and the sacred hands of God. And thus I will enable you fully to enjoy the imperishable treasures of Heaven.)

[2] Gabriele Zinano, *Almerigo* (Reggio, 1590), I, 2.

[3] Giovann'Agnolo Lottini, *Sacra rappresentazione di San Lorenzo* (Firenze, 1592), v, 2.

123

but the differences in style from the first to last are not as great as the similarities. The conversion speech from *Georgio* is a representative sample. Della Porta's poetic language, like the construction and moral orientation of his verse dramas, owes something to Giraldi but is more artistically controlled and consciously grand.

The style is frankly heroic. It adheres to a poetics which Della Porta could have formulated by a synthesis of classical techniques. Those he used were recommended by Aristotle, Demetrius Phalereus, and Longinus. But he may have allowed Tasso to save him the trouble. The author of the *Gerusalemme liberata* had made his own synthesis, read it to the Ferrara Academy in 1568 and 1570, and published it in two augmented parts as the *Discorsi dell'arte poetica* (1587) and the *Discorsi del poema eroico* (1594). The latter lists numerous rules and recommendations culled from the ancients and illustrated by quotations from Homer, Virgil, Petrarch, Ariosto, Della Casa, and Tasso himself, among others. Della Porta is not quoted, but if all Tasso's carefully chosen examples suddenly faded away on the page, replacements for them could be found somewhere among the lines of *Penelope*, *Georgio*, or *Ulisse*.

The passage from *Georgio* alone puts into practice nearly a dozen of Tasso's suggestions. His injunction to *"lunghezza de' membri e de' periodi"* [4] (*Discorsi del poema eroico*, v, 130) is heeded in *Georgio*'s long periods,[5] stretched out by the hyperbaton and enjambement also called for in Book v, 144 and 131 respectively. In his diction Della Porta aims at the Virgilian ideal delineated in the *Discorsi*, and only once or twice, when he undertakes to describe an autopsy or something equally stimulating to his scientific accuracy, does he descend to that particularity because of which Tasso declares Homer less magnificent than Virgil (vi, 169). Georgio's

[4] (length of parts and of periods)
[5] The punctuation in this edition, the only complete one of *Georgio*, seems to indicate oratorical, rather than logical, stops and pauses.

"Che dà nel Cielo eterno, eterna vita," illustrates Tasso's remarks on the effectiveness of repetition (v, 136), while "Che fiori, gemme, stelle, Sole, e Lune" puts his recommendations of pleonasm (v, 144) and asyndeton (v, 133–34) into simultaneous effect. Della Porta also favors the inversions endorsed by Tasso (v, 143). Sometimes he casts an entire period in tortured Latin syntax; often he moves only a word or two about, as in "Tutte sembianze son torbide, e vili" and "dalle di Dio sacrate mani."

The unmatched melodiousness of the *Gerusalemme liberata* makes it surprising that Tasso emphasizes the importance to heroic style of a degree of harshness, or *asprezza*, which "sente un no sò che di magnifico, e di grande," [6] an effect to be achieved by enjambement or by disturbing the meter and creating a hiatus from the collision of open vowels (v, 131). In Georgio's sermon, the latter technique produces the caesura in "Dell'eterna bellezza à quella solo. . . ." Tasso suggests obtaining further *asprezza* by means of "il suono ò lo strepito . . . delle consonanti doppie, che nell'ultimo del verso percuotono gli orecchi," [7] and cites Bembo's *vermi, arse, sparse,* as models (v, 132); a full third of the lines in Georgio's speech end in keeping with Tasso's suggestion.[8]

Tasso's recommendations owed something to the practice of Della Casa, who had turned Bembo's Latinizing methods to new enjambements and inversions, producing sonnets at once classical and more *aspri* than any vernacular poetry since Dante's. But although this style influenced Tasso's *ars poetica heroica,* in his own epic he used the smoothest

[6] (breathes an indescribable something of magnificence and grandeur)

[7] (the sound or clash . . . of double consonants which strike the ears in the last part of the line)

[8] At this time *versi piani,* or lines with a penultimate stress, were almost universally the choice for tragedy and epic. Annibale Caro had used *versi sdruccioli* (antepenultimate stress) in his translation of the *Aeneid,* and Bongianni Gratarolo had done so in his *Altea,* but most of Della Porta's contemporaries reserved *sdruccioli* for comic verse genres.

lyricism ever achieved in poetry.[9] Frank Templeton Prince cites Chiabrera as a disciple of the *Discorsi del poema eroico* and believes that the Italian poetic practice dictated by Tasso later influenced Milton's concept of vernacular epic style. When Della Porta employed the precepts of the *Discorsi* in tragedy, he aspired to a place in this tradition and to the title of "magnifico dicitore." [10]

Although Tasso is among the celebrated contemporaries not mentioned in Della Porta's skimpy correspondence, the

[9] In the *Mondo creato*, however, Tasso attempted to follow his own advice regarding heroic style. The result is not a particularly happy one.

[10] *The Italian Element in Milton's Verse* (Oxford, 1954). Prince's thesis that Milton's language was determined in part by the Counter-Reformation stylistic principles represented by Tasso gains additional support from the number of typically Counter-Reformation passages which sound like the first rumblings of Miltonic thunder. Della Porta's description of the dragon's deadly landing is a case in point:

> Poi gionta à terra spiega le grand'ali
> Distinte di color turchino, e verde.
> Hor par che tutta in se stessa se n'entri,
> E dietro à se ritiri la gran coda,
> Et forma hor torti auuolgimenti, hor groppi,
> Hor le ritorte ruote della coda
> In giro auuolte le disnoda. In somma
> Con la coda, vnghie, zampe, fiato, e denti
> Auuolge, sbrana, vccide, infetta, e tronca,
> Tal non si vidde ne' Catanei campi
> Quando i suoi incendi vomitando l'Etna
> Dalle cauerne sue sulfuree, & atre
> Le case, gli animali, alberi, e sterpi
> Rapido cioche intoppa e strugge, & urta.
> Hor così horribil angue, ouunque passa
> Strisciando 'l corpo . . .   (*Georgio*, I, 1)

(Then, alighting, he spreads his great wings bright with color of turquoise and green. Now he seems to withdraw into himself; behind, his great tail retreats and forms now tangles, now knots, now the twisted wheels of the tail in turning unties them. In all, with tail, claws, paws, breath, and teeth, he twists, rends, kills, infects, and chops. Such was not seen in the Catanian fields when Etna, vomiting fire from her sulphurous caves and black, swiftly consumes and fells all that hinders —dwellings, beasts, trees, and stumps. Thus now the horrid snake where'er it passes, winding its body . . .)

description of his eyes in *De humana physiognomonia,* III, 16 suggests personal acquaintance. It is impossible that these two Neapolitans could have avoided meeting through family connections, as fellow employees of Cardinal d'Este in Ferrara, or later in Naples, when Tasso was protected by Manso, Della Porta's friend and colleague in the Accademia degli Oziosi.[11] The literary tradition of Ferrara had reached Della Porta in Giraldi's works, making a decided impression on his ideas of the form and purpose of drama. Receptive as he was to Ferrarese influence, it is impossible that he could have ignored the theories of the only poetic genius in the Counter-Reformation Este circle. Nevertheless, Della Porta's debt to Tasso's theory remains hypothetical. The classical sources of the *Discorsi* were independently available and the stylistic tradition of Bembo and Della Casa was revered and promulgated elsewhere. Among the Oziosi, in fact, Basile made analytical tables and concordances of the two poets' lyrics.[12] But if Della Porta formed his verse style without knowing the *Discorsi del poema eroico* both before and after its publication, it is an odd coincidence that his practice so closely followed Tasso's theory.

The three levels of style discussed by the ancients, and augmented to four by Demetrius Phalereus, were important but confusing to Counter-Reformation poets determined to support classicism but driven to strange mixtures by their need to elaborate contemporary themes which had no classical precedents. They found it sometimes difficult to distinguish between epic and tragic style, and as the seeds of Marinism were sowed, the difficulty increased. Tasso says in the *Discorsi dell'arte poetica* (III, 25) that heroic style lies between the simple gravity of tragedy and the flowery beauty of the

---

[11] Angelo Solerti asserted definitely that Della Porta knew Tasso intimately when the two were in the cardinal's service together (*Vita di Torquato Tasso,* Torino, 1895, I, 837).

[12] *Osservationi intorno alle* . . . *rime del Bembo e del Casa. Con la tavola delle desinenze della rime, & con la varieta de testi nelle rime del Bembo* (Napoli, 1618).

lyric, but in the technical analysis of the *Discorsi del poema eroico* he applies most of his principles to tragedy and epic alike: some ornament is suitable to tragedy and epic, but not as much as to lyric poetry (v, 149–50); only the bitter sort of laughter is appropriate to tragedy and epic (v, 153), etc. When Tasso himself actually wrote a tragedy, he used the style he recommended for the epic but allowed it to lean markedly toward the lyric.

This blurring of the line between the "simple gravity" of tragedy and the somewhat more ornamental style of epic is evident in the comments of Orazio Toscanella, another Este protégé, who attempted to boil down Aristotelian theory for easy consumption. The only differences of language Toscanella remarks between the two genres are the appropriateness of humble style for characters of tragedy who have temporarily fallen from royal to plebeian estate [13] and the variety of verse forms possible to tragedy but forbidden to the epic.[14]

Although he ignored a classical distinction in forming his tragic verse style on epic principles, Della Porta was following a relatively conservative line. Tragedy after Giraldi was becoming linguistically more and more ornate. With Seneca's authority behind him, Groto laced his *Hadriana* with antitheses and labored similes. After Guarini took the stage, lyric style was no longer restricted to the chorus.[15] Tragedy was shifting into the Lydian mode. Music and wordplay pre-

[13] *Precetti necessarie, et altre cose utilissime, parte ridotti in capii parte in alberi; sopra diverse cose pertinenti alla grammatica, poetica, retorica, historia, topica, loica, et ad altre facoltà* . . . (Venetia, 1562), 74.

[14] *Ibid.*, 83.

[15] Ingegneri charged that Tasso's *delicatezza*, admirable in him and productive of many good effects, nonetheless caused many poets to study only striking *sententiae* and flowery style, resulting in plays beautifully worded, but unsound in principle, not didactic, and unapt for staging (*Della poesia rappresentativa & del modo di rappresentare le favole sceniche* . . . , Ferrara, 1598, 3–5).

empted first place, even in weighty political tragedies like *Solimano*, although Bonarelli boasted of its "grave style." [16] In romanesque tragedies especially, among them *Alvida* and the others descended from *Il Re Torrismondo*, linguistic ornament exceeded the bounds of sense and provided Scipione Errico with targets for his lampoon of *Seicentismo*.[17] But Tasso maintained in theory that a minimum of lyrical embellishment went a long way in tragedy and epic (*Discorsi del poema eroico* v, 148–50), and although he agreed with Demetrius that antithesis and melodic cadences in small doses can produce magnificence, he condemned the excessive use of them by contemporary poets as enervating to heroic style (vi, 162).

Della Porta accordingly curbed the talent for word games and striking contrasts happily unleashed in his comedies and preserved his tragic style from any contact with pastoral lyricism. Ignoring a ubiquitous metrical fashion, he introduced no short lines into the *versi sciolti* and adhered consistently to Giraldi's use of eleven syllables for the dialogue line, come what may, with verses of various metres and rhymes for choral divisions.[18] He inherited also from the author of *Orbecche* the rhetorical tirade and the Senecan *sententiae*. But because he used his legacy in moderation, Della Porta's verse is less prolix than Giraldi's and never as sententious or bombastic as that of Dolce and others in the direct Cinthian line. Tasso specifically warns against excess in these matters (vi, 162).

[16] Roma, 1632, preface, a2₁.

[17] *Le rivolte di Parnaso* (Venezia, 1625).

[18] Trissino had established the eleven-syllable unrhymed line for tragedy, interspersing it with a seven-syllable line, especially for choral parts. In *Canace* Speroni used more seven- than eleven-syllable lines, and even introduced a number of five-syllable lines. He did not reserve the short lines for the chorus. After *Canace*, this fashion caught on and was encouraged by pastoral influences. Della Porta, however, never capitulated to it.

Della Porta's Verse Style

There are some variations in style among Della Porta's three verse dramas, springing from their widely separated positions in the chronology of his works, and from their generic differences. *Penelope* is the earliest and, in Della Porta's opinion, the least tragic, in spite of being much bloodier than *Georgio*. Undoubtedly he felt that in a *tragedia di fin lieto*, or *tragicomedia*, as he himself called it, a certain latitude of style was permissible. He drops heroic style completely in some of Eurimaco's speeches, but the lyric style he substitutes is Petrarch's, not Guarini's. The third and lowest level of style is represented here too. Rather than sacrifice dramatic effect to strict decorum by unnecessarily replacing action with narration, Della Porta availed himself of the stylistic freedom allowed by critics like Toscanella. He exhibits Ulisse in lowly disguise, conversing with riffraff in humble, though circumspect, language. When the unrecognized king trades insults with Melanthio the herdsman (III, 1), or fights the beggarly Iro (III, 5), his speech is as plain as it can be without descending to prose. In another scene, Della Porta even allows Ulisse a pun, imbedding it, however, in a spate of highflown diction: "S'à te de' casi miei, e degli errori/ Mi bisognasse dar contezza, e lume,/ Più tosto il dì, che il dir mi verria meno," [19] (I, 3).

As Demetrius and Tasso advise, Della Porta uses yoked antonyms and extended antitheses sparingly. Ulisse's long soliloquy in Act III, Scene 8, is a rhetorical exercise, employing an ironically shifting contrast between pity and cruelty as a structural tool for marking off the sections of the oration. Simultaneously, the proposition to be demonstrated by the account of Ulisse's suffering is that pity can be cruel, and cruelty merciful. After a general comment on the unsatisfactory situation in which he finds himself, Ulisse begins with an apostrophe to Neptune, "Pietosa crudeltà sarebbe stata/

[19] (If I had to recount to you my affairs and my wanderings, I would run out of day [*dì*] before speech [*dir*].)

La tua ò Nettuno, . . .": Neptune's cruelty would have been merciful had he succeeded in one of his many attempts on Ulisse's life. Their enumeration is followed by a contrary exclamation, "Crudel pietà Mercurio fù la tua, . . .": Mercury's pity was cruel, for Ulisse would now be peacefully dead had the winged god not rescued him from a situation he now describes at length. Therefore, he concludes, "O pietade infelice, . . .": the quality of mercy is positively malignant, as far as Ulisse is concerned, because through its working in heaven, he has survived his trials, which he briefly summarizes in nine lines, only to find things in a tragic snarl at home. The rhetorical structure of the soliloquy is elaborate, but, by baroque standards, the antithesis is not. It smacks more of Seneca than of Marino.

Georgio, written at an unspecified date, later than *Penelope*'s debut, but before 1608, is stylistically more ornate. It is the only one of the verse dramas to contain images drawn from its author's scientific studies: he refers here to planets, comets (ii, 7) and to earthquakes (i, 1, 2; ii, 7). Perhaps because hagiographical tragedy was a genre unknown to the ancients, Della Porta felt that in *Georgio* he might indulge his fancy for unclassically mannered wordplay. Juggling words just for the fun of it, however, can unfit them for serious communication. The dialogue between Mammolino and Deiopeia, when he promises to try to save her daughter, is a sad example:

MAMMOLINO

Io ve'l prometto, e del promesso assai
Più forse attenderoui, e spero forse
Far sì, che lodarete e'l fatto, e l'opra,

DEIOPEIA

Quel forse, oime, m'inforsa ogni mia speme,
La gratia che mi fai in forse pone,
E colui la promessa, e'l fatto niega,

Che co'l forse promette, è'l mio mal certo,
E la speranza è in forse, e io viuo in forse,[20]

. . . . (II, 7)

Many of the embellishments in *Georgio* are successful, however. Alcinoë's speech as she faces death, if a shade contrived
and paradoxical for such a moment, nonetheless creates the
intended effect of pathetic *meraviglia:*

> Ecco io l'essequie fò della mia morte
> Porto à me stessa il mio funereo rogo,
> Et io meno me stessa alla mia tomba,
> E sarò sepellita pria, che muoia,
> Et in un tempo mi sarà quel drago,
> Feretro, sepoltura, essequie, e morte.[21]   (III, 4)

The lyrical extreme is marked by the Nuntio's description of
Alcinoë's awakening from her swoon, which comes as close
as Della Porta ever comes to Tasso's own lush style, in defi-
ance of his caveat against smoothness in heroic verse (*Discorsi,*
v, 131):

> Sol la chioma mouea l'aura, che sciolta
> Per la fronte ondeggiaua, e'l capel doro
> Increspa in mille nodi, e mille giri.
> L'acqua del lago le spruzzò su'l volto.
> La virtù irrigidita, e quasi spenta
> Cominciò à rauuiuarsi, ecco che'l cocco,
> Comincia arder nel volto, e già la rosa
> Porporeggiaua del pallor nel mezo
> Delle viole, e apriuansi nel volto

[20] (MAMMOLINO. I promise it to you and I shall perhaps [*forse*] expect rather more in return, and I hope perhaps [*forse*] so to act
[*far sì*] that you will praise the deed and the doing.
DEIOPEIA. That "perhaps," alas, makes uncertain [*inforsa*] all my
hope, the favor you do me puts me in uncertainty, and this negates the
promise and the deed, for the uncertain promise makes certain my misfortune, and hope is uncertain and I live in uncertainty.)

[21] (ALCINOË. I observe the obsequies of my own death, I carry my
own funeral torch, and I conduct myself to my tomb, and I shall be
buried before I die, and that dragon will be to me simultaneously bier,
tomb, funeral, and death.)

Della gloria di amor candidi i gigli,
E s'erano poco anzi quei begl'occhi
Torbidi, e sbigottiti, hor spiran fiamme,
E sfauillano ardori, e vibran strali
Qual nuoua Aurora, che dal cielo scaccia
Le tenebre notturne, e'l mondo rende
La bellezze, e ornamenti suoi già spenti.
Tal l'Aurora d'amor scacciando giua
Della tema il pallor rauuiva il volto,
E di rossor di Paradiso il cinge,
E colorea le scolorite stelle,
Che gratia, e leggiadria raggin per tutto.[22]   (v, 1)

But when Della Porta turned in old age to secular tragedy, he totally rejected the ornaments, conceits, and soft Lydian airs then more in vogue than ever, and wrote exclusively in his most austere style. Neptune's opening exclamation, "Mi vince Vlisse, Vlisse pur mi vince" (1, 1), is a line taken from *Penelope* (1, 1), a reference to the continuity of the two plots. That continuity is evident in the style as well, which in *Ulisse*, however, acquires a uniformity and a new assurance. The long periods, the *asprezza* forced by enjambement and clashing consonants, inversions, and repetitions prescribed by Tasso roll on in many a stately passage like the following:

Consiglier io sò ben, e sò ben ancho
Che tu saper lo dei, che un debil freno
Può destrier furioso in mezo al corso

[22] (The breeze moved only the tress which waved unbound on the brow, and the golden hair curled in a thousand knots and ringlets. The lake water sprinkled her face. Her nerveless forces, almost exhausted, began to revive, now the color begins to glow in her face, and if those beautiful eyes were formerly heavy and dazed, now they breathe flames and sparkle fires, and hurl arrows. Like the new dawn which drives from heaven the nocturnal shadows and returns to the world its extinguished beauties and ornaments, so that dawn of love moves, chasing away the pallor of fear, revives the face and encircles it with the rosiness of Paradise, and colors the faded stars which beam grace and charm everywhere.)

Ratto frenar, ma non si trouò mai
Così gagliardo fren, che frenar basti
Superba ambition animo vasto
Del regnar, perche sẽpre ingordo, & ebro
Di dolcezza ammassando nuoui regni;
Nuoui domini, anzi non satio mai,
Anchor che possedesse mille regni.
E per ciò conseguir, sossopra il mondo
Riuolge, e poco cura huomini, e dei.[23]   (III, 1)

Few Counter-Reformation tragedies are so grave in style; Anguillara's *Edippo* comes to mind, but it was forty-seven years earlier. Although one of the aims of Counter-Reformation literary policy was to preserve the order and form which the early Renaissance had recovered from antiquity, the greater number of late sixteenth-century poets, like Tasso, paid earnest lip service to Aristotle's *Poetics*, but remodeled it drastically, neglected the spirit for the letter, or separated theory from practice. Truly neoclassical practitioners were scarce. Della Porta's tragedy proves that they were not yet extinct. His heroic style, like the other aspects of his serious plays, manifests that deeply rooted classicism which is the half-hidden but all-determining foundation of his finest work, the comedies.

[23] (Counselor, I know well, and I know too that you must know it, that a light rein can quickly restrain a wild charger in mid-course, but no one ever found a rein strong enough to restrain a great spirit's high ambition to rule, for ever greedily and drunk on sweetness, it piles up new realms, new dominions, and is never satisfied, even if it possessed a thousand. And to do that, it overturns the world and cares little for men and gods.)

Learned Comedy
Between 1550 and 1614

WHEN the young Della Porta set himself to writing his first comedy, he had no shortage of models. He inherited a tradition of sophisticated *commedia erudita* descended from Latin comedy and cultivated by two generations of Italian dramatists. Ariosto and Machiavelli had brilliantly established a pattern which was modified only gradually and never entirely discarded. Subsequent comedies might be predominantly novellesque, like *La mandragola;* Roman, like *La cassaria;* or, like Bibbiena's *Calandria,* an equiproportioned cross between the two. They might be in prose or in verse; this choice troubled many comic playwrights, a few of whom followed Ariosto's example of revising prose comedies into verse. But whatever their sources and meters, *commedie erudite* throughout the century were always *imbrogli* in which young men, aided by sprightly servants, cleverly succeeded in tricking miserly fathers, winning wives of their own choice, or cuckolding elderly husbands. More often than not, the denouement depended on the classic device of agnition—timely revelations of birth and reconciliations between longlost children and parents. The characters were usually drawn from the contemporary middle and lower classes (until quite late in the century), the setting a residential street in a specific Italian town, the number of acts five, and the required time rarely more than a day.

In comedies of the first few decades, the emphasis was entirely on cleverness; the dialogue was neat and well-turned, the lovers witty rather than sentimental, the humor dry. A more Terentian than Plautine spirit moved playwrights like Lorenzino de' Medici, Benedetto Varchi, and Luigi Alamanni. They excited chuckles instead of guffaws, and their targets were avarice, stupidity (especially that of cuckolds), and the hypocrisy of bawds and corrupt friars.

Before the middle of the century declarations of independence became the fashion. Following the earlier example of Aretino, up-to-date dramatists like Francesco D'Ambra, Giovanmaria Cecchi, and "il Lasca," the emphatic Anton Francesco Grazzini, claimed emancipation from the Greek-Latin yoke.[1] A few, like Cecchi, even championed the rustico-romantic *farse* made famous by the plebeian Sienese guild, the Rozzi. But the kind of freedom which permitted the development of English comedy, for example, was never achieved by the Italian comic playwrights. "New comedy," as Professor Herrick calls it,[2] continued to conform to neo-classical tenets and drew on *novelle* only a little more than the older comedy had done. But there were undeniably some changes, which appeared more and more marked as the century progressed.

The shape of comedy to come could be seen early in the works of Aretino, the most original as well as the most versatile playwright of his generation, if not of his century. For all his gibes at scholarly imitations of the classics, Aretino retained most of the conventions inherited from Plautus and Terence. Also, however, he added elements of popular farce and naturalism in *La cortegiana*, dialects and "humours" characters in all five comedies, and foreshadowed the Coun-

---

[1] These four playwrights announced their revolt against Athens and Rome in the prologues to *La cortegiana* (1525), *I Bernardi* (1547), *L'assiuolo* (1550), and *La gelosia* (1551), respectively, as well as in other of their writings.

[2] *Italian Comedy in the Renaissance* (Urbana, 1960). See Chapter IV.

ter-Reformation style in the excessively embroiled *Talanta* (1541) and in the romantically serious *Ipocrito* (1542).[3]

The reciprocal relationship between the *commedia erudita* and the rising *commedia dell'arte* was responsible for some of the changes. The masks of improvised comedy existed outside the limits of any particular plot. They needed no introduction, for the audience recognized them at sight, enabling each character to launch immediately into his characteristic foolery. In learned comedy the broad caricatures and roughhouse farce of the popular stage began to be reflected by a gradual exaggeration of the stock types: the *davos* became cleverer and adept at rapid physical *lazzi*, the *senex* more grotesque and prone to prat falls, the Hispanized *miles* more bloated. Moreover, adulterations of the Tuscan dialogue with other dialects resulted in new comic types, like the ridiculously ceremonious Neapolitan, bursting with vanity and literary misquotations. Giovanni Battista Cini (in *La vedova*, 1569) and Cristoforo Castelletti (in *I torti amorosi*, 1581) used the figure with success, Della Porta with brilliance. The *innamorati* became more languishing and more articulate. Writers of early *commedia erudita* had inherited no language of love from their sources in *novelle* and Roman comedy, and therefore had to develop their own over the years, from a basically Petrarchan vocabulary. The tendency of the *comici dell'arte* to exaggerate and then to "freeze" their characters sped the evolution of an attributive language and a set of gestures for *innamorati*.

Perhaps the strongest pressure behind the "new comedy" was the spiritual, intellectual, and artistic atmosphere created

[3] So accurately did Aretino anticipate many of the styles to follow that his comedies were reprinted during the Counter-Reformation period, despite his memory's being anathema to all right-thinking Catholics. In order to avoid scandal, Luigi Tansillo's name was used as a cover to the late editions of *L'ipocrito* (*Il finto*, Vicenza, 1610), and *Il marescalco* (*Il cavallarizzo, comedia . . . nuova*, Vicenza, 1608), and *Il filosofo* (*Il sofista*, Vicenza, 1610).

by the Counter-Reformation. Because content was more and more strictly censored, form became paramount. As the characters were exaggerated, so too were the *imbrogli*. Terence's example and Giraldi's championing of the double plot justified late sixteenth-century playwrights in weaving increasingly complicated intrigues, only to disentangle them with a show of technique. The omnipresent taste for *meraviglia* encouraged such exhibitions of legerdemain, sometimes to the point of absurdity; in the *Intrichi d'amore*, sometimes attributed to Tasso,[4] the superfluity of disguises, recognitions, and misunderstandings forces the conclusion that the comedy was intended as parody.

Another striking change in comedy after 1550 appeared in the playwrights' avowed purpose. Prefaces began to promise moral profit more often than delight. Although the comedies themselves usually failed to keep the promises, most of them at least avoided the grosser immoralities of an earlier time. Didacticism in comedy was hardly an innovation; Horace and Terence had authorized, Ariosto and Machiavelli had employed it subtly. But during the Counter-Reformation period, faced with ecclesiastical charges that comedy corrupted public morals, scores of *commediografi* tried to prove the opposite. Some few, among them Lodovico Dolce and il Lasca, persisted in regarding pleasure as the end of comedy, but most of their contemporaries and successors were compelled by a need for the censors' approval to proffer moral intentions, whether or not their works bore them out, to cease condoning adultery, and to insert instructive squibs between their jests. Late in life Cecchi illustrated the change by purging some of his early comedies of their licentious speeches.

4 Published as "*Comedia del sig. Torquato Tasso. Rappresentata in Caprarola*" (Viterbo, 1603). Sanesi dates its composition 1585. A. Solerti was of the opinion that Tasso began the comedy and the members of the Caprarola Academy finished it (*Vita di Torquato Tasso*, Torino, 1895, 1,474), an opinion supported by the dedication of the 1603 edition.

Not all forms of moralizing were acceptable however. Satire, especially of religious abuses, was unthinkable, unless it was directed at some attitude or practice outlawed by the Council of Trent. The figure of the venal cleric, familiar in novellesque comedies from *Mandragola* to Dolce's *Marito* (between 1540 and 1550), utterly disappeared from the stage.

Adultery and concubinage now being frowned on as aims of comic intrigue, the courtship of young lovers was left as the sovereign theme. The sentiment and pathos of Iacopo Nardi's *Comedia di amicitia* (between 1502 and 1512), Alessandro Piccolomini's *Amor costante* (1536), or Aretino's *Ipocrito* had in their time been the exception; now they became the rule. At first, emotional scenes were simply interpolations in comedies which claimed to teach by presenting examples of folly to be avoided, but they soon gave rise to more positive didactic elements, providing examples of fidelity, chastity, and general highmindedness.

Eventually these lofty elements brought comedy close to tragicomedy. Distinct from *tragedia di fin lieto* by virtue of its admixture of low characters and jokes, the serious comedy foreshadowed by Luca Contile's *Pescara* (1537) and represented by such works as Sforza Oddi's, Raffaello Borghini's, and Girolamo Bargagli's, contained threats of death, a leavening of highly placed characters, and large doses of pathos and passion. Not without reason, plays of this genre—Diomisso Guazzoni's *Quintilia* (Mantova, 1579), for example—were occasionally even dubbed *tragicomedia* by their authors. An almost Corneillian concept of moral conflict—love versus friendship or duty or filial ties—often obtained, as it does in *La donna costante* of Borghini, *L'erofilomachia* of Oddi, or relatively early in Girolamo Parabosco's *Marinaio* (1550). Sometimes the humor was overpowered by moralizing and emotional intensity; the comedies of G. F. Loredano, Bernardino Pino da Cagli, and Girolamo Razzi contain more tears than laughter. A few playwrights like G. B. Cini managed to use the new seriousness to effect, without sacrificing the traditional gaiety of the *commedia erudita*. In this, Della Porta was Cini's heir.

Although the centers of theatrical activity until late in the century were in the north, comedy was not neglected in the south. The Neapolitan generation before Della Porta's could boast *commedie erudite* by Angelo di Costanzo, Scipione Ammirato, and Bernardino Rota. Among later southern masters of the genre were Luigi Tansillo and Giordano Bruno. Mario Apollonio discerns a geographical shift of comedy in the last part of the sixteenth century, when the south inherited the fully developed tradition of the north.[5] If Naples seems then to have become a theatrical center, it was not because there were many playwrights there and few elsewhere —for they were everywhere legion—but in large part because Giambattista Della Porta was a Neapolitan.

[5] *Storia del teatro italiana*, II (Firenze, 1951), 184ff.

Della Porta's Comedy

IN DEDICATING the first edition of Della Porta's earliest play, *L'Olimpia*, Pompeo Barbarito hailed it as a renewal of the "stile antico," a serious, artistic, and useful comedy able to inspire other "bell'ingegni" to recreate a taste for "commedie gravi ed artificiose."[1] Croce interpreted Barbarito's hope as a declaration of war between the *commedia erudita* and the *commedia dell'arte*, between *letterati* and *istrioni*.[2] But by November 1586, the earliest possible date for the magnificent court debut before the Count of Miranda, Spanish Viceroy of Naples,[3] the script had been in circulation for some years and had come to belong to the *istrioni* as much as to the *letterati*. Composed sometime after 1550, *Olimpia* "was praised by those few who saw her at home" (Prologue, A2). It must have been privately performed in houses and academies often enough to acquire a reputation, for in 1584 it

[1] Napoli, 1589, 4. Although early separate editions are cited for dedications, etc., the basic text used in this study is Gennaro Muzio's edition, *Delle commedie di Giovanbattista de la Porta Napoletano* (Napoli, 1726), 4 vols., based on first editions of the fourteeen comedies published in Della Porta's lifetime. Muzio corrected typographical errors and modernized the spelling of the first editions. Otherwise, he followed them exactly. In the absence of a modern critical edition—V. Spampanato's edition of eight comedies, *Le commedie* (Bari, 1910–1911), 2 vols., cannot, for lack of notes and introduction, be considered such—Muzio's is the most convenient and correct text available.

[2] *I teatri di Napoli: Secolo XV–XVIII* (Napoli, 1891), 70.

[3] Croce guessed that the performance was given in 1588 or 1589 (*Teatri*, 69); Apollonio dates it 1585 (*Storia del teatro italiano*, Firenze, 1951, II, 185); Fiorentino revealed that Juan de Zuñiga, conde de Miranda, took up his viceregal duties in November, 1586, *Studi e ritratti della Rinascenza* (Bari, 1911), 263.

appeared in Paris as *Angelica,* in performance by Fabrizio de Fornaris and his troupe.[4] With its new name and a few insignificant changes, *Olimpia* easily fitted into the repertory of the Confidenti; obviously it was not a declaration of war against the *commedia dell'arte in toto.* Its challenge was, rather, to two specific elements proper to one form of activity of the *comici dell'arte:* the licentiousness and the shapelessness which often characterized their improvised three-act farces. *Olimpia* represented a kind of comedy welcomed equally by learned amateurs and professional players as an answer to the demands of both moral reformers and neoclassical critics.

The fundamentals of Della Porta's dramatic theory, expounded in his lost Latin treatise on the art of comedy,[5] can be reconstructed from pieces of his seven prologues. Those attached to *Fantesca, Cintia,* and *Trappolaria* were intended mainly to amuse and flatter an audience, but the others contain statements of Della Porta's principles. The *Olimpia* prologue, diffident as befits a first effort, asks recognition of those attributes which the author apparently valued most in a comedy: *"armonia . . . proporzionata . . .* [,] *lingua . . . melata . . .* [,] *salsi scherzi . . .* [,] *gravi piacevolezze"* [6] (A2verso). The prologue to *Furiosa* is a classical defense of drama as a means of moral instruction, supported by ancient authority. Nevertheless, Della Porta declared himself a Modern in his most significant prologue, the only one he used twice, first for *Fratelli rivali* and then, slightly altered, for *Carbonaria.* Here he asserted his independence of

[4] See Chapter II and Chapter VIII. *Angelica* was known in Italy before its French debut, to judge by the prologue to Cornelio Lanci's *Mestola* of 1583. Lanci was given to plagiarizing his prologues, and in this case he borrowed, with minor changes, the prologue to *Angelica,* which was in turn a slight modification of the prologue to *Olimpia.*

[5] Pompeo Barbarito's mention of it in the dedication to *La Penelope* (Napoli, 1591) proves that it was finished by 1591.

[6] (proportioned harmony, . . . honeyed language, . . . saucy jokes, . . . seemly amusements)

the Ancients, as a number of his predecessors had done, and in answer to charges that his language was not like Boccaccio's and his procedure un-Aristotelian, he defined what he judged to be the first aim of comedy:

Ignorantissimo, considera prima le favola, se sia nuova, maravigliosa, piacevole, e se ha l'altre sue parti convenevoli, che questo è l'anima della Commedia: considera la peripezia, che è spirito dell'anima, che l'avviva, e le dà moto, e se gli antichi consumavano venti scene, per farla cadere in una, in queste sue senza stiracchiamenti, e da se stessa cade in tutto il quarto atto; e se miri più adentro, vedrai nascere peripezia da peripezia, ed agnizione da agnizione: che se non fossi così cieco degli occhi dello 'ntelletto, come sei, vedresti l'ombre di Menandro, di Epicarmo, e di Plauto vagare in questa Scena, e rallegrarsi, che la Commedia sia giunta a quel colmo, e a quel segno, dove tutta l'antichita fece bersaglio. Or questo è altro, che parole del Boccaccio, o regole di Aristotile, il quale se avesse saputo di filosofia, e di altro, quanto di Commedia, forse non avrebbe quel grido famoso, che possiede per tutto il mondo.   (A2verso-A3) [7]

The second time this prologue appeared, the derogatory remark about Aristotle had been cut; despite his modernity, Della Porta was too respectful of Aristotle to be comfortable in criticizing him. In the dedication of *Sorella*, Lucrezio Nucci reported that Della Porta constructed this comedy on

[7] (Ignoramus, consider first whether the plot is new, marvelous, pleasing, and well-proportioned, for this is the soul of the comedy: consider the peripety, which is the soul's spirit, which gives it life and motion, and if the ancients used up twenty scenes in order to make the peripety occur in one, in these [*i.e.*, the comedies of Della Porta], without distortion, the peripety occurs naturally in the course of the fourth act; and if you look more closely, you will see peripety born of peripety, and agnition of agnition: if the eyes of your intellect were not blind, you would see the ghosts of Menander, Epicharmus, and Plautus wandering on this stage, rejoicing that comedy has reached that height and the mark at which all antiquity aimed. This has nothing to do with the vocabulary of Boccaccio or the rules of Aristotle, who, if he had known only as much of philosophy and other things as of comedy, would perhaps not be so generally admired.)

the principle of peripety and agnition used by Sophocles in *Oedipus tyrannos*, because Aristotle praised it.

Barbarito's dedication of *Penelope* actually describes the plan of the lost treatise on comedy, revealing how Della Porta leavened classical precept with originality, always concurring, however, in Aristotle's emphasis on plot. It was to be:

. . . vn trattato doue si vede l'arte vera di comporle, [commedie] intesa sin hora da pochi, con le regole, cauate non pur d'Aristotele, & dalle antiche Comedie, ma inuentate, & osseruate da lui, in altra maniera di quel che han fatto tanti altri moderni, acciò non ardischi ogni vno di porsi ad vna impresa tanto difficile, con lasciarsi ingannar chè dal ridiculo, che si caua da alcuni motti impiastrati in certe scene le loro compositioni meritino nome di Comedie; non accorgendosi, che bisogna che'l ridicolo sia sparso per la Comedia, non solo per mezzo di facetie, & di motti intramessi, & nati legitimamente nella fauola, ma che la fauola per se stessa sia tale & habbia talmente proprie de peripetie vnite con l'agnitione, che raccontandosi faccia marauigliar, & muoua riso à chi l'ascolto . . .[8]   (A3)

Such views, borne out by the comedies themselves, testify that Della Porta's theater was shaped by the same two forces which guided his pseudo-scientific and philosophical investigations: the delight in marvels to which *Magiae naturalis* owes its existence, and the passion for order and design propelling him toward systems which, like the Doctrine of Signatures, affirmed the unity of all existence, temporal or spiritual, animate or inanimate, past or present.

[8] (a treatise on the true art of composing comedies, heretofore understood by few, with rules drawn not only from Aristotle and ancient comedies but discovered and observed by himself [Della Porta], in a way different from that of so many other moderns, who not daring to attempt so difficult an undertaking, deceive themselves that their compositions deserve the name of comedy by virtue of humor derived from a few words plastered on to certain scenes; not aware that humor [the ridiculous] must be spread throughout the comedy, not only by means of inserted jests and words, and rising appropriately from the plot, but also that the plot itself must be of a sort in which the peripeties are so tied to the agnition as in the telling to make the hearer marvel and laugh . . .)

Della Porta's Comedy

Essentially it was his love of the marvelous which made Della Porta a Modern. His natural inclination toward that *meraviglia* so fashionable just then is manifest not only in his demand that plots be "marvelous" but also in his very concept of the ridiculous, based firmly on the principle of exaggeration, which is the prime tool of *meraviglia*. When Della Porta took up the classical stock types he found them exaggerated into Italian caricatures by half a century of contact with the *commedia dell'arte*, and he proceeded to exaggerate them still further. He stylized them beyond all pretense to realism, enabling them to express and to act the greatest absurdities with the greatest grace, in an atmosphere of hilarious unreality, or more accurately, of uncompromisingly theatrical reality. In these characters the popular and the learned are delicately balanced. They act like the latest *commedia dell'arte* personages—the *Innamorati*, the *Capitano*, the *Zanni*, the *Servette*, the *Magnifico*—but they wear no masks and their conversation is often as elegantly literary as their names.

The pre-established personalities of his characters permitted Della Porta to dispense with explanatory details, providing him from the first with a stout fabric for embroidery, freeing him to concentrate on plot. He invigorated his *commedie erudite* with color, spirit, and theatricality borrowed from the *mestieranti*; he gave elegant line to his *commedia dell'arte* material by replacing improvisation with planned and focused effects, by polishing and elevating its language, and above all by subordinating its profusion of motifs to a unified design.

For, of course, Della Porta's prime consideration was always structure, into which entered both his loves, *meraviglia* and order. His aim was to achieve perfect order by means of marvelous complications, and at a time when fashion demanded *ingenium* of form, he was the most ingenious of dramatists. Zannetti's description of some of the lost comedies reveals how far Della Porta was fascinated by structural complexity and unity; the quintet of comedies on one plot, each complete in itself and yet intended to be performed as one fifth of the whole, marks the extreme limit.[9]

The relative seriousness of Della Porta's comedies was another sign of his modernity. The moral purpose he declared in the prologue to *Furiosa* was hardly original; such claims had been made since the birth of erudite comedy. But, strikingly, in Della Porta's work there actually seems to be some correlation between theory and practice. His earliest and his latest comedies are lighter than those of his middle period, but all fourteen of them sound the moral, sentimental, and pathetic notes approved by Counter-Reformers and rarely heard in pre-Tridentine *commedia erudita*. From time to time, moreover, a non-didactic seriousness shows briefly under the studiously frivolous surface of Della Portean comedy. He brought a mature knowledge of psychology to the ingenuous old stories he reworked, and he preferred as sources those which presented a clash between pretense and reality.[10] He was also given to troubling his characters with doubts of their identities, a dramatic theme from which a large measure of *meraviglia* can be extracted and which pointed three centuries ahead to another southern playwright haunted by the *commedia dell'arte* and the question of identity.

Della Porta's most joyous pursuit of *meraviglia* was linguistic. His comic language is a rich *macedoine* of spicy proverbs, city slang, learned allusions, alliterative and antithetical love laments, hyperbolic parodies, and whizzing crosstalk—all perfectly artificial and perfectly natural to artificial characters in artificial surroundings. With each new comedy Della Porta's prose became more dazzlingly decorative, far more so than he had ever allowed his *versi sciolti*

[9] Della Porta, *Elementorum curvilineorum libri III* (Romae: per Bartholomeum Zannettum, 1610), 99.

[10] This clash is not to be confused with the opposition between appearance and reality which Lionel Trilling discovers at the base of all literature worthy of the name. (*The Liberal Imagination*, New York, 1951.)

to be. It is because of his comic prose style more than anything else that he is often ranked with Tasso, Bruno, and Guarini as a trailblazer of the transition from the sixteenth to the seventeenth centuries.[11]

At his most modern, however, Della Porta remained a classicist, more profoundly so than most of his contemporaries who observed the unities and quoted Aristotle. His very statement of independence betrays his sense of a bond with the ancients; the fragments of theory in his prologues and the practice of the comedies themselves reveal a neoclassicism that sprang rather from concurrence in the ancients' ideals than from any conviction that their plays could be imitated but not surpassed. He was aware of a tradition linking him and his Italian predecessors through the Romans to the Greeks, and he believed that each age could improve on the last. Such a concept of the dramatist's relation to the past permitted Della Porta to use all the attractive elements of contemporary comedy, to mingle modern and ancient principles. By the time he began writing, the *commedia erudita* was highly developed; inheriting its forms and conventions, Della Porta used them with perfect ease and finality, and by doing so, placed them firmly in the tradition of classical comedy. His love of order and system demanded as much.

Most of his predecessors who asserted their freedom from the ancients did so on the basis of their plots. In the prologue to *Assiuolo*, for example, Cecchi boasts that his story is a contemporary Italian one, not dependent for its denouement on opportune arrivals of longlost parents or other such devices. But Della Porta used old and new elements alike and was not in the least afraid to borrow Roman and Greek plots. His structural balance is as Terentian as Machiavelli's or

[11] Attilio Momigliano finds the transition illustrated by these four more important than its point of arrival (*Storia della letteratura italiana*, Firenze, 1954, 250–51). Giorgio Pullini's emphasis in his article on Della Porta's prose style is precisely on its transitional function. ("Stile di Transizione nel Teatro di Giambattista Della Porta," *Lettere italiane* VII, Padova, 1956, 299–310.)

Ariosto's, with complications as numerous as Salviati's or Beltrame's, but his material is like Aretino's and more than Aretino's, Plautine, compact of loud contrasting colors, sex, farce, and caricature. He also took plots from *novelle* and early *commedie erudite*, like other dramatists (although, unlike most of them, he never used pastoral elements), but even his novellesque plays were Plautine. He had translated all of Plautus' comedies before 1591 and possibly even before writing any of his own. Probably the reason why the translation was never published as such is that the greater part of it was incorporated into the translator's own comedies. Plautus became part of Della Porta's mind, a permanent storehouse of situations, resolutions, encounters, and character types for all occasions. Indeed, the principle of exaggeration on which Della Porta worked to achieve his most modern effects was one authorized and consistently invoked by Plautus.

Della Porta was also aware that the use of tragicomic themes, which put him in the avant-garde of Counter-Reformation fashion, had classical precedents in the moral works of Terence and in Plautus' *Amphytrion* and *Captivi*. Unlike most of the other writers of serious Italian comedy, Della Porta was unwilling to harm the tradition or change the essence of classical comedy, eager though he was to improve on it. Bargagli, Razzi, and Oddi regularly scuttled humor for the sake of sentiment and pathos, but in his dark middle period, Della Porta was true to his Plautine colors and never forgot that comedy is primarily a laughing matter.

Even his comic language, often cited as a model of early *Seicentismo* does not exceed the limits set by Plautus, who always enjoyed a round or two of word play. Demetrius expressly advises antithesis and hyperbole for comic effect; Plautus uses both and is no less profuse of vocabulary than Della Porta. Della Porta's comic prose is exaggerated, overblown, but its patterns are intellectual, based on *ingenium*, employing striking antitheses and, above all, hyperbole. It is rarely sensual, never lyrical or pastoral, and most surprising for the time, usually free from farfetched conceits. It is a language drier than Tasso's or Guarini's, more restrained than Bruno's, and infinitely more robust than the fullblown *Seicentesco* style represented by Marino. In forging what is, on the surface, a most unclassical comic prose, Della Porta seems to have taken seriously the neoclassical precepts to which everyone else paid mere lip-service and to have ruled his fancy by ancient doctrine and example.

Because Della Porta wrote over a period of many years, some of his plays were "scherzi della sua fanciullezza" (*Fratelli rivali* prologue, A2verso) or revisions of them, and others were "scherzi de' suoi studi più gravi" (*Carbonaria* prologue, A3); naturally there are progressive differences to be seen from first to last. The system of grouping usually followed for the comedies is that established by Milano.[12] It is based on subject matter and divides the plays into four categories: strictly Plautine, Plautine-novellesque, novellesque-romantic, and "realistic." These categories are quite misleading and do nothing to illustrate the development of Della Porta's thought and technique. Among the earliest and the latest comedies are close Plautine imitations, but they are less similar to each other than to the semi-novellesque works of their respective periods. As one period succeeded another, Della Porta used his Latin material in different amounts and for varying effects. He began to adapt more from the *commedia dell'arte*, he conceived of romantic love in increasingly noble terms, his moral sensibility grew more delicate, his language became more fantastic. And yet all the characteristic elements of Della Portean dramaturgy are already present, at least in embryo, in *Olimpia*. The most reasonable order in which to study the other comedies would seem to be determined by the degree to which each manifests growth or change in the model represented by *Olimpia*. Such an arrangement is doubly warranted by the fact of its coinciding

[12] "Le commedie di Giovanbattista della Porta," *Studi di letteratura italiana* (Napoli, 1900), II, fasc. 2, 315.

with the likeliest chronology for the composition of the comedies.[13]

L'OLIMPIA

SYNOPSIS: While visiting her aunt in Rome, Olimpia falls in love with Lampridio. On her return to Naples she is promised by her mother, Sennia, to Trasilogo, a braggart captain. Aided by Mastica, a glutton, Lampridio comes to Naples disguised as Olimpia's brother, Eugenio, who together with her father, Teodosio, was captured by pirates years ago and is presumed dead. Lampridio is accepted by Sennia as her longlost son, and thus gains free access to Olimpia. Trasilogo learns of the deception and, hoping to discredit Lampridio, plans to hire a pair of vagabonds to impersonate Teodosio and Eugenio. The men he approaches for the purpose are, by coincidence, the real Teodosio and Eugenio, returned from captivity and eager to be reunited with Sennia and Olimpia. Warned of Trasilogo's plot, Lampridio persuades Sennia to turn the wanderers away from her door. Lampridio's own father, Filastorgo, arrives from Rome, but his son pretends not to know him. Teodosio and Eugenio succeed in convincing the police of their identity, however, and Lampridio is imprisoned. Sennia realizes that her daughter's honor is lost and vents her rage on Mastica. Lampridio's tutor persuades Filastorgo to forgive his son, and Filastorgo persuades Teodosio and Eugenio to drop their charges and to accept Lampridio as Olimpia's husband. Trasilogo finds another bride, Mastica is forgiven, the family is reunited, and the lovers are married.

The *favola* of *Olimpia* derives in part from Plautus' *Mercator*, and to a lesser degree from *Epidicus* and *Miles gloriosus*.[14] But for the slave girl of *Mercator*, introduced into her lover's house as his mother's maid, Della Porta substitutes the well-born Lampridio, masquerading as Olimpia's lost brother. Leaving Plautus behind, the intrigue is doubled by

[13] See Chapter III.
[14] For details about the sources of Della Porta's comedies, see Milano, *op.cit.* In his analyses, Milano was concerned almost exclusively with sources, despite which he missed a few. In the case of *Olimpia*, he mentioned only *Mercator*, 325.

Trasilogo's counterplot, tripled by the lovers' counter-counterplot, and quadrupled by the transformation of pretense into reality when the true brother and father return. Altered in every dimension, the plot satisfies his own demand for "la favola . . . nuova, maravigliosa, piacevole" (*Fratelli rivali* prologue, A2verso–3), and illustrates how Della Porta, always bent on marvelous order and orderly *meraviglia*, improved on the ordinary *imbroglio*. D'Ambra's much-admired *Bernardi* (1549), in comparison, requires four pairs of lovers and five *vecchi* to make it as tangled as it is, and to the same end the author of the celebrated *Intrichi d'amore* concocted a dozen unconnected disguises for as many characters. Della Porta uses characters economically and avoids confusion by making the plots and counterplots reflections of each other, all motivated by desire for Olimpia and dependent on the absence of her father and brother. The effect of *meraviglia* is achieved not by the sheer number of coincidences but by marshaling the workings of chance toward a confrontation of the deceivers with the very truth they have been counterfeiting. Della Porta retraces this ironic pattern in most of his comedies.

His characteristic method of elaborating his fable is already apparent in *Olimpia*. He accomplishes the major part of the exposition in the first scene, but adroitly avoids the pitfalls of this time-honored course. Disdaining to use an argument, a soliloquy, or a bare recital of facts by one character to another whose ignorance of them is hardly credible, Della Porta begins with an encounter between Olimpia's nurse and her crony, Anasira. Olimpia has just confided to the former her plan to pass off Lampridio as her brother, and Anasira smells a secret in the nurse's air of self-importance. The utility of the scene is camouflaged by the humor of the garrulous old soul's gradual capitulation to her friend's clever interrogation, which does not stop short of blackmail. The nurse's moral strength lies in aphorisms, and at first she resists temptation by warning herself that "chi ha gran voglia di udire, ha gran voglia di ridere." [15] But Anasira can match her, saw for saw, and resolves the conflict between the duty of secrecy and the delight of indiscretion with the observation that all women are born with wagging tongues. Comforted by this reminder that her shortcoming is universal, the nurse tells all, satisfying Anasira's curiosity and gracefully instructing the audience.

Compared with the host of Renaissance intrigue comedies in which the plots proceed by fits and starts, dropping lumps of humor, characterization, or sentiment along the way, Della Porta's plays are masterpieces of coordination. His integration of action with other dramatic elements is the more remarkable for the unusual variety of the latter. Smooth procedure is less difficult to achieve in comedies like Lorenzino's *Aridosia* (before 1537), for example, with its deliberately restrained tone, practical characters, and uniformly dry wit. Della Porta could be dry whenever he chose, and he chose to be so whenever he delineated a clever servant, but he indulges in the juicier sorts of humor too: rollicking slapstick, amorous banter, coarse *double-entendre*, fantastic parody, and absurd hyperbole. The last of these, in particular, is with Della Porta more than a stylistic device, rather a mode of conceiving character, language, even action. Mastica, the glutton of *Olimpia*, is the first product of this conception. Descended from Plautine parasites like Stichus, he outdoes his ancestors and is transported by his obsessive hunger into a marvelous world of food fantasy which is the special realm of Della Portean gluttons. Like his creator, Mastica seems to hold with the Doctrine of Signatures, but for him the headquarters of universal meaning is not the Divine Mind but the human stomach. In everything he sees, hears, and experiences he finds an association with some part of the nourishment process. The word *agnolo* sounds to him like *agnello* (I, 2). The mention of his own name moves him to lament his starvation, ". . . non vò esser Mastica, che non mastico, se

[15] (he who greatly desires to listen, greatly desires to laugh)

non sputo e vento." [16] Like the nurse, he tends to proverbs and aphorisms, but only to those which hinge on hunger. He can barely wrench his mind into communication with those of differently oriented characters. The nurse has trouble making him listen to her instructions: ". . . odi un poco." Mastica: "Che vuoi tu, ch'oda? Ventre, che non rode, mal volontier ode." [17] Yet the progress of the *imbroglio* is never interrupted for these comic manifestations. Mastica is very busy as a go-between, and though he is constantly haunted by visions of edibles and potables, he is always in the thick of the plot. His motivation to this strenuous activity is, of course, hunger.

In the same way the braggart, Trasilogo, is central to the story and makes no move without advancing the action, yet he expatiates fully on his delusions of carnage. Being on opposite sides of the intrigue, Mastica and Trasilogo are bound to run afoul of each other. In their meetings utility is again wed to delight; while new knots are tied in the story line, obsessions collide. To Trasilogo's boasts of the havoc he wreaked among the fabulous *Grimei, Dinamei, e Dicei,* Mastica replies that he can do as much to the *Panettarii, Piscatorii, Tavernarii,* and *Salcicciarii* (1, 5). The clash of personalities gives piquancy to the formal conflict.

Olimpia herself is the author of the original conspiracy and though she actually appears in only two scenes, she is no mere pawn like the *innamorate* in scores of earlier comedies. She is exaggerated in her way as the braggart and the glutton in theirs, and as she charges Mastica with messages for Lampridio, a new obsession heaves into view:

. . . digli a bocca, che l'ho amato assai più in assenza, che non l'amai in presenza; e che solo un refrigerio ho avuto in questa lontananza, che mi sono trasformata in pensiero, e stata tanto

[16] (I don't want to be Mastica, for I masticate nothing but spit and wind.)

[17] (What do you want me to do—listen? It's hard to listen on an empty belly.)

sospesa in lui, che mi sono dimenticata di me stessa, e dell'affanno, dove viveva; che non l'ho lasciato scompagnato per un sol passo; che gli sono stata sempre intorno, come l'ombra sua; e che si dimentichi Iddio di me, se per un sol punto me sono io dimenticata di lui; . . ." [18]

But no single mood is allowed to dominate; beneath Olimpia's impassioned melody runs a ground bass of mildly cynical commentary from the impatient Mastica. The antagonism between humor and sentiment creates a beneficial tension and provides an additional occasion of interplay among parts of the comedy. In a corresponding scene, the pedantic Protodidascalo, annoyed by Lampridio's lovesick rhapsodizing, answers it with an equally wordy flight of humanistic misogyny (II, 1). Thus it is with most of Della Porta's servants and tutors; they are helpful but risible, and thoroughly enjoy deflating or parodying their masters' amorous frenzies. These continuous exhibitions of humor and sentiment result from the characters' being tied so closely together that what affects one necessarily elicits reactions from all. Meanwhile the general pace never falters, because each character is assigned an important function in the plot and their jostling against each other pushes the action forward, causing "peripety to be born of peripety."

The consequent effect of inevitability and natural motion was what Della Porta piqued himself on when he criticized the ancients' distortion of twenty scenes for the sake of peripety in one. In *Olimpia* he used exactly the method described in the *Fratelli rivali* prologue: in Act IV, the second part of the epitasis, the return of Teodosio and Eugenio sets off a chain reaction of reversals and recognitions leading to

[18] (. . . tell him face to face that I have loved him more in absence than when we were together; and that my only solace in this separation was that I was transformed into thought and became so fixed on him that I forgot myself and the distress in which I lived; that I never left him alone for a single step; that I have been always about him, like his shadow; and that I wish God may forget me if I have forgotten him for a single instant . . .)

the grand peripety, thence to the catastrophe. The total damage has been done by the end of the act, though it requires three scenes of the next act to spread the ill tidings to those concerned. The low point for all the sympathetic characters is reached in Act v, Scene 4, but rather than weigh down the action with individual expressions of woe, Della Porta uses Mastica as a barometer, and in the glutton's ludicrous wailing over the mouthwatering goodies lost to him forever, conveys the general misery. The resolutions come thick and fast thereafter, one producing another until Mastica again gives voice to the predominant mood, this time one of joy, as he delivers the *envoi*. He is fulfilling one of the traditional functions of the clown, but his role of spokesman also is symbolic of the comedy's admirable unity, and his joy is a "sign" of a universal contentment.

This complex simplicity of design and execution is a triumph of clarity and control. But it breathes a dizzy carnival atmosphere. The fantastic dialogue sounds utterly natural on the lips of these abnormal characters. They belong unreservedly to this world of erotic, bellicose, and culinary fixations, hyperbole of word and gesture, and perfectly timed *lazzi*. Olimpia and Lampridio pant, weep, and pule in ornamental patterns, Mastica bellows hymns to bellyfodder, Lalio sets off a firecracker under Protodidascalo, Trasilogo's servants, armed with mops and brooms, fall all over each other in a household drill. The spirit of the *commedia dell'arte*, ritualistic, rambunctious, and always gloriously artificial, has penetrated the *commedia erudita:* the result is wellbred farce.

But another, more earnest spirit of the times lurks in the corner. Although Della Porta's earliest comedies are not expressly didactic, in *Olimpia* there is already evident a moral awareness, a lack of viciousness which distinguishes the Counter-Reformation theater. The prologue promises:

. . . se ben non è isconcia nella faccia, ha molto buona roba sotto i panni. E ancora piena d'onesti costumi, e lontana da viziose

azioni: onde non è men bella nella bellezza, che buona nella
bontà." [19]   (A2verso)

And indeed *Olimpia* is relatively circumspect. There are no
alluring prostitutes, religious hypocrites, nor venal clerics in
the *dramatis personae*. Adultery is not condoned; a little for-
nication takes place, it is true, but it is accompanied by a
private exchange of vows and soon mended by public marriage. There is a suggestive joke or two, usually about Protodidascalo's supposed homosexuality, but they are very
mild. Much worse obscenity and sensuality were winked at
by the censors, who reserved their outright condemnations
for unorthodoxy, anticlerical satire, and illegalities. Della
Porta apologized for *Olimpia*'s being "un poco vana, o
lascivetta, . . ." [20] (Prologue, A3), but he offered no excuses
and obviously considered it one of "her" charms.

Thus far the moral improvements instituted in *Olimpia*
were external, indicating observance of the new rules of
propriety rather than any revolution in ethical standards. But
there is an inner change as well, small but prophetic of Della
Porta's later attitude. Lampridio has a conscience. It is not a
very sensitive or powerful one, but its mere existence is surprising. He perpetrates the deceit unhesitatingly, and even
when he begins to suspect that Teodosio and Eugenio are in
fact the lost husband and son of Sennia, Lampridio heart-
lessly turns them away from their home, but at the end he is
distinctly repentant. His elders are slow to forgive him, and
he is made to understand the wickedness of his behavior.
What a change from the hundreds of earlier comedies in
which everyone takes it for granted that young men will
stoop to any sort of baseness to satisfy their desires, and no

[19] (. . . though she is far from ugly in the face, she also has many
beauties beneath her garments. She is still full of virtuous habits and
far from vicious actions: whence she is no less beautiful amid beauty
than good amid goodness.)
[20] (a little frivolous, or mildly risqué)

apology is expected! The characters in *Olimpia* are weak and inclined to sin, but they are not corrupt, nor is their society.

In admitting his ill-doing, Lampridio pleads only one mitigating circumstance, the fact of his love. He is not misusing the word. *Olimpia* belongs to the group of Counter-Reformation comedies in which love is substituted for lust. Olimpia's and Lampridio's feelings for each other are not in the least noble; love is not yet idealistic nor connected with morality, but it is unmistakably love, tender and intoxicating. The deliberate sweetness in art fostered by the Jesuit-directed aesthetic reform, the southern warmth of the Neapolitan character, the passion and love of exaggerated ornament brought from Spain by the occupation, meet in Della Porta. When Lampridio, disguised as an ex-captive still in chains, is permitted to greet his "sister," they vie with each other in elaborate compliments:

LAMPRIDIO

Ecco il vostro schiavo in catene, che ha eseguito, quanto dalla sua divina padrona gli è stato imposto, acciò conosca l'ardentissimo desiderio, c'ha di servirla, e mostri il simulacro del cuor suo, qual stia avvento intorno di catene.

OLIMPIA

D'oggi innanzi cominciarò ad avermi in più stima, e gloriarmi di questa mia bellezza: poich'è piaciuta a persona tale, che è posta in tanto pericolo per amor mio.

LAMPRIDIO

La contentezza, che ho di mirarvi a mio modo, e di servirvi, saria stato ben poco, se l'avessi comperata con pericoli di mille vite.

OLIMPIA

In me non conosco tal merito; ma ringrazio di ciò il cortese animo vostro.

LAMPRIDIO

Ringraziatene pur colui, che vi creò di tal pregio, che sforza ognun, che vi vede, a servirvi, ed onorarvi.

OLIMPIA

Desidero non essere intesa da vicini, o da quei di casa, e sopra tutto bramo vedervi sciolto da queste catene, che temo non v'offendano: che a questo collo dilicato, ed a questi fianchi ci convengono le braccia di chi v'ama a par dell' anima, e della sua vita.

LAMPRIDIO

L'offesa me la fate ben voi, anima mia, con dir, che queste m'offendano: che mentre mi stringono appo voi, mi fanno più libero della stessa libertade: e che sia vero, ecco, che da me stesso son venuto a farmevi prigione. Ma quelle, che mi stringono nell'amor vostro, sempre ch'io pensassi disciorle, m'allacciarebbono in duri ceppi, ed in amarissima prigione.

OLIMPIA

Ho tanta speranza ne' meriti dell'amor mio, che con mille catene più dure di queste ci legheremo con nodi d'inseparabil compagnia; ne basterà alcun accidente a schiodarle, se non la morte.

LAMPRIDIO

O Dio, non è questa Olimpia mia? non è questa la sua figura angelica? non la tengo abbracciata io? o forse sogno, come ho soluto sognarmi altre volte?

OLIMPIA

Sento genti venir di su. Camminate, fratello.[21]   (III, 3)

[21] (LAMPRIDIO. Here is your chained slave who has done everything required by his divine mistress so that she may know his ardent desire to serve her and so that he may show the simulacrum of his heart which has been enchained.

OLIMPIA. From this day forward I shall begin to esteem myself more and to glory in my beauty: because it has pleased such a person, who has put himself in such danger for my love's sake.

LAMPRIDIO. My joy in seeing you at will and serving you would have been cheaply purchased had I paid with a thousand mortal dangers.

OLIMPIA. I do not merit this; but I thank your courteous spirit.

LAMPRIDIO. Thank Him, instead, Who created you of a value that forces everyone who sees you to serve and honor you.

OLIMPIA. I do not wish the neighbors or the members of the household to hear us, and above all I want to see you shed of these chains, which I fear offend you: for this delicate neck and these sides should

Sentiment and style are one in such passages. Della Porta's *innamorati* are not at all sensuous or melting; their feelings are, however, exaggeratedly strong, obsessive, like the gluttons' feelings for food or the braggarts' egotism, and they are sharp-witted and active in their pursuit of each other. The language is exactly the same: fulsome, but rather clever than languid, and never soft at the center. In fact, this description fits every aspect of *Olimpia* and of the thirteen comedies to follow, despite the changes visible in Della Porta's work over the years.

LA FANTESCA

SYNOPSIS: Essandro, scion of the Genoese Fregosi family, has been separated from his father by the latter's exile and has been reared by his uncle Apollione in Rome. Following a quarrel with Apollione, Essandro has come to Naples and has fallen in love with Cleria, daughter of the physician Gerasto and his wife, Santina. Disguised as a servant girl, or *fantesca*, named Fioretta, Essandro takes service in Gerasto's house and works at persuading Cleria to love "Fioretta's" twin brother. Essandro's servant, Panurgo, is quartered at a nearby inn and provides his master with advice and male attire whenever the courtship requires either. Gerasto fatuously falls in love with "Fioretta," arousing the jealousy of Santina and of the housekeeper, Nepita. Essandro's plans are threatened by the announced arrival of the Roman pedant Narticoforo and his son Cintio, to whom Cleria has been betrothed for years. Panurgo undertakes to break the engage-

---

wear the arms of her who loves you as much as her own soul and life.

LAMPRIDIO. It is you who offend me, my soul, by saying that these chains offend me: for while they bind me close to you, they make me freer than liberty itself: and truly of my own will I came to make myself a prisoner. But those chains which bind me in your love, whenever I think of loosing them, would fasten me to heavy blocks and in a most bitter prison.

OLIMPIA. I believe my love so strong that with a thousand stronger chains than these we will bind ourselves with knots of inseparable companionship; nor will anything but death un-nail us.

LAMPRIDIO. Oh God, is not this my Olimpia? Is not this her angelic face? do I not embrace her? or perhaps I dream, as I have often done?

OLIMPIA. I hear people coming from above. Walk this way, brother.)

ment. As Gerasto and Narticoforo have never actually met, it is easy for Panurgo, dressed in stolen robes, to pass himself off as each in turn, introducing the disguised glutton Morfeo first as Cleria to Narticoforo, then as Cintio to Gerasto. On both occasions Morfeo acts the part of a diseased half-wit, sowing discord between the prospective fathers-in-law, who thereupon hire a pair of braggarts, Captains Dante and Pantaleone, to settle their grievances. Meanwhile Gerasto obtains a rendezvous with "Fioretta" but is met instead by his irate wife. The deception is discovered, and Essandro and Panurgo are in danger, until Apollione arrives to announce a general amnesty in Genoa, and recognizes Panurgo as his lost brother, the father of Essandro. Cleria is given to Essandro, her sister to Cintio, Gerasto swears off philandering, and the Fregosi family is reunited.

In Milano's opinion, *Fantesca* represents Della Porta's transition from his "old" to his "new" style and reflects a hesitation between Plautine and novellesque plots, later resolved in favor of the latter in *Cintia*.[22] But Milano also regarded *Fantesca* as the second comedy in order of composition, antedating several others in the allegedly "old" style of "schietta imitazione plautina." [23] Such are the contradictions engendered by overemphasis on sources.

Admittedly, the sources of *Fantesca* are heterogeneous, as those of *Olimpia* are not. The intrigue is akin to *Hortensio* (1560) and *Suppositi* (1509), as Milano observed.[24] It is even closer to the novellesque *Calandria* (1513) and the Plautine *Clizia* (ca. 1515). But the Intronati, Ariosto, Bibbiena, and Machiavelli had no monopoly on disguised lovers, old men in love with transvestites, and old women who outwit their lustful husbands. Through each of its situations, *Fantesca* can claim kinship with dozens of earlier Renaissance comedies. They, in turn, are related to Roman plays: *Calandria* to *Menaechmi*, *Suppositi* to *Captivi* and *Eunuchus*,[25] and so on.

---

[22] *Op.cit.*, 350.
[23] *Ibid.*, 313. (frank Plautine imitation)
[24] *Ibid.*, 344.
[25] See the prologue to the prose version in *Commedie e satire di Lodovico Ariosto annotate da Giovanni Tortoli* . . . (Firenze, 1856).

But Della Porta also had a direct connection with Plautus, whose *Casina,* as much as any Renaissance comedy, is an obvious source of *Fantesca.*

It is not by its sources, however, that *Fantesca* can be categorized among Della Porta's plays. A more significant difference between it and *Olimpia* is the relatively greater number of references to its author's scientific interests. The realistic details in Gerasto's description of the hanging in store for Panurgo (v, 7), Narticoforo's graphic word picture of a hanged man's face (IV, 1), and his exchange of insults with Gerasto, "faccia di boja . . . faccia d'appiccato" [26] (IV, 2), were surely suggested by Della Porta's own experiences during the preparation of *Della Chirofisionomia* and *De humana physiognomonia.* The apothecary's recipe for taming a shrew (v, 2) might have been one of the myriad "secrets" collected for *Magiae naturalis;* it is no more absurd than the charm for testing a wife's chastity in the *Magiae* (7. lvi), or the preservative against envy (8, xiv). In wooing "Fioretta," (I, 3), Gerasto develops a pun on her name into an image which includes planting, pruning, watering, and the other horticultural chores performed by Della Porta himself and recorded in *Pomarium* and *Olivetum.* His works on physiognomy, botany, and indeed the *Magiae* itself were completed or first published in the 1580's. *Fantesca* appears to have been revised between 1581 and 1591,[27] so that it is not surprising to find it sprinkled with allusions which would not have occurred to Della Porta years earlier while he was composing *Olimpia.*

The revisions, however, are superficial, and the determining features of *Fantesca* seem to belong, if not to exactly the same year as *Olimpia,* at least to the same stage in Della Porta's development. The morality which obtains in both is perfunctory and external, compared to that in the late comedies. Cleria is somewhat harder to seduce than Olimpia, it is true; Milano, indeed, intensely admires the former's self-defense, which "fa onore veramente al filosofo napole-

---

[26] (hangman's face . . . hanged man's face)
[27] See Chapter II.

tano." [28] But this praise is undeserved; after all, Cleria does give in. Counter-Reformatioon comedy boasts scores of firmer heroines, several of them fashioned by Della Porta during his serious phase.

Moral questions are touched on twice in *Fantesca*, but only as a gesture in imitation of Plautus; Della Porta himself was not ready to utilize his unobjectionable but as yet irrelevant moral values as a basic element of drama. The short argument on honor (v, 3) is, like the parallel scene in *Penelope*, the Renaissance version of Cleostrata's argument with Myrrhina in *Casina* (ii), and Nepita's cynical speech (v, 5) on the uselessness of locking girls up is a twisted imitation of the tolerant stand taken by Plautine fathers like Demaenetus in *Asinaria*. Both scenes touch lightly on matters which Della Porta later thought worthy of serious attention.

Like the morality, the sentiment in *Fantesca*, though a shade more ornately expressed, goes only as deep as that in *Olimpia*, sincere but easy, unhampered and unfortified by high-mindedness.

But it is structure, more than anything else, which marks *Fantesca* as an early comedy. Della Porta's attention to form was constant throughout his life, but only in his first years of playwriting was it a preoccupation, a conscious effort to create "order out of disorder" (*Fantesca* v, 9). Eventually the construction of *imbrogli* became second nature to him, but at the beginning he was intrigued by *meraviglia* of form and seems to have been experimenting in the early comedies with different means of achieving it. Most likely it is in this period that Della Porta wrote the lost *La notte*, in which several *imbrogli* arise from the throwing of one pebble, and the seven nameless comedies which appear from Zannetti's description to have been exercises in structural complexity and unity. [29]

In *Fantesca* Della Porta successfully tests the principle of

[28] *Op.cit.*, 344. (truly does honor to the Neapolitan philosopher)
[29] See Chapter ii.

exaggeration-by-multiplication and the catalytic effect of a reiterated motif. He discards the concentric pattern of *Olimpia* for a design of eccentric circles of action tangential to each other. Situations, motives, and roles are multiplied by two. Essandro is both an *innamorato* in pursuit of Cleria and a *fantesca* pursued by Gerasto, who is, in his turn, simultaneously the heavy father and the *senex amans*. In Narticoforo the roles of paternal *vecchio* and pedant are joined, and Morfeo is a rare specimen of transvestite glutton. One braggart will not suffice; Capitano Dante must be complemented by Capitano Pantaleone. Panurgo appears for the best part of the play to be merely a superior *davos* with a craftsman's pride in his machinations, thus refuting Pullini's charges that Della Porta's servants never enjoy their games of deceit.[30] But at the end Panurgo too assumes a second role. His metamorphosis from roguish servant into the well-born father of the hero is, incidentally, a dramatically successful breach of neoclassical decorum [31] which Della Porta never repeated.

The doubling trick in *Fantesca* is extended even to the love scenes, in which Della Porta uses it, as he regularly does his deflating technique, to drain off excess sentiment or to add a dash of bitters. The love between Essandro and Cleria is reflected crazily in Gerasto's grotesque passion for "Fioretta"; Gerasto's declaration (I, 3) is a travesty of courtly wooing, and when, in the following act (Scene 3), Essandro besieges Cleria with persuasive love-battle conceits, his speeches are tongue-in-cheek reminders of his own ludicrous courtship by his *innamorata*'s father.

While the unity of action in *Fantesca* is assured internally by the multiple involvements of the characters, it is further emphasized by the externally imposed theme of jealousy. Gelosia speaks the prologue, identifying "herself" as the

[30] *Op.cit.*, 300.
[31] Giovanni Battista Giraldi Cinthio, *Discorse . . . intorno al comporre de i romanzi, dalle comedie, e delle tragedie, e di altre maniere di poesie* (Vinegia, 1554), 259.

hinge of this comic action and the indispensable friend of all women in love. Thereafter, this motif is kept in constant play. It is made the occasion of the exposition (I, I), when Essandro reveals his true sex and intentions to Nepita in order to allay her jealousy of the love his female disguise has aroused in Gerasto. Domestic jealousy is twice deplored (I, 4; II, 3). An unpleasant encounter between Gerasto and the jealous Santina (II, 7) is followed by Essandro's encomium to the love without jealousy which he and Cleria share (II, 8). At last, when all fortunes are at their lowest ebb, Gerasto blames Santina's jealousy as the cause of all their present troubles (V, 4). In none of the comedies from which Della Porta may have borrowed situations for *Fantesca* could he have found a theme so used to reinforce structural unity.

Were all of Della Porta's comedies like *Fantesca*, Spampanato's claim that Della Porta was influenced by Bruno [32] might be acceptable. *Fantesca* has the wildly Neapolitan exuberance and unceasing physical action, without the bitterness, violence, or moral force of *Candelaio*. Perhaps the influence of Rabelais on both might account for the similarities. But *Fantesca* need not depend for admiration on any slight resemblance to other comedies. It has sufficient charms of its own: design, pace, and theatricality so engaging that Apollonio chooses this comedy to represent Della Porta's work in his distinguished anthology.[33]

LA CINTIA

SYNOPSIS: Cintia, sired out of wedlock by Arreotimo, has been reared as a boy because only by lying about the child's sex could her late mother persuade Arreotimo to matrimony. The so-called "Cintio" loves her childhood friend Erasto, who loves "Amasia," in reality Amasio, disguised as a girl by his father Pedrofilo to

32 "Somiglianze tra due commediografi napoletani," *Rassegna critica di letteratura italiana* (Napoli, 1906), XI, 145–67.

33 *Commedia italiana. Raccolta di commedie da Cielo D'Alcamo a Goldoni* (Firenze, 1947).

protect him from their political enemies. Amasio loves Erasto's sister Lidia, but Lidia loves "Cintio." Promising to help Erasto to "Amasia's" bed, Cintia herself has kept the appointment in the dark and is now in an advanced stage of pregnancy. She describes the situation to Erasto in a version adapted to fit her alleged manhood, but his shocked disapproval discourages her from telling the truth. Meanwhile "Amasia" tries to prepare Lidia's mind for the seduction he plans, and is himself importuned by Erasto and an amorous braggart captain. "Cintio" and "Amasia" pretend to act as go-betweens for Erasto and Lidia, respectively, and arrange a double rendezvous for the evening. Dressed in "Amasia's" clothes, Cintia barely escapes unmasking by Erasto. The captain spies on them and is convinced of "Amasia's" unchastity. Amasio in "Cintia's" clothes keeps the appointment with Lidia and takes her by force. Erasto learns "Amasia's" true sex and vows revenge on "Cintio" for foisting a prostitute on him. Lidia's father accosts Arreotimo and charges "Cintio" with rape. Unable to shake Cintia's determination to die at Erasto's hands, the nurse reveals the secret of her sex, which Cintia promptly confirms by giving birth to a baby. Erasto is delighted to learn that Cintia was his unknown *innamorata*. Amasio is forgiven and betrothed to Lidia, whose father rejoices with Arreotimo over the birth of their grandchild.

For several reasons *Cintia* is unique among the comedies. To begin with, Della Porta either named his daughter after the heroine or the heroine after his daughter. It is not known which came first. Although it was probably revised late, *Cintia* is generally classified as an early work.[34] That fixation on structure which made Della Porta's first two comedies manifest attempts to perfect the intrigue plot was clearly as strong when he wound up *Cintia* with Erasto's exclamation, "Ecco distrigato l'intrigo d'una intrigatissima Commedia"[35] (v, 3). Throughout the play one can feel Della Porta straining for more marvelous complications and more closely knit order. After *Olimpia*'s corolla of variations on one situation

[34] See Chapter II.
[35] (Here now the tangle of a most entangled comedy is untangled.)

and *Fantesca*'s cluster of situations on one theme, he tried out in *Cintia* a square design with a lover at each corner. The two couples, their parents, nurses, and servants all work at cross purposes because of misunderstandings arising either from Cintia's masquerade or from Amasio's. Whereas technically *Olimpia* has no subplot and *Fantesca* several, *Cintia* has one, but that one is of the same proportions as the main plot and proceeds side by side with it. After *Cintia* Della Porta invented no new structural patterns; he was content to retrace those of *Olimpia*, *Fantesca*, or *Cintia*, or to synthesize elements from all three. Apparently he particularly liked the arrangement of *Cintia*, for he used two sets of lovers in what were probably his next six comedies.

Nevertheless, *Cintia* resembles none of the comedies but *Fantesca*, and that only a little. In none of the others do *imbrogli* turn on disguises of sex or do heroes suffer political exile. *Fantesca* is the only other comedy which is more novellesque than Plautine. But *Cintia* is hardly Plautine at all. Except for the anonymous braggart captain and a degree of kinship several times removed to the *Menaechmi* theme, it owes its characters and situations to comedies in *Calandria*'s wake, specifically to the Intronati's *Hortensio* and Secchi's *Interessi*.[36] The clever servant, usually indispensable to Della Portean comedy, the glutton, the procurer, the pedant: all are missing from *Cintia*. The braggart's part is small, and of the three *vecchi*, not one is miserly or amorous. True to form, "peripety is born of peripety," but the customary reconciliation between long-separated parents and children or spouses is replaced by the purely sexual agnitions through which Cintia and Amasio come into their own. The construction and motivation which J. L. Klein so admired in *Cintia* and

---

[36] See Milano, *op.cit.*, for a detailed comparison of the Intronati's and Della Porta's treatments of the story. See also Florindo V. Cerreta's proof that *Hortensio* is not Piccolomini's, but the collective work of his fellow Intronati ("Clarifications concerning the real authorship of the Renaissance comedy *Ortensio*," *Renaissance News*, x, 63–69).

termed a Plautine-Ariostean improvement on *Hortensio* [37] are really, if anything, more Terentian than Plautine.

The absence of the stock comic underlings leaves the field to Cintia herself. She is at once heroine, wooer, and mastermind of the plot. The enlargement of the *innamorata*'s role in comedy as the sixteenth century progressed is usually attributed to the influence of the *commedia dell'arte* and its professional actresses.[38] Certainly Della Porta's heroines, beginning with Olimpia, owe something to this popular innovation. But Cintia inherits her character from the erudite comic tradition, in which dominating ingénues made rare but memorable appearances, nearly always as tranvestites.[39] Cintia, who doffs her male garb for one scene only, is in the line of Bibbiena's Santilla and is therefore singular among Della Porta's *innamorate*.

Her emotions, however, are characteristic of the Counter-Reformation. There is a touch of the masochist about her, and the pigheaded death-wish she reiterates (IV, 6; IV, 9) is worthy of Tasso's Erminia. This aspect of her nature confirms her as a marvel of wholehearted devotion. Otherwise, she is more like Clorinda, independent and resourceful, but also, in contrast to any of Tasso's ladies, witty. Her foil is Lidia, an endearingly helpless mooner, easily distracted from one infatuation by another, terrified when actually confronted by a determined lover. The *innamorati* are as carefully opposed. Erasto is an introvert, a bit prim, markedly contemplative and idealistic; Amasio, although successfully disguised as a girl, is impetuous, thoughtless, something of a fire-eater. There are more striking characters in Della Porta's other comedies, but no such contrasts between pairs of lovers.

The frantic bustling to and fro, the mistakes of the night in

[37] *Geschichte des Drama* (Leipzig, 1856–1876), v, 650.

[38] See R. C. C. Perman, "The Influence of the *commedia dell'arte* on the French Theatre before 1604," *French Studies*, IX (1955).

[39] See Norman B. Spector, "Odet de Turnèbe's *Les contens* and the Italian Comedy," *French Studies*, XIII, no. 4 (October, 1959), 312, note 8.

Act III, the absurd conversation à quatre, a double *double-entendre* (II, 5), are familiar landmarks of Della Portean farce, but despite these, *Cintia* is not truly farcical. Speeches like Erasto's denunciation of "Cintio" (IV, 5) or her pathetic defense (IV, 8) would not be out of place in serious comedies like *Il moro* or *La furiosa*. But even these later works contain larger doses of broad humor than *Cintia*.

Yet the language of *Cintia* is that of *Olimpia* and *Fantesca*. Amasio's conceit on bowing with the knees of his heart (III, 6) is not representative and was probably added at the same time as Mizieto's rebuke of Cintia for cursing her stars (I, 1) —a line unnecessary to the comedy but useful to an author suspected of believing in judiciary astrology. Otherwise, *Cintia*'s style is as involuted and curveting as that of Della Porta's first comedies but generally simpler and more realistic than the language he began using in *Astrologo*.

The strangest element in *Cintia* is the moral contradiction it presents. The three fathers and two nurses manifest a kindness and responsibility common to the serious comedies. But the young people behave more licentiously than any of Della Porta's other *innamorati*. Cintia, tricking Erasto into sleeping with her, and Amasio, raping Lidia, are as unscrupulous as any early sixteenth-century libertines, be they Bibbiena's or Aretino's. Moreover, Della Porta seems to have approved, for he spread himself in Cintia's praises (V, 1; V, 2). And yet there are conversations between Cintia and Erasto which equal the best in *Moro* for moral sensibility and idealism. To test Erasto's reaction, Cintia describes the deception she has practiced on him as though she were the man Erasto thinks she is and the victim an anonymous lady.

ERASTO

Ogn'uno si può ingannare, ma non un'innamorata.

. . . .

Cintio mio caro, per dirvelo alla libera, come conviene fra tali amici, come noi siamo, da che nacqui io, non vidi più brutto, e più infame atto di questo; o non più mai inteso tradimento al mondo, indegno non solo d'immaginarsi da un gentiluomo par vostro, ma da un barbaro, e ben' incolto; nè so, come in un bell' animo, come il vostro è, abbia potuto capire così brutto pensiero. Avete ingannato una donna, il cui sesso è esposto all' ingiurie di ognuno, poi innamorata: e chi si può dir peggio . . .

CINTIA

O che sentenza crudele! O che giudice precipitoso! Come pro-rompete in un così rigoroso decreto senza ascoltar le mie ragioni, e legittima difesa?

. . . .

Accecato di amore non sapeva quello, che mi facessi.

ERASTO

Amor non fu mai cagion di atto discortese, ed infame.

. . . .

Non si deve mai commettere inganno.

. . . .

Chi veramente ama, non fa così

. . . .

Chi ama, proccura l'amor della sua amata; non le proccura biasimo, o disonore.

. . . .

Il matrimonio non è valido, perchè non è contratto con colui, col quale ella avea l'animo; . . . nè so, come non vi morde la coscienza.

. . . .

Ma che dolcezze eran le vostre di godere quel corpo, di cui l'animo non concorreva col piacere con voi? Godevate un cadavero.[40] (II, 1)

[40] (ERASTO. Anyone can be deceived, but not a woman in love. My dear Cintio, to speak freely, as friends like us should do, in all my life I haven't seen an uglier, more infamous deed than this; nor heard of worse betrayal in all the world, not only unworthy the consideration of a gentleman of your quality, but even of a barbarian and oaf; nor do I know how such an ugly idea could have entered a beautiful soul like yours. You deceived a woman, whose sex exposes her to the injuries of everyone, and moreover, a woman in love: and who, to say worse . . . ,

CINTIO. Oh what a cruel judgment! What a precipitous judge! Will

Here Della Porta achieves a marvel of dramatic irony, which is intensified in retrospect at the end of the play when Erasto is delighted to find that he was wrong. But Della Porta's sense of good theater cannot account for his choice of arguments. Erasto could have been unconsciously ironic without waxing so moral. Not hazarding a guess at the author's intentions, Milano observed of this scene that Erasto is like the sixteenth-century comic playwrights who claimed in their prologues to be moralists, but in their comedies "aretineggiavano e peggio." [41] Klein rather too sweepingly declared Della Porta the only Italian playwright of his time to state the principle of love, as opposed to lust, and considered Erasto's opinions a criticism of the immorality of this genre of comedy.[42]

Because he was not concerned with *Cintia*'s relation to the other thirteen comedies, Klein omitted to mention that Della Porta nowhere else condones such flagrantly loose behavior. But Klein's comment provides an insight to Della Porta's frame of mind at this period. He was in the process of developing the more deeply moral view which distinguishes the late comedies. Erasto's overriden arguments may reflect the changes taking place in Della Porta's attitude. But the fact

---

you burst into so stern a decree without hearing my reasons and lawful defense? . . . Blinded by love, I did not know what I was doing.

ERASTO. Love was never the cause of a discourteous and infamous deed.

. . . .
One must never perpetrate a deceit.

. . . .
He who loves truly does not behave thus.

. . . He who loves obtains the love of his loved one; he does not bring blame or dishonor to her.

. . . .
The marriage is invalid, because it was not contracted with him she chose; . . . nor can I understand why your conscience doesn't gnaw you. . . . But what delight had you in enjoying a body the soul of which was not participating in the pleasure with you? You were enjoying a cadaver.)

[41] *Op.cit.*, 358. (Aretinized and worse)
[42] *Op.cit.*, v, 653–54.

that they are overridden, that the unusually reprehensible actions of Cintia and Amasio are justified, is most significant. It gives the comedy a satirical coloring. The only two of Della Porta's works heretofore associated with satire are *Astrologo* and *Turca*, neither of which *Cintia* resembles at all. But perhaps there is some connection. If *Cintia* was the third to be written, it directly preceded the satirical *Astrologo*. It is not unreasonable to look for seeds of the latter in the former. If the tension between Erasto's pronouncements and the unwonted licentiousness of the action is interpreted as embryonic satire, Cintia can be related to a period in the development of Della Porta's thought which produced his only two satirical comedies.

L'ASTROLOGO

SYNOPSIS: The Neapolitan widowers Pandolfo and Guglielmo have agreed to marry each other's daughters, but Guglielmo is now presumed to be lost at sea, and his son Lelio, wants to bestow his sister, Artemisia, on Eugenio and to marry Sulpizia, respectively son and daughter to Pandolfo. Pandolfo and his servant, Cricca, who is secretly loyal to Eugenio, consult the astrologer-magician, Albumazar, and are told that Guglielmo lies dead at the bottom of the sea, but that his external appearance may be transferred by Albumazar's magic to a living man, who will then be in a position to choose Artemisia's husband. Pandolfo persuades his clownish vintner, Vignarolo, to undergo the transformation and, according to instructions, leaves him blindfolded and alone with the astrologer in a room filled with Pandolfo's treasures, which Albumazar's henchmen proceed to carry out through the window. While the rogues convince Vignarolo that he has been metamorphosed, the real Guglielmo returns, but is repulsed by his son, to whom Cricca has revealed the astrologer's plot. Guglielmo at last proves his identity and agrees to help his children against Pandolfo. Vignarolo's sweetheart locks him in the cellar to prevent him from spoiling the counterplot, while Guglielmo pretends to be Vignarolo pretending to be Guglielmo, in which guise he decrees the nuptials of the four young lovers. Then he reveals himself and persuades Pandolfo to relinquish the pleasures of youth for the contentment of old age. There is a falling out among the thieves, Albumazar loses the rewards of his dishonest labor, and Pandolfo recovers his treasure.

LA TURCA

SYNOPSIS: Gerofilo and Argentoro, rich inhabitants of the Island of Lesina, having lost their old wives in a Turkish raid, plan to marry each other's daughters, unaware that Clarice is already secretly married to Gerofilo's son, Eromane, and Biancofiore is pregnant by Argentoro's son, Eugenio. Eugenio's gluttonous servant, Forca, member of a disreputable gang, suggests that the lovers and their friends stage a fake Turkish raid, abduct the girls and return them later, pretending to have redeemed them from the pirates but to have compromised their honor, thus necessitating the desired marriages. The plan goes well until a band of real Turks led by Dergut Rais captures the lovers and their companions. The governor of the island and his men are called in aid, but they arrest several of the fleeing false Turks by mistake. Forca saves the day by luring Dergut alone with tales of hidden treasure to Argentoro's house, where he pushes the corsair into a pit. Forca uses Dergut's ring to redeem the lovers from the pirate ship, then turns his prisoner over to the governor, who gives him to the hangman. The governor ends the quarrel between the lovers and their fathers by restoring to the reluctant old men their nagging wives, whom Forca has recognized among the captives on the pirate ship. Just before Dergut is to be hanged, his request for Christian sacraments leads to the discovery that he is the governor's longlost son. Everyone is happy, except Gerofilo and Argentoro, who have no faith in their wives' promises to reform.

Astrologo and *Turca* are so much alike that they may be examined more profitably together than separately. External evidence suggests that of the fourteen extant comedies, they were respectively fourth and fifth in order of composition, written in the 1570's, near the time of Della Porta's trouble with the Holy Office.[43] It has not been remarked before that

[43] See Chapter II, p. 60.

they have in common a bitter tone alien to the other comedies, which might well have been the temporary result of an inquisitional ordeal. Milano classified this pair of comedies as *realistiche*,[44] an inaccurate adjective to apply to any of Della Porta's works. But *Astrologo* and *Turca* are undeniably distinct from the rest in being primarily satirical, not only of universal types but also of abuses immediate to late sixteenth-century Naples.

The plots of both comedies are typically Della Portean syntheses, solidly indebted to Plautus. The basic rivalry between fathers and sons comes from *Casina*, and Vignarolo of *Astrologo* resembles the clownish dolt in the same play. The expressions of filial hatred in *Turca* echo the last scenes of *Bacchides*. The governor's discovery of a son in his supposed enemy (*Turca* v, 2) parallels the agnition in *Captivi*, and Eugenio's routing of the cooks (*Turca* II, 5 & 6) is borrowed from *Aulularia* (III, 1 & 2). Interspersed with classical situations are incidents from various *novelle*. Vignarolo's mischance with the barrel (*Astrologo* III, 7 & 8) was inspired by the *Decameron*, VII, 2.[45] Guglielmo's loss of identity is reminiscent of Grazzini's *Grasso legnaiuolo*, and Vignarolo, vintner turned gentleman, is a bit like Aretino's Maco, yokel turned courtier. The Turkish abduction recalls a score of Renaissance *novelle* modeled on the *Decameron*. Milano and Klein agreed that the astrologer is related to Ariosto's *Negromante*,[46] although Albumazar Meteoroscopio [47] is a more polished and grandiose caricature than Iachelino, and his trio of witty thugs more theatrically effective than Ariosto's solitary factotum.

But the sources from which *Astrologo* and *Turca* derived

[44] *Op.cit.,* 325.

[45] See Hugh G. Dick, "The Lover in a Cask: a Tale of a Tub," *Italica*, XVIII (1941), 12–13, for an analysis of this incident as it is treated by Boccaccio, Sercambi, Apuleius, Della Porta, and Tomkis.

[46] *Op.cit.,* 372, and *op.cit.,* v, 621, respectively.

[47] See Thomas Tomkis, *Albumazar: a Comedy (1615)* . . . edited by Hugh B. Dick (Berkeley, 1944), 162, for the origins of the name.

their unusual flavor were contemporary life and Della Porta's own experiences. His wide acquaintance with both charlatans and serious astrologers like himself (before his forced recantation) is the basis of the caricature he named Albumazar. His research for the *Chirofisonomia*, which took him to Neapolitan gallows, jails, and hospitals, where he examined large numbers of dead and live criminals, also provided him with raw material for comedy. *Astrologo* opens with a description of Naples as a city of thieves, and an introduction to a sinister fraternity of footpads who meet at the Cerriglio, an inn which actually flourished locally in Della Porta's day.[48] *Turca* has its share of criminals, too; they pose as servants, but their names, Capestro, Forca, Boja, and their manners give them away as brothers to the *Astrologo* gang rather than to the harmless intriguers of the other comedies. Boja doubles as the town hangman, and though he is a highly stylized caricature, he was almost certainly born of Della Porta's traffic with Antonello Cocozza, the Neapolitan hangman who made his contribution to science by sending a message round to the Via Toledo whenever an execution took place.

The Turkish motif also touched close to home, especially in southern Italy, where the coastal inhabitants were regularly preyed upon by pirates, even after the victory of Lepanto. Milano suggested that Della Porta had in mind a Turkish raid led by a renegade of the Del Vasto family against Naples in 1563,[49] but there is no proof that *Turca* refers to any specific incident. The character of Dergut Rais, however, has a historical original ignored by the few scholars who have treated of Della Porta. Giovanni Antonio Summonte narrated the exploits of the redoubtable Dragutto Rais, a Turkish corsair who harassed Italy for more than twenty-

---

[48] See Benedetto Croce, *La Spagna nella vita italiana durante la Rinascenza.* 4ª ed. riv. ed acc. (Bari, 1949), 242, for details about this popular haunt.
[49] *Op.cit.*, 359.

five years, until his death in 1565. He outwitted Andrea D'Oria brilliantly and though he was once captured by Giannettino D'Oria and sent captive to the Emperor, Dragutto managed to escape. One Sunday in 1548, Dragutto raided Castell'à mare di Stabia, but was forced to flee, leaving behind twenty of his men. He took with him, however, eighty prisoners, all of whom he later returned for ransom, "salvo che d'una bellissima fanciulla, che la volse per sua sposa." [50] Such deeds soon made him a legend among the Italians, by whom he was as much admired as feared. Not only in name, but in boldness and intelligence, the Dergut of *Turca* resembles Dragutto as Summonte described him. After his death his erstwhile victims seem to have forgotten their rancor and to have made him a hero, or so the sympathy and salvation Della Porta provides for him would indicate.

Structurally, the main plots of *Astrologo* and *Turca* adhere to the principle of pairs employed in *Cintia* and the intrigue depends, like that of *Olimpia*, on a calculated pretense which is unexpectedly impeded by the reality it stimulates. Neither play has a prologue, but the author's intentions are clearly defined by the way in which he effects them. Eromane's words testify to Della Porta's continued interest in techniques of plot complication:

O che intrighi, o che favole si veggono ogni giorno nascere dagli amori, e da porgere soggetto a mille Commedie: poichè le cose sempre riescono diverse da quel fine, dove dirizzate sono! [51]

(*Turca* IV, 8)

But the emphasis is no longer on structure. Della Porta has learned his trade, and instead of experimenting with *imbrogli*, he builds *Astrologo* and *Turca* out of tried patterns, and devotes his attention to the satire. Neither play is a structural

---

[50] *Historia della città e regno di Napoli*, 2ª ed. (Napoli, 1675), IV, 253–57. (except for a very beautiful girl, whom he wanted for his wife)
[51] (Oh, what intrigues, oh, what plots are seen every day to arise from love affairs, fit to provide subjects for a thousand comedies, since things always turn out differently from the way they are planned.)

triumph. Despite Klein's unbounded admiration for the intricacies of *Astrologo*, behind which he discerned a scientific mind intriguing with the skill of a Lodovico Sforza or a Richelieu [52](!), the action is occasionally jerky, the love story and the dirty work not as perfectly coordinated as is usual with Della Porta. In *Turca* some details of the pirate raid are excessively confusing (IV, 2), and Dergut's story wants integrating with the rest of the plot. But both comedies are basically well-designed, and their structural faults are glossed over with the visual humor of *commedia dell'arte lazzi* and the colorful spectacle of picturesque thieves and exotic Turks.

In *Astrologo* and *Turca* Della Porta's growing didacticism dominates from the first, not in the form of instructive examples it was later to take, but in that of satire. Although satire was usually disapproved by the Counter-Reformers, it was encouraged when its target was an object of the authorities' censure. The occult arts constituted such a target. As for the targets which *Astrologo* and *Turca* have in common, why should religious and political censors object to criticism of domestic abuses and the petty criminality of the lower classes? Besides, Della Porta so far stylized his subject matter as to render his attack indirect. But satire was nevertheless uppermost in his mind in these two comedies; the characters and the language seem to have been chosen for their satirical potentialities.

Among Della Porta's plots, only those of *Astrologo* and *Turca* turn on sexual rivalry between fathers and sons. In both comedies strong criticism is leveled at abuse of parental authority and at the figure of the *senex amans*. In each case the conflict involves two pairs of lovers and a couple of *vecchi*. Although Professor Dick's dismissal of the characters in *Astrologo* as stock types of *commedia erudita* [53] cannot be challenged, the lovers in this and its sister comedy are not

[52] *Op.cit.*, V, 620.
[53] *Albumazar* . . . , 14.

cut to an identical pattern. Lelio is a shade more decisive than
Eugenio, as befits a young man who has managed a household
since his father's disappearance (II, 6), and Eromane is far
more determined and practical than the Eugenio of *Turca*
(II, 3, 8).[54] Neither these four nor their sweethearts are
remarkable for their chastity or highmindedness, but they
are virtuous compared to their fathers, old Guglielmo of
Astrologo excepted, and are cast as victims of the lust, harshness, and avarice of the *vecchi*. From Cricca's first obscene
response to Pandolfo's confession of love for Artemisia (I, 2),
through the lovers' various discussions of their fathers' selfish
brutality (II, 6, 8), until the moral underscored for Pandolfo
(V, 2) and his acceptance of it (V, 5), the plot of *Astrologo*
never strays far from the subject of parental tyranny. In
Turca the attack is much more vicious. Whereas the guilty
father in *Astrologo* repents and his children never lose their
affection for him, in *Turca* there is real hatred between both
pairs of sons and fathers and only a forced and grudging
reconciliation at the end. Eromane and Eugenio wish fer-
vently for their fathers' deaths (*Turca* II, 3), and Eugenio
resorts to violence to thwart Argentoro (II, 5). The *innamorate* of *Astrologo* hold an interesting discussion of the
subservient position of women, in connection with which
they bring up the question of feminine honor, touched upon
more casually in *Fantesca* (V, 3) and *Penelope* (III, 1). Sulpizia inveighs against the double standard of sexual morality
and echoes the lament of many heroines of contemporary
Spanish comedy that so weighty a matter of family honor
should depend on the chastity of the weaker sex (II, 8). In
Turca the fathers themselves testify to the evils of excessive
parental authority. In his youth Gerofilo was forcibly married to Medusa for her money, as Argentoro was to Gabrina
for her rank (I, 4). So much hatred resulted that the *vecchi*

---

[54] The latter's character is confused by a careless mix-up of names
perpetrated by the printer of the first edition and perpetuated by
Muzio. In II, 8 and 10, and IV, 1, the lovers are paired off incorrectly.

have refused to ransom their wives from the Turks, the wives in revenge have incited the Turks to prey on their husbands' wealth (III, 1), and when the four are at last reunited, it is with corrosive regret.

A much smaller target of satire, set up briefly in *Astrologo* alone, is social climbing. Professor Dick does not recognize this folly in *Astrologo*,[55] and indeed, compared to its English adaptation, which interests him primarily, the Italian original contains very little mockery of the would-be gentleman. But Vignarolo's exultation over the new intellectual forces he feels in his brain now that he is "diventato gentiluomo" (III, 4), and his gratification at being called a gentleman by Guglielmo (IV, 7), were surely intended as digs at social pretension. The most arresting aspect of Vignarolo's transformation is that it illustrates Della Porta's penchant for the riddle of identity. For a brief but bewildering time, faced by Vignarolo's claims, poor Guglielmo is driven to wonder whether or not he is himself and, indeed, what "self" is. In this quandary he speculates on the Pythagorean theory of transmigration of souls (IV, 7), a subject, incidentally, on which Gian Vincenzo Della Porta once wrote a book. No conclusion is reached in *Astrologo;* its author had a weakness for these teasing questions, but he never did more than flirt with them.

The first object of satire in *Astrologo*, of course, is the complex of occult arts on which swarms of Renaissance confidence men traded for their livelihood. It is significant that Della Porta's attack is not only on charlatanism but also on astrology, necromancy, and methods of magic and divination in general. The villainous Albumazar has a fluent command of general scientific jargon, and he is an adept at Della Porta's pet pseudo-science of physiognomy (I, 4 & 5). His judgment of Pandolfo,

. . . [chi] dà credito all'astrologia, e alla negromanzia: chi si può dire più? che se fosse un Salomone, dando credito a queste

[55] *Albumazar . . . ,* 14.

sciocchezze, basterebbe a farlo la maggiore bestia del mondo. Mirate fin dove giugne l'umana curiosità, a per dir meglio, asinità! [56]   (I, I)

states the attitude to be taken toward all such lore throughout the play. Professor Dick wonders why anyone so given to occult learning should satirize it so uncompromisingly,[57] but when the scattered facts about Della Porta's life are put together and examined, it seems clear that the attack was a necessary recantation of his former beliefs, wrung from him by the Holy Office's command to disband his academy, cease his occult practices, and write a comedy. *Astrologo* was most likely offered as the first proof of his reformation.

In *Turca*, although he does not mention astrology, Della Porta implicitly renounces it by pointedly stating the orthodox belief in Divine Providence as opposed to the pagan notion of fortune or fate (III, 2; IV, 3). He also speaks slightingly of alchemy, another of his serious pursuits suspect to the authorities, by causing Leccardo to grumble, "più tosto gli Alchimisti caverebbono argento di una pomice, che un carlino dalle mani di questo vecchio" [58] (II, 7).

The shots discharged in the service of orthodoxy did not exhaust Della Porta's supply of ammunition. Albumazar was not only a symbol for the heresies of occult learning; he was also a common criminal. He and his henchmen in *Astrologo*, together with their colleagues in *Turca*, constitute Della Porta's comment on the Neapolitan underworld, of which he had such peculiar knowledge. Albumazar declares at the outset ". . . siamo in Napoli, città piena di ladri e furbi . . ." [59] (I, I). In addition to the thieves the cast includes a prostitute, a familiar figure of erudite comedy which Della Porta, how-

[56] ([who] believes in astrology and necromancy: what more need be said? for if he were a Solomon, believing in such nonsense would be enough to make him the greatest beast on earth. See to what lengths human curiosity, or rather asininity, will go!)

[57] *Ibid.*, 17.

[58] (the Alchemists could sooner get silver from a pumice stone than a sixpence out of the hands of this old man)

[59] (we are in Naples, city full of thieves and rogues)

ever, uses only this once. In *Turca* the representatives of low life are part-time servants, and the most charming of these is Boja, the hangman, whose exchange with Dergut is a deliberately macabre travesty on a closely reasoned philosophical discourse. He is greedily appreciative of Dergut's rich clothing, which by law falls to the executioner after the hanging. Milano admired the playwright's anti-Spanish courage and realism in satirizing the hangman's rights,[60] but there is no evidence that Della Porta thought his overlords or their laws unjust, and as for realism, what real hangman ever talked like this?:

DERGUT

Misero me, che ho da morire.

BOJA

Fratello, chi ai visto, che non abbia da morire? Non bisogna nascere, chi non vuol morire: la morte è comune a tutti.

DERGUT

Morirò innanzi il tempo.

BOJA

Niuno muore innanzi il suo tempo, o dopo, ma tutti nel suo tempo; e a ciascuno è prefisso il suo, che non si può preterire: e se questo non fosse il tempo del tuo morire, non moriresti.

DERGUT

Ho voluto dire, che muojo giovane.

BOJA

Chi ti ha rivelato, che dovevi morir vecchio? Non ai visto morire bambini, primachè fossero nati, ed altri subito nati, ed altri giovani; e per lungo tempo, che tu avessi vissuto, pure al morire ti parrebbe aver vissuto poco tempo.

DERGUT

Muojo contra mia voglia.

BOJA

A questo non sei solo, che ognuno muore contro sua voglia,

60 *Op.cit.*, 366.

perchè niuno vorrebbe morire; e se pure avessi vissuto cinquecento anni, venendo il tempo di morire, pur moriresti contro
tua voglia.

DERGUT

Dico, che muojo per forza.

BOJA

Qui ci è rimedio: muori di buona voglia, che così non morirai
per forza. Tu sai certo, che ai da morire, e non potrai scampare:
se muori per forza, averai due dolori, l'uno della morte, e l'altro,
che muori per forza; però per aver manco dolore, muori di buona
voglia, perchè ogni cosa per difficile, che sia, faccendola di buona
voglia, è sempre facile.

DERGUT

Ed il peggio è, che muojo infame, e disonorato.

BOJA

L'onore, e l'infamia sente l'uomo mentre è vivo: che dopo morto,
niuno verrà all'altro mondo a rinfacciarti, che fosti appiccato.

DERGUT

Quanto aspro, ed acerbo è il morire appiccato.

BOJA

Dimmi sei stato appiccato altre volte?

DERGUT

Non io.

BOJA

Come dunque sai, che il morire appiccato è molto aspro, ed
acerbo? o forse è risucitato alcun' appiccato, e te l'ha detto? Tu
a te stesso con le tue fantasie ti fai la morte più orribile, e
spaventosa. Non sai tu di quel Tedesco, che si fece appiccare per
conversazione? Ti prometto della morte farti sentir poco, o niun
dolore. Ti farò morire con tanta dilicatezza, che prima ti troverai
morto, che te ne accorgerai; anzi sarai morto, e ti parrà di esser
vivo: e quando ti avrò appiccato, se non sarà così, vò, che tu
appicchi me. Io ti accomoderò una cordicina sotto il capestro,
che per essere sottile, fa il groppo stretto, e ti strangolerà senza,
che lo senti: ti parrà un pulice, che ti morda il collo: ti salto

sopra le spalle con tanta destrezza, come un daino: non dubitare, che per esser ricco, ed uomo, che lo meriti, io ti farò molte carezze.

DERGUT
Carezze da boja; o che manigoldo amorevole!

BOJA
Se dopo morto resterai con gli occhi aperti, stralunati, e guerci: se ti uscirà la lingua fuori, e che un'occhio miri il cielo, e l'altro la terra, ti gli chiuderò, e ferrerò la bocca; se ti caderanno le bave, le asciugherò, e farò, che parerai il più bell' appiccato, che fosse mai.

DERGUT
Muojo per le mani del più vil' uomo del mondo.

BOJA
Anzi del maggior'uomo del mondo. Io ammazzo Signori, Principi, e Reggi, senza esser gastigato; anzi ne son pagato: ho libero dominio sopra tutti: a me è licito abbassare le più superbe teste del mondo, e calcare il collo de' maggiori: io ho posto sotto il giogo i Romani, che hanno posto sotto il loro giogo tutte le nazioni dell'universo: a me è lecito cavalcare, e servirmi per istaffe delle spalle degli uomini valorosi: io dispenso corone, e come consigliero son padrone della ruota; e quando sedo in quel tribunale, sono spaventevole a tutti. Trionfo sopra i carri, e nel mio trionfare, il popolo con grandissima confusione, e moltitudine mi riempie le porte un pezzo prima: per dove ho da passare, ho soldati, e birri intorno, che fanno far largo: sopra il carro mi stanno uomini nudi, attaccati intorno, ed io in mezzo a loro con regal maestà, e con bojesca degnità, taglio mani, seco braccia, e con tanaglie infocate, abbrucio quelle membra, che voglio: e se gli altri Signori han giurisdizione sopra le robe de' loro vassalli, io son padrone del corpo, e della membra, perchè taglio, tronco, appicco, e squarto, come a me piace. Pajonvi poco questi miei privilegi?

DERGUT
O che strani conforti!

BOJA
Fratello, più pena è il pensare a morire, che la stessa morte:

quella ha manco pena, che ha men tardanza; e però per sentir poco dolore, fatti appiccar presto, caldo, caldo. Chi ha tempo, non aspetti tempo: poichè ai questa comodità di farti appiccare, spediscila presto, che io per farti piacere, ti spedirò or'ora.[61]

(IV, 6)

Certainly Della Porta never caught such gems falling from the lips of Antonello Cocozza. Yet his business with Cocozza probably gave him some ideas for the character of Boja and it may be that *Turca* is set on the Island of Lesina, the first comedy to be set outside Naples, in order to avoid immediate identification with Cocozza.

The criminals in *Astrologo* are as eloquent as Boja; in fact, they are the first to give full vent to that exuberant style characteristic of the mature Della Porta, reveling in word-play and mouthfilling exaggerations. Albumazar briefs his cohorts with a breathless rhapsody:

. . . tu, Ronca, roncheggiando, tu Arpione arpizzando, e tu Gramigna stendendo le tue radici per tutto, e gramignando quanto afferri; e come nuovi Soloni, che il giorno attendeva alle cose pubbliche, e la notte scriveva le leggi d'Atene, così voi virtuosamente spendendo l'ore, il giorno insidiando alle borse, e falsando monete, scritture, processi, e polizze false al banco, e la notte dando caccia alle cappe, e a' feraioli, faccendo sentinelle per la strade, per dare assalti alle porte de' palazzi, e batterie alle botteghe, che sono le nostre sette arti liberali . . .[62]   (I, I)

Turca contains a similar gathering parodying high councils of state (II, 8), and Forca echoes Albumazar when he re-

[61] Translations of passages over a page in length will be found in Appendix C.

[62] (You, Weed-hook, hooking stolen goods, you, Grappling-hook, thievishly grappling, and you, Dog-weed, spreading your roots everywhere, and weeding up whatever you grasp; and like modern Solons, who by day managed public affairs and by night wrote the laws of Athens, you virtuously pass the hours, by day ambushing purses, counterfeiting money, receipts, contracts, and false policies at the bank, and by night stealing capes and cloaks, standing watch in the streets in order to assault palace doors and storm shops, all of which are our seven liberal arts . . .)

marks, "Veramente l'arte della furberia dovrebbe annoverarsi fra le sette arti liberali" [63] (IV, 4). *Albumazar* surpasses all the others, however, for in many of his speeches macaronic Latin and astrological jargon are allowed to run riot, achieving a blend of high absurdity, ringing sound, and acute satire (I, 5; II, 3).

The *innamorati* of both comedies also communicate in the most elaborate style their author had yet permitted himself. Of the two, *Turca* contains the more conceited language, very like that of the later comedies. It reflects Della Porta's taste for the parlour-game of *imprese* [64] and his passion for botany and the Doctrine of Signatures he applied to it and expounded in the *Phytognomonica* of 1588. The first love scene between Eugenio and Biancofiore, for example, is conducted entirely in the language of the flowers. In order to foil eavesdroppers, he pretends to be addressing the lily he wears in his hat (!), she the flowers in her windowbox:

EUGENIO

. . . già veggio il collo languido in giù piegarsi, e la sua candidezza divenir pallida, e scolorita, qual calcata viola: le sue immacolate frondi veggio liete, e ridenti, ma parmi qual doloroso giacinto abbia nelle sue frondi descritto col sangue, ahi, ahi, ahi.

He throws her the lily with a cypress branch, signifying *do or die*, to which she responds with a mixed bouquet of

. . . sempreviva, . . . fiammola, . . . voglia dire, che sempre vive in fiamma . . . mirto . . . assenzio, forse che ella è morta nell'amarezza; o forse quel mirto, che è dedicato a Venere, vuol dire, che ama, e disia godere i frutti d'Amore; e quell'assenzio vuol dire assenza, che assenza mia ella è più amara dell'assenzio.[65]

[63] (Truly the art of rascality should be numbered among the seven liberal arts)

[64] The Linceo Ms. Codice 9, 20–23verso, at the Lincei Academy Library in Rome, contains some twenty-five *imprese* which Della Porta concocted for his friends.

[65] (EUGENIO. . . . already I see the languid neck bending, and its whiteness become pale and faded, like a trampled violet: I see its im-

As in all Della Porta's comedies, the extravagances of the love in *Astrologo* and *Turca* are parodied by the comic characters. Forca performs this duty in *Turca* (II, 1; II, 4), and in *Astrologo* Armellina and Vignarolo do it uninhibitedly in their coarse love scenes (II, 1), when he addresses her awkwardly in the grandest terms he can dredge up and she answers in what Professor Dick calls "nauseating *double-entendre*," [66] goading her swain at last to curse the god of love saltily.

Despite the unwonted bitterness which flavors them both, *Astrologo* and *Turca* are, on the whole, gay and farcical. The characters are extreme caricatures and their world is deliberately theatrical and unreal, quite lacking in the sordidness which made Aretino's satires of contemporary vice so biting. Yet it cannot be doubted that Della Porta meant his criticism seriously. Guglielmo's sermon to Pandolfo, Albumazar's contempt for the arts he practices, and the gullibility of his victims, and Dergut's frequent comments on the excess and stupidity he observes among Christians, are full of good sense and moral implications. *Turca* and *Astrologo* are too stylized to be realistic, as Milano would have had them, but they are for that no less effective as satires on contemporary ills and they introduce Della Porta as an active, if left-handed, moralist.

LA TRAPPOLARIA

SYNOPSIS: The miserly Callifrone orders his son Arsenio to Barcelona, there to marry his stepsister Elvira and to bring her back to Naples together with his twin brother Lelio, a second step-

maculate leaves happy and shining, but it seems to me like the sad hyacinth with the leaves on which *ahi ahi ahi* is written in blood. . . . house-leek [always living] . . . clematis [flame flower] . . . means that she lives always in flame . . . myrtle . . . wormwood, perhaps that she is dead of bitter sadness; or perhaps that myrtle, which is dedicated to Venus, means that she loves and wants to enjoy the fruits of love; and that wormwood [*assenzio*] means absence, and my absence is more bitter to her than wormwood.)

[66] *Albumazar . . . , 13.*

sister, Eufragia, and Elionora, the Spanish wife from whom Callifrone has been unavoidably separated for fifteen years. Arsenio, however, is in love with Filesia, bondservant to Lucrino, a procurer who has guarded her from harm only that he may eventually make a profit on her. Filesia feels sure that she is well-born, despite her present circumstances, and she dreads the dishonorable union which Lucrino plans for her with Captain Dragoleone, a braggart. Arsenio has no money with which to buy Filesia's freedom and is so much distressed by the prospect of leaving her that his servant, Trappola, devises the following plan: Arsenio is only to pretend to sail. When Dragoleone's servant, Dentifrangolo, arrives with his master's money and ring in exchange for Filesia, he is to be met by Fagone, a glutton, and Trappola, posing as Lucrino and his assistant. They will give Fagone's ugly wife, Gabrina, to Dentifrangolo, and Fagone will then pose as Dentifrangolo, using the money and ring to obtain Filesia for Arsenio. The plan works very well until Gabrina returns from playing her part and finds Filesia in her house, brought there by Fagone to wait for Arsenio. Not having been told the whole plan, Gabrina jumps to the conclusion that Filesia is Fagone's mistress, throws her into the street, and lays waste the banquet Fagone has ordered. Arsenio finds Filesia and, at Trappola's suggestion, the lovers present themselves to Callifrone as Lelio and Eufragia, his Spanish son and stepdaughter. He is deceived by their Spanish manners and speech and accepts them without suspicion until Dragoleone, Dentifrangolo, and Lucrino compare notes, realize they have been tricked, and denounce the lovers. In Arsenio's temporary absence, Filesia almost persuades them to believe her story, but suddenly Elionora arrives from Spain and asserts that Filesia is an impostor. The real Eufragia is at the pier with Lelio, waiting to disembark. Elionora reveals that her other stepdaughter, Arsenio's intended, was stolen by pirates several years ago. After a series of questions, it becomes apparent that Filesia is the lost Elvira. Before Callifrone can rejoice at this news, he is informed that the ship on which he sent Arsenio to Barcelona has sunk. In his grief the old man is led by Trappola to promise anything to whoever can offer him comfort, whereupon Trappola produces Arsenio, alive and well. Trappola is freed of servitude, the young couples are united, and the family is reconciled.

Della Porta's Comedy

Trappolaria is what Milano calls "schietta imitazione plautina," and is the only one of Della Porta's comedies in which
the debt is explicitly acknowledged. The prologue informs
the audience that the heroine is "parente alla Fenicia di
Plauto, e di questo parentado piu si gloria, che d'esser di
casa di Moncada" [67] (A2verso). Specifically, *Trappolaria* is
a synthesis, and it is not to be expected that it resemble
Pseudolus as obediently as classical imitations like Varchi's
Suocera, for example, resemble their sources. The main *imbroglio* is identical with that in which Plautus' Phoenicium
finds herself, but the rest of *Trappolaria* consists of pieces
adapted from other Plautine comedies. Milano numbered
Curculio, Mercator, Miles gloriosus, and *Persa* among the
sources.[68] Sometimes the contributions are specific and meas-
urable, like the framework provided by *Mercator* for the
Filesia-Gabrina scene (III, 10), and others are very general,
like the influence of the character of Curculio upon that of
Trappola. Milano neglected to mention either the more
marked debt of the same character to the title-figure of
Epidicus or the agnition which *Trappolaria* borrows from
Cistellaria. There are traces here, too, of Della Porta's familiarity with Ariosto's Plautine comedies, in particular *Cassaria,*
which includes a *davos* named Trappola and a ruffian Lu-
cramo.[69] The variety of sources employed in this comedy,
which Della Porta frankly admits is imitative, is very revealing of his methods of composition, his complete familiarity
with Plautus' works, and his extraordinary powers of organization.

[67] (a relative of Plautus' Phoenicium, and she is prouder of this kinship than of belonging to the house of Moncada)

[68] *Op.cit.,* 329.

[69] A scene between the two (III, 3) probably offered Della Porta
hints for a parallel encounter (III, 4). Even Della Porta's disquisition
on physiognomy may have been inspired by the exclamation of
Ariosto's Trappola on first seeing the procurer, "Gli altri hanno i
segni di loro arti sul petto, e l'ha costui sul viso" (prose version).
("Others wear the marks of their trades on their breasts, but he bears
his in his face.")

The prologue to *Trappolaria* is an index to Della Porta's aims, once he felt himself to be in full control of his technique. He takes the assured tone of an experienced and successful playwright. Consistent in his pursuit of the ideal in comedy, he now appears ready for a high-handed move. The acknowledgment to *Pseudolus* and the subsequent blending of exclusively Plautine elements suggest that *Trappolaria* was intended to be a "perfect" comedy, the comedy Plautus never wrote, the ideal arrangement of Plautine material.

Della Porta does not make any such claim, to be sure, but he implies it, while ostensibly concentrating on the relatively paltry aim of pleasing the Spanish lords of Naples. Crying up the charms of his heroine, "La Spagnuola," he pays various compliments to all the ladies of her nation. The prologue and at least the final version of the play itself were probably written for performance before a largely Spanish audience, possibly at the Neapolitan vice-regal court. With its charge of pro-Iberian feeling, its interlarding of Spanish phrases, and its final reference to the strong kinship of sentiment, temperament, and climate between Naples and Spain, this prologue is one of many pieces of evidence which refute Milano's and Lionello's Cecchini's wishful assertions that Della Porta was openly resentful of the Spanish yoke.[70]

The dramatic elements which Della Porta emphasizes in the prologue to *Trappolaria* are style and seriousness. He promises "lingua pronta, arguta, faceta, festosa, e mottegevole"[71] (A2verso). This phraseful of adjectives may be taken as an announcement of the flowering of his comic prose, the "prebaroque" language which Momigliano praises and Pullini criticizes as Della Porta's trademark. The florid style which came and went in the first three comedies, then billowed into Rabelaisian hyperbole in *Astrologo* and ceremonious puns in *Turca*, has in *Trappolaria* been ordered, confirmed, and extended, so that Della Porta's fantastic and stylized plot pat-

[70] "Giovanni Della Porta e 'la Cintia,'" *Meridiano di Roma* (15 dicembre 1940), viii.
[71] (quick, sharp, witty, gay, and facetious language)

terns are at last integrated with a language equally fantastic, stylized, and appropriate to this admirably artificial genre. In grief, joy, or anxiety, Arsenio spouts learned allusions and ingenious linguistic tricks:

(*As Filesia faints in his arms*) Non vedi, o Trappola, che ho morta in braccio la vita mia, ed in me pur vive la morte mia? O morte, come puoi dar morte a chi puo dar vita ad altri? Se tu sei stata pietosa a lei, togliendola d'impaccio, perche sei cosi crudele a me, facendomi sopravivere a tanto dolore? Ai acquistato titolo di crudele, uccidendo lei: acquistalo or di piestosa, uccidendo me ancora. Oimè, ella e tutta raffreddata, è tuttavia le manca nel cuore il calore; e par, che con questo suo morire m'inviti alla morte. . . .   (I, 4)

. . . Deh se t'ho in queste braccia, ti stringerò così forte, che non ne scamperai più mai; e chi penserà di svellertene, penserà prima di svellerne quest' alma. Dubito, che farò come la simia, che per troppo stringere i figli in braccio, gli uccide. . . . vorrei, che Cerere mi prestasse il suo carro, col quale andò cercando la sua Proserpina, per andarla cercando a voglia mia. Andrò a tutti i trombetti di Napoli, che la bandiscono, e prometterli per mancia la vita mia. . . .[72]   (IV, 3)

Fulfilling the promise of dialogues between *innamorati* in Della Porta's earlier comedies, the scenes between Arsenio and Filesia are full-blown love-duets of the type which was winning more and more applause on public and private stages

---

[72] (Do you not see, oh Trappola, that I hold my life dead in my arms, and yet my death still lives in me? Oh, death, how can you give death to one who can give life to others? If you have been merciful to her, removing her from this trouble, why are you so cruel to me, making me survive so much grief? You earned a name for cruelty by killing her: now earn one for mercy by killing me too. Alas, she is quite cold, and her heart is still cold; and it seems by her death she invites me to die . . . Ah, if once I have you in these arms, I shall hold you so close that you will never escape; and whoever thinks to tear you from them must resolve first to tear out this soul. I fear I shall do as does the ape who kills its children by embracing them too closely. . . . I wish that Ceres would lend me her carriage, in which she went searching for Proserpine, so that I might search for her [Filesia] as I wish. I shall go to all the buglers [*i.e.*, town criers] of Naples so that they will publish her loss, promising my life as the reward . . .)

and which became a necessity to any *commedia dell'arte* scenario:

ARSENIO

O anima mia, che non è misura, che possa misurar' il contento del cuor mio: sono attuffato in un mar d'ineffabil gioja: ma può in me il rispetto dell'onor tuo, che mi vieta, che non ti baci quegli occhi. O stelle, che sete scese dal cielo, per porvi in questa fronte! Vorrei aver tanti occhi, quante stelle il cielo, o vorrei esser tutt'occhi, per satiarmi di mirarti.

FILESIA

Ed io vorrei esser tutta cuore, per esser capace di tanto amore, e poter tutta amarti: perchè tanto amo te, che non posso amar me stessa. Che conoscendo, che ne' tuoi degni costumi, e leggiadre fattezze consiste la mia beatitudine, da che mi ti diedi, feci ferma deliberazione, che l'anima mia, mentre sarà viva, abbia ad esser vostra ancella.[73] (IV, 3)

The images and vocabulary in *Trappolaria* are drawn from general comic and romantic commonplaces of the period, except for frequent references to criminal physiognomy, which support the consensus that *Trappolaria* belongs to the period shortly after the composition of *Astrologo* and *Turca*. The pseudo-scientific parodies are shot through with the bits of gnomic wisdom treasured by all Della Porta's clowns and rogues. Trappola, pretending to recognize Dentifrangolo from Dragoleone's description, enumerates the features:

Ecco il naso corvino, e i diti con l'unghie arroncigliate come nibbio, che è segno, che sei un solennissimo ladro: ecco l'orecchie

[73] (ARSENIO. Oh, my soul, there is no measure which can measure my heart's contentment: I am plunged in a sea of ineffable joy: but a more powerful influence on me is my respect for your honor, which forbids me to kiss your eyes. Oh, stars, you have descended from heaven to place yourselves in this brow. I wish I had as many eyes as there are stars in heaven, or I wish I were all eyes, so that I could sate myself with looking at you.

FILESIA. And I wish I were all heart, to be capable of that much love and of loving you with my whole being. For knowing that my happiness consists in your worthy behavior and charming features, ever since I gave myself to you, I firmly determined that while my soul lived, it would be your handmaid.)

lunghe, che dimostrano, che sei un asino. Poco barba, e men colore; sotto il ciel non è peggiore.[74]   (III, 1)

This and similar passages seem to be aimed at private audiences familiar enough with the playwright's "scientific" works to be able to laugh at these travesties and allusions. Only his personal acquaintances, however, could have seen the exclusive joke in Callifrone's residing in "la strada Toledo, vicina alla Carità" (v, 1)—the Della Porta family's street address in Naples.

Della Porta's second promise of the prologue is that "La Spagnuola" or Trappolaria "è tutta piena di gravità" (A2). *Olimpia* had gained him recognition as a champion of respectable comedy, and *Trappolaria* is more respectable still. Perhaps because of his eagerness to atone for his scientific transgressions by convincing the authorities of his piety and orthodoxy, or else merely because the Counter-Reformation attitude was growing daily more scrupulous and more unsympathetic to risqué comedies full of bad examples, Della Porta builds *Trappolaria* around an unprecedentedly straitlaced love affair. For all her misfortunes and condition of servitude, Filesia is triumphantly virginal at the end of the play. The preservation of her chastity is the more remarkable for her being a prominent and active figure in the plot. Unlike Cintia, Filesia owes her importance to the *commedia dell'arte's* emphasis on meaty roles for professional actresses. The non-tranvestite heroines of Della Porta's first comedies, though infinitely more articulate and strong-minded than the invisible or shadowy *innamorate* of standard *commedie erudite*, were nevertheless kept offstage as often as possible. Filesia, on the other hand, has nine full scenes and wanders the streets in her own proper dress.

She and Arsenio take their predicament much more seriously than it deserves and more seriously, too, than do their

[74] (Here is the hooked nose and the claws curved like a kite's which shows that you are a most solemn thief: here are the long ears, which show that you are an ass. Little beard, and less color; under heaven there is nothing worse.)

predecessors in Della Porta's comedies. Filesia talks wildly of death, faints, threatens suicide, and harps constantly on her honor, showing herself to be a cousin to the heroines of *capa y espada* comedy and first of a bevy of Della Portean *ingenues* who guard their virginity with Counter-Reformation zeal. Cleria of *Fantesca* makes some show of resistance, but eventually sacrifices honor to love. Cintia and Erasto go so far as to discuss the relationship between the spirit and the body, but not until *Trappolaria* are love and morality actually joined. The pathos, tenderness, and tentative supraphysicality of love in *Cintia* is confirmed in *Trappolaria* as sentimental love with heroic overtones; love becomes the guardian, instead of the enemy of morality, and the mind and spirit take undisputed precedence over the body. As an inevitable consequence, the element of pathos grows stronger and edifying emotions come into play among all the characters. Arsenio's repentance for his deception, and Callifrone's for his avarice present an emotional and ethical contrast to the relatively lukewarm filial affection in *Olimpia* or the frank antagonism in *Turca*.

Despite Della Porta's pride in its gravely moral tone, sentimental pathos, and high-sounding speeches, *Trappolaria* owes its excellence to its author's sense of the ridiculous. The stylization of his characters kept pace with that of his plots and language; his variations on Plautine caricatures grew more exaggeratedly absurd. The glutton Fagone and his shrewish wife Gabrina, with their malicious repartee and furious cavorting, reveal how expert Della Porta had become at blending Plautine substance, *commedia erudita* eloquence, and *commedia dell'arte* vigor. He also exploits the tension between sentiment and humor further than ever in *Trappolaria*. A perfectly balanced double outburst occurs when Arsenio and Fagone learn that Gabrina has mistakenly turned Filesia out of her house and has overturned the loaded banquet table. The distressed lover and the hungry glutton break simultaneously into a lament at cross-purposes, ending thus:

ARSENIO

E cieca che non vedeva, e non riveriva contanta bellezza?

FAGONE

Più cieca fu, quando percosse quel fiasco, che stava con una ciera allegra, e brillante, con un bocchin, che parlava, e dicea, baciami, t'invito a bere; e me l'ha rotto in mille parti.[75]   (IV, 2)

But the soul of the comedy is Trappola, the clever servant par excellence. Plautus provides a model for Trappola in the figure of Pseudolus, which Della Porta enlarges with borrowings from the characters of Curculio, Epidicus, and his own Panurgo of *Fantesca*. Plautus' sly trickster blooms into an outrageous genius of comic intrigue. Trappola is a perfectionist, a self-conscious artist in the laying of traps. He punctiliously announces to the procurer and to Callifrone that he intends to deceive them, and calmly recites his aims in the face of their indignant threats. When Arsenio suggests that it might be unwise thus to alert the enemy, Trappola replies loftily that he scorns to take mean advantage and that the glory of his tricks must be augmented by forewarnings to his victims (I, 5). Later, when it seems momentarily that his plot will fail, he neither fears nor laments, but bolsters himself with the reminder, "sei gran maestro delle trappole, inventore ed essecutore peritissimo" [76] (V, 3). The characteristics of the stock clever servant are exaggerated to the point of *meraviglia*, making Trappola a marvel of wit and trickery.

Thanks largely to this *tour de force* of characterization, or caricaturization, *Trappolaria* comes close to being what its author intended, a perfect Plautine comedy. But it smacks of the Counter-Reformation in its moral flavor, style, and sen-

[75] ARSENIO. Is she blind, that she did not see and revere such beauty?
FAGONE. She was blinder when she broke that flask which stood there with a happy, shining face, with a little mouth which spoke and said, kiss me, I invite you to drink; and she broke it for me into a thousand pieces.)

[76] (you are a great master of traps, a most expert inventor and executor)

timent, and these least Plautine aspects are what Della Porta emphasizes in the prologue. It seems very likely that he wrote it on the brink of a new phase in his playwriting career, the period of the serious romantic comedies, occasionally called tragicomedies.

LA SORELLA

SYNOPSIS: Attilio has just returned to Nola, supposedly from Constantinople, where he was to have ransomed his mother and sister, kidnaped years before. Unknown to his father Pardo, Attilio has gone no farther than Venice, where he fell in love with a bondservant, Sofia, used the ransom money to buy her freedom, and secretly married her. Since Pardo has not seen his daughter for years, he accepts Attilio's story that his mother Costanza is dead, and that Sofia is his sister Cleria. But to the young couple's dismay, Pardo determines to marry Attilio to Orgio's niece Sulpizia, and "Cleria" to Trasimaco, a braggart captain. Attilio's servant Trinca undertakes to solve the problem, and as a first step, persuades Pardo that Trasimaco is a slanderous villain, and suggests that "Cleria" be married instead to Attilio's friend Erotico. The news of this engagement distresses Sulpizia, who is in love with Erotico and does not realize that Trinca's plan is for the two pairs of lovers to live in Pardo's house after the invalid marriages, and exchange partners at night. Meanwhile, Trinca brews trouble between the gluttonous Gulone and Trasimaco, in order to distract the latter from urging his prior claim to "Cleria." All proceeds smoothly until Pedrolito arrives from Constantinople, bearing a letter from Costanza and a report that the real Cleria has disappeared. Pedrolito goes on an errand, leaving behind his little son, who speaks only Turkish. When Pardo confronts Attilio, "Cleria," and Trinca with their deception, the latter pretends to speak Turkish and "translates" the child's answers so as to convince Pardo that Pedrolito is moonstruck. When Pedrolito returns, however, Pardo realizes that Trinca has tricked him again. In the meantime Costanza arrives in Nola and meets Attilio and Trinca. When Attilio remorsefully admits to his mother that he used her ransom money to buy Sofia, she forgives him and agrees to pretend for Pardo's benefit that Sofia is her daughter. A warm reconciliation scene follows, but when Attilio congratulates Costanza on her performance, he is horrorstruck to learn that the reunion was genuine; his wife is his sister, the missing Cleria. The other pair of lovers is almost as unhappy. Sulpizia is more jealous than ever, and her nurse chides Erotico for his supposed infidelity. Orgio sees them together, and beats the nurse for acting as a go-between. The nurse revenges herself by revealing to Pardo that Sulpizia and Cleria were exchanged in their cradles, and that Orgio has been keeping the secret for fear of losing Sulpizia's inheritance. Pardo makes peace with everyone and blesses the two young couples.

Milano linked *Sorella* with *Olimpia* as a descendant of *Mercator*, but with additional Plautine elements, specifically from *Epidicus, Poenulus* (v, 2, 3, 4), *Mostellaria* (III, 1), *Trinummus* (IV), and Terentian elements from *Andria* (I, 5; II, 1: IV, 1). He observed also that a few short passages in *Sorella* (v, 6), are direct translation from *Mercator* (IV, 2), and *Andria* (II, 2).[77] Here is proof that Della Porta shared the general sixteenth-century admiration for Terence, although his first allegiance was to Plautus. *Sorella* is not without analogies in earlier Italian drama; ill-matched lovers and secret marriages are common enough in *commedie erudite*, among them Ariosto's *Negromante*, and a similar case of incest averted occurs in Razzi's serious comedy *La balia* (1564). Essentially, however, *Sorella* is a synthesis of classical situations, and among Della Porta's comedies, its true sibling is not *Olimpia* but *Trappolaria*.

Sorella owes less to *Mercator* than it does to *Poenulus*, companion-piece to *Pseudolus*, Plautus having written the two comedies as variations on a single theme.[78] Despite the general problem of dating, it is fairly safe to place *Trappolaria* and *Sorella* next to each other in chronological order,[79]

[77] *Op.cit.*, 325.
[78] Milano, *op.cit.*, 329.
[79] See Chapter II.

and their plots, style, and moral tone are so similar as to suggest that Della Porta in some sort intended them as a pair, following the example of his Latin precursor. That is not to say that he tried to make them just alike; it seems that he had begun experimenting again and that *Sorella* is his attempt to make the nobler spirit glimpsed in *Trappolaria* dominate the neo-Plautine farce he had there perfected. In quality, the sentiment and morality are the same in both plays, but in quantity and consequence they are not. In *Trappolaria* the serious element is subordinated to the comic; in *Sorella* it is the other way around. Trinca, for all his wit, does not reproduce the gay atmosphere created by Trappola, but functions rather as a humorously worried participant in the romantic *imbroglio*. The gluttons and braggarts are equally funny in both comedies, but in *Trappolaria* they determine the general mood, while in *Sorella* they provide comic relief.

The structural design of *Sorella* is four-cornered like *Cintia*'s, but the two pairs of angles on either side are unequal, so that the square becomes a trapezoid. The complications again arise from the ironic coincidence common to *Olimpia*, *Astrologo*, and *Turca*. Lest the *meraviglia* be lost by repetition, however, Della Porta doubles the coincidence: the masquerade is first threatened by reality, and then turns out to *be* reality. This *imbroglio* is sustained in the busy manner of *Trappolaria*, though not as well, because the Trasimaco episodes are imperfectly fused with the main section.

Like *Trappolaria*, *Sorella* offers abundant examples of Della Porta's prose in bloom. One of the traditional *topoi* of Renaissance lyrics, the experience of falling in love, is given a full treatment in the first act:

ATTILIO

Venne l'ora della cena, e ci sedemmo a tavola, ed una giovane, chiamata Sofia, ci serviva. Ella, nel volgermi gli occhi sopra, mi lanciò una fiamma nel core, che non cessò mai serpire per tutto, finchè non fece bene l'uficio. Io, sentendomi le vene diseccate

dal fuoco, chiedeva da bere, e per rinfrescarmi, e per godermi
quella divinissima vista più da presso. Ma facea contrario effetto,
perchè Amor avea mischiato veleno e fuoco in quél vino, che mi
avvelenava, e uccideva in un tempo. Così, tra vivo, e morto non
sapeva che mangiava, o beveva, o aveva, ma parea un di quei, che
si sognano mangiare, che la mia cena fu la sua bellezza. Si levò la
mensa, a tutto innebriato di amore, me ne andai . . .[80]   (I, 3)

This passage is like several from *Trappolaria*, with one difference. Della Porta is not so intent on leavening excessive
passion with comic mockery. He still laughs at lovers' exaggerations, but his sympathy for them seems less patronizing
and more respectful.

In general, the language of *Sorella* is that of *Trappolaria*,
except that the vocabulary has changed slightly. Besides a
hint about physiognomy in II, 6, there are relatively few
references to the playwright's pseudo-scientific and scientific
studies. He draws his images from common human experience, and his allusions for the most part from philosophy and
literature. His predilection for *imprese* betrays itself in the
nurse's exclamation "O mondo immondo!" (II, 5); among
the *imprese* described in Della Porta's private papers is one
captioned *Mundus immundus*.[81] But there is nothing else to
indicate that his mind was running on any of his other interests during the composition of *Sorella*.

The comic figures, like their fellows in *Trappolaria*, are

[80] (The dinner hour came, and we sat down at the table, and a
young girl named Sofia served us. In turning her eyes on me, she shot
into my heart a flame which did not cease to circulate until it had
completely done its work. Feeling my veins desiccated by fire, I asked
for something to drink, both to refresh myself and to enjoy a closer
view of that goddess. But the effect was contrary, for Love had mixed
poison and fire in that wine, which simultaneously poisoned and killed
me. Thus, half alive and half dead, I did not know what I ate or drank
or what was wrong with me, but I seemed like one who dreams of eating, for my meal was her beauty. The table was cleared, and quite
drunk with love, I left . . .)
[81] Linceo Ms. Codice 9, 20.

sharply defined, brimming with *commedia dell'arte* vitality, revealing their ludicrous obsessions in ripe, allusive speeches and learned parodies fostered by erudite comedy. Gulone is a superb example of the Della Portean glutton, a *gourmet* as well as a *gourmand*, who can discourse on methods of cooking and serving like a sixteenth-century Brillat-Savarin (ii, 3). Poetic and passionate about food, Gulone proves that he is learned as well by undertaking to disprove the philosophical thesis often "spit out by sages" that "Nature is a benign mother to man" (ii, 1). He makes his point by citing a number of animals to whom Nature has given a superior capacity for ingestion, envies all ruminants their cuds, and ends with a fervent wish that the human stomach were equipped with buttons. Gulone's enemy, Capitano Trasimaco, like the majority of Della Porta's braggarts, is Italian instead of Spanish, and is rather well-versed in *romanzi* and classical mythology, comparing himself now to Orlando or Astolfo, now to Mars or Hector. Both the *commedia erudita* braggart and his brother on the popular stage became very literary as years passed,[82] but of course the former usually surpassed the latter in learning. Trasimaco is an erudite braggart par excellence. He is also an inveterate name-dropper; most braggarts are, but Trasimaco has a record-breaking list of desirable acquaintances, ranging from his "pupil in the arts of war," the King of France (ii, 6), to the King of Transylvania, who wants him for a brother-in-law, not to mention the Queen of England, who begs him to marry her for the safety of her country (iii, 6). Trasimaco is so expert with words that he can even talk his way out of a fight and, in full retreat, can manage to justify his cowardice to the bystanders (iii, 8 & 9). Trinca, the clever servant, though not a master-mind, is as charming as Trappola. Affectionate to his employers, inclined in a jolly way to virtue and gnomic wisdom, he possesses the inestimable merit of being able to laugh at himself. When the tangle of his plans is miraculously unraveled by

[82] See Daniel C. Boughner, *The Braggart in Renaissance Comedy* (Minneapolis, 1954), 98–99, 112 *passim*.

the nurse's revelation, Trinca gives a relieved chuckle: "Questa volta abbiamo avuto più ventura, che senno!" [83] (v, 6).

It is Trinca who first indicates that *Sorella* is a determined departure from the lighthearted farce. In the opening scene he makes a startling statement. To Attilio's plea for help, Trinca replies, "Ben sapete, che il volersi soddisfare di illeciti amori, e di poco onesti desideri, suol partorire mostri d'infamia. . . . Ho da servirvi nelle cose oneste, non nelle scelerate." [84] (I, I). And, in fact, it is only after Attilio has buttressed his request with moral arguments that Trinca will take the case in hand. The genre of *commedie gravi* reinaugurated by *Olimpia* has become grave indeed when a *davos* can entertain such scruples. To be sure, *Sorella* is no homily; the hero commits a heartless crime when he allows his mother to languish in captivity and lies to his father for his own amorous ends, but he eventually admits the enormity of what he has done and exhibits throughout the comedy great moral sensibility, shared by the other characters. For all Della Porta's sympathy toward love, he emphasizes the potentially destructive force of its passion; Pardo's description of Attilio's exemplary life before falling in love (I, 5) is deliberately comic, but, like Polonius' advice to Laertes, the tedious preaching of a platitudinous old fogey, it is also invulnerable in principle. There is a loosely similar scene in *Il negromante* (I, 4). Ariosto's comedies have been cited as forerunners of the didactic Counter-Reformation drama,[85] but when the paternal doctrine of his Massimo is compared with that of Pardo, it becomes obvious that, in this instance at least, Ariosto teaches mere propriety, and Della Porta virtue.

[83] (This time we've had more luck than sense!)

[84] (You well know that the wish for satisfaction by means of illicit love affairs and unchaste desires usually engenders monsters of infamy. . . . I am supposed to serve you in honest enterprises, not in wicked ones.)

[85] Michael Ukas, "Didactic Purpose in the *Commedia Erudita*," *Italica*, No. 3 (September, 1959), 198–205.

The love affair between Erotico and Sulpizia is striking for its spirituality. She jealously denounces male lust (IV, 8), but despite his name, Erotico is of all men least guilty of this vice. In fact he is a confirmed neo-Platonist, declaring,

> . . . mi servo di quella sua bellezza, come occhiali, per innalzarmi a piu sublime grado di contemplazione, a quel sommo bene, a quella celeste ineffabile bellezza, anzi fonte, onde scaturisce ogni bellezza.[86] (I, 2)

and goes so far as to add that he has no need of seeing Sulpizia often because he carries her image in his heart. The purity of his love is so extreme that Sulpizia's nurse is suspicious of its sincerity, a sure sign that Della Porta wrote this passage half tongue-in-cheek. But he expounds the same doctrine with utter gravity in *Georgio*, and though he may have intended Erotico to be part caricature, he does not mock neo-Platonism itself but regards it rather as an ideal system which might give rise to humorously exaggerated avowals by sonneteers or doting lovers, but which nonetheless lent dignity to the comedies which he reputedly liked to think of as moral lessons.[87]

From his first comedy to his last Della Porta exhibits sentiments in impressive contrast to the callous opportunism condoned in innumerable earlier *commedie erudite*. But it is neither the first nor the last comedies that Professor Herrick has in mind when he counts Della Porta among the "comic writers of the century who introduced romantic and pathetic arguments that made some of the comedies at least approach tragicomedy."[88] Specifically, *Fratelli rivali*, *Moro*, and *Furiosa* make the nearest approach, but *Sorella*, if farther behind, is unmistakably on the same road.

Even the main characters' social position is a clue to the

[86] (. . . I use her beauty like eye-glasses, in order to rise to the most sublime level of contemplation, to that highest good, to that ineffable celestial beauty, indeed the fountain from which all beauty springs.)

[87] Giuseppe Gabrieli, "Giovan Battista Della Porta Linceo," *Giornale critico de filosofia italiana*, VIII (1929), fasc. I, 428.

[88] *Tragicomedy, Its Origin and Development in Italy, France, and England* (Urbana, 1955), 124.

connection of *Sorella* with the serious comedies of Della Porta, Oddi, Borghini, and the romantic Spanish drama which influenced them all. Pardo is not a prosperous burgher, like all the previous *vecchi*, but a minor ex-courtier, once employed as steward to Queen Bona of Poland (I, 3). This hardly makes him an aristocrat nor *Sorella* a court comedy like Oddi's *Prigione d'amore*, but it links this play with the rise of the semi-tragicomedy, which followed the Spanish fashion of depicting life in higher social circles than the *commedia erudita* traditionally dealt with, and which presented actions of a correspondingly more serious nature. The characters have rather more noble principles than those in Della Porta's preceding comedies. Pardo is an admirable old man, tenderly faithful as a husband, conscientious as a father, a just master to his servants, wise and self-controlled toward his neighbors. Costanza is a wonderfully magnanimous and self-sacrificing mother, and Erotico proves himself a precursor of the heroes of many earnestly romantic comedies when he gratuitously offers to go into exile with Attilio for the sake of friendship (V, 5).

Although Della Porta has not yet moved from marvelous situations and caricatures to marvels of virtue and feeling, he packs the various reconciliations in *Sorella* with pathos and serious emotion, and develops the threat of incest hanging over the lovers melodramatically, if not tragically. One of Attilio's typical laments goes thus:

Solo al mio male non può trovarsi rimedio. O voi, che con medicine cercate fuggir la morte, venite a scambiarla con la mia vita: che quanto più chiamo la morte per rimedio de' miei mali, ella da me più s'allontana: che sia maladetta l'ora, che nacqui; maladetto chi mi pose nella cuna; e maladetta chi me diede il latte, che bevei.[89]   (IV, 6)

[89] (For my ill alone there is no remedy. Oh, you who through medicine seek to flee death, come exchange it for my life: for the more I call on death as the remedy to my ills, the farther it moves away from me: cursed be the hour I was born, cursed he who placed me in the cradle, and cursed she who gave me the milk I drank.)

Della Porta's Comedy

This is strong language, stronger than farce can support for long without changing generically. *Sorella* represents Della Porta's comedy in evolution.

I DUE FRATELLI RIVALI

Synopsis: During a bullfight, Ignazio, nephew of the Viceroy of Salerno, has fallen in love at first sight with Carizia della Porta, daughter of an impoverished nobleman, and hopes to win her without interference from his brother Flaminio, who has always been his rival in everything. Ignazio and his servant Simbolo try to allay Flaminio's possible suspicions by requesting him to arrange a match between Ignazio and the Count of Tricarico's daughter. By instructing his brother to ask a very large dowry, however, Ignazio assures himself of a refusal. Unknown to Ignazio, Flaminio is also in love with Carizia, and has begun laying siege to her virtue, aided by his servant Panimbolo and the glutton Leccardo, a dependent of the della Porta family. Leccardo is also solicited for help by Capt. Martebellonio, who desires Carizia's sister Callidora. Ignazio obtains an appointment with Carizia, and after much persuasion, she agrees to marry him, if her father, Eufranone, approves. The latter is suspicious of so advantageous an offer for his dowerless child, but eventually yields to Ignazio's pleas and agrees to a wedding the next morning. When Flaminio hears of the betrothal he stifles the objections of his conscience and, urged on by Panimbolo, falls in with the following plot: Leccardo is to make an appointment with the della Porta's lustful maid, Chiaretta, asking her to dress in her mistress' clothes. He will also promise Martebellonio an assignation with Callidora, for whom he will substitute Chiaretta in the dark. Flaminio is to tell Ignazio that Carizia is unchaste and, as proof, will take him to the della Portas' gate, show him the clothes Leccardo will smuggle out while the maid and the captain are at their pleasure, and then disappear for a time into the house, ostensibly to lie with Carizia. The deception is successful, and when Eufranone comes at dawn to greet the bridegroom, Ignazio denounces Carizia. Eufranone returns home quietly, but shortly afterward the horrified Leccardo emerges to report that Carizia has fallen dead of fear as her father prepared to stab her. Flaminio is overcome by remorse and confesses his perfidy to Ignazio, begging for death. Ignazio leaves revenge to Eufranone, who demands the public restoration of Carizia's good name and takes the case before the viceroy. Don Roderico condemns Leccardo to death and declares that a marriage between Callidora and his guilty nephew will clear the della Portas' honor. Flaminio is delighted, but Ignazio considers the punishment too much like a reward and demands Callidora for himself. As the angry brothers prepare to duel, Eufranone's wife appears to announce that her daughter has awakened from her deathlike swoon. Carizia enters, forgives Flaminio, and gives her hand to Ignazio. Callidora is wed to Flaminio, and Leccardo is released by the hangman.

Della Porta's boast that Plautus, Menander, and Epicharmus would rejoice at the improved state of modern comedy [90] is remarkable for the sense of independence and of tradition it reveals simultaneously. Although his specific reference is to structural modifications, Della Porta widened the applicability and significance of this passage by inserting it in the prologue to *Fratelli rivali*, a comedy removed from classical drama by more than a few mechanical innovations. Together with *Moro* and *Furiosa*, it represents its author at his most modern, venturing into the latest Counter-Reformation fashion in comedy. It is clear from the prologue, however, that Della Porta himself considered the venture, not a break with, but an extension of classical comic tradition.

Della Porta was bound to be attracted by the serious and sentimental genres crowding the Counter-Reformation stage. His firsthand knowledge of Spain and the necessarily close contact he enjoyed with Spanish culture in Naples made him particularly susceptible to the influence of the cape-and-sword drama then in incubation. Not from any specific play, perhaps, but from the general flavor of Spanish romanticism not uncongenial to his nature, Della Porta formed a taste for bittersweet comedy. His pride in being intellectually and artistically *à la mode* made him sensitive to the various pressures and shifts in taste which were pushing *romanzi* matter

[90] See above, p. 143.

into both tragedy and comedy. His own preference for
commedie gravi was encouraged by the censors and by the
success which playwrights like Borghini were achieving
with their lachrymose comedies. Accordingly, after some
preliminary exercise in the use of weighty elements, Della
Porta produced a trio of serious comedies peopled by noble
characters, aristocratic either in fact or in spirit. Their moral
standards are high, their conflicts go beyond mere trickery,
they are deeply concerned with honor, friendship, and exalted love. Their misfortunes are excruciatingly pathetic and
romantic, they are threatened with death, madness, and other
calamities to which they react with appropriately highflown rhetoric.

Of the three, *Fratelli rivali* was the first to be published,
and perhaps the first to be written. Its main source is Bandello's *novella*, i, 22, a story first told in the late fourth- or
early fifth-century Greek romance of *Chaereas and Callir-
rhoe* by Chariton and retold in *Orlando Furioso* iv and v,
Much Ado About Nothing, *The Faerie Queene*, ii, 4, Jacob
Ayrer's *Comedia von der Schönen Phaenicia* (ca. 1595), and
Peter Beverley's *Ariodanto and Ienevra* (1583). Della Porta
was indebted for his version only to Bandello and Ariosto.
From the same sources he had already borrowed the trick
whereby a lover is convinced of his mistress' unchastity and
had used it in *Cintia* iii, 3. Now he recharged this old material with suspense and *meraviglia* by reorganizing it around
the motif of fraternal rivalry and embellishing it with veri-
similar details from recent history and from the annals of
his own family. For thirteenth-century Messina, the setting
of Bandello's *novella*, Della Porta substitutes sixteenth-century Salerno, and for the poor but noble Fenicia, a heroine
named Carizia della Porta, whose father has lost his fortune
supporting the Sanseverino's unsuccessful rebellion against
the Spanish opposition (i, 1). On the basis of research in
Neapolitan and Salernitan archives, Spampanato revealed that
the historical Della Portas were landowners in that province,
that they were connected with the counts of Tricarico, a

family also mentioned in the comedy (1, 1 ff.), and that the
Don Roderico di Mendozza of the play, Spanish viceroy and
uncle to the rival brothers, was a historical personage, Don
Rodrigo de Mendoza, governor of Salerno sometime after
1541. These facts led Spampanato to identify Eufranone as a
member of a branch of the playwright's family which remained loyal to Ferrante Sanseverino in the uprising of
1551.[91]

These novellesque, historical, and original ingredients are
stirred skillfully into a romantic intrigue which Milano declared superior to any of Oddi's or Borghini's serious comedies and close to English and Spanish excellence in the
genre.[92] But it must not be supposed that Plautus was neglected. Milano referred to Plautine elements in *Fratelli rivali*
without pointing them out. Perhaps he had in mind the braggart, the glutton, and the clever servants. But this comedy
and the other two of its type are far removed from Plautine
farce. Romantic, moral, almost tragicomic, they evoke the
spirit, not of *Casina* or *Pseudolus*, but of *Captivi*. Its epilogue
might serve equally well at the end of *Fratelli rivali*, *Moro*,
or *Furiosa:*

Spectatores, ad pudicos mores facta haec fabula est, necque in
hac subigitationes sunt neque ulla amatio nec pueri suppositio nec
argenti circumductio, neque ubi amans adulescens scortum
liberet clam suum patrem: huius modi paucas poetae reperiunt
comoedias, ubi boni meliores fiant.[93]

The unaccustomed seriousness and nobility of *Captivi* undoubtedly moved Della Porta to emulation, as every other

[91] "I Della Porta ne' *Duoi fratelli rivali*," *Anomalo* (Napoli, June
1918 ?), 200.

[92] *Op.cit.*, 399.

[93] Plautus, *Works*, The Loeb Classical Library, 1 (London, 1937).
(Spectators, this story has been wrought according to modest customs, neither in it are there subtle tricks nor any love-making nor
substituted children nor shady plots to obtain money, nor does any
young lover, unknown to his father, buy the freedom of a prostitute:
poets invent few comedies of this kind, by which good men are made
better.)

aspect of Plautus' theater did at one time or another. Even at his least classical, Della Porta could claim classical authority and, in a broad spiritual sense, could feel that he was building on and in the tradition of Latin comedy.

Captivi's theme of loyalty is matched in *Fratelli rivali* by the motif of honor. The action hinges on the brothers' competition, receiving its impetus from Ignazio's attempt to win Carizia before his brother can challenge him and its complications from Flaminio's subversive counterplot, resulting in a nearly tragic disaster which is remedied by fortune and good counsel. The motives of the minor figures, Chiaretta's lust for Leccardo, Martebellonio's for Callidora, Leccardo's for food, are all made to work toward the aims of one or another of the brothers. The movements of the underlings and the technical twists and turns of the intrigue never obscure the weighty concerns of love, sibling rivalry and, above all, honor.

From the beginning the latter concept sets the general tone. The main characters belong to the class by which such high-flown notions may properly be entertained. The brothers are grandees of Spain, nephews to the most powerful noble in Salerno, and Carizia's family is of the petty aristocracy; even her *vecchia* is no ordinary *balia* or nurse, but a duenna, who is addressed as *Madonna* and *Mon'*Angiola and who calls Carizia her *nipote*, indicating that she is a poor relation rather than an employee. Ignazio loves Carizia in the most honorable way, aiming only at marriage, valuing her virtue as much as her beauty and scorning mercenary considerations: "L'onestà, e gli onorati costumi sono i fregi dell'anima: ricchezze ne ho tante, che bastano per me, e per lei." [94] (I, I). Flaminio's intentions are less pure (I, 2), although he is willing to marry Carizia should all other bribes fail (II, 9), but he too is greatly concerned with his own honor and is loth to sully it by participating in Panimbolo's plot, until the wily servant manages to convince his master that all is fair and honorable in love and war (III, I). When the ruse boomerangs, Fla-

[94] (Chastity and honorable behavior are the ornaments of the spirit: I have riches enough for myself and for her.)

minio's first thought is for his lost honor (iv, 5). Eufranone is as touchy about his family's reputation as a *declassé* aristocrat might be expected to be; he receives Ignazio's proposal courteously but is suspicious of the rich young man's sincerity and delivers a pathetic discourse on the irreplaceability of honor to one whom fortune has robbed of all else (ii, 6). Later, when Flaminio's plot has seemingly caused Carizia's death, Eufranone does not press for revenge but is adamant in his demand that his daughter's good name be vindicated (iv, 7). Eufranone's scenes are the most touching of the play's tearful portions. It is to Della Porta's credit that he stiffens the pathos with dignity sufficient to prevent sogginess. Carizia herself rejoices in an absolutely impregnable honor and an astounding facility of expression on the subject. She is no ordinary *innamorata*. She is, in fact, Della Porta's first real heroine. For resolution and spirit she is superior to Hero, her counterpart in Shakespeare's verison of the story; her graceful parries of Ignazio's verbal thrusts (ii, 3), her demure apology for disrupting her own funeral (iv, 4) conjure up the shadow of Beatrice. In so adorning Carizia, however, Della Porta seems to aim at creating less a woman than a marvel of feminine honor.

The fullblown, antithetical prose of *Fratelli rivali* is particularly appropriate to the elevated concepts and grand passions of such characters. It is noteworthy, however, that even in the most elaborate passages, Della Porta avoids the far-fetched conceit, the startling adjective, the lyrical cadence, the mind-wrenching comparison and sensual image of Seicentist style in flower. He makes his appeal rather to the mind than to the senses, exciting wonder by means of marvelous paradoxes. He favors the extended simile, a judicious scattering of hyperbole, measured antithesis and resounding vocabulary. Ignazio's account of his falling in love represents Della Porta's romantic prose at high tide:

IGNAZIO

Appena entrammo nello steccato (come in un famoso campo di mostrare virtude, e valore) che furono stuzzicati i tori, i quali furiosi, e dalle narici spiranti focoso fiato, vennero incontro noi. Onde se mai generoso petto fu stimolato da disio di gloria, fu il mio in quel punto; perchè sempre volgea gli occhi in quel Cielo di bellezza, parea, che da quelle vive stelle de' suoi begli occhi spirassero nell'anima mia così potentissimi influssi, così infinito valore, che io feci fazioni tali, che a tutti sembrarono maraviglie, che io non solo non andava schivando gli affronti, e i rivolgimenti de' tori, ma gl'irritava ancora, acciocchè con maggior furia m'assalissero. Di quelli molti ne distesi in terra, e n'uccisi. Ma in quel tempo, che io combatteva con i tori, Amor combatteva con me. O strana, e mai piu intesa battaglia! Onde un combattimento era nello steccato apparente, ed un'altro invisibile nel mio cuore: il toro alcuna volta mi feriva nella pelle, e ne gocciolavano alcune stille di sangue, e'l popolo ne avea compassione; ma ella con i giri degli occhi suoi me fulminava nell'anima; ma perche le ferite erano senza sangue, niuno ne avea compassione. De' colpi de' tori alcuni ne andavano voti d'effetto; ma quelli degli occhi suoi tutti colpivano al segno. Pregava Amore, che crescesse la rabbia a' tori, ma temperasse la forza de' guardi di Carizia. Al fine io rimasi vincitore del toro, ella vincitrice di me: ed io che vinsi, perdei, e fui in un tempo vinto, e vincitore, e restai nella vittoria per amore. Del toro si vedea il cadavere disteso in terra, il mio vagava innanzi la sua bella immagine. Il popolo con lieto applauso gradiva la mia vittoria, ed io piagneva la perdita di me stesso. Ahi quanto poco vinsi! ahi quanto perdei! Vinsi un toro, e perdei l'anima.

SIMBOLO

Faceste tanto gagliarda resistenza a'fieri incontri de'tori, e non poteste resitsere a'molli sguardi d'una vacca.[95]

[95] (IGNAZIO. We had no sooner entered the ring (as it were a celebrated field for proving spirit and valor) than the bulls were goaded and charged us, furious and breathing fire from the nostrils. Whereupon if ever generous heart was stirred by desire for glory, mine was at that moment; because I constantly turned my eyes toward that heaven of beauty; it seemed that the living stars of her beautiful eyes breathed into my soul such powerful influences, such infinite courage, that I performed feats that made everyone marvel, for not only did I not avoid the charges and reversals of the bulls, but I even aggravated them so that they would attack me more furiously. I laid many of them out on the ground and killed them. But while I fought the bulls, Love

Della Porta's Comedy

Obviously the comic characters of *Fratelli rivali*, far from being awed, are stimulated by the fine company in which they find themselves. They chatter a good deal in the easy impudent manner typical of Della Porta's rogues, but they also push his parody of pathetic and heroic style to new rhetorical heights. Leccardo describes Carizia's "death" in the most tearfully heart-rending similes ever invented by glutton, likening it first to the roasting of a lamb, then to the touching demise of a suckling pig (IV, 5). And in the verbal contest between him and Martebellonio, a *tour de force* of hyperbole and epic allusions, braggadocio, gluttony, and bathos go as far as they can go:

MARTEBELLONIO

Ti vò raccontar la battaglia, ch'ebbi con la Morte . . . Sappi, che la Morte prima era viva, ed era suo uficio ammazzar le genti con la falce: ritrovandomi in Mauritania stava alle strette con Atlante, il qual per essere oppresso dal peso del mondo, era mal trattato da lei: io, che non posso soffrir vantaggi, li toglio il mondo da sopra le spalle, e me lo pongo su le mie . . . al fin lo posi sopra questi tre diti, e lo sostenni, come un melone.

LECCARDO

Quando voi sostenevate il mondo, dove stavate, fuori, o dentro del mondo?

---

was fighting with me. Oh, strange, unheard-of battle! In which a visible combat went on in the ring and an invisible one in my heart: the bull sometimes scratched my skin, from which some drops of blood fell, at which the public felt pity; but she, by the movement of her eyes, struck me like lightning in my soul; but because the wounds were bloodless, no one pitied me. Some of the bulls' blows missed me, but those of her eyes all hit the target. I prayed Love to increase the bulls' fury but to temper the force of Carizia's glances. In the end I emerged victor over the bulls, she victress over me: and I who won, lost, and was at once vanquished and victor, and I remained in victory for love. The bull's corpse was seen extended on the ground, mine was wandering before her beautiful image. The public received my victory with pleasure and I wept for the loss of myself. Alas, how little I won! alas, how much I lost! I vanquished a bull, and I lost my soul.

SIMBOLO. You so vigorously resisted the fierce onslaughts of the bulls, and you couldn't resist the soft glances of a cow.)

MARTEBELLONIO

Dentro il mondo.

LECCARDO

E se stavate di dentro, come lo tenevate di fuori?

MARTEBELLONIO

Volli dir di fuori.

LECCARDO

S se stavate di fuori, eravate in un'altro mondo, e non in questo?

MARTEBELLONIO

O sciagurato, io stava dove stava Atlante, quando anch' egli teneva il mondo.

LECCARDO

Ben, bene, seguite l'abbattimento.

MARTEBELLONIO

Mona Viva, sentendosi offesa, ch'avessi dato ajuto al suo nemico, mi mirava in cagnesco, con un'aspetto assai torbido, ed aspro, e con ischernevoli parole mi beffeggiava: la disfido ad uccidersi meco: accettò l'invito, e perchè avea l'elezion dell'armi, si volle giucar la vita al pallonetto . . . constituimmo per lo steccato tutto il mondo: ella n'ando in Oriente, io in Occidente.

LECCARDO

Voi eleggeste il piggior luogo, perchè il Sole vi feriva negli occhi; e poi quello occidente porta seco male augurio, che dovevate esser ucciso.

MARTEBELLONIO

L'arte tua è della cucina, e a pena t'intendi, se la carne è bene allesa; Che tema ho io del Sole? . . . Il pallonetto era la montagna di Mauritania: a me toccò il primo colpo: percossi quella montagna così furiosamente, che andò tanto alto, che giunse al cielo di Marte, e non la fece calar giù in terra per segno del valor del suo figlio.

LECCARDO

Così privasti il mondo di quella montagna. Ma quella, che ci è adesso, che montagna è?

Della Porta's Comedy

MARTEBELLONIO

O, sei fastidioso! Ascolta, se vuoi; se no, và, ed appiccati.

LECCARDO

Ascolterò.

MARTEBELLONIO

Ella dicea, aver vinto il giuoco, perchè era imboccato il pallonetto; la presi per la gola con due dita, e'l uccisi, come una quaglia, talchè non è più viva, ed io son rimasto nel suo ufficio. . . .

LECCARDO

Ma io ti vò narrare una battaglia, ch'ebbi con la Fame . . . La fame era una persona viva, magra, sottile, che a pena avea l'ossa, e la pelle; e soleva andare in compagnia con la carestia, con la peste, e con la guerra, che n'uccideva più ella, che non le spade. Ci disfidammo insieme: lo steccato fu un lago di brodo grasso, dove notavano caponi, polli, porchette, vitelle, e buoi interi, interi: qui ci tuffammo à combattere co'denti: primache ella si mangiasse un vitello, io ne tracannai due buoi, e tutte le restanti robe; e perchè ancora m'avanzava appetito, e non avea che mangiare, mi mangiai lei, così non fu più fame al mondo, ed io sono suo luogotenente, ed ho due fami in corpo, la sua, e la mia. Or presto andiamo a mangiare, altramente mi mangierò te intero, intero: Dio ti scampi dalla mia bocca.

MARTEBELLONIO

Tu sei un gran bugiardo.[96]   (I, 4)

There is, however, one significant difference between the scheming servants of *Fratelli rivali* and their predecessors. In

---

[96] See Appendix C for translation. Martebellonio's speech looks forward to the standard memorized baggage of the professional stage braggart. Cf. Francesco Andreini, *Le Brauure Del Capitano Spavento* . . . (Venetia, 1615, 1st ed. 1607), "Ragionamento 36. Dell'abbattimento nello steccato hauuto con la Morte," a dialogue between the famous braggart of the Gelosi and his straightman, by the Della Portean name of Trappola. Leccardo's answering boast is reminiscent of the fifteenth-century *ottava rima* poem, "Il Gran Contrasto e la Sanguinosa Battaglia di Carnouale, e di Madonna Quaresima" (Firenze, n.d.)

the earlier comedies, tricksters plotted against each other, and the arch-trickster was in the lovers' camp. But Leccardo and Panimbolo are in positions charted according to a moral system. For all their charm, they are conspicuously on the wrong side. The external conflict is between the tricksters and the tricked and arises from the internal conflict between Flaminio's envious love and his honor. The moral alignment is against him and the masterminds in his employ, and the outcome of the plot is a lesson to schemers and to those who forfeit their honor.

Luigi Tonelli regards *Fratelli rivali* as Della Porta's master-piece, worthy of Lope de Vega.[97] Certainly many of Lope's comedies are not nearly as good. But the comparison is mis-leading. Lope and Della Porta did not write in the same genre; despite its cape-and-sword elements, *Fratelli rivali* contains too much of its author's Plautine heritage to belong to the anticlassical Spanish tradition. Ireneo Sanesi accused Della Porta of spoiling this comedy by inconsistency in the last scenes, when the supposedly inconsolable Ignazio agrees to marry his lost bride's sister and the remorseful Flaminio forgets his self-recrimination and urges his own right to the sister.[98] Milano argued that Della Porta intended to illustrate thus the inconsistency of the Spanish character.[99] Neither heeded Ignazio's explicit disavowal of love for the sister and declaration that he wants her in memory of Carizia and as satisfaction to his honor (v, 3). Nor did Milano call in aid of his defense the obvious intention of the author to emphasize the brothers' rivalry. The very title of the comedy indicates that Della Porta wished to give a subtle but strong psycho-logical motivation to the entire conflict; Flaminio's challenge to Ignazio in the midst of the regretted ruin caused by his last challenge is exactly the opposite of psychological incon-sistency. A total reformation of character would have been

[97] *Il teatro italiano dalle origini ai giorni nosti* (Milano, 1924), 150.
[98] *La commedia.* 2ª ed. riv. acc. (Milano, 1954), I, 415.
[99] *Op.cit.,* 397.

not only unlikely in terms of realistic psychology but harmful to the unity of a comedy carefully built around the themes of strict honor and fraternal rivalry. It would, moreover, have outraged the neoclassical law of decorum which demanded continuous integrity in every character. With his bent toward experiment and innovation, Della Porta was pleased to enlarge and develop the potentialities of comedy, but he could not transgress the neoclassical rules.

IL MORO

SYNOPSIS A: Pirro has been absent from Capua for ten years, ever since his wedding day, when the jealous Capitano Parabola convinced him with false proofs that his bride was unchaste. The still faithful Oriana is now being courted by Erone, son to the governor. Her father, Omone, desires the union and only Pirro's brother, Filadelfo, supports Oriana's vow of fidelity and shares her belief that Pirro is alive. Pirro returns disguised as a Moor and, after questioning Oriana's nurse, realizes that he has been deceived and is enraged that Erone should aspire to Oriana's hand. He attacks Erone but is overpowered by guards and, when he refuses to explain the assault, is condemned to death. Meanwhile Filadelfo challenges Erone to single combat, of which the victor will decide Oriana's future. Erone is impressed by the "Moor's" noble features and stance, releases him from his dungeon, and makes a friend of him. When Filadelfo's challenge is delivered, Erone accepts it, but his father will not allow him to fight. Erone asks his new Moorish friend to fight in his place. After much soul-searching and weighing of his love for Oriana and Filadelfo against his debt of honor to the magnanimous Erone, Pirro decides in favor of the latter and manages to defeat his brother without killing him. Pirro's honor is put to an even more severe test when Erone asks his help in winning Oriana by posing as an eye-witness to his own death. Oriana does not see through the Moorish disguise but feels drawn to the stranger and when he proves his claim to have known her husband by recalling intimate details which only Pirro himself could have told him, she is overcome by painful memories and swoons. Lacerated by love but still unwilling to betray his friendship and break his promise to Erone, Pirro takes poison. Erone finds him and takes advantage of his weakened condition to elicit the truth from him. Erone forces Pirro to take an antidote to the poison and insists that they go to Omone, with whom they find Pirro's father, prepared to oppose Oriana's re-marriage. Capitano Parabola is also present, still hoping that Oriana will favor him. When he reminds her that she owes him something for saving her life from Pirro ten years ago, the Moor reveals his identity and worries a public confession of the whole truth from the braggart. Oriana obtains a pardon for Parabola, and there are tender reconciliations and eulogies all round.

SYNOPSIS B: (Alternating with the main action) The glutton, Ventraccio, rages that his food has been dosed with an emetic, and on learning that Parabola is the culprit, swears revenge. Erone's pedantic tutor, Amusio, irritates the governor with his macaronically unintelligible account of the Moor's attack. A mischievous page drives Amusio into a rage by jeering at him and tripping him with a string tied across his path. The angry Amusio treats Oriana's nurse haughtily when she asks him to read a note for her. She takes his learned gobbledygook as a personal affront and accuses him of attempted rape. Despite the effeminate pedant's protests, the governor orders his arrest. Pannuorfo, a fatuous Neapolitan, pays court to Oriana. Erone is annoyed at such presumption and gives permission to his servant, Cricca, to discomfit both Pannuorfo and Parabola with practical jokes. Cricca enlists the aid of Ventraccio, who dresses up as a Moor and beats Parabola. After Parabola has worn himself out trying to climb walls, dashing first in one direction, then in another, he is allowed to escape. Pannuorfo boasts to Cricca that Oriana is in love with him, although he feels no more than pity for her, but when Cricca tells him that Oriana is fond of birds, the Neapolitan grasps at the information as a means of gaining access to her chamber. Announcing that he wishes to present her with a giant turkey-parrot, he rushes off to put on a parrot costume, and returns cackling Neapolitan love songs in what he hopes is a parroty voice. Cricca pretends to be deceived and prepares to hoist Pannuorfo through Oriana's window in a cage attached to a pulley. Cricca halts the cage half-way up and leaves Pannuorfo stranded in mid air. The page throws rocks at him, and Pannuorfo insists he is a parrot until Omone orders him to be beaten and driven away.

Although *Fratelli rivali*, *Il moro*, and *La furiosa* must, by virtue of their tragicomic qualities, be classified as a trio in the midst of Della Porta's lighter dramatic works, they are not nearly as much alike in design and atmosphere as are, for example, *Astrologo* and *Turca*. The plot of *Moro* is derived from a typically Della Portean variety of sources. Croce declared it "ricalcata sui *Torti amorosi*" of Castelletti (1581).[100] Milano traced it to the *Odyssey*, the Ruggiero-Bradamente-Leone incident in *Orlando Furioso*, and the *Decameron* x, 9. He also suggested a general kinship with Oddi's *Erofilomachia* and *Morti vivi*, and specifically attributed Pannuorfo's misfortunes to a *novella* of Pietro Fortini.[101] Since Milano saw fit to comment on resemblances as slight as those *Moro* bears to Boccaccio's *novella* and Oddi's comedies, it is surprising that he overlooked the similarity of Act I Scene 4 to Plautus' *Stichus* I, 2; of IV, 6 to Giraldi's *Orbecche* (II, 1); of the entire main action to Razzi's *Gostanza* (1565) and, above all, to Della Porta's own *Penelope*.

Moro is a play in two parts, which belong at opposite ends of the dramatic scale. The main plot is the most highflown and romantic, the most nearly tragic that Della Porta ever used in a comedy. Indeed, when the hero speaks of the situation, he explicitly calls it "la tragedia de' nostri amori" [102] (IV, 6). For the only time in Della Portean comedy, moreover, the *envoi* is spoken not by one of the comic characters but by the heroine's dignified father (V, 5). The moral seriousness and elevated sentiment of *Fratelli rivali* reappear here in a *romanzo* rather than a *capa y espada* setting. Only in *Georgio* does Della Porta reproduce this atmosphere. The action of *Moro* is turbulent, its ingredients those of adven-

[100] *Saggi sulla letteratura italiana del '600*. 3ª ed. riv. (Bari, 1948), 300.
[101] *Op.cit.*, 390, 385.
[102] (the tragedy of our loves)

ture drama: a disguised and heartsick hero who has wandered in foreign lands for ten years; a lady in distress; an armed skirmish; a duel between brothers, one incognito; a love triangle; several tests of honor; and an attempted suicide. The standards of behavior and morality celebrated in the *romanzi* are adapted to the drama and pushed to an incredible perfection. To the *meraviglia* born of coincidence, agnition, and sheer intricacy in his earlier comedies, Della Porta here, as in *Fratelli rivali*, adds marvels of virtue, in this case fidelity, gratitude, and courtesy.

For the first time he creates a romantic plot in which none of the protagonists look to their servants for guidance or resort to sly trickery against each other. When the play opens, the malicious fraud responsible for the misunderstanding is ten years old, and its perpetrator, the braggart, has no part in moving the immediate action of the main plot. Pirro's masquerade as a Moor and Erone's substitution of Pirro for himself in the duel are deceptions forced upon them by circumstances and are not aimed at obtaining selfish ends at other people's expense. All the characters in the primary action are noble-minded and well-intentioned, and their dramatic conflict consists in internal struggles of conscience between duties set in opposition by their bizarre situation. In keeping with their high ideals of virtue and honor are their exquisite manners, unanimous adherence to a lofty concept of courtly love, and elevated prose style.

Oriana, like Carizia della Porta a full-fledged heroine, was praised by Milano as a passionate, typically Neapolitan woman.[103] Her gaiety in the comic scenes does much to justify this estimate, but her behavior in the main action shows her to be a manufactured marvel like Della Porta's Penelope, through whom Oriana is also related to the wives in *Stichus* who must withstand the urgings of a beloved father in order to remain true to their husbands. Torn between conjugal and

---

[103] *Ibid.*, 390.

filial duty, she eases her heart and mind in speeches which Milano admired for their lack of "sdolcinature e le antitesi secentistiche": [104]

ORIANA

Piangerò, pregherò, me gli butterò a i piedi, me smenticherò di me medesima, mi porrò ad ogni indegnità, pur che resti moglie del mio Pirro. E che mi può avvenir peggio in questa vita, che non esser moglie di Pirro? O che crudel battaglia, se debbia obbidire al padre, o al marito? sto in mezzo a due morti, non so qual' eleggermi. Se obbedisco a mio padre, torrò per isposo il figlio del Governatore, ma sarò contraria al mio desiderio, e all'amore, il quale mi sforza, e mi minaccia, e vuol, che sia moglie di Pirro, che è gli occhi, e il cuor mio. Obbedirò dunque al padre? Ah moglie traditrice. Obbedirò al marito? Ahi figlia poco amorevole: a chi dunque debbo obbedire, sposa, e figlia? Ahi Pirro sposo infelice d'un infelice moglie. Obbedendo al padre, mi legherò con uomo, che abborro io, e arò in odio tutto il tempo della mia vita; e amore mi spaventa con odj orribili, e con morti crudeli. Obbedendo ad amore, mancherò del debito a mio padre, al qual debbo obbedire più di tutti gli uomini del mondo: sarò detta figlia disamorevole, e indiscreta, m'acquisterò l'odio suo, de' parenti, e di tutto il mondo. Sarò mostrata a dito fra mille: che dunque far debbo? se fuggirò una morte, incorrerò in un' altra. Qual dunque mi eleggerò fra queste due? meglio è disobbedire al padre, e obbedire ad amore: avendo così a morire, arò manco pene: morrò almen soddisfatta dell'amor mio, nè sarò la prima, o la seconda, che per seguire amore non han fatto conto di cosa alcuna, arò molte compagne. Ahi sciocca voglia, ahi vana elezione. Dunque per seguire un disordinato appetito d'amore, arò da disobbedire al mio padre? e negli esempli poco onorevoli, e disonesti d'altre donne si serbino per autorità del mio male? Il fallo non ha scusa, che s'elegge per propia volontà. Muojasi dunque, e obbediscasi al padre. Morendo almeno arò questa soddisfazione d'aver obbedito a mio padre: sarò commendata per figlia onorata, e di buona fama. Ahi se farò così, come mi porto coll'infelice Pirro, che m'ha amato con tanto affetto, e or pate per me sì lungo esilio, lontano dagli agi di sua

[104] *Ibid.*, 388. (cloying sweetness and Seicentist antitheses)

casa, e forse in misera servitù di schiavo, e che uomo di tanto pregio, e di tanto valore debbe essere stimato così poco? Questo è dunque il premio del suo amore? del suo valore? del suo esilio? Ahi muojasi più tosto, a si servi a lui la fede; se noi povere donne non potremo contrastar con gli uomini con l'armi, e con le forze, contrastiamo almeno con la costanza, e con la fede.

BALIA

Taci, ecco tuo padre.

ORIANA

Questi mio padre! Questi è il maggior nimico, che io abbia: cerca tormi dal mio marito, e darmi ad un'altro. Ma che parole potrò rispondergli, che non sieno rabbia, e disperazione: che altro, che rabbia, e disperazione parlar non posso, essendo tutta rabbia, e disperazione . . .[105]   (I, 3)

If her words sound empty and illogical compared to those used in similar situations by the heroines of Corneille or Racine, still Oriana's dilemma represents a more mature concept of dramatic conflict than is usual in sixteenth-century Italian comedy and shows growth in Della Porta himself, whose Penelope in the same case hesitated not an instant to reject her father's arguments. More credible as a woman, Oriana is also a more versatile moral marvel than Penelope, and she exhibits a very un-Neapolitan sort of magnanimity. When Parabola's evil deception is finally discovered, she objurgates against *vendetta*, pardons him for all he has made her suffer, and persuades his other victims that forgiveness is divine (v, 5).

Pirro, like Ariosto's Ariodante, is faithful to his lady even though for ten years he believes her false. He proves that his love is as pure, i.e., spiritual, as it is courtly, when he stills her fears about her aging beauty with an assurance that it is her agelessly beautiful soul which he loves (v, 5). Oriana does not seem to notice that his answer is beside the point. But however exalted his love, Pirro is able to subordinate it to the de-

[105] See Appendix C for translation.

mands of honor that constitute the *meraviglia* which is the first aim of this play. Filadelfo is a pattern of fraternal loyalty and his challenge to Erone a model of knightly courtesy, as is the response to it (II, 5). Erone is likewise large-souled, appreciative of valor and generous in bestowing praise where it is deserved. He has fallen in love not so much with Oriana herself as with her reputation for chastity and highmindedness. But among these *nonpareils* Pirro is foremost, as Erone himself states, "è possibile trovarsi uomo di tal qualitade? . . . Io resto molto stupefatto della cortesia, la quale avanza quante ne sieno state fatte infino adesso." [106]   (V, 2)

So many praiseworthy characters in such an unusual situation offer Della Porta many opportunities to exercise his considerable gifts for creating pathos and irony, which mingle and reinforce each other in this comedy as in no other. Erone muses aloud on the happiness to which his Moorish friend will help him, while every word is a dagger to the disguised Pirro, who knows that in requiting Erone's kindness to him, he buries his own happiness together with that of Oriana and Filadelfo. (IV, 4). This leads to an even more ironically touching scene between Oriana and the Moor, who proves that he knew her Pirro by recounting tender intimacies and revealing the pet-names the lovers used only for each other (the familiar device used also in *Penelope* and *Ulisse*). Loyal to his friend but heartbroken, the Moor assures her that Pirro is dead and urges her to marry Erone. She faints in anguish and, waking in the Moor's arms, murmurs pathetically that she dreamed her husband was holding her (IV, 6). Nothing could be more lachrymose, more sentimental, nor more theatrically effective.

The other part of *Moro* is the comic subplot, which is no plot at all but a series of *burle*, of tricks and countertricks which provide light relief from the romantic action. The comic plot is as farcical as the other is serious; the two are

[106] (is it possible that such a man exists? . . . I am quite astounded by his courtesy, which surpasses any ever seen.)

juxtaposed and employ some of the same characters but are not in the least interdependent. This is the first of Della Porta's plays to be constructed in this way, more akin to the English manner than the Italian.

Comic types of various origins and colors rub elbows in *Moro*. Amusio is one of Della Porta's most erudite pedants, and Ventraccio is a classical glutton in *commedia dell'arte* dress. Capitano Parabola differs from other Della Portean braggarts in one way: he is not a simple poltroon but a villain. His wickedness has simmered down into low knavery over the years, but the memory of the treachery by which he originally separated Oriana and Pirro hangs over the otherwise comic shape of his character and gives a sinister hue to his boasts about the force of his ireful and concupiscent passions. The stock braggart always piques himself on his wrath and his lust, but whereas these are venial sins in comedy, they become mortal in the milieu which *Moro* shares with Counter-Reformation *romanzi*.

These stock types and their fellows, the *balia*, the servant, and the page, to whom Della Porta always imparts a measure of fantasy and liveliness borrowed from popular rather than from written comedy, all behave in *Moro* like jumping jacks from the *commedia dell' arte*. Perhaps because they are bent on *burle* instead of on the usual intrigues, they are more physically active in their humor than ever before; they brawl, feed each other emetics, throw buckets of slop (III, 8), trip each other with lengths of string (III, 7), and chase one another about in an endless ballet of *lazzi*.

The most hilarious *burla* is the one reserved for Pannuorfo, a new addition to Della Porta's stable of comic types. His antecedents and age have been argued more than once but never satisfactorily determined. Although he is a Neapolitan and speaks entirely in dialect, suggesting popular origin, Pannuorfo is not an ancestor of Pulcinella, as Fiorentino claimed.[107] His type seems to have grown out of *commedia*

---

[107] See Michele Scherillo, *La commedia dell'arte in Italia, studi e profili* (Torino, 1884), 134.

dell'arte practices but was embellished with learned touches and made several appearances in the *commedia erudita*. Among the pre-Della Portean comedies which contain some version of the comic Neapolitan are (Tasso's?) *Intrichi d'amore* (1585), *L'Hortensio*, Piccolomini's *Amor costante* (1536), Aretino's *Cortegiana*, Cini's *Vedova* (1569) and the comedies of Cristoforo Castelletti. Croce believed that *Moro* owes something in this respect to Castelletti's *Torti amorosi* (1581),[108] and certainly the Neapolitan Giovan Girolamo of the latter, overflowing with ceremony, conceit, and bad poetry, is very like Pannuorfo. But Croce's statement that Della Porta had to pump new life into the tired type [109] is unconvincing. So relatively few appearances of the comic Neapolitan have been noted in the vast number of sixteenth-century comedies that the type can hardly have been worn out by Della Porta's time. Its heyday in comedy, which Croce called its decadence,[110] was in fact in the seventeenth century, when D'Isa, G. C. Sorrentino, Alfonso Torello, and other Neapolitan comic playwrights [111] made frequent and successful variations on the Della Portean model. Later, the type flourished again in the eighteenth-century *opera buffa*.

Whatever his history, Pannuorfo is one of Della Porta's best characters. His peacock-prancing and ludicrous affectations, the self-infatuation which prompts his complaint "O gran travaglio è l'essere bello! tutto lo juorno lettere . . ." [112] (III, 5), his miraculous ignorance and his horrible Petrarchizing steal the show. Even Oriana, beset with tragicomic cares, has to laugh at Pannuorfo's announcement of the "stãtie" he has written on her virtues (III, 4). The perfect conclusion to his absurd courtship comes in the *burla* of the birdcage. Possibly it was inspired by Parabosco's *Marinaio* (between 1546 and 1557), in which Lamberto woos a courtesan and is

108 *Saggi*, 300.
109 *Ibid.*
110 *Ibid.*, 304.
111 *Ibid.*
112 (Oh, what a bother it is to be handsome! letters arriving all day long . . .)

turned by a necromancer into an invisible parrot (IV, 8), but Croce suggested a more likely source. He observed that Pannuorfo takes literally a popular Neapolitan song of the sixteenth century:

> O Dio, che fosse ciaola, e che volasse
> A ssa fenesta a dirte na parola;
> Ma no che me mettisse a na caiola . . .
> Ed io venesse, e ommo retornasse
> Com'era primma, e te trovasse sola;
> Na no che me mettisse a na caiola! [113]

It would have been like Della Porta to put these words into action onstage. He appreciated popular entertainment and possessed a gift for mixing its elements with those produced by conscious art and application of theory.

Della Porta never indulged his love of *meraviglia* more freely than in *Moro,* which, with its marvels of virtue and of absurdity, is at once the most serious and the most ridiculous of his comedies. Oriana's debates of conscience and Pannuorfo's sojourn in the birdcage mark the limits of Della Porta's comic-romantic world. The harmony in which these opposite elements merge is owed to his perception that there was no room for realism in his work; the total artificiality of all his plots, scenes, and characters, the constant emphasis on theatricality give consistency to even the most unlike parts. *Moro* illustrates this to perfection; Oriana and Pannuorfo are equally at home in the footlighted unreality of Della Portean comedy.

LA FURIOSA

SYNOPSIS: Agazio of Palermo and his erstwhile neighbor, Bizozero of Milano, meet in Naples, searching for their respective children, Vittoria and Ardelio, who have run away from home to

---

[113] *Ibid.,* 301, note 2. (Oh, Lord, that I were a bird and could fly to your window to speak to you; but don't put me in a cage . . . And that I would come and turn back into a man as before, and find you alone; but don't put me in a cage!)

find each other and to confirm the betrothal which their fathers had first made and then broken for financial reasons. Unknown to Agazio, Vittoria is nearby, overcome by fatigue but insisting to her disapproving nurse that she will not rest until she finds Ardelio.

Foiana, wife to a doctor specializing in madness, tells her maid Nespila that she is weary of her impotent old husband and intends to take as her lover the stupid but vigorous braggart, Capitano Basilisco. Reluctantly, Nespila agrees to act as go-between. Basilisco is delighted by the invitation and instructs Lupo, a glutton, to order a banquet in celebration.

The sailor Gripo pulls a bejeweled cap from the sea and is challenged for it by Orea the fisherman. Vittoria and her nurse pass and are asked to hold the cap while the two men fight. Vittoria recognizes the cap as Ardelio's and learns from Gripo that her lover has drowned in a shipwreck. She abruptly loses her mind, is barely restrained from throwing herself into the sea, and at last flees from her nurse. Just then Ardelio clambers, dripping, from the sea and is told the bad news by the nurse. Vittoria returns but cannot recognize or understand her lover and again flees. Consequently he too goes mad and flees in the opposite direction. Noticing the distracted lovers in the street, Foiana is inspired to suggest that Basilisco disguise himself as one of her husband's mad patients in order to gain admission to the house.

Agazio and Bizozero meet the nurse and together they find Vittoria and Ardelio, who think themselves dead, rave in Spanish and Neapolitan dialect, and again run away. Consulted by the fathers, the doctor orders porters to find the children while he arranges a way to trick them into swallowing the pills which will cure them. Believing themselves dead, they refuse to eat, but the doctor plans to hire some people to masquerade as corpses and to eat in the presence of Vittoria and Ardelio, hoping to persuade them by example. The disguised Basilisco is mistaken for Ardelio, is beaten for resisting his keepers, and is locked in the cellar for refusing to eat. Ardelio is mistaken for Basilisco and is greeted by Nespila and Foiana, whom he beats. Discovering the error, Nespila frees Basilisco from the cellar and he joins Foiana. The doctor catches them *in flagrante delicto*, forgets his patients, and runs off to fetch Foiana's brothers as witnesses. Nespila manages to substitute Vittoria for Basilisco, so that the doctor's accusation is discredited and he is forced to apologize to his wife.

Disconsolate, the doctor returns to his patients and is able to restore their wits, to the joy of their fathers, who bless their union.

Milano dismissed *La furiosa* rather cursorily as a romantic blend of Boccaccesque and Plautine elements which does not meet the standards set by *Fratelli rivali* and *Moro*.[114] Specifically, the scenes in which Ardelio's cap is fished from the sea (II, 3 and 4), the shipwreck and the name of the sailor Gripo come from the *Rudens* of Plautus (II, 1 and IV, 3). The search of Plesidippus for Palaestra in that comedy may also have suggested the search of Vittoria and Ardelio for each other. Foiana's invitation to Basilisco (II, 2) is mildly reminiscent of the fake offer made to Pyrgopolynices in Plautus' *Miles gloriosus* (IV, 1). If Della Porta needed a source for the general idea of love-madness, there were many available, most obviously *Orlando Furioso*. The trick by which Foiana deceives her husband is found in the *Decameron* VII, 8, as well as in a number of *commedia erudite,* among them *Calandria* and Cecchi's *Assiuolo* (1550).

Milano's evaluation of *Furiosa* is as incomplete as his terse reference to its sources. Although it is not his best, Della Porta's last serious comedy cannot be disposed of by a single derogatory adjective. The author himself distinguished this play by attaching to it a weighty, if graceful, prologue in which he formally defines the function of comedy. Arguing with *Momo, La Verità* depends on Horace for her defense of comedy as a mixture of "l'utile e'l dolce," a mirror of human actions which encourages lowly folk and, by representing bad people and actions, teaches youth what to avoid (p. 7). This statement was a theoretical commonplace often used to cover a multitude of sins. But because *Furiosa* contains an example of sin most uncharacteristic of Della Porta, its prologue should probably be taken seriously as an explanation or

[14] *Op.cit.,* 385.

excuse for a subplot which otherwise would seem to condone immorality.

In many ways *Furiosa* proceeds according to Della Porta's customary formula. Here are the lovers opposed by their fathers, here too the old *balia*, the braggart, the clever *fantesca*, the glutton who waxes poetic about food. The physical movement and slapstick of the *commedia dell'arte* never lags; there is constant darting and scurrying about, and the characters come to blows every other scene or so. The love speeches are more precious and less heroical than those in *Moro*, but the style is essentially the same, rich and antithetical. Like Eugenio of *Turca*, Ardelio wears on his cap an *impresa* borrowed from Della Porta's private list of ingenious devices: a gold medal bearing an insignia of cypress and palm branches entwined, with the motto *O Vittoria, o morte* (II, 4).[115] And, as usual, the low characters manifest the comic side of this sort of wit, their language now absurdly hyperbolic, now breezily colloquial, now slily obscene.

But in other ways *Furiosa* is *sui generis* among Della Porta's comedies. Its structure is that of an *imbroglio*, but the comic and the romantic actions are self-contained entities; they converge, and the characters pass back and forth from one to the other, but they are separate plots, leading to different conclusions and foreign to each other in atmosphere.

The romantic plot is serious but not courtly like those of *Fratelli rivali* or *Moro*. Rather, it constitutes Della Porta's excursion into domestic tragicomedy, highly pathetic. The lovers are childhood friends, extremely young and sheltered, but their attachment is profounder than Oriana's and Pirro's. As Vittoria describes it, it is not noble love but true love, not "founded on childish fancy" but on a sense of their acquaintance even before birth (I, 2). The underlings are not permitted to poke ribald fun at these romantic excesses; even the rough Gripo admits reverently, "Or questo sì, che sono

---

[115] Linceo Ms. Codice 9, 20.

amori fini, e non da scherzi" [116] (II, 4). The strange form
which the lovers' madness takes testifies to the depth and
sincerity of their feelings; they accept literally the conceits
repeated in innumerable love lyrics. Now Vittoria thinks her
soul has left her body to search for Ardelio's (II, 6), now
each claims to be the disembodied soul of the other (III, 2),
and now both believe themselves to be corpses which move
and breathe but cannot live in the absence of their lovers
(III, 2).

The doctor to whom this pathetic case is entrusted is appropriately serious and high-minded, a *gran medico* (III, 2)
rather like Della Porta himself. He has a store of curative
"secrets," prescribes hellebore for insanity (III, 3),[117] pub-
lishes many books (I, 3), and practices medicine not for
money but for "gloria" (III, 3).

The *commedia dell'arte* comic plot belongs to quite another world, one in which the prize is to the quickest wit and
a cuckold deserves no pity. When Boccaccio opens the door
to that world, its values become for the moment acceptable
and its atmosphere seductive, but Della Porta presents its
sordidness. The intrigue of Foiana and Capitano Basilisco is
the only adultery to occur in any of Della Porta's extant
comedies. Foiana herself is delineated with unaccustomedly
misogynistic malice; lacking the high-spirited grace of her
counterpart in the *Decameron*, she is only lustful, sly, and
low in her tastes. She prefers the captain because he "ha
dell'asino" [118] (I, 3). But she prospers and triumphs over her
helpless husband; the doctor whose behavior is so admirable
in the romantic plot becomes the most ludicrous of cuckolds.
His character changes completely under the stress of domes-

116 (this, it must be admitted, is a refined love, not one to be taken
lightly)

117 Cf. Della Porta's own prescription in *Magiae naturalis*, VIII, 2, of
mandrake, belladonna, and henbane for causing temporary insanity and
vinegar or lemon juice for curing it.

118 (he is something of an ass)

tic troubles; he forgets his disinterested professional ethics and neglects his patients until he is heavily bribed to care for them (IV, 9).

The contrast between the idealistic love story and the scabrous comic plot is too striking to be anything but deliberate. The clue to Della Porta's intentions lies in the prologue and, more unmistakably, in the motif of madness threaded through both plots. It is not a major unifying principle as the same theme is in Bruno's *Candelaio*, but rather a leitmotiv like the refrain of jealousy in *Fantesca*. Madness determines the title and the main action. Vittoria and Ardelio run mad when their love is frustrated, first by their parents, then by apparent death. Agazio's comment on the event is to the point: ". . . tra l'amore, e la pazzia ci è un gran parentado" [119] (III, 1). Much the same idea is expressed in a totally different context by Basilisco, as he feigns madness to satisfy his lust: "l'amor non è altro che pazzia. Cupido è pazzo, e chi lo segue pazzissimo: . . ." [120] (III, 5). Finally, the doctor, once more in the character of the magnanimous healer, apologizes for his recent metamorphosis by calling it a *furia* (V, 1).

The adultery is successfully committed and concealed, but is deliberately made ugly. Even the clever servant who arranges the affair disapproves of it (I, 3). Perhaps it is too much to suggest that Basilisco's counterfeit madness is symbolic of the insanity, i.e., unhealthiness, of lust, but in any case, the illicit incident is presented so as to provide what the prologue demands from comedy; an example of what to avoid. The same can be said of the doctor's temporary *furia*, brought on by his impotent love, returned by hate, which distracts him from his best pursuits. The moral of the romantic plot is stated explicitly: when true love is thwarted,

[119] (between love and madness there is close kinship)

[120] (love is nothing but madness. Cupid is mad and he who follows him very mad . . .)

madness rules. The fathers recognize that their avarice has produced chaos (III, 2) and agree that it is wrong to ignore the signs of a heavenmade marriage.

Della Porta's serious intentions are clear enough, but they are imperfectly carried out. Because he does not reconcile the two plots, he fails to teach a well-reasoned moral lesson and succeeds only in celebrating what the *balia* in her grave envoi calls "meraviglie di amore."

I DUE FRATELLI SIMILI

SYNOPSIS: Senecio has sent his son, Giacinto, under the care of the pedant, Gaio Roderico, and the glutton, Polifago, to Palermo, in order to marry Eufragia, daughter of Senecio's friend, Argentino, and bring her home to Naples. Giacinto loves Egeria, who is pregnant by him, but dares not reveal it to his father, unaware that Senecio's conscience is troubled by a similar sin of his own youth. Twenty years ago he fathered a child on Lippomena of Riggio, but was forced to marry another girl chosen by his family. Since his wife's death, Senecio has tried unsuccessfully to find Lippomena. Gaio and Polifago return to Naples with Eufragia and her bridegroom who looks exactly like Giacinto but is really Lepido, son of Lippomena. Shipwrecked off Riggio and mistakenly believing Giacinto drowned, Gaio and Polifago have been sheltered by Lippomena, of whose connection with Senecio they are unaware. Fearing to lose Senecio's patronage should Giacinto's death be discovered, Gaio has persuaded Lepido to pose as Senecio's son. Egeria and her nurse, Brunetta, greet Lepido joyfully, taking him for Giacinto, but he repulses them coldly and proceeds to Senecio's house, where he is welcomed according to Gaio's expectations.

The true Giacinto also finds his way home. He goes first to Egeria but neither she nor Brunetta will have anything to do with him. After he leaves in bewilderment, Egeria repents her vindictiveness and sends Brunetta after him, but Brunetta again mistakes Lepido for Giacinto and again is denied recognition. Lepido and Giacinto grow more and more confused, as one is dunned by the other's old creditors, and the other is asked to pay the bill which Polifago has just run up at an inn.

Argentino arrives in Naples and is ignored by Giacinto, then embraced by Lepido. Gaio also takes Giacinto for Lepido and unwittingly reveals the conspiracy but realizes his mistake before Giacinto can do anything about it and arranges for the latter's creditors to have him jailed. Gaio then instructs Lepido to pose as a "false Giacinto" in order to discredit the true Giacinto when he frees himself and comes looking for Senecio.

Lippomena arrives from Riggio to join Lepido and is joyfully recognized by Senecio. In a general confrontation, Gaio's treachery is revealed and the half-brothers are correctly identified. Senecio is delighted to have two sons instead of one. The fathers bless the two young couples, and the pedant suffers no graver punishment than the loss of his beard, pulled out by the furious Brunetta.

On the brink of tragicomedy Della Porta turned back to farce. Between 1606 and 1614 he published a final quartet of plays, in all of which comedy once more takes precedence of romance. How many parts of these may have been drafted much earlier cannot be determined. Uncertainty about original dates and the length of time between composition and printing in each case make it possible that all of Della Porta's comedies were revisions of youthful works or of his translations of Plautus. The possibility remains a possibility, except in the case of *Fratelli simili*.

Although this was the last comedy to be published, it was ready for the printer in 1610 under the title of *I simili*,[121] and may have circulated even before 1591 as *Il pedante*.[122] The least important of Della Porta's comedies, it has the earmarks of an attempt rejected at a time when the author's reputation was in the making, and unearthed when his fame was established beyond the range of criticism. In plot, *Fratelli simili* is a cross between *Menaechmi* and *Cistellaria*. Following the pattern set by *Olimpia*, it centers on a coincidental collision between pretense and reality. Della Porta's prime aim here

---

[121] Zanetti, *op.cit.*, [99].
[122] See Chapter II, p. 67.

seems to be that of his earliest comedies: to complicate the intrigue as far as possible without rendering it unintelligible. In this he partially succeeds; the structural design is very intricate yet not confusing, but it is executed as mechanically as an exercise.

Moreover, the design is marred by carelessness. If Lepido wants to pass himself off as Giacinto, why does he not pretend to recognize those who address him familiarly by that name? How is it that Lippomena, who was present at the conception and fruition of Gaio's plan, is unaware that the victim of the deception is the long-lost father of her son? Why does Giacinto persist in denying the possibility of a connection with Argentino, even after the latter mentions by name the girl Giacinto has been sent to marry? Either Della Porta overlooked these details or intended, for some comic effect that never comes off, to introduce a singularly stupid collection of characters.

Uncharacteristically of Della Porta's mature technique, these stock types are not developed to the limits of their fixed roles. The pedant is unusually wicked, the glutton more alcoholic than most, but these distinctions are not comic; neither Gaio nor Polifago is touched with that exuberant fantasy which increased over the years in Della Porta's humorous characterizations.

Della Porta's affinity for the *commedia dell'arte*, which grew stronger as he grew older, is hardly apparent in *Fratelli simili*. The comic "lead" is the pedant, the only *commedia erudita* type never successfully adapted to the public stage. The caricatures are mild and few; there is no braggart, no clever servant, no sprightly maid. The action is rarely physical. The role of Giacinto-Lepido requires considerable walking, and Polifago indulges briefly in a slapstick rampage at the inn (ii, 8), but otherwise, cavorting in the manner of popular comedy is at a minimum, and the dialogue suggests no *lazzi*. The result is the closest Della Porta ever came to stiffly old-fashioned *commedia erudita*.

A stronger indication of *Fratelli simili's* early date is its

comparative lack of that sentiment and pathos which Della
Porta exhibited sparingly in *Olimpia*, increased subsequently
to a high emotional pitch, and thereafter retained in con-
densation, even in his last comedy, the farcical *Tabernaria*.
Like Shakespeare, Della Porta added to Plautus' story a scene
of reconciliation between the long-separated parents (v, 3);
the incident is mildly touching, but less so than the parallel
encounter in *Olimpia*. The young lovers are no warmer.
Egeria fills several scenes with ornate laments, but despite her
flow of words and her truly pitiable situation, she has neither
the dramatic emotional presence nor the gracefully helpless
droop of Della Porta's other late *innamorate*.

The degree of moral sensitivity possessed by the characters
of *Fratelli simili* is likewise low by Della Porta's mature
standards. The *balia* speaks glibly in Petrarchan terms of the
meeting between Egeria and Giacinto in childhood, when
their love was born (1, 2), but they themselves say nothing to
indicate any deeper or finer affection between them than the
sort shared by Olimpia and Lampridio, nor does Egeria put a
fine point on pre-marital chastity. Like those of the early
comedies, these *innamorati* are not corrupt, but they care
more for propriety than for private morality. As for the villains, Gaio and Lepido outdo the plotters of Della Porta's first
comedies in criminal selfishness. Between them they hope to
have Giacinto executed or sent to the galleys for life (IV, 9),
and like their ancestors in pre-Counter-Reformation *commedia erudita*, they feel no remorse.

But the language of *Fratelli simili* smacks of Della Porta's
late years. The dialogue abounds in verbal games like Gaio's
outburst, "o Parche porche, perchè non troncate lo stame
della mia vita?" [123] (1, 4). Laments like Egeria's represent
Della Porta's style at its farthest reach of antithesis:

Oimè, che or fuoco, or ghiaccio, ora speranza, or timore, ed ora
disperazione con disusate tempre me tormentono l'anima: or la

[123] (Oh piggish [*porche*] Fates [*Parche*], why [*perchè*] do you not
cut my life's thread?)

speranza s'impaurisce, or la paura s'insperanza, or l'amor si dispersa, or la disperazione s'innamora, il ghiaccio s'infoca, ed il fuoco s'agghiaccia, ed io misera resto preda delli loro insopportabili dolori.[124]   (III, 5)

The elaborate style, however, seems to be only a sauce poured over a leftover comedy, after a last-minute decision to serve it up.

LA CHIAPPINARIA

SYNOPSIS: Cogliandro wishes his daughter, Drusilla, to marry Capitano Gorgoleone, a braggart, but she loves Albinio, the next-door neighbor. Though locked in her room, Drusilla manages to converse from the window with Albinio and to show him a letter she has stolen from her father. It reveals that a bearkeeper and his charge are to pass through Naples en route to the Duke of Tuscany's private zoo, and are to spend a night in Cogliandro's house. Albinio's servant, Truffa, decides to disguise Albinio as a bear in order to get him under the same roof with Drusilla.

Panvino, the glutton, and Truffa use the stolen letter to convince the bearkeeper that they are Cogliandro and his servant. They put the bear, Chiappino, in Albinio's house, dress Albinio in a bearskin and deliver him to Cogliandro, persuading the latter that Panvino is the keeper he was expecting.

Gorgoleone's servant, Rompiguerra, peeping into Drusilla's window, sees her in Albinio's arms and tells his master, who in turn tells Cogliandro. Panvino creates a distraction by pretending the bear has escaped. Albinio retreats before Drusilla is confronted by her father, to whom she swears that what he witnessed was an optical illusion planned by Gorgoleone. The latter flees when he is told that the bear is just around the corner. Still posing as the bearkeeper, Panvino tells Cogliandro that his Chiappino needs some exercise, and by throwing the bearskin over Drusilla, smuggles her out of her father's house into Albinio's. Shortly thereafter, Cogliandro spies Drusilla embracing Albinio at a window in the latter's house. Suspicious of these

---

[124] (Alas, now fire, now ice, now hope, now fear, and now despair with unusual force torment my soul: now hope frightens, now fear causes hope, now love despairs, now despair enamours, ice burns, fire freezes, and I remain prey to their unbearable pains.)

"optical illusions," Cogliandro pays Albinio a visit, but finds no trace of his daughter; hurrying home again, he finds her there, for Panvino has again used the bearskin to transport her. Announcing to Cogliandro that he must now proceed to Tuscany, Panvino for a third time leads the disguised Drusilla away before her father's eyes, but before they reach Albinio's door, they are accosted by the municipal customs officer and forced to accompany him to his office in order to pay the duty on imported bears. Albinio is in despair, but Truffa takes the real bear to the customs house and manages to substitute it for Drusilla, whom he delivers once more to her lover. On Truffa's instruction, Panvino flatters Gorgoleone, reveals that Albinio has had great success with the bearskin, and persuades the captain that Drusilla wishes him to come to her in the same disguise. The real bearkeeper demands his charge back from Panvino, and as he is leading Chiappino away, Gorgoleone appears with Cogliandro, intent on unmasking Albinio. The former boastfully attacks Chiappino, realizes too late that the bear is real, and is mauled for his pains.

Gorgoleone hopes to recoup his losses by enjoying Drusilla and forthwith allows Panvino to drape him in the bearskin. The real bear and his keeper leave Naples, but Panvino tells Cogliandro the departure has been delayed and again requests shelter for himself and the disguised Gorgoleone. Truffa arrives with a band of thugs disguised as policemen, who beat and unmask Gorgoleone. Convinced of the captain's duplicity, Cogliandro bestows Drusilla on Albinio.

A surprisingly unsentimental and amoral frivolity separates *La Chiappinaria* from the genre of *commedie gravi* to which all of Della Porta's other comedies, even his last light ones, belong. *Chiappinaria* is unrelieved and unrelenting farce, undidactic and unpathetic, reminiscent of Della Porta's earliest *imbrogli* in the predominance of its structural pattern over every other element of the play. Early composition is suggested also by a detail of diction: Cogliandro is thrice referred to as a cuckold (II, 6; II, 8; IV, 8). In accordance with his declared moral intentions in writing comedies, Della Porta usually avoided the subject of adultery, once the most popular situation in *commedie erudite* in the line of Machiavelli and Bibbiena. But before his definitive choice of Ariostean over Machiavellian models, Della Porta may have sketched *Chiappinaria* as a farce about December's cuckolding by May. He may then have finished or revised the comedy to meet Counter-Reformation standards, substituting a daughter for a wife in the intrigue, but neglecting to omit the humorous references to *"le corna"* or even to change Cogliandro's name, with its built-in sexual gibe.

Milano considered *Chiappinaria* too close to its Plautine source, *Miles gloriosus,* to deserve any praise except as a good translation.[125] Not to disagree with this judgment would be to do Della Porta an injustice. He borrowed his main plot from *Miles* and added a trick from *Pseudolus* (the roundabout way in which Truffa obtains the bear), but he limited and unified the action and invented a motif on which his comedy turns and depends for its considerable charm, i.e., the bear, Chiappino himself. The name appears to connect Della Porta with Giulio Cesare Cortese's jovial Neapolitan academy, the "Schirchiate de lo Mandracchio e Mprovesante de lo Cerriglio," in which, to judge from several publications of the members, "lo chiappo" was a private joke.[126] Perhaps *Chiappinaria*'s total lack of seriousness results from its having been aimed at this company of intellectual roisterers.

The characters are the streamlined and fantastic caricatures of Della Porta's mature production. The braggart, the glutton, and the clever servant are bespangled archetypes. The lovers are morally unlike and emotionally like the *innamorati* of the serious comedies, and strike the same melodramatic poses, albeit with comic results. Albinio laments a trifling setback in his amorous game of hide-and-seek with all the

[125] *Op.cit.,* 337.

[126] Camillo Minieri-Riccio, "Cenno storico delle Accademie fiorite in Napoli," *Archivio storico per le province napoletane,* v (1880), fasc. III, 585. The words *chiappo* (noose) and *chiappino* (sly) were both played on by the academicians. By christening the bear "Chiappino," Della Porta worked the bear motif and the theme of trickery into the title of his comedy.

tragic fervor manifested by Pirro of *Il moro* at the point of death, but the only effect of this or any of his tirades is hilarity among his fellow conspirators.

The grandiloquent and antithetical rhetoric of Della Porta's late comic style resounds in every act of *Chiappinaria*. The vocabulary reflects the interest in astronomy which grew stronger than ever in the playwright's waning years. Albinio, Drusilla, and Gorgoleone all draw on the heavens, stars, and comets for their similes (I, 4; V, 10, for example). Some of the images come closer than usual to the tortuousness of *Seicentismo;* Panvino announces, "Il tempo è comodissimo che già in Cielo s'accendono le torce per andare a seppellire il giorno, che è oscuro, e si vedono sorgere le corna della Luna" [127] (II, 6). But even this brief essay in preciosity reveals Della Porta's neoclassical concern for total unity; *le corna* is a reminder of the central issue, the "cuckolding" of Cogliandro. This wedding of image to theme and action is a late development of the Della Portean style. As Ignazio borrows terms from the bullring in the very Spanish *Fratelli rivali*, and as images of madness screech through *Furiosa,* so Truffa uses a straightforward simile from Della Porta's knowledge of "unnatural natural history" to describe his method of intriguing in this "Bear Comedy":

L'invenzione così a primo è imperfetta: ma come l'orso, producendo il suo parto imperfetto, leccandolo, a poco a poco li dà la sua forma perfetta; così noi leccandola col cervello, e ripolendola a poco a poco, la ridurremo alla forma perfetta.[128]   (I, 5)

The absence in this comedy of genuine tenderness, of moral example, and of Della Porta's expert blending of pathos and irony, is not a shortcoming as it is in *Fratelli simili.*

[127] (The time is right, for already in Heaven, the torches are lighted for the day's burial, it is dark, and the moon's horns are seen to rise)
[128] (The idea is imperfect at first: but as the bear, on producing its imperfect issue, by licking it little by little gives it its perfect form, so by licking this with our brains and repolishing it little by little we will reduce it to its perfect form.)

Weighty elements simply have no place in *Chiappinaria*. Its merit consists primarily in the design and pace of its insistently frivolous action. It includes no longlost husbands, wives, parents, or children; there is not even an agnition to endanger the pervasive gaiety by so much as a single tear. Like so many of Della Porta's intrigues, this one depends on the juxtaposition of pretense and reality, but here reality is represented by a bear and pretense by a bearskin.

Chiappinaria is so purely farcical that it might even be a deliberate foil to the lachrymose comedies, written in reaction to an overindulgence in tears and didacticism. The *commedia dell'arte* style of humor, at which Della Porta had become so adept and which he used so effectively as comic relief to his romantic plots, is given its head in *Chiappinaria*. The action is not even a plot in the usual sense: it is a giant *burla*, punctuated by *lazzi*. Physical humor is paramount. The characters and the bear ceaselessly pop in and out of Cogliandro's and Albinio's houses, in a dizzy round of impersonations, snatched kisses, collisions, dodges, and fistfights. On the printed page *Chiappinaria* may seem to deserve Milano's poor opinion. But it should not be examined by the standards of the *commedia erudita;* for all its affinities with the learned comedy, it is essentially an *un*improvised *commedia dell'arte* farce, a work as much of choreography as of dramaturgy. *Chiappinaria* should be seen onstage or else read with the aid of strong visual imagination before it can be appreciated for what it is—a light-footed ballet in bearskin.

LA CARBONARIA

SYNOPSIS: Pirino, son of Filogenio, loves Melitea, bondservant to a procurer, Mangone, who plans to sell her to a doctor in need of an heir to replace his kidnapped daughter. Pirino's servant, Forca, defrauds Filogenio of one hundred *scudi* by telling him that the doctor plans to kill Pirino for jealousy and can be stopped only by a bribe. Forca plans to use the money in the following way: Pirino's friend, Alessandro, will give the money to

Filogenio, asking him to buy a male slave for him from Mangone. Pirino will blacken his skin with carbon and will be sold to Mangone by the glutton, Panfago, masquerading as Raguseo, the slave-trader newly arrived in Naples. Once inside Mangone's house, Pirino will exchange clothes and color with Melitea, whom Filogenio will credulously buy for Alessandro. Panfago will send gifts to Mangone by some porters. One of them, a deaf-mute in Alessandro's service, will change places with Pirino.

The deception is successful until Panfago goes to collect his reward and cannot find Pirino. The glutton jumps to the conclusion that he has been betrayed, and reveals the plot to the doctor. Together they go to Mangone, discover the deaf-mute in blackface, beat him to make him talk. He in turn beats all three of them and escapes.

Forca and Pirino spy on Panfago and the doctor, as they prepare to seize Melitea, who is in Filogenio's house, waiting to be delivered to Alessandro. While the doctor informs Filogenio of the deception and assures him that he had no evil intentions toward Pirino, Forca quickly replaces Melitea with the deaf-mute, who is shortly afterward led home by the doctor. Discovering the fraud, the doctor brings the mute back, just as Forca and Alessandro are having Panfago arrested for theft of the clothes he used for his disguise.

Meanwhile Mangone meets the real Raguseo and accuses him of taking part in the deception. As they fight, they are approached by Melitea's foster father, Isoco, who has been seeking her in all the slave-markets. He had believed her to be the child of his late wife, Galasia, but discovered after Melitea's abduction by pirates that Galasia had played the kidnaper in order to revenge an insult offered her by Melitea's real father.

When the doctor hears the story, he realizes that Melitea is his lost child. He forgives Forca's deception because it has saved him from incest. All would now be well, had the lovers not run away. Forca is able to overtake them, however, and when they are assured that they will not be separated, Melitea and Pirino embrace their parents and friends in a general reconciliation.

The two remaining comedies are made rich by a blending of elements old and new in Della Portean dramaturgy: the form of traditional written comedy, the comic content and movement of *commedia dell'arte*, and the sentimental and moral refinements of Counter-Reformation serious comedy. *Carbonaria* is the earlier and the better of the two. Milano called it the finest example of Della Porta's frankly Plautine imitation, declared its source to be *Poenulus*, and linked it with *Trappolaria*, on the basis of the latter's derivation from *Pseudolus*, Plautus' variation on the theme of *Poenulus*.[129] But *Carbonaria* is not as much like either *Trappolaria* or *Poenulus* as *Sorella* is, nor is it as close to any single source as *Trappolaria* is to *Pseudolus*. Milano admitted that the black-face disguise which gives *Carbonaria* its name is missing in *Poenulus* and hints that the trick might have been inspired by Aretino's *Talanta* or Dolce's *Fabritia*.[130] He ignored, however, the similarity of this part of the plot to the disguise engineered in Plautus' *Persa* and the specific debt of the scene between Mangone and Pirino (III, 2) to that between Dordalus and Saturio's daughter (*Persa* IV, 4).

The Plautine origin of *Carbonaria* may account for a minor but curious omission in its prologue. This prologue is nothing more than a revision of the sharp defense with which Della Porta prefaced *Fratelli rivali*. In the *Carbonaria* version he made only one change which seems more than stylistic in purpose. He repeats the original praises of his plot and structure but cuts the concluding sentence,

Or questo è altro, che parole del Boccaccio, o regole di Aristotile, il quale se avesse saputo di filosofia, e di altro, quanto di Commedia, forse non averebbe quel grido famoso, che possiede per tutto il mondo.[131]   (A2verso)

The omissions may be of no significance whatsoever, but equally well it may indicate that Della Porta preferred to attack Aristotle only when absolutely necessary, i.e., in defense

---

[129] *Op.cit.,* 329.
[130] *Ibid.,* 333.
[131] See page 143, end of note 7 for translation.

of the novellesque romantic genre of *Fratelli rivali*. The tradition behind *Carbonaria*, descended through Plautus from Greek comedy, exempted its author from disagreeing with the Stagirite. That Della Porta occasionally denied Aristotle's authority in science as well as in drama, reveals his independence; that he was reluctant to do so and avoided it when possible is symptomatic of chronic neoclassicism.

The forces are marshaled and the action accelerated in *Carbonaria* according to the stylized *commedia erudita* strategy of which Della Porta had long been a master. The plot poses a problem in love which is coaxed into *imbroglio* by the joint efforts of comic and romantic characters, and solved at last by a fortuitous agnition. In addition, *Carbonaria* includes the best of what Della Porta had learned from the *commedia dell'arte*. The black-face disguise is exploited for the same choreographic effect achieved with the bearskin in *Chiappinaria;* the continual changes of complexion and the unceasing procession of tricksters and tricked in and out of Mangone's and Filogenio's houses provide an abundance of that visual and physical movement characteristic of improvised comedy; and the singing and dancing required of the "slave," as well as the general horseplay assigned to several of the low characters, was clearly suggested by professional comedians' repertories of jigs, jingles, and *lazzi*.

Into this charming unreality, Della Porta injected some ironic comment on the ways of the real world. Perhaps because his research into Neapolitan crime had ended with the publication of the *Physiognomonia*, he painted no more vignettes of life in the underworld after *Astrologo* and *Turca*. But in *Carbonaria* he returned briefly to that sort of satire. The procurer Mangone provides some telling details of his repellent trade when he discusses the profit he intends to make on three of his acquisitions, Gobba, Magrina, and Demonica (i, 2), each of whom boasts special talents which promise to bring a high price and to maintain Mangone's reputation for professional discernment and variety of stock.

The Ragusan slave-dealer comes in for similar criticism. In a scene which echoes Albumazar's declamation on the "seven liberal arts of thievery," Forca puts Panfago through a cate-chism of evil in order to determine his qualifications for the job of impersonating Raguseo (II, 3). The satire is pointed up by a quarrel between Mangone and Raguseo (V, 2), in which each takes a righteously censorious view of the other's profession and the pot calls the kettle black with absurd earnestness. But at no time is the general fantastico-comic effect weakened by bitterness or by lapses into realism, as it had been in *Astrologo* and *Turca*.

As though to express in *Carbonaria* all the tenets of his ma-ture art, Della Porta added to its classically balanced intrigue, *commedia dell'arte* pace, and timely satirical tone the roman-tic and moral sensibility he had developed in his semi-tragicomedies. Despite the farcical nature of the situation in which they move, the characters of the lovers and their fathers are protected from ridicule. The doctor is no *senex amans;* he wants to marry Melitea so that he may have an heir to replace his lost daughter. When Melitea is proved to be his child, he even seems glad to be relieved of the necessity for further procreation. Both the doctor and Filogenio hold serious and enlightened views on parental responsibility. The latter takes a conscientious interest in his son's education, and though distressed by Pirino's temporary neglect of his stud-ies, forces himself to be intelligently tolerant of youthful vagaries (I, 5).[132] The doctor displays more good sense than

---

[132] Corsano (*op.cit.*, 81, note 1) regards Filogenio's discourse on the education of youth as an example of the unctuous bigotry and cau-tious respect for authority which Della Porta fearfully assumed after his reprimand by the Inquisition. Filogenio says, "Perché introducendosi ne' teneri intelletti il zelo della santa religione, con quella se vien a dar l'imperio alla ragione, freno agli affetti e termine alla volonta." (Because by introducing love of holy religion into young minds, one can there give rule to reason, curb to desires and limit to will) Corsano interprets Forca's gibe, "Oh, gran pedagogo, sarebbe stato il mio padrone" (Ah, my master would have made a great teacher), as Della Porta's hint that the preaching is insincere. Corsano does not mention

many fathers in erudite comedy possess by recognizing that his daughter's virtue is in no way diminished by any outrages to which the pirates and slave-dealers may have subjected her (v, 3), for which civilized opinion he is rewarded with the news that her virginity has been preserved by good luck.

The *innamorati* are still more high-minded than their parents, and strongly resemble the lovers of Della Porta's most serious comedies. When Forca urges the necessity of robbing Filogenio's strongbox in order to rescue Melitea, Pirino suffers a severe conflict between filial duty and romantic love, which he examines with nearly tragic intensity before deciding in favor of the latter (i, 4). Like Melitea, he expresses his feelings in the flowery and antithetical language which had developed apace with Della Porta's increasingly sentimental lovers, becoming finally their natural and exclusive mode of communication. Pirino can use easy colloquialisms with Forca and his friends, but he is stylistically most at ease in such utterances as:

Sempre quello, che più si desidera più si teme. Tremo, non so se di paura, o di allegrezza. Il pericolo, dove mi trovo, mi spaventa, l'allegrezza dell'acquisto mi rallegra, il timor turba l'allegrezza, talchè provo in uno stesso tempo una timida allegrezza, ed un'allegro timore.[133]   (iii, 1)

Although he avoids the extremes suffered by Ardelio of *Furiosa*, Pirino feels likewise that in Melitea's absence he is a body without a soul (i, 1). The concept of love and the moral of *Carbonaria*'s love story also are identical with those of the darker comedy. Pirino and Melitea are transfigured by love; they consider that their first duty is to each other, so

---

that Roman comedy was full of moral *sententiae* mocked by servants' jests. Della Porta may have borrowed the device as he did so many others, without moral purpose, sincere or insincere.

[133] (What one desires most he always fears most . . . I tremble, I know not whether from fear or from joy. The danger in which I find myself terrifies me, the joy of possession delights me, fear disturbs the joy, so that I feel simultaneously a fearful joy and a joyful fear.)

much so that Melitea displays a surprising independence in warning that she will acknowledge the doctor as her father only if he blesses her union with Pirino; otherwise she is prepared to flee with her lover to the wilderness. Both fathers are properly impressed. Filogenio acknowledges that "i loro amori non erano fondati in vani desiderj giovanili, ma su salde leggi di santissimo matrimonio," [134] and the doctor concedes that such marriages are made in heaven (v, 5). In semi-tragic plays like *Moro* and *Furiosa* such emotional and didactic attitudes are signs of changing fashions in drama; the introduction of these elements in full force in a farcical intrigue comedy like *Carbonaria* measures the degree to which the Counter-Reformation and the romantic sentiment it encouraged had transformed the gracefully malicious and astringent *commedia erudita* of an earlier generation. Simultaneously, *Carbonaria* is proof that Della Porta was one of the few comic playwrights who could employ the latter-day sweetness and light without sacrifice of wit, line, or comic pace.

LA TABERNARIA

SYNOPSIS: Giacomino and Antifilo both love Altilia, daughter of their erstwhile tutor, Tito Melio Strozzi, Salernitan pedant. Altilia returns Giacomino's love, but his miserly father, Giacoco, forbids the match. Hearing that Tito Melio and his family will stop in Naples on his way to Rome, Giacomino's servant, Cappio, plans to take advantage of Giacoco's temporary absence to bring the lovers together. The pedant has sent ahead his gluttonous servant, Lardone, to take rooms at the Cerriglio, an inn owned by a German. Cappio bribes Lardone to direct Tito Melio instead to Giacoco's house, where Cappio will pose as the innkeeper and Giacomino will be waiting to receive Altilia. The plot is overheard by Antifilo, who hurries to Posillipo, where Giacoco is transacting some business, and spreads a false alarm of a Turkish raid, hoping that Giacoco will return for safety to Naples that night and upset Cappio's plans. Antifilo also meets a

[134] (their love is not based on silly childish desires but on the firm laws of most holy matrimony)

Spanish braggart, Don Juan de Cardon de Cardona, and hires him to go to Giacoco's house, demanding tavern service.

Cappio does all he can to discourage the unwelcome guest, pretending singlehandedly to be a gang of fierce foreigners, dashing in and out in various costumes and threatening the braggart in several dialects. Nevertheless Don Juan stays on to greet Altilia and her nurse, Lima, when Tito Melio and Lardone leave them at the "inn." The braggart's flirting earns him a blow from Giacomino, but their fight is interrupted by the approach of Giacoco. While Giacomino puts the house in order, Cappio poses as the innkeeper and turns Giacoco away, then emerges in his own person to show his bewildered master the way home. Wrapping Giacoco up to the eyes against the cold wind, Cappio leads him in a circle, stalling to give Giacomino time, and at last brings Giacoco to his own door. The old man is suspicious of Don Juan's presence and grows very angry when Tito Melio appears, demanding his daughter and his rooms. Convinced at last that the pedant has lost his way, Giacoco directs Cappio to take the wanderers to the Cerriglio, where the real innkeeper denies that the pedant's daughter and her nurse were left with him. A fight is averted by the arrival of Antifilo and his father, Limoforo, who offer shelter and aid to the pedant.

Altilia and Lima are cared for meanwhile by Giacomino and Cappio. Lima reveals that Altilia is really the child of a rich Neapolitan but was reared by Tito Melio after she and Lima were separated from her parents during the plague. Lima supposes that Altilia's father is now dead, but suggests that someone be hired to play his part, demand her back from the pedant and give her to Giacomino. Giacomino and Cappio agree to the plot, take Altilia to the Cerriglio, and bribe the German innkeeper to say she was there all the time. When Limoforo, Tito Melio, and Antifilo arrive with the police to search Giacomino's house, they find no trace of Altilia and again repair to the Cerriglio, where she is waiting for them. After Limoforo and Antifilo leave, Giacomino's friend, Pseudonomo, presents himself as Altilia's father. Lima pretends to recognize him and the pedant is easily deceived. But when he goes to tell Limoforo, the latter realizes on hearing the facts that he himself is Altilia's real father. Limoforo confronts Pseudonomo and at last the truth triumphs. Antifilo is downcast by the news that Altilia is his sister, but everyone else is delighted. Limoforo is won by Giacomino's frank apology and honorable intentions. Tito Melio is gratified by the offer of a home with his foster daughter. Giacoco is pleased by his son's rich alliance and his daughter-in-law's beauty.

According to the dedication written for the edition of 1616,[135] *Tabernaria* was Della Porta's "ultimo parto in questo genere." Its absence from Zannetti's list indicated that the comedy was written after 1610 or that it was re-christened before publication. It is probable, though by no means certain, that *Tabernaria* is identical with the mysterious *Bufalaria*, mentioned only by Zannetti.[136] The title under which the play has survived applies also to a type of Roman comedy developed by Titinius about the middle of the second century B.C. Departing from the Greek-inspired *palliata* cultivated by Plautus and Terence, the new style of comedy was known as the *togata* or *tabernaria*, because its characters wore the Roman *toga* and were of the lower class, dwelling in *tabernae*. The two names were interchangeable. The *tabernaria* had no connection with taverns.[137] In the sixteenth century the terms survived, but their definitions were uncertain. Orazio Toscanella lists among the species of comedy "*Pretestata, Tabernaria, Togata*," [138] apparently unaware that the first of these was technically not comedy but historical drama,[139] and that the last two were identical with each other. It is not clear whether or not Della Porta understood the Roman use of the terms. Except in the freedom he gives his female characters and his treatment of love between young people of respectable families, his comedies are Renais-

[135] See p. 58, note 5.

[136] See p. 68.

[137] George E. Duckworth, *The Nature of Roman Comedy. A Study in Popular Entertainment* (Princeton, 1952), 68, note 69.

[138] *Precetti* . . . , 12verso.

[139] According to Duckworth, probably not tragedy, either, though the only surviving complete example is Seneca's (?) *Octavia*, a tragedy (40, note 3).

sance versions of the *palliata* rather than of the *togata*. The title of *Tabernaria* is a reference to the Neapolitan tavern, the Cerriglio, scene of some of the action of the comedy, and presumably the meeting-place of Cortese's academy. Clearly *Tabernaria* had no connection with the type of Roman comedy denoted by the term. Either Della Porta was ignorant of the original meaning, or he was deliberately playing on it in calling his last comedy a "tavern-play."

The Plautine source of *Tabernaria* is *Aulularia*, as Milano observed,[140] and perhaps *Mostellaria* as well.[141] But *Tabernaria* owes less to Plautus than to Ariosto. This was not the first time Della Porta succumbed to the influence of his Ferrarese predecessor; *L'astrologo* is indebted to *Il negromante*, and *Trappolaria* bears traces of *La cassaria*. In *Tabernaria* the debt is larger, for the entire central situation is borrowed from *La scolastica*, in which young Claudio loves the daughter of his former tutor and hopes to win her when she and her father journey through the city on their way to a new abode. Eurialo is also in love with a girl who passes through town and he takes advantage of his father's absence to shelter her in his home. Della Porta merged the four *innamorati* into a single couple but retained the Ariostean situation and many of the details as well.

Ariosto (as well as the brother who finished *Scolastica* for him), like other comic playwrights of his generation, expected his audience to take on faith the strength and tenderness of his lovers' feelings, but Della Porta inserted a generous number of his usual love-scenes into the borrowed story, and endowed his *innamorati* with a portion of that moral sensitivity characteristic of his serious comedies. If the love affair is not quite as spiritual as that in *Carbonaria*, it is nevertheless a superior sort of relationship, engaging the

---

[140] *Op.cit.*, 399.
[141] With the recent recovery of Menander's *Dyscolos* (1st ed. Ed. V. Martin, Papyrus Bodmer IV, Cologny-Genève, 1958-1959), the specific source of *Aulularia* has at last been established.

mental, moral, emotional faculties as fully as the physical. Although the intrigue places Altilia in an equivocal position, she proves herself a model of cultivated refinement. Reared by a scholar, she is an accomplished rhetorician; her letter rejecting Antifilo's devotion is an exquisitely correct mixture of courtesy, logic, and ornamental phrasing (1, 3). Like all of Della Porta's heroines, Altilia corresponds to the traditional Petrarchan ideal of physical beauty, but in her case, this loveliness is emphasized. With the exception of Carizia in *Fratelli rivali*, no other *innamorata* is so often praised for her ideal beauty. She has "ore ne' capelli, zaffiri negli occhi rubini nelle labbra, e perle ne' denti" [142] (1, 2). She inspires not only Petrarchan admiration and time-honored images but heartfelt and untutored Neapolitan rhapsodies as well:

O che bello piezzo de femmena! O che uocchie cernarielle! o che faccia vasarella! o che bocca cianciosella! o che labbra mozzecarelle! o com'è ghiocarella, . . .[143]

Her moral character is worthy of such a mind and body. She is deeply and articulately grateful to her foster father, and declares with warmth and spirit that she will not be separated from him, even though she has found her real father and is about to acquire a husband (v, 6).

Though Altilia's relationship with Giacomino can hardly be called a kinship of souls, it is serious and very strong. He is generally solicitous of her honor, and if he takes full advantage of the unlooked-for opportunity to be alone with his idol, his crime may be excused by his youth, love, and hot blood. He makes clear his moral intentions by announcing his reinforced determination to marry Altilia. The same heat persuades Giacomino to deceive his father; the same basic innocence of intention and goodness of heart make him un-

---

[142] (gold in her hair, sapphires in her eyes, rubies in her lips, and pearls in her teeth)

[143] (Oh, what a beautiful bit of femininity! Oh, what dancing eyes! oh, what a kissable face! oh, what an adorable mouth! oh, what luscious lips! oh, how delicious she is . . .)

easy and repentant (IV, 1; and V, 4). He and Altilia are not heroic lovers but they are more sentimental and well-meaning than the *innamorati* of those comedies Della Porta wrote before he had discovered how far he could go with emotion and morality.

Like *Chiappinaria* and *Carbonaria*, *Tabernaria* reveals the bond with the *commedia dell'arte* which was strongest near the end of Della Porta's career. Though *Tabernaria* remains a *commedia erudita*, it is infinitely more theatrical than its erudite model, *La scolastica*. The witty but restrained and Terentian characters of Ariosto have become broad, Plautine, fantastic caricatures. The landlord, Bonifazio, prime mover of *Scolastica*, has been replaced by the clever servant indispensable to improvised comedy. A blustering Spanish braggart, darling of the public stage, has been added to the cast of characters. The scholar Lazzaro, to whom Ariosto gives no comic function, cedes his place to Tito Melio, a rare and charming hybrid of Della Porta's cultivation: a stock, macaronic pedant typical of one sort of post-Ariostean erudite comedy, enriched by Lazzaro's kindliness and a new touch of pathetic dignity. Certainly Tito Melio belongs to an erudite tradition and was aimed at an educated audience; spouting Latin and references to *romanzi*, passionately defending Queen Dido's good name (III, 9), he reflects the literary fashions and pedagogical jokes of the period. But in the extremity of his caricature the influence of the *commedia dell'arte* shows itself. The strong, broad line, the immediately identifiable and deliberately exaggerated caricature, though hardly an invention of the *commedia dell'arte*, was nevertheless its trademark. For Della Porta, in whom Plautus and Renaissance popular comedy met, it was the only natural method of characterization.

With the exaggeration and multiplication of comic characters goes the physical and visual action of *Tabernaria*. Where *Scolastica* moves at an elegant walk, Della Porta's comedy follows a dance measure. The *burle* are carried and the *lazzi* are performed rapidly and rhythmically. For once, the action is not limited to the street but moves indoors, or at least partly so. The guests sit down to dinner at the "tavern," perhaps at an outdoor table or beneath a ground-floor *loggia* (III, 1). In the absence of written stage directions, it can only be supposed that the set combined a street scene with some suggestion of an interior facing the street, an arrangement frequent in the *commedia dell'arte*. Plautus also presented banquet scenes onstage, however, and Della Porta may have borrowed this device from his Roman model. In either case, he must have justified it by Plautine authority. The device constitutes a break with the strictest classical tradition, a break which both Plautus and Della Porta were happy to make for the sake of popular theatrical effect. For the most part, however, the action of *Tabernaria* occurs on the street; there is a steady *courante* performed by the characters in and out of the Cerriglio and surrounding private houses.

In several earlier comedies Della Porta had used Spanish for some of his dialogue, and in *Il moro* he used Neapolitan to great effect, but in *Tabernaria*, perhaps for the delectation of Cortese's dialect-conscious academy, he went further than ever in mixing dialects in the *commedia dell'arte* manner. The braggart, Don Juan, speaks Spanish; Giacoco, Neapolitan; il Tedesco, owner of the Cerriglio, Germanic pidgin-Italian; and Cappio, a master linguist, switches easily from Sicilian to Venetian to Piedmontese (II, 3). Giacoco's language is particularly charming. In character he resembles Ariosto's Bartolo, a penurious but kindly father. But in temperament Giacoco is a true Neapolitan, excitable, susceptible to female beauty, garrulous, easily moved to tears or laughter; and his singsong dialect, loaded with deformations and diminutives is that of Pulcinella, as yet unknown to written comedy.

Tabernaria's merits are eclipsed by those of several other Della Portean plays, but this last comedy is valuable as an example of its author's final synthesis of the erudite and popular traditions. *Tabernaria* shows how far he was willing to go. The dialects, the *lazzi*, the caricatures and color belong to the *commedia dell'arte*, but beneath them and around them always is the classical framework, the character types of the *palliata*, the carefully measured proportions of the intrigue, the learned allusions, and, of course, the polished and predetermined dialogue. Della Porta is occasionally credited with imparting popular flavor to the erudite comedy, but he cannot be properly considered a modernizer. Nor was his theater a reversion to the *stile antico* hailed in the *Olimpia* dedication, but rather an extension of it, by which he rounded out the tradition. Around him comic playwrights were grafting pastoral, musical, and tragic shoots onto the intrigue comedy, and in the early years of the seventeenth century the form had already swollen out of the classical shape. There was a group of Della Porta imitators at this time, noted for their mixtures of erudite and popular elements, fashioned on the pattern of *Tabernaria*. The relation in which Della Porta stood to theatrical innovation is adumbrated by the term applied to these playwrights who continued in his line: Sanesi calls them "i ritardatori." [144]

[144] *Op.cit.,* I, 637ff.

Della Porta's Influence on Written Comedy

ITALY

THE earliest instance of Della Porta's influence on Italian written comedy appeared in 1584 when Fabrizio de Fornaris presented *Angelica*, his adaptation of *Olimpia* in Paris, where he published the comedy a year later.[1] Fornaris was a professional actor-manager, and *Angelica* bears the stamp of the *commedia dell'arte*, but it remains essentially a *commedia erudita* and closely follows its original. Fornaris claimed to have obtained the comedy in Venice "some years ago . . . from a Neapolitan gentleman," probably Della Porta himself, who spent a considerable time in Venice in the seventies and eighties. Fornaris' comedy is the only known example of such full-scale borrowing by any Italian playwright, but while it proves Della Porta's appeal to the *comici dell'arte* and is important as the means by which his comedy was first introduced to France, *Angelica* does not illustrate his general influence on Italian written comedy. That was to appear a decade or so later.

By the time of Della Porta's death, the limits of the *commedia erudita* had been extended to embrace all manner of elements—pastoral, romanesque, tragic. Most noticeable of all was the influence of the cape-and-sword drama. Napoli-

---

[1] See below, p. 263, and Appendix B.

Influence on Written Comedy

Signorelli dated the introduction of the Spanish style about the middle of the seventeenth century,[2] but in fact it took the stage much earlier, pushing neo-Latin comedy into the wings and permitting it only an occasional walk-on. The romantic traits recognizable in the comedies of Oddi, of Borghini, and of Della Porta himself quite dominate seventeenth-century comedies. Lorenzo Guidotti's *L'imbriachezza d'amore* (Roma, 1625) is a conservative example: it includes a prince and a duke in disguise, a pair of princesses in male clothing, vaguely indicated shifts of scene, Spanish sonnets, much word-play on the conceit of love-intoxication, threats of death, and careful consideration of the rules of honor. There are still traces of the earlier comedy, to be sure, in the five-act construction and in the persons of Paragrafo the pedant and Gerundio, a variation on the Neapolitan type in the tradition of Gialoise, Pannuorfo, and their colleagues.

But the regular comedy was not snuffed out all at once. Until fairly late in the seventeenth century there existed an ever-diminishing number of *classicheggianti* or *ritardatori*, whose subjects were Plautine, Terentian, or novellesque, who adhered to the unities of time and place, whose characters were the stock *innamorato, servi, capitani, pedanti, parasiti,* and *napoletani* evolved in the Cinquecento. But this was no return to the spirit of early northern comedy. The effects of the Counter-Reformation—the emphasis on morality and didacticism, the greater attention to female characters, a certain increase in pathos and emotional intensity—were visible in the works of the *ritardatori*. In short, their neoclassicism was that of the late sixteenth century and of Della Porta.

Napoli-Signorelli was perhaps the first to link the names of several seventeenth-century *commediografi* by reason of their common predilection for "la regolarità latina." Those he cited were: [3] Niccolò Lepori (*Il finto moro*); Scipione Teo-

---

[2] *Vicende della cultura nelle Due Sicilie.* 2ª ed. napoletana (1810–1811), v, 530.

[3] *Ibid.,* 529–30.

doro (*Gl'amanti ingelositi*, Napoli, 1634); [4] Girolamo Comes or Gomez (*Lu bravazu*, in Sicilian dialect, Palermo, 1654); Lorenzo Stellato of Capua (*Il furbo*, Napoli, 1638; and *Il ruffiano*, Napoli, 1643); Filippo Gaetano or Caetani, duke of Sermoneta (*L'Ortensio*, Napoli, 1609; *Li due vecchi*, Napoli, 1612; and *La schiava*, Napoli, 1613); [5] Francesco D'Isa (a Franciscan priest who wrote under his brother Ottavio's name, *La Fortunia*, Napoli, 1612; *L'Alvida*, Napoli, 1616; *La Flaminia*, Viterbo, 1621; *La Ginevra*, Napoli, 1622; and *Il malmaritato*, Napoli, 1622); Luigi Eredia of Palermo (*La trappolaria*, Palermo, 1602); Giulio Cesare Torelli of Naples (*L'anchora*, Napoli, 1602).[6] It is not surprising that Napoli-Signorelli, reared in the heyday of neoclassicism, should have admired the *ritardatori*. Of the last two he went so far as to say that they sometimes approach Della Porta's excellence.

Croce gave Della Porta's name to the whole genre, "la commedia regolare sul tipo del Porta," [7] citing the comedies of D'Isa, G. C. Sorrentino (*L'astuta cortegiana*, 1631) and Alfonso Torello as examples,[8] and branding as pale imitators of Della Porta, G. C. Torelli, Caetani, Fabrizio Marotta (*Il ratto*, Napoli, 1603), Bernardino Moccia (*La Flaminia*, 1611), and Ottavio Glorizio of Tropea (*Le spezzate durezze*, Venezia, 1605; and *L'impresa d'amore*, Venezia, 1607). Croce's pronouncement is enough to discourage study of the "imitators":

[4] According to Lione Allacci, this is a pseudonym of Scipione Errico of Messina, Ozioso, author of *Le rivolte di Parnaso* (Venezia, 1620) and defender of Marino. (*Drammaturgia . . . accresciuta e continuata fino all'anno MDCCLV*, Venezia, 1755, 40).

[5] Written earlier, according to its prologue, and presented before the Count of Lemos, who did not become Viceroy of Naples until 1610.

[6] Croce dated the writing of this comedy 1599 (*I teatri di Napoli: secolo XV-XVIII*, Napoli, 1891, 80), but Marotta's letter about the play, prefacing the 1604 edition, is dated 1598.

[7] (the regular comedy along the lines of Della Porta's)

[8] *Saggi sulla letteratura italiana del '600* (Bari, 1924), 304–305.

Ne ho lette quante ne ho potuto trovar citate e repescar nelle nostre biblioteche. Che miseria! Il solito intreccio, non rivestito più degli splendori dell'ingegno del Porta, è ripetuto a sazietà.[9]

Sanesi adds to the lists of Napoli-Signorelli and Croce the names of Ubaldino Malavolti of Siena (*I servi nobili*, 1602; *L'amor disperato*, 1605; *La menzogna*, 1612); the Genoese Anton Giulio Brignole Sale, marquis of Groppoli; Giovanni Villifranchi of Volterra (*La fida turca*, 1612; and *La greca schiava*, Firenze, 1618); and Paolo Veraldo,[10] but Sanesi does not blame all these *ritardatori* on Della Porta.

Although all these playwrights shared Della Porta's neo-classical-cum-Counter-Reformation standards, it does not follow that they all imitated him. He was not the only exponent of the classically regular but romantic genre which Professor Herrick recognizes as "serious comedy." [11] He had several rivals, among whom Sforza Oddi was perhaps the most successful and influential. Oddi's kind of neoclassical comedy was like Della Porta's in many ways but it was also unmistakably Oddi's tragicomic own. He, too, had his imitators.

Giovanni Villifranchi, for example, revealed in the prologue to *La greca schiava* that the comedy was tailored to fit the cast of Oddi's *I morti vivi*, which his academy had recently performed. The plot and atmosphere as well seem to have been borrowed directly from Oddi's serious comedy. Like Oddi's Alessandra, Villifranchi's Filena is a foreigner, living in bondage, hoping to discover the whereabouts of her erstwhile lover. Like Oddi's Ottavio, Villifranchi's Delio has meanwhile involved himself with a rich widow. And so it

---

[9] *I Teatri di Napoli . . .* , 80. (I have read as many of them as I could find mentioned and could dig up in our libraries. What poverty! The usual plot, no longer clothed in the splendors of Della Porta's wit, is repeated to satiety.)

[10] *La commedia.* 2ª ed. riv. ed acc. (Milano, 1954), I, 635-38.

[11] *Italian Comedy in the Renaissance* (Urbana, 1960).

goes. Villifranchi dispensed with braggart and glutton, contenting himself, as did Oddi, with a highly literary pedant, and subordinating the comedy to the semi-tragic love passion, expressed at great length and without the relief of servants' parody with which Della Porta's most pathetic love scenes are leavened.

The work of Ottavio Glorizio, one of Croce's "pale imitators" of Della Porta, admittedly contains Della Portean features, in particular the stock characters of braggart, glutton, and comic Neapolitan, but Glorizio's *Impresa d'amore*, with its *imbroglio* consisting of Settimia's plan to force her elders' consent to her marriage by fleeing to Rome with her lover's twin sister (both in male disguise), and the plan of the rich courtesan Delia to recapture the affection of Oratio, has little of the neo-Plautine flavor of Della Portean comedy and is conducted more in the manner of the (Tasso's?) *Intrichi d'amore*, or of the comedies of Cristoforo Castelletti.

Some of the *ritardatori*, however, were obviously indebted to Della Porta. G. C. Torelli's *Anchora*, for example, is prefaced by Fabrizio Marotta's statement of the requirements of good comedy. Derived from a synthesis of Greek and Roman principles, most of them are the common aims of all *ritardatori:* unity of time and place, decorum of character determined by type and social position, progression from bad to good fortune, polished language, sharp and appropriate jests. Counter-Reformation desiderata are also included, articulated with a Della Portean emphasis: sound precepts and moral examples, discourses which move the affections and, above all, ingenuity and complication of plot combined with harmonious balance of parts and natural, inevitable resolution. In words similar to Della Porta's own in the prefaces to *Fratelli rivali* and *Carbonaria*, Marotta makes plot the first consideration and *meraviglia* the ultimate effect:

. . . si vede la favola esser una, e di una sola attione, non semplice, ma attrecciata, possibile, e maravigliosa, e bene ordinata, e disposta, e rallargata con le digressioni convenevoli alla favola . . .[12]

The comedy which follows this manifesto attempts to realize the ideal in specifically Della Portean terms. Here is the servant who gibes at his master's love while laying snares to further it, here the pedant, the glutton, the braggart captain, and the comic Neapolitan. Here too the complicated tangle of mistaken identity, punctuated by *commedia dell'arte lazzi* mixed with literary speeches, resolved by the reunion of long-separated parents and children through recognition of an anchor-shaped birthmark. On the serious side there are disquisitions on worldliness and eternity, a suggestion of incest, a noble contest of friendship, and threatened death fortuitously averted. Not half as good as any of Della Porta's serious comedies, *L'anchora* nevertheless owes all it is to them.

Marotta's own comedy, *Il ratto*, is even more specifically indebted to Della Porta; the situation of old Menicoantonio, who wants to marry again in order to replace his child stolen years ago, is borrowed from *Carbonaria*, and his character is a cross between Pannuorfo's of *Moro* and Giacoco's of *Tabernaria*. The pedantic Glottocrisio, the boastful Capitano Encelado, the parasitical Sarcofago are copied from Della Porta with more fidelity than imagination. Marotta also uses occasional *lazzi* and gives a *commedia dell'arte* pace to his Plautine plot, but *Il ratto* is nonetheless a *commedia eruditissima*, and in this one way differs from its Della Portean originals. Not only the pedant but the other characters as well spout literary allusions and launch into Jesuitical discussions of abstractions at the drop of a hat. In sheer prolixity Marotta quite outdoes Della Porta.

Filippo Caetani, duke of Sermoneta, apparently admired

[12] Giulio Cesare Torelli, *L'anchora* (Napoli, 1604), prefatory letter, p. 4. (. . . the plot is seen to be unified and built on single action, not simple, but complicated, plausible, marvelous, well-ordered and distributed, and augmented with digressions appropriate to the plot . . .)

Della Porta's plots and sentiment more than his humor, for in his own three comedies, Caetani borrowed Della Portean intrigues, expanded the moral discourses, and reduced the number and activity of the comic characters. *Li due vecchi*, its plot adapted from *Fantesca*, contains neither braggart nor Neapolitan dialect, pedant nor glutton, and no scenes intended as primarily comic. It leans on the clever servant Lucrino for a *motus motandi* and for occasional quips to justify the appellation *commedia*. *L'Ortensio* owes something of its plot to *L'erofilomachia*, but here Caetani avoids Oddi's semi-tragic tone and concentrates unsuccessfully on achieving maximum complication with minimum confusion. *L'Ortensio* contains a braggart and a clever servant of the Della Portean stamp, the latter named Giovanni but, significantly, called Trinca sometimes by those who admire his wiles (II, 7). In Caetani's *La schiava*, the clever servant bears the equally Della Portean name of Truffa, and two scenes are stolen outright: II, 5 from *Carbonaria* II, 1–2—Eurialo disguises himself as a slave named Amorat and is sold to the procurer who has possession of his sweetheart; and II, 9 from *Trappolaria* III, 4—the procurer is tricked by two servants, one posing as a buyer, the other disputing his identity in such a way as to establish it. Caetani is more austere than Della Porta in his humor and more profligate in his language, which is extremely elaborate and precious in the love scenes. He occasionally waxes didactic but he aims first at ingenious structure; lacking Della Porta's fine sense of balance, however, Caetani entangles his plots in obscure incidents and is forced to abrupt or unnatural resolutions.

The best of Della Porta's imitators was Francesco D'Isa, the Franciscan who published his five comedies under his brother's name in order to keep the cloth unbesmirched. With the exception of the sympathetic courtesan, all of D'Isa's characters are modeled on Della Porta's. Like the *innamorati* of *Fratelli rivali* and *Moro*, the protagonists of *Alvida* and *Ginevra* are aristocrats; one of them, Camillo of *Ginevra*, goes mad like the lovers in *Furiosa*. The heroine of *Fortunia* has a touch of true heroism rare in the genre; she has the *animo virile* (II, 3) of Della Porta's Carizia or Oriana, or of one of Oddi's strong-minded ladies. D'Isa's comic characters are borrowed from Della Portean comedies of all vintages, not only from the serious period. Tofano, the *vignarolo* of *Malmaritato*, is a bumpkin with social ambition like Vignarolo of *Astrologo;* Mambrino, the glutton of the same play, argues with the braggart by comparing eating to fighting, in direct imitation of Della Porta's formula:

Il General è la Fame, l'Appetito il Mastro di Cāpo, i Cuoci sono i Capitani; i Trincianti l'Alfieri, i Scalchi i Sergeti, gli huomini d'arme i Galloni d'India: che se ne vengono armati con quelle corazze all'Inglese; i caponi i cavalli leggieri, & i pollastri fanti; i spiedi vi rappresentano al vivo le spade, i schidoni le lāce, le caldaie le corazze, le pentole le celate, & i taglieri le rotelle: il campo è la tavola, e questia pācia è il corpo della battaglia, le spie sono gli occhi, che gentilmente spiano i luochi de buō bocconi: e per fine i vinti sono gli animali arrosti, e allessi, il vincitore è questo braccio, che con la furia di questa mano mette a sacco, & appiano il capo e dove là ci si perde la vita, quà ci si guadagna! [13]   (*Malmaritato* II, 3)

In D'Isa's *Fortunia*, Capitano Squarciabandiera and Scompiglio lament the lack in modern times of heroic fighters and heroic eaters, respectively (II, 10). Unfortunately, the verbal intoxication which possesses Della Porta's gluttons and braggarts never seizes on D'Isa's. He does somewhat better by the

[13] (The General is Hunger, Appetite is Field Commander, the cooks are the captains; the carving knives the standard-bearers, the carvers the sergeants, the soldiers the turkeys: for they come armed in English-style cuirasses; the capons are the light cavalry, and the cockerels infantry; the skewers are exactly like the swords, the spits are the lances, the kettles the cuirasses, the pots the helmets, and the trenchers the shields: the field is the table and this belly is the battle corps, the spies are the eyes, which nicely spy out the location of the best mouthfuls: and finally the losers are the roasted and boiled animals, the winner is this arm, which, with the fury of this hand, sacks and clears the field, and while life is lost there, it is gained here.)

Neapolitan figure borrowed from *Moro,* the amorous and conceited Colambrogio of *Fortunia,* who sings, "Cor mio, si non me daie quarche repuoso/ E muorto il molt'Illustre Colambruoso" [14] (III, 7). In the characters of Capitano Squacquera Spaccatruono of *Alvida* and Capitano Colafanfaro of *Ginevra* the braggart and the comic Neapolitan merge. D'Isa's other comic figures are merely repetitions of the stock types employed by Della Porta: the pedant who speaks macaronic Latin, the clever servant, the *fantesca,* the procurer, the *balia* and so on. D'Isa also joined Della Porta's pursuit of *meraviglia.* He strains after the marvelous in complexity of conflict and simplicity of resolution. In *Ginevra* he presents a marvel of virtue: like the purposely exaggerated examples of moral and emotional power in *Furiosa, Penelope,* and *Moro,* the behavior of D'Isa's hero is intended as a "maraviglioso dimostramento d'amore" (Prologue, A2verso). D'Isa's superiority to other *ritardatori* rests in his handling of plot. His excruciatingly twisted intrigues are conducted with harmony and grace akin to Della Porta's. Less serious than Caetani, D'Isa was more faithful to Della Porta, weaving comic scenes tightly into the fabric of his love stories, but judiciously adding the pathos, moral earnestness, and romantic sentiment so highly regarded in the Counter-Reformation.

A definitive classification of those *ritardatori* who merely wrote in the genre of Della Porta and those who came under his direct influence must wait upon a complete investigation of the *ritardatori* in general, an investigation in which tracking down the comedies themselves will not be the least task. But even so cursory a study as the present one reveals that Torelli, Marotta, Caetani, and D'Isa stand apart from other *ritardatori* as the immediate heirs of Della Porta. These playwrights were all Neapolitans, either from the city or from one of the towns in the surrounding Regno di Napoli. Caetani

[14] (Heart of mine, if you do not give me some rest, the most illustrious Colambrogio is dead.)

and Marotta were Della Porta's fellow members in the Accademia degli Oziosi, and Torelli was associated with Marotta. D'Isa, publishing in the same genre, city, and general period, almost certainly was connected with the circle in some way.

It would seem, indeed, that the tradition of the Neapolitan *commedia erudita* was fostered by a literary intelligentsia with a continuity of more than one generation. In Della Porta's childhood, Bernardino Rota, Scipione Ammirato, and Angelo di Costanzo had tried their hands at neoclassical comedy. These older poets belonged to the circle of Della Porta's uncle, and Rota was much impressed by the young Giambattista.[15] It seems that the bonds linking Neapolitan comic playwrights of different generations were identical with the bonds of their social life. Della Porta's influence on Italian written comedy in his own time and immediately afterwards is manifest in the work of Torelli, Marotta, and Caetani because, in effect, they all belonged to the same club.

There were other dramatists among the Oziosi and their friends, all of whom probably felt Della Porta's influence, although not necessarily in the same way. Milano reported that Carlo Noci of Capua owed the plot of his *La Cinthia* (Napoli, 1594) to Della Porta's comedy of the same name.[16] There is, in fact, little similarity between the two. Noci's work in *versi sciolti* mixed with rhyme is a *favola boscareccia* about a flock of nymphs and shepherds who live on the banks of the Tiber. It has in common with Della Porta's comedy only two proper names, Cintia and Ergasto, and the fact that the heroine is in male disguise. Noci's printers were Carlino and Pace, with whom Della Porta often dealt, and his dedicatee was Giovanni Battista Caracciolo, marquis of Brienza, member of the Oziosi. Noci probably borrowed a few external touches in order to advertise his work by Della Porta's

[15] *Delle poesie* . . . (Napoli, 1737), 199, 206.
[16] "Le commedie di Giovanbattista della Porta," *Studi di letteratura italiana* (Napoli, 1900), II, fasc. 2, 350, note 1.

reputation and to pay homage to the great man. But Noci's debt to Della Porta was small and his *Cinthia* is remote from the tradition of the *ritardatori*.

Among those listed as *ritardatori* by Napoli-Signorelli, Croce, or Sanesi, are others who moved among the Oziosi and whose comedies should be found and studied for signs of Della Portean influence. Among the *commedie erudite* of charter members were Scipione Errico's *Gl'amanti ingelositi*, Fabrizio Carafa's *Il fedele amante*,[17] Giulio Cesare Capaccio's comedy of forgotten name,[18] and the Count of Lemos' Spanish comedy, *La casa confusa*.[19]

Napoli-Signorelli's eighteenth-century admiration notwithstanding, the comedies of the *ritardatori* after Della Porta were monotonous relics of a once robust genre. In 1615 G. C. Capaccio, despite his own excursion into *commedia erudita*, damned the genre for its meaningless action and its use of Spanish and of Neapolitan dialect, which he considered respectively too highflown and too low, and praised the superiority of the *commedia dell'arte*.[20] Nevertheless even professional actor-managers like Barbieri and Silvio Fiorillo continued to write occasional semi-regular comedies [21] and as late as 1642, Prospero Bonarelli included a braggart, a pedant, and several other *ritardanti* conventions in his *I fuggitivi amanti*.[22] For all practical purposes the regular comedy of neo-Latin stock types was finished by the middle of the seventeenth century. Della Porta was the last important writer in the genre; as such he must be considered in any study of the later and lesser *ritardatori*, but his direct influence is visible only in the plays of his Neapolitan imi-

17 Allacci, *op.cit.*, 40, 335.

18 Croce, *I teatri di Napoli . . .* , 81.

19 *Ibid.*, 88; and Cayetano Alberto de la Barrera y Leirado, *Catalogo bibliografico y biografico del teatro antiguo espanol . . .* (Madrid, 1860), 209.

20 Croce quoted Capaccio's letter in *I teatri di Napoli . . .* , 81.

21 Sanesi, *op.cit.*, i, 639–643.

22 *Ibid.*, i, 638.

tators. In the eighteenth century Niccolò Amenta penned seven comedies somewhat anachronistically containing braggarts, comic Neapolitans, and all the other conventions of the late *commedia erudita*,[23] but his brief resurrection of the genre cannot be attributed specifically to the influence of Della Porta.

Camerini rightly placed Della Porta squarely in the major tradition of Italian drama, calling him "il più valente, se non il più fecondo dei precursori del Goldoni," adding incorrectly that like his greater successor, "coltivò con gloria la commedia improvvisa e la scritta." [24] Della Porta's mastery of plot and judicious utilization of *commedia dell'arte* traits in his academic stock types, giving discipline to one and body to the other, point in the direction that Goldoni was to take. There are also signs, unknown to Camerini, of a more tangible debt. One of Goldoni's unpublished French plays, *Les vingt deux infortunes d'Arlequin,* which is probably a later version of the *Le trentadue disgrazie d'Arlecchino* (1739), was discovered by Pietro Toldo to owe its main plot to Della Porta's *Sorella.*[25] Whether Goldoni took the situation directly from the Italian or from the well-known adaptation of Rotrou is uncertain. It may be mere coincidence that both Goldoni and Rotrou give the name of Lélie to Della Porta's Attilio. Goldoni's first-hand acquaintance with at least some of Della Porta's plays was proved by Maria Ortiz from the frontispiece to the Pasquali edition of Goldoni's comedies. The preface, written by Goldoni himself, affirms that the etching is a portrait of him surrounded by his books of comedy. One of the books is plainly labeled "Della Porta." [26] But Della

[23] Croce, *Saggi . . . '600,* 305.

[24] *I precursori del Goldoni* (Milano, 1872), vi. (the worthiest, if not the most prolific, of Goldoni's precursors. . . . he gloriously cultivated improvised and written comedy.)

[25] "Tre commedie francesi inedite di Carlo Goldoni," *Giornale storico della letteratura italiana,* xxix, fasc. 2–3 (1897), 377–91. The play is to be found in the Bibliothèque Nationale Ms. 9254.

[26] "La cultura del Goldoni," *Giornale storico della letteratura italiana,* xxxviii, fasc. 1–2 (1906), 76.

Influence on Written Comedy

Porta's significant contribution to the eventual development of a Goldoni was to have written good Italian regular comedy, to have proved as few others had done how literary elegance and popular humor can join and thereby improve each other.

FRANCE

The triumph of French classical drama in the seventeenth century, surpassing anything ever achieved by the Italian theater, was preceded by decades of cultural importation from Italy. From the middle of the sixteenth century on, French playwrights translated, adapted, or simply pilfered an as yet undetermined number of Italian plays, among them some of Della Porta's.

Although for a long time comedy was a neglected genre in France, some of the *commedie erudite* which arrived there in print were welcomed unreservedly. The earliest adaptations, such as Charles Estienne's *Comédie du Sacrifice* (1547), later called *Les abusez*, and Jean de la Taille's *Corrivaux* (1562), were in prose, like their originals, as were the translations of Pierre Larivey (formerly Pietro Giunti), who published his first six in 1579. Eventually French playwrights handled and mixed their sources more freely. By 1580, Odet de Turnèbe's *Contens* (published 1584) had illustrated how borrowings from Parabosco, Secchi, and Piccolomini could be melded into a subtle, distinctively French verse comedy. Until the seventeenth century, however, little was built on this excellent foundation.

Traveling actors also were carriers of Italian comedies, and it was by this means that French audiences were first acquainted with Della Porta's work, if not with his name. Italian *comici dell'arte* began wandering into France singly during the reign of Francis I,[27] and various troupes began arriving regularly from 1571 on.[28]

[27] Armand Baschet, *Les comédiens italiens à la cour de France sous Charles IX, Henri III, Henri IV et Louis XIII d'après les lettres royales, la correspondance originale des comédiens, les registres de la "Trésorerie de l'Epargne" et autres documents* (Paris, 1882), 2ff.

[28] *Ibid.*, 13.

Among them were *I Confidenti*, the company of Fabrizio de Fornaris, who in 1584 twice performed his prose comedy, *Angelica*, based on Della Porta's *Olimpia*. Fornaris published it the following year, acknowledging in the dedication that "gl'anni adietro mi fu da un gentil-homo Napolitano virtuosissimo spirto, donata questa comedia." [29] From prologue to curtain line, *Angelica* is a close paraphrase of *L'Olimpia;* the notable changes are the substitution of a dull old servant for Della Porta's pedant, and the promotion of the braggart to star billing. Translated into Spanish and greatly enlarged, the role was played by Fornaris himself, who was permanently identified with the mask of Capitano Coccodrillo. The main effect these changes had on Della Porta's comedy was to make it a more suitable vehicle for an actor with a specialty.

Angelica's success warranted a French translation, made in 1599 by one "L. C." [30] perhaps (Pierre) Larivey-Champenois. During the years when French comedy became increasingly romantic, tragic, Spanish, and lachrymose, nothing more was heard of *L'Olimpia*, alias *Angelica*, but in 1653, after the dramatic genres had been clearly separated and the time was ripe for Molière, Tristan L'Hermite adapted *Angelica* in verse as *Le parasite* and published it the following year.[31]

Fornaris had done little more than change Della Porta's wording, but Tristan completely recast the comedy in an elegant French mould. Without altering or adding to the

[29] *Angelica* (Paris, 1585), dedication, aij. (a few years ago, this comedy was given me by a most gifted Neapolitan gentleman).

[30] Charles Brunet, . . . *Bibliothèque dramatique de Monsieur de Soleinne* (Paris, 1845), IV, 72, and Arthur Ludwig Stiefel, "Tristan L'Hermites *Le Parasite* und seine Quelle," *Archiv für das Studium der neueren Sprachen und Literaturen*, LXXXVI (1891), 76.

[31] The source of *Le parasite* was discovered by Stiefel (see note above). The most recent editor of *Le parasite* does not mention the possibility that Tristan used "L. C.'s" translation, taking it for granted that he knew *Angelica* in Italian (*Le parasite. Comédie*. Edition annotée par Jacques Madeleine, Paris, 1934, Introduction, v).

incidents of the intrigue, he redistributed the action, omitted scenes, monologues, and characters, enlarged the role of the *innamorata*, and trimmed that of the braggart, in order to give comic emphasis to Fripesauces, the plotting parasite. Only this last change brings *Le parasite* closer to *L'Olimpia*, in which Mastica is the most prominent comic character, than to *Angelica*, dominated by Capitano Coccodrillo. Tristan translated the colorful colloquial prose of his source into classical burlesque verse, and in so doing, restrained the humor and the sentiment as well. Although Lucinde and Lisandre are in fact as intimate with each other as are Angelica and Fulvio, or Olimpia and Lampridio, their behavior is not made the subject of bawdy jokes by the comic characters. And in their own speeches, the French lovers are emotionally more self-contained than their Italian prototypes. Lisandre expresses his feelings fully but without raving or tears. Tristan was even stricter with his heroine. Olimpia and Angelica make only one or two appearances each, at which times they pour out their hearts. Lucinde takes part in many scenes and speaks of many matters, but never of love. *Le parasite* is not a different genre from its source; it remains *commedia di viluppo* of the sixteenth-century neo-Latin sort, but it has been admirably dandified. Tristan utilized the genre to display his mastery of style; the polished verses, the sprightly artificial comic tone, the perfect balance, and emotional restraint are modifications he imposed on Della Porta's firstfruits, a sentimental Neapolitan *imbroglio*, to make of it a detached and graceful French game.

By the time Tristan adapted *Angelica,* some of Della Porta's other work had reached the French stage by a quite different route. A gradual mingling of genres in the sixteenth century had produced tragicomedy, which flourished in the seventeenth century despite the neoclassicists' efforts to separate comedy and tragedy. The first French examples do not truly deserve the name of tragicomedy. Professor Herrick prefers to call Louis Le Jars' *Lucelle* a *"drame libre,"* [32] for it is melodramatic but closer to the romantic comedy of its source, Piccolomini's *Amor costante*, than the true romanesque tragicomedy to come, represented by Garnier's *Bradamante* (1582). Between 1630 and 1650, during the height of its popularity, French tragicomedy was primarily influenced by Spanish drama, but some of the most active practitioners of the genre continued to draw occasionally on Italian sources. Jean Rotrou, for example, the best and most prolific of these French "baroque" dramatists,[33] leaned often on Lope and Francesco de Rojas, but also adapted Oddi's *Erofilomachia* as *Clarice*, Girolamo Bargagli's *Pellegrina* as *La pèlerine amoureuse*,[34] and Della Porta's *Fratelli rivali* and *Sorella* as *Célie, ou le viceroi de Naples* and *La soeur*, respectively.[35]

Fratelli rivali and, to a lesser degree, *La sorella* contain moments of melodrama bordering on tragedy, but the balance of both plays is unequivocally comic. Rotrou made tragicomedies of them by banishing the braggarts and gluttons, together with all the frankly comic scenes, and concentrating exclusively on the romantic problems which

[32] *Tragicomedy, Its Origin and Development in Italy, France, and England* (Urbana, 1955), 176.

[33] What Raymond Lebègue calls "baroque" in French drama contains, of course, a large infusion of neoclassicism. See "La comédie italienne en France au XVIᵉ siècle," *Revue de littérature comparée* (Paris, 1950), 5–24. For a fruitful study of Rotrou's development, see Francesco Orlando, *Rotrou dalla tragicommedia alla tragedia* (Torino, 1963). Published too late to aid me, this book makes a valuable contribution to the investigation of the baroque, from which, in any case, I have attempted to separate my own study.

[34] Antero Meozzi, *La drammatica della Rinascita italiana in Europa. Secolo XVI-XVII* (Pisa, 1940), 26.

[35] Joseph Vianey, "Deux sources inconnues de Rotrou," *Archives historiques, artistiques et littéraires* (Paris, 1890–91), II, 241–50; A. L. Stiefel, "Unbekannte italienische Quellen Jean de Rotrou's," *Zeitschrift für französische Sprache und Literatur*, Supplement No. 5 (1891).

threaten serious consequences to various pairs of highborn lovers. Because the characters of *La soeur* are bourgeois, and those of *Célie* noble, the former was published as a *comédie* and the latter as a *tragi-comédie*,[36] but, aside from this technicality, they belong to the same genre.

Of the two, *La soeur*, first performed in 1645 and published in 1647 [37] is the closer to its source. The plot corresponds exactly to that of *La sorella* except in a few details of construction. Rotrou dispensed with all the soliloquies save one (v, 2), and avoided repeated rehearsing of the intrigue by making the characters merely whisper it to each other after the first exposition.[38] The *imbroglio* and the participants' reactions to it became profoundly serious. Rotrou raised to its highest power every potentially tragic element in his source; the *cri du sang*, for example, acknowledged casually by Della Porta in more than one comedy, becomes a roar in *La soeur*.[39] Moreover, Rotrou suppressed all traces of Della Porta's clowning, slapstick, and parody, leaving of the original collection of comic characters only Ergaste, the scheming valet, and Lydie, the pretty *suivante* who replaces the old *balia*. Rotrou permitted them to be sharp-witted but not funny, and with a Gallic insistence on symmetry, paired them off in the last scene, which ends not with a Della Portean jest, but with earnest rejoicing, "*O favorable hymen*, . . ." (v, 6). There is deliberate humor in the valet's pretense of speaking Turkish by spouting nonsense syllables (III, 4), but the stateliness of Rotrou's alexandrines deprives the scene of the hilarity which pervades it in *La sorella*.

H. C. Lancaster damned *La soeur* as mere intrigue, without

[36] Jean Rotrou, *Oeuvres*, IV (Paris, 1820).

[37] Vianey, *op.cit.*, 242.

[38] See, for example, the scene (IV, 2), in which Lélie explains the situation *sotto voce* to Constance.

[39] For a full discussion of the *cri du sang* as a dramatic motif, see Clifton Cherpack, *The Call of Blood in French Classical Tragedy* (Baltimore, 1958).

character or manners.[40] A. L. Stiefel, after a detailed examination, declared it one of the best French comedies before
Molière's.[41] Both were wrong, Lancaster to condemn intrigue comedy per se, Stiefel to judge *La soeur* superior to
La sorella. The qualities to be admired in the former are the
neat complication of the plot and the tender sensibility of the
lovers; both exist in the original, in addition to many other
admirable touches which Rotrou would have done well to
preserve.

He was more imaginative in *Célie, ou le viceroi de Naples*,
also first performed in 1645. Despite its subtitle, it is set in
Salerno, like its source, *Fratelli rivali*. Rotrou omitted all the
comic *contretemps* and decreased the number of characters,
thereby simplifying the *imbroglio*. He heightened the melodrama in the remaining action and exploited its innate irony
by additions like the scene between the heroine and her
sister, a character developed for the purpose. Célie, questioned by Ismène, who has overheard her lamentations, answers that she is rehearsing a comedy, and unburdens herself
on the pretext of recounting its plot (III, 4). Other scenes
are closely copied from Della Porta, but become entirely
different by virtue of the language. Alvare's recital of his
falling in love (I, 1), for example, is largely a paraphrase of
Ignazio's first speech (I, 1), but the effect of *meraviglia* created by paradoxes in *Fratelli rivali* is no longer paramount in
Célie. The same paradoxical thought is expressed but the
antitheses are fewer, for the substance is subject to the demands of rhyme; the appeal is first to the ear, and the mind
is not compelled to marvel:

> Aussitôt les taureaux,
> Soufflant avec fureur le feu par les naseaux,
> Et près de nous donner un sanglant exercice,

[40] *A History of French Dramatic Literature in the Seventeenth Century*, Part II, Vol. II (Baltimore, 1932), 479.
[41] *Op.cit.*, 103.

A sauts précipités bondirent dan la lice:
Alors, san vanité, si dans un noble sein
Un grand coeur fut jamais piqué d'un grand dessein,
Ce fut le même coeur qui s'étoit laissé prendre,
Ce glorieux captif qui venoit de se rendre.
D'abord, pour exciter sa générosité,
Je tournai mes regards vers ce ciel de beauté,
D'où ces astres brillans, ces étoiles vivantes,
Ces yeux, ces beaux auteurs de mes ardeurs naissantes,
M'influèrent au sein des transports si puissans,
Que ma valeur passa la croyance des sens.
Je sus avec tant d'art, vigueur et de feintes,
Assaillant les taureaux, éviter leur atteintes,
Que, loin d'apprehender qu'aucun me put heurter,
Je devins insolent jusqu'à les exciter:
La mort de cinq ou six dont je jouahai la terre
Dans une mer de sang acheva cette guerre:
Enfin en ce combat je demeurai vainqueur;
Cependant que l'amour triomphoit de mon coeur:
Mais qui vit ma victoire ignora ma défaite;
Car l'une fut publique, et l'autre fut secrète.[42]

Ingenuity is no longer the distinguishing characteristic; the antitheses have been diluted by words, and the matter is diffused. The language throughout the play is like this, all on the same level; everyone speaks in large, noble alexandrines, even the valet and the *suivante*.

As an example of French tragicomedy *Célie* is interesting, and somewhat superior in structure to *Fratelli rivali*. By not revealing the plot against the heroine's honor until very late, Rotrou procured new tension and suspense for the entire play. But nothing he did could justify Lancaster's comment that "It makes a distinct improvement upon the Italian original, but in spite of Rotrou's efforts, he did not succeed in turning his crude model into a masterpiece." [43] Neither play is a masterpiece, but *Fratelli rivali* is far from crude, and its

[42] See above pp. 207–8 for the original speech.
[43] *Op.cit.*, 534.

relative value is that of polychrome to monochrome—one may be more consistent, even more tasteful, but the other is richer in contrast and vitality.

According to Pietro Toldo, Rotrou may again have borrowed something from Della Porta for *L'Hypocondriaque, ou le mort amoureux*.[44] The motif of love madness in this tragicomedy, the belief of each lover that the other is dead, the parents' severity, the refusal of Cloridan to eat, because he believes himself (i.e., his *true* self, Perside) dead, and Cleonice's attempt to save his temporarily mad friend from starvation by ordering actors disguised as hungry cadavers to persuade Cloridan that eating is a proper function of the dead: all are to be found in Della Porta's *Furiosa*. Beyond this, however, there is not the slightest connection between the two plays. The plot of *L'Hypocondriaque* is derived from Doni's story of Girolamo Linaiuolo, or from some version of a similar story in the *Gesta Romanorum*. But Toldo's theory is perfectly plausible. At the time, Della Porta's comedies were available in numerous editions, and the adapter of *La sorella* and *I fratelli rivali* probably knew them all.

It was inevitable that some contact should have occurred between Della Porta, famous in his own country and known through adaptations in France, and the greatest of French comic writers, to whom the Italian theater was a lifelong interest and source of ideas. But the nature of the contact is arguable. There is no doubt that Molière borrowed parts of the Turkish scene in *Le bourgeois gentilhomme* from *La soeur* ii, 4, which is merely a translation into alexandrines of *La sorella* iii, 4, in which the valet pretends to interpret some Turkish speeches, remarking that in that language much can be said in two words. Despite Max J. Wolff's insistence on a direct debt of Molière to Della Porta,[45] there is nothing to

[44] "Les morts qui mangent," *Bulletin italien* v (1905), No. 3, Année xxxvii, 291–97.
[45] "Molière und Della Porta," *Archiv für das Studium der neueren Sprachen und Literaturen,* cxxxiv (1916), 148.

indicate that Molière took the suggestion from *La sorella;* everything he used was in Rotrou's scene. The same is true of other similarities between Molière comedies and *La sorella;* the exposition in *Les fourberies de Scapin* I, 1, 2 (used also in *Mélicerte* II, 1), is like that of *La sorella,* but even more like that of *La soeur,* I, 1, 3.[46]

The possibility of Molière's acquaintance with Della Porta's comedies *is* suggested, however, by *L'étourdi,* a veritable grab-bag of intrigues, three-fourths of them derived from Barbieri's *Inavvertito.* The similarity of the scene in which the hero tries to pass as the longlost son of his *innamorata's* guardian (IV, 1) to *Le parasite* III, 2, was noticed by Eugène Rigal [47] and interpreted by Jacques Madeleine [48] as an instance of Tristan's influence on Molière. It may well be that Molière borrowed the ruse from *Le parasite,* but he might as easily have remembered it from *Angelica,* or even from the ultimate source of both, Della Porta's *Olimpia.* In the last act (Scenes 1–4), moreover, Mascarille's representation of himself as a Swiss innkeeper and his absent master's house as an inn, a trick for which Lancaster could suggest no source,[49] is strongly reminiscent of *La tabernaria.*

It is highly probable that among the numerous Italian plays which Molière had seen or owned were some of Della Porta's, either in *commedia dell'arte scenari* or in the original ver-

---

[46] See Molière, *Oeuvres* . . . ed. Eugène Despois et Paul Mesnard, VIII (Paris, 1883), 410, note 1, and VI (1881), 171–172, note 1. Lancaster (*op.cit.,* 581) asserted that *Le Médecin malgré lui* contains echoes of *La soeur,* but did not cite specific passages. Martine's vow of vengeance (*Médecin* I, 3) is in a general way like the nurse's revenge in *Soeur,* which originates with the *balia* in *Sorella* V, 1, but a claim of Della Porta's influence in this instance would be far-fetched. The same may be said of Mélicerte's doubting of Myrtil's fidelity (I, 1), which is similar to Sulpizia's suspicions (*Sorella* I, 1), but no more so than to the corresponding scene in *Soeur.*

[47] "*L'Etourdi* de Molière et *Le Parasite* de Tristan l'Hermite," *Revue universitaire* (15 février 1893), reprinted in *De Jodelle à Molière* (Paris, 1911), 292ff.

[48] *Le parasite* . . . Introduction, xvii.

[49] *Op.cit.,* I, 107.

sions. Scraps of them perhaps remained in Molière's mind, to be used whenever the need arose. On the other hand, it cannot be proved that Molière studied Della Porta's comedies or consciously imitated them. There is little to support Wolff's theory that Molière took the name of Tartuffe from the line "Sei un tartufo" in *Astrologo* IV, 7, or that Georges Dandin's conjugal problem is a deliberate combination of Gerofilo's troubles in *La turca* and the cuckolded doctor's in *La furiosa*.[50] Every detail of the situation except for the apology Dandin makes to his wife can be found in the *Decameron* VII, 8, which Wolff admits as the principal source of the situation. The apology occurs in *La furiosa*, it is true, but to set too much store by it is pointless. That two playwrights happened to add a similar prosaic incident to a story they told in common can hardly be admitted as evidence of influence.

Although for Molière, Della Porta may have been only an occasional convenient source of *burle*, he held more substantial attractions for Tristan and Rotrou. It is proof of the variety of his work that it could provide a basis for the dry high comedy of the one and the tearful tragicomedy of the other. In the more pathetic and serious plays of Della Porta's middle period, Rotrou found semi-tragic situations which lent themselves easily to his further romanticizing. But ultimately, Della Porta's strongest appeal, to Rotrou probably as to Tristan certainly, lay in his ingenious Plautine *imbrogli* —timesavers for playwrights in search of plots. Even at its most romantic, the French mind is logical and Della Porta, the superlative plot mechanic, consistently provided his adapters with neoclassically balanced and harmonious structures.

GERMANY AND SPAIN

Through *Fratelli rivali* Della Porta's name has been linked mistakenly with other traditions of continental drama. Sanesi has persistently connected him with the German theater

[50] *Op.cit.*, 148.

through Jacob Ayrer's *Comedia von der Schönen Phaenicia*,[51] although Milano rejected this possibility.[52]

Ayrer's play, written about 1595, is based on the Bandello *novella* which inspired Ariosto, Shakespeare, and Della Porta. Albert Cohn listed it with those of Ayrer's works composed under the influence of English acting troupes in Germany,[53] and believed that both Shakespeare and Ayrer knew the Bandello story through some lost Italian dramatization of it which included comic episodes from which the Beatrice-Benedick and Johan-Anna Maria scenes might have been developed by their respective authors. Cohn was apparently not deterred from this theory by the total dissimilarity of Shakespeare's and Ayrer's comic additions, nor by the consideration that any dramatist adapting a serious *novella* as a comedy would insert comic scenes as a matter of course. If *Phaenicia* is unlike *Much Ado*, it is even less like *Fratelli rivali*. In fact, it is much closer than either (and closer than Cohn would admit) to the original Bandello *novella*, even in the characters' names.

Sanesi also directs Della Porta scholars to Spain by remarking a "certain conformity" between *Fratelli rivali* and *Los enemigos hermanos* of Guillen de Castro. In this case, however, there is not a common source or even a resemblance of plot. Written not during Castro's days of political prominence in the Kingdom of Naples, but in the last period of activity before his death in 1621, *Enemigos hermanos*[54] has all the characteristics of the nonclassical Spanish tragicomedy which was so popular in the seventeenth century. Its plot is a complicated problem in mistaken identity and se-

---

[51] *Op.cit.*, I, 435. Here Sanesi repeats the claim made in the first edition of 1911.

[52] *Op.cit.*, 392.

[53] *Shakespeare in Germany in the Sixteenth and Seventeenth Centuries* (London, 1865), lxi. This work also contains the text of the play from Ayrer's *Opus Theatricum* (Nuremberg, 1618).

[54] *Obras*, III (Madrid, 1927) Biblioteca selecta de clásicos españoles. 2ª serie.

crets of royal birth on which the throne of Spain depends, told without respect for unity of time or place in three *jornadas*. The two brothers turn out to be unrelated, and the story has nothing to do with Bandello's *novella* in any of its versions. The titles constitute the only point of resemblance between *Enemigos hermanos* and *Fratelli rivali*.

Sanesi's laudable eagerness to spread Della Porta's fame and influence resulted in a third unjustified linking, this time of *Fratelli rivali* with the anonymous Spanish comedy *La Laura*, found in manuscript in Naples and thought to be the work of a Spaniard at the Neapolitan viceregal court in the late sixteenth century.[55] Sanesi thinks that *Laura* owes its action to Della Porta and to the anonymous *Ingannati*,[56] but *Fratelli rivali* has in common with the Spanish comedy only the notion of deceit practiced by a lover to turn his rival and his beloved against one another. There are no brothers, no supposed death of the heroine, the ruses employed are quite different from that in Bandello's *novella* and in Della Porta's play. *Laura* is very Spanish in form, divided into *jornadas*, written in mixed rhymes, independent of neoclassical unities or decorum. Its atmosphere is pastoral, smacking of Montemayor and Cervantes.

Satisfying as it would be to show that Della Porta was known and imitated in Spain, it must be admitted that the influence was the other way around. *Fratelli rivali* reveals Della Porta's awareness of the contemporary fashion for the *capa y espada* drama and the Spanish tragicomedy, but there is nothing to prove that the Spanish dramatists were aware of him.

ENGLAND

Considering the significant and long-acknowledged debt which Tudor and Stuart dramatists owed to Italy, it is sur-

[55] The text can be found in A. Restori, "Appunti teatrali spagnuoli," *Studi di filologia romanza*, VII, fasc. 20 (Roma, 1898), 426ff.
[56] *Op.cit.*, I, 432.

prising that in Mary Augusta Scott's itemized account of the debt a mere ten out of the scores of Italianate comedies written during the reigns of Elizabeth I and James I could be traced to specific sources in Italian drama.[57] Only in recent years have some scholars begun to suspect in the *commedia erudita* an influence as strong as that of the *novella* and likely to justify Stephen Gosson's complaint that English playwrights "ransackt" the Italian stage to furnish their own.[58] Ariosto, Secchi, Grazzini, Oddi, and Pasqualigo attracted Elizabethan and Jacobean adapters, but none as often as Della Porta, from whom five comedies were borrowed in the early seventeenth century.

How Della Porta's plays traveled north and across the Channel remains in question. Kathleen M. Lea has shown that *commedia dell'arte* troupes were known in England from the late sixteenth century on,[59] presumably acting their usual versions of innumerable Italian plays. Della Porta's popularity with the *comici dell'arte* [60] guaranteed the place of his comedies in such repertories. Of those demonstrably used by English adapters—*Sorella, Astrologo, Trappolaria, Fratelli rivali,* and *Cintia*—the first three are contained *in scenario* in the Correr Collection [61] and the fourth in the Locatelli Collec-

---

[57] *Elizabethan Translations from the Italian* (Boston, 1916).

[58] *Playes Confuted in Five Actions* (London, [1582]), D42verso. See David Orr, *The Influence of Italian Drama of the Sixteenth Century on English Drama before 1623.* Unpublished Doctoral Dissertation (University of North Carolina, 1960, Library of Congress Microfilm 60–4853) for an examination of English dramas proved to be influenced by the *commedia erudita*, and for a lucid statement of the traditional view of the Italian drama as without significant influence in England.

[59] *Italian Popular Comedy. A Study in the commedia dell'arte 1560–1620 with Special Reference to the English Stage,* II (Oxford, 1934), 352ff. John A. Lester reported mention of Italian *histriones* in Scotland as early as 1514 "Italian Actors in Scotland," *Modern Language Notes,* XXIII (1908), 240–42.

[60] See Appendix B for further discussion.

[61] See Vittorio Rossi, "Una commedia di G. B. della Porta ed uno nuovo scenario," *Rendiconti del R. Istituto Lombardo,* 2ª ser., XXIX, fasc. 16 (1896), 881–895; and Tina Beltrame, "Gli scenari del Museo Correr," *Giornale storico della letteratura italiana,* LXXXXVII, fasc. 1–2 (1931), 1–48.

tion.[62] Although the collections themselves postdate the English adaptations of Della Porta's comedies, the individual scenarios had certainly been in use for some time in Italy and, conceivably, in England as well. The *scenari* are so very sketchy, however, containing no dialogue, and only an outline of the action, redistributed over three acts, as compared to the five prescribed for written comedy, that they can hardly have been the link between Della Porta's comedies and their English versions, all but one of which follow the original five-act pattern and, to varying degrees, reproduce in detail the scenes and dialogues of their sources.

But of course the *comici dell'arte* did not limit themselves to improvisation from scenarios. Their repertories included full-length *commedie erudite*, which they performed as written, or with minor changes. Fornaris' *Angelica*, as played by the Confidenti on tour in France, is an illustration: except for modifications in two of the characters, it is a fairly close paraphrase of *Olimpia*.[63] If it was in this sort that traveling companies played Della Porta's comedies in England, and if the future adapters saw, understood, and took detailed notes on the performances, then the *comici dell'arte* must be credited with effecting the liaisons. Otherwise, it is more likely that Della Porta reached his adapters in print. Each adaptation appeared only after its source had become available in at least one edition. The case for derivation from printed texts is made stronger by the first four English versions' being made in the learned atmosphere of Cambridge University, where Italian drama had been in vogue for several decades.[64]

The first of the five "English" adaptations is, like the next two, in Latin. It is the work of Walter Hawkesworth, an indistinct but attractive figure, fellow of Trinity, amateur actor and playwright, who left Trinity in 1605 for a brief

[62] See "Carletta" [pseudonym of A. Valeri], "Gli scenari di Basilio Locatelli," *Nuova Rassegna* II (Roma, 15 sett. 1894), 441–56.

[63] See above, p. 263.

[64] See G. C. Moore Smith, *College Plays Performed in the University of Cambridge* (Cambridge, 1923).

political employment which ended in his early death abroad the following year.[65] At about the turn of the century he provided his fellow players at Trinity with two Latin comedies, *Leander* and *Labyrinthus*. The first of these was declared in 1914 by F. S. Boas probably to be a Latin adaptation of Della Porta's *Fantesca*,[66] which error has been repeated parrot-fashion more than once since then, even after J. M. Lothian proved in 1930 that *Leander* was borrowed from Oddi's *Erofilomachia*.[67] To search for the source of *Leander* among Della Porta's comedies was a natural mistake, however, for its companion piece, *Labyrinthus*, is a verse translation of *Cintia*.

Although there is no question that *Labyrinthus* is the earliest known case of English plagiarism of Della Porta, its exact date has not been established. In the St. John's College Ms. I.8, which contains both comedies, *Leander* is dated 1599 [Circumcision Style], because of which, presumably, George B. Churchill and Wolfgang Keller,[68] Miss Scott,[69] Felix Schelling,[70] and Hugh G. Dick [71] assign the same date to *Labyrinthus*. An allusion in the text (v, 5) to the marriage "heri" of Leander and Flaminia suggests that the two comedies were presented on consecutive nights. It is likely, however, that this manuscript is a copy made for the revival at Trinity in 1602/3, as was probably the Trinity College Ms. R.3.9, in which *Leander* is labeled *"Acta est secundo A.D. 1602* [Annunciation Style] . . . *ut primo acta est A.D. 1598*

[65] *Dictionary of National Biography*, ed. Leslie Stephen and Sidney Lee, IX (London, 1908), 205.

[66] *University Drama in the Tudor Age* (Oxford, 1914), 317.

[67] "Sforza d'Oddi's 'Erofilomachia'—The Source of Hawkesworth's 'Leander,'" *Modern Language Review*, XXV (July), 338–41.

[68] "Die lateinischen Universitäts-Dramen Englands in der Zeit der Königen Elisabeth . . . ," *Jahrbuch der Deutschen Shakespeare-Gesellschaft*, XXXIV (1898), 309.

[69] *Op.cit.*, 211.

[70] *Foreign Influences in Elizabethan Plays* (New York, 1923), 73.

[71] Thomas Tomkis, *Albumazar: a Comedy (1615* . . . edited by Hugh G. Dick, Berkeley, 1944), 54, note 6.

[A.S.]." Both manuscripts may be even later copies, but since in the Trinity manuscript, as well as in a third manuscript (Cambridge University Library Ms. Ee.5.16), Hawkesworth himself is on the actor-list of *Labyrinthus*, the performance it refers to cannot have been later than 1606. With some misgivings, E. K. Chambers has dated *Labyrinthus* between 1602 and 1606,[72] and Alfred Harbage echoes the guess as fact.[73]

If the choice of dates is between 1598/99 and 1602/3, the latter seems more likely for the Latin comedy's debut, if only because its Italian source was not printed till 1601. Admittedly, however, Hawkesworth could have known *Cintia* in manuscript; it had been completed by 1591. In either case, *Labyrinthus* corresponds so nearly to its source as to force the conclusion that whether or not Hawkesworth had seen a performance of *La Cintia*, he must have worked from the text, making minor changes. Florence replaces Naples as a setting, two characters are slightly expanded, and a few scenes are added to link *Labyrinthus* with *Leander*. The characters are re-christened in Latin, except for the braggart, who becomes "Don Piedro Pacheco D'Alcantara" and spouts a mixture of Latin and Spanish, but says little more than the nameless *Capitano* of *Cintia*. This modification might have been inspired by the Spanish braggart in *Fantesca*. Obviously, Hawkesworth knew more than one of Della Porta's plays. His reference to "Il cavaliere Marte bellonio di Mantua" (I, 7) as a celebrated braggart, suggests acquaintance with Capt. Martebellonio of *Fratelli rivali*, published in the same year and city as *Cintia*.

Rather incongruously, Hawkesworth discarded *Cintia*'s

---

[72] *The Elizabethan Stage* (Oxford, 1923), III, 337.

[73] *Annals of English Drama 975–1700* (Philadelphia, 1949), 72–73. Inconclusive but persuasive evidence in support of the 1602/3 date is provided by an inscription in a seventeenth-century hand and ink on the title-page of the Cambridge University Library copy of the first edition of *Labyrinthus* (Londini, 1636): "Exhibita est haec comoedia in Col. Sᵃ. Trinit. anno 1602. . . ."

Christian frame of reference, making his characters swear by Roman gods and worship in a temple instead of a church (IV, 3), but he preserved and even heightened the color of Counter-Reformation didacticism which Della Porta cast over even his early comedies. In *Cintia* the nurse refuses to answer Lidia's half-reluctant pleas to be saved from rape (III, 6); in *Labyrinthus* she is prevented from answering (III, 7). And lest the audience remain in doubt of his moral intentions, Hawkesworth tried to justify the action in the play in an original *envoi:*

Spectatores, Labyrinthus hic noster quantos errores habuit,/ Honestas fraudes, amoris furta licita, nemo sibi unusquisque, idem, & alter alteri;/Ubi & decipere justum, & decipi amabile . . .[74]   (V, 8)

Labyrinthus was so successful at Trinity that it was revived for the Bachelors' Commencement attended by King James in 1622, and, in commemoration of this occasion, was printed in London in 1636. But it owed little of its success to Hawkesworth; despite a few alterations, *Labyrinthus* is, after all, merely *Cintia* in a toga.[75] But as the first adaptation of Della Porta's work in England, it is significant, for it seems to have established a precedent.

The next English adapter of Della Porta was not only a Trinity man like Hawkesworth, but eventually became Master of the college. At other stages of his career, Samuel Brooke was chaplain to Prince Henry, archdeacon of Coventry, and presiding clergyman at the clandestine marriage of John and Anne Donne. He helped to promote interest in Italian drama at Cambridge with his three Latin plays: *Melanthe,* 1614/15, a pastoral in the Italian style; *Scyros,*

[74] (Spectators, however many faults our Labyrinthus had, in the honorable deceits and permissible tricks of love, it is every man for himself, and both fair to deceive and amiable to be deceived.)

[75] Perhaps some readers would agree with Mr. Orr that the somewhat more farcical tone of the adaptation is an improvement on the original (*op.cit.,* 107).

1612/13, an adaptation of Bonarelli's *Filli di Sciro;* and *Adelphe,* 1611/12, a comedy discovered by J. S. G. Bolton in 1928 to be a reworking of *La sorella.*[76] *Adelphe* was performed several times at Trinity, first between Michaelmas, 1611, and March 25, 1612. The second performance on March 2, 1613, was part of the festivities for the visit of the Elector Palatine of the Rhine and his new brother-in-law, twelve-year-old Prince Charles. There were Trinity revivals of *Adelphe* after the Restoration, in 1662 and 1669, but despite its academic popularity, the comedy was never published.[77]

La sorella was Della Porta's most often adapted comedy, perhaps because of its theme of incest, an evil which had a special piquancy for late Renaissance taste, but more certainly because its plot lends itself with equal ease to comic variations like Middleton's or to serious ones like Rotrou's. Brooke produced neither sort. He adapted *Sorella* by rearranging a good many scenes and speeches, without adding to the plot or to the characters. Searching for originality in *Adelphe,* Professor Bolton discovers the hero to be more virtuous than his prototype in *Sorella*—more virtuous, too, than an impartial reader can admit. A further claim that the adaptation reflects "high respectability and clerical interests"[78] is but slightly supported by Brooke's toning down the theme of incest and altering the character of Gulone; indeed the claim seems even to be contradicted by his omission of the final moral, spelled out by Della Porta: evil is sent that good may be derived from it.

For the most part Brooke followed Della Porta, and would have done better to follow him altogether, for all his changes are either useless or harmful. The Latin which he substitutes for Della Porta's sprightly Italian is as flat as Hawkesworth's.

[76] Samuel Brooke, *Melanthe, A Latin pastoral play of the early seventeenth century* . . . edited with a biographical introduction by Joseph S. G. Bolton (New Haven, 1928), 5, note 19.
[77] Stage-copies for the second and fourth performances are in Trinity College Library Mss. R.3.9 and R.10.4, respectively.
[78] *Op.cit.,* 50.

The modifications in length and position of scenes, speeches, and so forth, succeed only, as even Professor Bolton reluctantly admits, in blurring the outlines and dissipating the dramatic force of Della Porta's comedy.[79]

Professor Bolton tries to redeem a portion of Brooke's sins against his source by pointing to "a not unpleasing dialogue" in which "the tone of Brooke's adaptation may be seen at its best." [80] The passage in question, for which there is no equivalent in *Sorella*, is a boasting contest between Martepalvenerius, the braggart who has wrestled "ipsam mortem," (II, 11). It is indeed a very funny scene, but, alas, does credit not to Brooke's imagination but only to his taste, for he found the scene ready- (and better) made in *Fratelli rivali* (I, 4). Other details reminiscent of *Fratelli rivali* appear elsewhere. Perhaps out of reverence for royalty, Brooke chose not to translate several of the passing references in *Sorella* to crowned heads of Europe; one of the substitutions he inserted is the name of "Gherardij, comitis de Tricarico" (II, 11), probably the same Count of Tricarico proposed as a father-in-law for Don Ignazio of *Fratelli rivali*. And in rechristening the characters of *Sorella*, Brooke named one of his heroes Flaminius, perhaps after the second of the rival brothers, and one of his heroines Charitia, like the memorable Carizia Della Porta of *Fratelli rivali*. Whatever pain these discoveries might cause a Brooke fancier must be counterbalanced by the satisfaction they give to the Della Porta scholar. They provide the first proof that *Fratelli rivali* was known at Trinity or, for that matter, in England. It still remains for someone to determine whether *Adelphe* is simply a Latin translation of an embellished version of *Sorella* acted by *comici dell'arte*, or a result of Brooke's reading of Della Porta's comedies.

When King James visited Cambridge in March 1614/15, he was regaled with a sort of Italian drama festival. Brooke con-

[79] *Ibid.*, 45.
[80] *Ibid.*, 47.

tributed to it his *Melanthe,* and perhaps it was owing to his influence that two of the other offerings were borrowed from Della Porta. The king's favorite among them was *Ignoramus,* a Latin prose comedy derived from *Trappolaria* by George Ruggle, graduate of Trinity College and Fellow of Clare Hall until his death in 1622. The king liked the comedy so well, in fact, that he commanded another performance, for which he returned to Trinity.[81]

Ignoramus marks a change in Della Porta's fortunes in England. *Labyrinthus* had a single "prestige" printing, and *Adelphe* was never published at all, but *Ignoramus* went into five editions in its own century and five more in the next.[82] It became a standard school piece at Cambridge and later at Westminster.[83] Moreover, it was the only one of the Latin adaptations to pass into English and onto the popular stage. In 1622 Robert Codrington's literal translation was published [84] and Ferdinando Parkhurst's *Ignoramus, or The Academical Lawyer,* was performed at court,[85] and in 1677 Edward Ravenscroft's abridged version, *The English Lawyer,* was acted at Drury Lane.[86]

Ignoramus was the first of the English adaptations to differ

---

[81] See John Chamberlain's letter to Sir Dudley Carleton, March, 1615, reprinted by J. S. Hawkins in his edition of *Ignoramus* (George Ruggle, *Ignoramus, Comoedia; scriptore Georgio Ruggle, A. M. Aulae Clarensis, apud Cantabrigienses, olim socio; nunc denuo in lucem edita cum notis historicis vita auctoris, et subjicitur glossarium vocabula forensia dilucide exponens: accurante Johanne Sidneio Hawkins ARM.,* Londini, 1787, xxvi–xxxvi, and xli, note a); an anonymous article, "The Latin Plays acted before the University of Cambridge," *Retrospective Review,* xii, Part 1 (London, 1825) 1–42; G. C. Moore Smith, *op.cit.,* 95; and E. K. Chambers, *op.cit.,* iii, 475.

[82] Entered in Stationers' Register in 1615, first and second editions in 1630, followed by editions in 1658, 1659, 1668, 1703, 1731, 1736, 1737, 1787. See Chambers, *op.cit.,* iii, 475, for further details.

[83] George Dyer, *An English Prologue and Epilogue to the Latin Comedy of Ignoramus* . . . (London, 1797), 6.

[84] *Ignoramus: a comedy* . . . *translated into English by* R. C. (London).

[85] Harbage, *op.cit.,* 126.

[86] Published in London, 1678.

greatly from its source. Ruggle paraphrased twenty-one scenes from *Trappolaria* and more loosely imitated another sixteen, but unlike Hawkesworth or Brooke, he added something of his own: eighteen new scenes and seven characters, which turn *Ignoramus* into a satire. Once before, Ruggle had satirized the conflict between town and gown, in *Club Law*,[87] and now he did so again, aiming his attack specifically at Francis Brackyn, deputy recorder of Cambridge,[88] in whose honor Ruggle replaced the braggart soldier of *Trappolaria* with a braggart lawyer. Clad in the legal robes of Ignoramus, the bullying and cowardly *miles gloriosus* joins with another stock type of the *commedia erudita*, the pedant. He speaks a vile jumble of English and Latin: when he suffers a drenching, he demands, "rubba me cum Towallio," and when he wants to know the time, asks, "Quotu est Clocka nunc?" (I, 3). If his prose is bad, his poetry is atrocious, much like the compositions of the comic Neapolitan type represented by Della Porta's Pannuorfo, except that it is studded with technical terms: "Et dabo Fee simple si monstres Love's prety dimple,/ Farthingalos, Biggos, stomacheros, et periwiggos." (I, 5). But Ignoramus is not simply a composite of *commedia erudita* types. He is also a vehicle for anti-Puritan satire, and to make him so, Ruggle endowed him with some of the characteristics of Butler's Hudibras.[89] The combination of these varied old materials produced a new and distinctively English comic figure.

Ruggle's originality, however, is limited to the satire, and the satire is limited to the escapades of Ignoramus and his satellites. The other departures from *Trappolaria* are not exploratory: some are minor and inevitable results of the satire; others, equally minor, seem endless. All necessarily deny much of *Trappolaria*'s charm to *Ignoramus*. The char-

---

[87] See *Retrospective Review*, 29, note 22.
[88] See Van Gundy, *op.cit.*, 10ff. for an account of this town and gown quarrel.
[89] *Ibid.*, 16ff.

acter of Trappola, for example, Della Porta's *tour de force* of benevolent knavery, dwindles in the adaptation into a conventional *davos*, in order to make room for the new title character. As might be expected, the shift in emphasis throws the entire comedy off balance. Ruggle further rocked the poise of his play by making the non-comic characters more serious than Della Porta had allowed them to be. As stock types, moving with brilliantly artificial gestures, taking exaggerated poses, the lovers and parents of *Trappolaria* are both sentimental and comic. Ruggle's Antonius and Rosabella are more subdued and more earnest than Della Porta's Arsenio and Filesia, and Theodorus is not a traditional miser like silly, good-natured old Callifrone, but a heavy father of tragicomedy—proud and stern even to the point of cruelty, and by his own admission, violent in his passions (v, 7). This serious strain is not developed, however; *Ignoramus* bears no resemblance to the dark comedies of Della Porta's middle period. It arouses no *meraviglia*, neither by examples of extraordinary virtue or feeling, nor by its own extraordinary form. The exact proportions and the choreographic perfection of *Trappolaria* are lost. Instead, *Ignoramus* offers simultaneously a rather tedious love story and a boisterous satire.

But whatever its weaknesses, *Ignoramus* has a busy, heterogeneous atmosphere, compact of classical, romantic and contemporary English elements. In addition to the character of Ignoramus himself, Ruggle made two excellent additions, one which Della Porta might have liked, but would not have dared to use, and another which would probably not have occurred to him. The first is the bawdy exorcism of Ignoramus' "devils" by Cupes, a parasite, and Cola, a dissolute friar, who seize upon each of the lawyer's Latin words as if it were an evil spirit, and parody the solemn rite of casting out the powers of darkness by conjuring it to withdraw from specific parts of the victim's body (IV, 11). Here is double-edged satire on legal phraseology and on popery. It is ironic that one of Della Porta's plays, the only category of his works approved by the Inquisition, should become indirectly a vehicle for exactly the kind of blasphemous jesting which the Holy Office most abominated.

Ruggle's second conspicuous addition has nothing to do with the satire on lawyers and would, but for a difference in national temperament, have fitted nicely into *Trappolaria*. Ignoramus is warned that a fearsome character called the Sowgelder is looking for him, whereupon Cupes enters in disguise, blowing a butcher's horn and brandishing a knife (II, 8). Ignoramus flees, and throughout the rest of the play is terrified by offstage blasts from the horn. The English audience seems to have been vastly amused by this broad *burla*, but it is less in the Italian nature to laugh at such a threat.

Ignoramus had a great success, the scope of which was broadened by Codrington's translation and Ravenscroft's abridgement. The former was scrupulously faithful to the Latin comedy and even reproduced the original macaronic passages with their translations. Ravenscroft made several changes, mostly in the interest of brevity; the London public would hardly have suffered the six-hour original version of *Ignoramus*. Ravenscroft's other alterations also were dictated by popular taste. Ignoramus himself ceased to be specifically Francis Brackyn of Cambridge and became a more universal figure of the pompous lawyer, and the shady jokes were omitted in deference to lower and middle class propriety. In its economy *The English Lawyer* resembles *Trappolaria* more than *Ignoramus* does. But it, too, lacks Della Porta's disciplined fantasy. Obviously Ravenscroft did not consult *Trappolaria;* he was probably unaware of its existence. As an unacknowledged adaptation *Ignoramus* did nothing to spread Della Porta's name, but it introduced his work to a wide English audience.

The night after the debut of *Ignoramus*, King James was treated to yet another of Della Porta's comedies, the first to be adapted directly into English. This was the celebrated *Albumazar*, derived from *L'astrologo* and destined for a long life on the popular stage. It alone of the five adaptations in England has been exhaustively studied, and is available in the excellent edition of Hugh G. Dick.[90]

Professor Dick records quibbling over the authorship of *Albumazar* as late as the nineteenth century, when Henry Ingalls attributed it to Shakespeare. Today it is universally identified as the work of Thomas Tomkis of Trinity College, who wrote also for academic performance in 1607 an entirely dissimilar comedy called *Lingua: or the Combat of the Tongue and the Five Senses for Superiority.*[91] Following its first performance on March 9, 1614/15, *Albumazar* was often seen at the university, and may have reached London before the theaters were closed in 1642.[92] It was printed twice in 1615, twice again in 1634, and once in 1668, when its first authenticated public performance took place at Lincoln's Inn Fields. Among its subsequent appearances were the 1704 version by John Corey, *The Metamorphosis: or the Old Lover Out-Witted;* the American, James Ralph's adaptation, *The Astrologer,* published with a preface by Garrick in 1744; and Garrick's successful revivals of the original version in 1747, 1748, and 1773.[93] Dryden wrote a prologue to the 1668 performance, mistakenly claiming that *Albumazar* had influenced *The Alchemist.*[94] The two are similar only in theme, and there were several other plays at that time which treated of the same subject matter. Moreover, Jonson's comedy was performed as early as 1610, and there is no reason to suppose that *Albumazar* was written very long before its 1614 debut.

Tomkis' alterations of his source are not as immediately

[90] See above p. 173, note 47.

[91] Further biographical information about Tomkis is included in Professor Dick's introduction. See also Gerald P. Mander, "Thomas Tomkis," *Times Literary Supplement* (March 21, 1945), 151.

[92] Richard Brathwait, *The Honest Ghost* (London, 1658), 231, refers vaguely to "Tom Trinculo's" appearance on the "publick stage."

[93] Professor Dick traces the entire stage history of the play.

[94] *Covent Garden Drollery,* edited by G. Thorn-Drury (London, 1928), 87.

apparent as Ruggle's are, but they go deeper. Tomkis neither added nor subtracted characters and renamed only five. He changed nothing in Della Porta's story, but strengthened the structure somewhat by contracting and re-arranging scenes. But the improvements are not as great as Professor Dick would have them:

. . . his alterations show that Tomkis was conscious of the need for a swift pace in this kind of comedy. His most elaborate changes come in the last act, which he re-arranges by opening with the astrologer's betrayal by his confederates, thus foreshadowing the approaching climax in Scene v, when Pandolfo's plans go awry. By this means suspense is maintained, the climax comes late in the act, and the falling action is brief. Porta, on the other hand, places the climax early (v, ii), uses the betrayal of Albumazar as part of the falling action, and carries on for three leisurely scenes after the main source of suspense has disappeared.[95]

This particular bit of praise is misplaced. Professor Dick neglects to mention that Tomkis' fifth act contains eleven scenes exclusive of the epilogue, so that after the climax in Scene vi (not v), there are still five scenes of *Albumazar* to be got through, compared to a mere three in *Astrologo*. The suspense in Tomkis' counterplot, however, is much more effectively sustained than in Della Porta's. In *Astrologo* Cricca describes the plan out loud (iv, 9), but in *Albumazar* Lelio whispers it to Sulpitia (iv, 13), thereby keeping the secret until the audience actually witnesses the enactment of this hoax at the climax.

A sharper difference between *Albumazar* and *Astrologo* is evident in the characters and their surroundings. Despite their names, Lelio, Flavia, and all the others are Londoners, who chat, in a capricious mixture of prose, blank verse, and rhyme, of the Court, St. Paul's, the Exchange, the "university" and the East India Company. Della Porta's faint suggestion of difference between the two pairs of lovers is devel-

[95] Dick, *op.cit.*, 12–13.

oped into a strong contrast. Lelio becomes steadier and more mature than Eugenio, Flavia's timidity and helplessness are pronounced, and Sulpitia turns into such a witty and spirited creature that it is no wonder her part was prized by English actresses, among them Peg Woffington.[96]

The darling of the audiences, however, was Trincalo, Tomkis' variation on Della Porta's clownish Vignarolo. They are very like, except that the Italian oaf is merely amusing, the English one inspired. Vignarolo and his kitchen *innamorata* are simple and obscene in their wooing. Trincalo, on the other hand, has several modes of feeling and expression. Alone, he muses on his love in the homeliest terms:

I neuer see a yong wanton Filly, but say I, there goe's Armellina; nor a lusty strong Asse, but I remember my selfe, and sit downe to consider what a goodly race of Mules would inherit, if she were willing . . . (II, 1)

But he goes courting with highflown compliments on his lips and is answered as his affectations deserve:

TRINCALO
Sweete madame, I read nothing but the lines of your Ladiship's countenance, and desire onely to kisse the skirts of your garment, if you vouchsafe mee not the happinesse of your white hands . . .

ARMELLINA
Hence foole, hence. (II, 1)

There is no discouraging him; rebuffs only move him to verse:

> My heart in flames doth fry
> Of thy beauty
> While I
> Dy,
> Fy?
> And why
> Shouldst thou deny
> Me thy sweet company? (III, 8)

96 *Ibid.*, 59.

Like *Astrologo*, *Albumazar* is a satire, but with a difference in aim and intensity. Tomkis had no need to placate the Holy Office, and therefore did not assume the fierceness by which Della Porta hoped to convince the authorities of his new-found contempt for judiciary astrology. By using fewer astrological terms (possibly because he knew fewer), cutting much of the jargon and referring oftener to the gullibility of the public, Tomkis softened the satire and pointed it more decidedly at charlatanism in general. A target at which Tomkis aimed even more carefully was social climbing, for which Della Porta could spare only a couple of shots. One reason for Trincalo's dominating the play with a force impossible to his Italian original is that he is in part that figure so dear to Elizabethan and Jacobean audiences—the would-be gentleman, who rejoices in his magical transformation because he thinks it has raised him to the gentry (III, 5). Professor Dick, recognizing social climbing as "a problem of some reality in Jacobean England," [97] regards Tomkis' satire of it as without precedent in his source. But although it is undeniable that English dramatists excelled in attacking this particular folly, Della Porta provided a germ for it in *Astrologo* (III, 4; IV, 7), and in *Moro* he lightly satirized social pretensions in the person of the comic Neapolitan.

Inevitably, there are omissions to regret in *Albumazar*. Like all of Della Porta's adapters, Tomkis necessarily sacrificed the provocative prose of his source. His evocation of an English atmosphere, too, was achieved only at the cost of Della Porta's world of Neapolitan back streets. On the whole, however, *Albumazar* is a stronger play than *Astrologo* and is unquestionably superior to the three preceding adaptations.

A final look at the program arranged at Cambridge for King James in March 1614/15 yields one more hint to the Della Porta scholar. Five plays were scheduled, of which four were actually presented: *Ignoramus*, *Albumazar*, Brooke's Italianate *Melanthe*, and Edward Cecil's *Aemilia*. The latter is

[97] *Ibid.*, 14.

now lost, but we have John Chamberlain's word that it was a Latin comedy about a foolish tutor of physic.[98] This description brings to mind several Italian comedies, but especially Della Porta's *Fantesca* and *Furiosa*. Two of the four plays performed that week were adapted from his works, and the third was by another of his adapters; it is highly possible that when and if the lost manuscript of *Aemilia* is unearthed, it will prove to be one more result of the vogue Della Porta was enjoying at the university during this period.

Later performances of the adaptations kept alive the vogue, or at least its memory. Milton's references to comic stage lawyers in the *Elegia Prima* and to "Trinculos" in the *Apology for Smectymnuus* reveal that he, like most Trinity men, knew *Ignoramus* and *Albumazar*.[99]

The fifth known adaptation of Della Porta in England was the only one to reach the London stage without first graduating from Cambridge. The connection between Thomas Middleton's *No Wit, No Help Like a Woman's* and *La sorella* was not even noticed until the late nineteenth century [100] and has been very little studied since then. D. J. Gordon briefly compared the two plots in 1941,[101] and in 1944 Lucetta J. Teagarden promised readers of *Studies in Philology* an article on Middleton and Della Porta which, unfortunately, never appeared.[102]

Of all Della Porta's English adapters, Middleton is the best-known and the only professional playwright. *No Wit* is one

---

[98] Quoted by Hawkins, *op.cit.*, xxviii, xxx.

[99] See Warton's opinion that Milton knew *Ignoramus*, quoted in *Paradise Regained, The Minor Poems, and Samson Agonistes* . . . , ed. Merritt Y. Hughes (New York, 1937), 28, note 31; *Prose Selections*, ed. Merritt Y. Hughes (New York, 1947), 2d ed., 153, note 21.

[100] Stiefel, "Unbekannte italienische Quellen Jean de Rotrou's," . . . , 44–46.

[101] "Middleton's *No Wit, No Help Like a Woman's* and della Porta's *La Sorella*," *Review of English Studies*, XVII, 400–14.

[102] See Allan H. Gilbert, "The Prosperous Wittol in Giovanni Battista Modio and Thomas Middleton," *Studies in Philology*, XLI, 237, and Boughner, "Traditional Elements in Falstaff," . . . 426, note 83.

of his minor comedies, written sometime after 1610,[103] probably without a collaborator.[104] It was performed in 1613 [105]
and survives in a version made by James Shirley for performance in Dublin in 1638 and published in 1657.[106]

No Wit's appearance in London during the Della Porta
vogue at Trinity College and Clare Hall suggests some connection between Middleton and Cambridge. But Mark Eccles
has proved that Middleton matriculated at Queen's College,
Oxford, allowing, however, that he may have tried both universities.[107] Middleton's use of *Sorella* at about the time
Brooke was adapting the same comedy implies more than
coincidence, but there is nothing in the two adaptations to
link them to each other. The plots are identical in outline,
but none of Brooke's few variations on his source appear in
No Wit. Yet it cannot be concluded from this negative evidence that Middleton went directly to Della Porta, for his
play is so different from its source and Brooke's so similar
that it is not clear whether Middleton borrowed from either,
or from a version performed by some traveling troupe of
comici dell'arte. Middleton's frequent use of Italian material
in other plays—*Women Beware Women* and *The Witch*, for
example—suggest familiarity with the language.

Only half of *No Wit* comes from *Sorella*. The subplot, for
which the comedy is named, is an *imbroglio* of Middleton's

---

[103] Richard H. Barker, *Thomas Middleton* (New York, 1958), 181.

[104] Unless C. W. Stork is correct in following Fleay's suggestion and
discerning Rowley's hand in the Pickadill figure in Act ɪɪ and in Act
ɪv, Scene 2, *William Rowley his All's Lost by Lust, and a Shoemaker, a
Gentleman with an Introduction on Rowley's Place in the Drama*
(Philadelphia, 1910), 47–48. As Pickadill belongs to the subplot and is
not borrowed from Della Porta, however, the possibility of Rowley's
collaboration is irrelevant to this study.

[105] At Henslowe's Hope Theater, according to Felix Schelling,
Elizabethan Drama 1558–1642 . . . (Boston, 1908), ɪ, 496; at Lady
Elizabeth's, according to Harbage, *op.cit.*, 85.

[106] Gerald E. Bentley, *The Jacobean and Caroline Stage*, v (New
York, 1956), 1134.

[107] "Middleton's Birth and Education," *The Review of English
Studies*, vɪɪ, No. 28 (October, 1931), 6.

invention, turning on the wooing of a rich widow. It proceeds in parallel with the *Sorella* plot, both sets of characters meeting and moving together toward the denouement, but not actually involving themselves in each other's intrigues. In the main plot all the important incidents of the source are retained but transplanted from Nola to London, and longer, more unified scenes are substituted for the numerous street encounters characteristic of *commedia erudita*. Only in the resolution of the incest dilemma can the structure of *No Wit* be unfavorably compared with that of *Sorella*. Notwithstanding Professor Gordon's opinion that "Middleton cuts the knot most expeditiously,"[108] the denouement of the English play seems contrived. The saving revelation of the heroine's identity is made by a character from the subplot who has little reason for knowing the truth and none for publishing it, save that time is running short and a happy ending is due. The old nurse who performs the same function in *Sorella*, on the other hand, is in a natural position to have obtained such information, and her motive for betraying the secret is a credible desire for revenge, the cause of which has been witnessed by the audience.

Sorella is the most serious and romantic of Della Porta's comedies adapted in England. Middleton may have chosen it precisely because the mere facts of the plot provided romantic intrigue, without requiring elaboration. Left free to concentrate on humor, he avoided impassioned declarations of love or sorrow, substituting for them the steady stream of the valet Savourwit's caustic jests, which dissipate the pathos inherent in the situation. When forced to consider a serious problem, Middleton regarded only its practical aspects, allowing his characters little more than perfunctory expressions of their emotional disturbances. The question of incest, for example, is basic to the plot, and joking about it would be in the worst possible taste, so Middleton introduced it matter-of-factly, without dwelling on it as Della Porta has done.

---

[108] "Middleton's *No Wit* . . . ," 412.

The heartlessness in *No Wit* deplored by Schelling as an Italian importation [109] is, in fact, native to Middleton; Della Porta's characters, on the contrary, manifest the tenderest of Counter-Reformation sensibilities.

But if the omission of the sentimental and moral speeches rather flattens Middleton's *innamorati*, his comic characters have an individuality denied to Della Porta's glitteringly abstract marionettes. The braggart and the glutton disappear to make room for the very English caricatures of the subplot, and the *commedia erudita* figures who are allowed to remain trade their conventional foibles for eccentricities. Sir Oliver Twilight, the deceived father of the piece, for one, is fixed on the subject of grandchildren, to the point of rejoicing over his supposed daughter's pregnancy, although as far as he knows, she is neither married nor engaged. The evolution of "humors" characters from stock types, adumbrated in *Ignoramus* and *Albumazar*, is complete in *No Wit*.

Critical opinions of *No Wit* run the gamut from Schelling's phrase, "Extraordinary excellence" [110] through Barker's, "successful potboiler" [111] to Anthony Trollope's off-the-record comment:

No Wit is a bad play all round;—bad in language, bad in character, and bad in plot. And yet there is a certain activity about it that may have made it attractive on the stage to an audience devoid of all taste. The people with whom the reader in intended to sympathize are all bad;—and then there is not a single scene that is not badly told.[112]

Even if one makes all possible allowances for Victorian sensibility, Trollope's verdict is as unsatisfactory as the style in which it is couched, but neither will Schelling's or Barker's quite do. *No Wit* is, rather, a funny, well-balanced, and on

[109] *Elizabethan Drama* . . . , I, 514.

[110] *Ibid.*, II, 416.

[111] *Op.cit.*, 86.

[112] Marginal notes made in his copy of Dyce's edition of Middleton's works, March 10, 1877, now in the Folger Library.

the whole, better play than *Sorella*, which, for all its virtues, has the flavor of an experiment, one of Della Porta's first essays at injecting semi-tragic elements into the form of the neoclassical farce he had perfected. Yet *No Wit*'s superiority is not so much a result of Middleton's improving on Della Porta's material as of his wedding it to a new and amusing subplot.

Middleton's debt to Della Porta may not have ended with *No Wit*. Another of his comedies, *The Family of Love*, contains a scene, for which no source has been discovered, in which two would-be seducers of a physician's wife disguise themselves as patients, only to be foiled by the doctor and forced to swallow a massive dose of physic [113] (v, 1). Their misadventure is almost identical with that of Capitano Basilisco in *La furiosa* (IV, 5).[114] This incident in *The Family of Love* is in turn thought to have supplied Rowley with the comic subplot of *The Changeling*. N. W. Bawcutt distinguishes in it three themes, which he ascribes to separate English sources: that of the jealous husband; that of the madhouse; and that of the lovers disguised as patients.[115] But if Middleton knew *Furiosa*, which antedates the other suggested sources, he may have spared his collaborator this painful piecing-together of themes, for the three were already united in Della Porta's comedy.

It was only to be expected, as Della Porta's stock began rising among historians of English drama, that someone would attempt to link him with Shakespeare. Having noticed that in the Bandello *Novella* I, 22, usually designated as the source of *Much Ado About Nothing*, there is no parallel to the deception by means of servants' dressing in their betters' clothes, whereas such a parallel exists in *Fratelli rivali* (III, 4),

[113] *Works*, edited by Alexander Dyce (London, 1840), II.

[114] Massinger later used the same *burla* in *The Parliament of Love*, 1624.

[115] *The Changeling*, edited by N. W. Bawcutt (London, 1958), xxxvi.

D. J. Gordon has suggested that the plot may have reached Shakespeare through Della Porta.[116] Charles Tyler Prouty denies the possibility, on the grounds that *Fratelli rivali* existed only in manuscript, inaccessible to Shakespeare, until Spampanato's edition was published in 1911.[117] Because he is unaware of the various editions of *Fratelli rivali* from 1601 on, as well as of its popularity with acting companies before that, some of Professor Prouty's arguments are invalid, but his conclusion is not. Although the servants in *Fratelli rivali* discuss dressing in their masters' clothes in order to deceive Don Ignazio, they do not actually do so. In *Orlando Furioso* (v, 47–51) and in Beverley's *Ariodanto and Ieneura*, on the other hand, the same plan is really carried out. With such sources known to have been accessible to Shakespeare, it seems pointless to search for others.[118]

Any explanation of the success of Della Porta's comedies in England must begin with simple recognition of their availability. All of them were printed more than once, performed often in Italy, and carried abroad in their original versions and in scenarios by the *comici dell'arte*. In addition, each of Della Porta's adapters doubtless had particular reasons for his choice. Hawkesworth may have preferred *Cintia* because it presented so few costuming difficulties to the student actors. Ruggle found *Trappolaria* a suitable vehicle for satire. Tomkis saw the potentialities of the characters in *Astrologo*. In

[116] "*Much Ado About Nothing:* A Possible Source for the Hero-Claudio Plot," *Studies in Philology,* xxxix (1942), 279–90.

[117] *The Sources of Much Ado About Nothing: a Critical Study, together with the Text of Peter Beverley's Ariodanto and Ieneura* (New Haven, 1950), 14, note 18.

[118] See Daniel C. Boughner, "Traditional Elements in Falstaff," *Journal of English and Germanic Philology,* xliii (1944), 417–28, for a much more promising suggestion of connection between Della Porta and Shakespeare. Discussing Trasimaco of *La sorella* and Falstaff in the tradition of the stage braggart, Professor Boughner concludes, "If there is a chain of affinity reaching from Ruzzante to Falstaff, Della Porta and the *commedia dell'arte* may have forged the necessary links" (427).

general, however, Della Porta attracted English dramatists, as he was to attract French, by his ingenious mixtures of romantic intrigue and comedy. From the academic Hawkesworth to the professional Middleton, his adapters shared a practical need for sound plots and an ability to recognize good workmanship when they saw it.

Conclusion

IN VIEW of the number of secondary sources to which this study is indebted, it may seem paradoxical to say that Della Porta has been neglected. He has attracted many kinds of scholars, it is true: historians of science, collectors of curiosities, Neapolitan archivists, surveyors of Italian literature and drama, and analogue prospectors. But the inevitable result of such attraction is that Della Porta's works have been served up piecemeal or in capsules. Have his remarkable plays been denied an extended investigation because they are not readily available? If so, it is surprising that no one has undertaken a modern edition of the comedies, or at least completed Spampanato's attempt. Part of the answer lies in the general neglect of the "learned" drama of the Italian Renaissance. In the nineteenth century, especially, the *commedia erudita* was denigrated in favor of the myth of the *commedia dell'arte* which sprang from the spirit of the "people." The sudden spate of articles on Della Porta's comedy in the 1890's resulted solely from the notion that he wrote *scenari* for professional improvisation.

In recent years, however, new fashions in scholarship have directed attention to "the Counter-Renaissance," "mannerism," and "the baroque." Attempts to define and illustrate such terms have led scholars to many neglected poets and playwrights, and have brought about significant re-evaluations. While the resultant increase of interest in Della Porta is heartening, an unfortunate side effect is that the "pre-baroque" quality of his drama has been somewhat overemphasized, even before theorists of the baroque have reached an international agreement on definitions. Themes, motifs, and techniques which are "pre-baroque" to French or Italian critics may be "Renaissance manneristic" to Germans or Americans. Only after the terminology is standardized and Della Porta's place in literary history in a broader sense is established, can an exact analysis of the baroque element in his works be undertaken profitably.

Conclusion

Admittedly, his comedies are not austere imitations of classical models; they are, instead, rich in pathos, slapstick, sentiment, *commedia dell'arte* fantasy, and Counter-Reformation morality, all expressed in a prose which grows more florid from first play to last. Admittedly, too, his love of *meraviglia* moved Della Porta often to exaggerate these elements and to create with them comically monstrous effects. But love of *meraviglia* is not a uniquely baroque phenomenon. And it must be remembered that Della Porta built all his multicolored pleasure domes on the foundation of the neo-Latin *commedia erudita* and within the boundaries of his Plautine inheritance. His love of order and his education had made him profoundly a classicist. In his day, Counter-Reformation attitudes toward drama were leading to the hybrid forms and lyricism of the seventeenth century, but the original aim of Church policy had been to preserve the glories of classical form and style and, simultaneously, to elevate drama by purging it of paganism and licentiousness. Della Porta was a rare example of Counter-Reformation neoclassical theory in action. Not a reactionary, he delighted in the latest theatrical fashions—unless they violated the spirit of the classical tradition as he understood it.

The most melodramatic elements of his more serious comedies do not exceed the limits set by Plautus, whose plays also had ranged from the farcical to the moral. Even Della Porta's language, which in its progressive exuberance reflects the development of the baroque style, eschews the devices not authorized by the ancients and the early Renaissance. It avoids the pastoral, the lyric, and the farfetched conceit. In full bloom, Della Porta's style seems determined by the principles of Renaissance *copia* and of comic exaggeration dear to Plautus. If it is sometimes mildly Rabelaisian, it is never Marinistic.

The translation of Plautus which Della Porta made early in his career formed his dramaturgy. For the rest of his life he added ingredients, improved structure, deepened, but never cast aside, his Roman heritage. His comedies reflect his times,

Conclusion

and contain all manner of contemporary elements, but Della Porta was not an innovator. He felt himself linked by tradition with Menander and Plautus and wrote his comedies accordingly. Whatever new elements he brought to the tradition were intended not to destroy or subvert, but to continue it. If his comic style looked forward to the baroque, it was with many a carefully measuring backward glance at Plautus and his classical mentors, whose ghosts, he hoped, "flitted over the modern stage, rejoicing that comedy has progressed so well." He was equally well aware of a bond with the immediate past, and incorporating into his classical ideal the contributions of Ariosto, Aretino, and other Italian predecessors, Della Porta brought the *commedia erudita* to its peak.

Then, as it declined, he passed on its imperishable part. It was the essential classicism of his comedy which attracted foreign adapters. His classically firm plots and his restrained illustration of their modern flexibility encouraged dissimilar variations. He provided his French and English successors with foundations able to support tragicomedy, satire, caricature, and comedy of manners.

It is, perhaps, the fortune of Della Porta's comedy abroad that offers the richest field of investigation to students of comparative literature. There is much to be done by Italianists on Della Porta and his work at home, beginning with a full biography and a critical edition of his complete dramatic works. But it is equally important to determine his place in the history of comedy, a task made more necessary and more difficult every day by new discoveries and re-evaluations. The amount and kind of influence exerted by the *commedia erudita* outside Italy remains in question. Della Porta offers a perfect point of departure for future research along this line, for he claims the twofold value of being the best and last practitioner of an undeservedly neglected Italian genre and one of the most significant means by which it was made part of a broader international tradition.

APPENDICES · BIBLIOGRAPHY · INDEX

Dating the Plays

PUBLISHED COMEDIES IN SUGGESTED ORDER OF COMPOSITION	FIRST EDITIONS	DATES OF COMPOSITION	
		CERTAIN	SUGGESTED
1. *L'Olimpia*	1589	before 1580	ca. 1550
2. *La fantesca*	1592	revised 1581	ca. 1550
3. *La Cintia*	1601	before 1591	before 1572
4. *L'astrologo* (= *Il negromante?*)	1606	before 1591	before 1572
5. *La turca*	1606	in part 1572	1572
6. *I due fratelli simili* (= *Il pedante?*)	1614	before 1610	before 1591
7. *La trappolaria* (= *Lo spagnuolo?*)	1596		before 1591
8. *La sorella*	1604	between 1591 and 1598	between 1591 and 1598
9. *I due fratelli rivali*	1601	after 1591	before 1600
10. *Il moro*	1607	1598	1598
11. *La furiosa*	1609	between 1591 and 1603	by 1600
12. *La Chiappinaria*	1609	1600 or after	1600 or after
13. *La carbonaria*	1606	after 1591	1600 or after
14. *La tabernaria* (= *La bufalaria?*)	1616	——	before 1610

OTHER PUBLISHED PLAYS	FIRST EDITIONS	DATES OF COMPOSITION	
		CERTAIN	SUGGESTED
1. *La Penelope*, tragicomedy	1591	before 1581	before 1580
2. *Il Georgio*, sacred tragedy	1611	before 1608	1570's or 80's
3. *L'Ulisse*, tragedy	1614	1612	1612

UNPUBLISHED PLAYS	PROBABLE DATE	SOURCE OF INFORMATION
1. *Santa Dorotea*	before 1591	perhaps among sacred tragedies mentioned by Barbarito, 1591; by title, Zannetti, 1610; Chioccarelli, ca. 1646.
2. *Sant' Eugenia*	before 1591	

UNPUBLISHED PLAYS COMEDIES	PROBABLE DATE	SOURCE OF INFORMATION
1. *L'alchimista*	before 1591	Barbarito, Zannetti, Chioccarelli
2. *La notte* (also called *La pietra*)	before 1591	Barbarito, Zannetti, Chioccarelli Ghirardelli

3. *La strega* (also called *La santa*)	before 1591	Barbarito, Zannetti, Chioccarelli
4. *Il fallito*	before 1610	Zannetti, Chioccarelli
5–9. An untitled quintet of comedies on a single theme	before 1610	Zannetti, Chioccarelli
10–11. An untitled pair of comedies on a single theme	before 1610	Zannetti, Chioccarelli

OTHER UNPUBLISHED WORKS ON DRAMA	PROBABLE DATE	SOURCE OF INFORMATION
1. The works of Plautus translated	before 1591	Barbarito, Zannetti, Chioccarelli
2. Treatise on the art of comedy *Arte da comporre comedie* or *De arte componendi*	before 1610	Zannetti, Chioccarelli

SUPPOSEDLY UNPUBLISHED COMEDIES WHICH ARE PROBABLY ALTERNATE TITLES	PROBABLE DATE	SOURCE OF INFORMATION
1. *Lo spagnuolo* (= *La trapporaria?*)	before 1591	Barbarito
2. *Il negromante* (= *L'astrologo?*)	before 1591	Barbarito
3. *Il pedante* (= *I due fratelli simili*)	before 1591	Barbarito
4. *La bufalaria* (= *La tabernaria?*)	before 1610	Zannetti

SUPPOSEDLY PUBLISHED COMEDY WHICH WAS PROBABLY AN ALTERNATE TITLE		
1. *Gl'intrighi*	——	Crasso, 1666; Sarnelli, 1677

The Question of Scenari

IT IS ironic that although Della Porta's extant works have been only partially and sporadically studied, a small but intense scholarly war was at one time waged over some works which he did not write. The cryptic statement of a seventeenth-century bibliographer gave rise to the notion that Della Porta wrote *scenari* for the *commedia dell'arte*, a notion which was seriously investigated in the nineteenth century, when collections of *scenari* began to be unearthed in profusion, and which was at last quelled less than thirty years ago.

The earliest suggestion of such activity was made in 1683 by Lionardo Nicodemi, who, in augmenting the Neapolitan bibliography of Niccolò Toppi, distinguished between Della Porta's *La notte*, mentioned by Toppi, and Parabosco's comedy of the same title, adding of the former "la quale ordinariamente suole rappresentarsi all'in pröto in pubblici Teatri, ed in case private." [1] Nicodemi produced no authority for this assertion, which was next quoted verbatim by Gennaro Muzio, in the preface to his 1726 edition of Della Porta's comedies.[2] Napoli-Signorelli passed on the information [3] and Settembrini added to it the hypothesis that Della Porta's other lost comedies were "canevacci." [4] Set-

---

[1] *Addizioni copiose . . . alla Biblioteca Napoletana del Dr. Niccolo Toppi* (Napoli, 1683), 118 (which is usually performed in improvisation, in public theaters and private homes).

[2] *Delle commedie . . .* (Napoli), I, a5.

[3] *Vicende della cultura nelle Due Sicilie.* 2ª ed. napolteana (1810–1811), v, 528.

[4] *Lezioni di letteratura italiana* (Napoli, 1869–1881), II, 317.

tembrini's disciple, Carlo Tallarigo, asserted definitely that Della Porta wrote *scenari* for the *comici dell'arte*.[5]

The first challenge to this loose assertion was thrown down by Fiorentino, another disciple of Settembrini and friend of Tallarigo. Fiorentino pointed out that *La notte* was listed by Zannetti in 1610 among the works ready for the press,[6] inferring logically that it must have been a complete comedy, because *scenari* were not dignified by publication. Fiorentino also scouted the idea that Della Porta wrote any other *scenari* and pointed to references in several of his prologues to the social position of his actors and audiences as proof that all of the comedies were originally intended for private performance by amateurs, not by professionals capable of improvisation.[7]

The opposing view was now earnestly espoused by Michele Scherillo, who resurrected Andrea Perrucci's *Dell'arte rappresentativa premeditata e all'improviso*, for "proof" that Della Porta wrote *scenari*. In discussing comedy *"del Soggetto all'improviso,"* Perrucci declared, *"porterò l'esempio d'un Autore in ciò classico, che sarà la Trapolaria di Gio:Battista della Porta Napolitano"* [8] and reproduced in full a three-act *scenario* in which the sketchily indicated action follows that of Della Porta's *Trappolaria* with the omission of two characters and the substitution of more modern *commedia dell'arte* names (Trappola becomes Coviello, for example).[9] On the basis of this, Scherillo decided that Della Porta developed the *scenario* from *Pseudolus* and later augmented it into his five-act *commedia erudita*.[10] The evi-

---

[5] *Nuova crestomazia italiana per le scuole secondarie* (Napoli, 1884), II, 235.

[6] "Del teatro di Giovan Battista de la Porta," *Studi e ritratti della Rinascenza* (Bari, 1911), 328, reprinted from *Giornale napoletano di filosofia e lettere, scienze morali e politiche*, Nuova serie, Anno II, vol. III, fasc. 7 (marzo, 1880). Fiorentino did not mention that Barbarito had listed *La notte* in 1591 among the comedies of Della Porta which he hoped to publish (*Penelope* dedication).

[7] *Ibid.*, 329.

[8] (Of comedy improvised on a plot . . . I shall print the example of an author classic in that, the *Trapolaria* of the Neapolitan Gio:Battista della Porta)

[9] Napoli, 1699, 353-62.

[10] *La commedia dell'arte in Italia, studi e profili* (Torino, 1884), 121.

dence points to a contrary order. The exposition is indicated as follows:

> Tartaglia e Fedelindo vengono discorrendo di volerlo inviare a Barcellona per prendere la matrigna, il fratello e la cognata, facendo il racconto dell'argomento della commedia de' *Due figli simili* . . . ,[11]

of which Scherillo commented that Della Porta had cleverly tacked the ending of a contemporary comedy onto the action of *Pseudolus*. Scherillo did not identify the comedy, and Allacci listed no play of this title. It is mentioned in a manner which suggested that it was in the repertory of the company for which the *Trappolaria scenario* was prepared. Perhaps it refers to *Menaechmi*, perhaps to a lost Italian or Spanish comedy, or perhaps to Della Porta's own *Due fratelli simili*, also called *I Simili*. The exposition of the latter could easily be fitted into the action of *Trappolaria*, and if the company was already familiar with *Fratelli simili*, they would certainly have used it, or any part of it, freely. In any case, the *scenario* seems to have been extracted from the play or plays, not *vice versa*, as Scherillo insisted.

Croce accepted Scherillo's view of the *Trapolaria canevaccio*, and despite Fiorentino's strong argument to the contrary, continued to regard the missing *La notte* as a *scenario* also.[12] Meanwhile Albino Zenatti's discovery of a manuscript containing one hundred *commedia dell'arte scenari* in the Biblioteca Corsiniana in 1885 brought to light a new pair, *I due fratelli rivali* and *La trappolaria*. But on examination, these *scenari* were found to have nothing whatever to do with Della Porta's comedies of the same titles.[13] The next discovery was made in 1890 and in the Biblioteca Casanatense, where "Carletta" (the pen-name of A. Valeri) turned up 103 new *scenari* among them six with titles suggesting connections with Della Porta: *I due fratelli rivali, I due fratelli simili, La fantesca, La trappoleria, La turchetta,* and *La tavernaria*. But by establishing that all of these *scenari* had been extracted from complete comedies and written down between

---

[11] (Tartaglia and Fedelindo come on discussing [Tartaglia's] wish to send him to Barcelona to fetch his stepmother, his brother and his sister-in-law, recounting the plot of the comedy of *Due figli simili* . . .)

[12] *I teatri di Napoli: secolo XV-XVIII* (Napoli, 1891), 79.

[13] Francesco De Simone-Brouwer, "Due scenari inediti del secolo XVII," *Giornale storico della letteratura italiana*, XVIII (1891), fasc. 3, 277–90.

1618 and 1622 by one Basilio Locatello or Locatelli,[14] "Carletta" considerably weakened the case for Della Porta's having had a hand in the adaptation of his comedies for the *commedia dell'arte*.

A systematic denial of the possibility was undertaken next by Vittorio Rossi after he had unearthed in 1895 fifty-one more *scenari* in the Correr Collection at Venice. Rossi declared that Perrucci's phrase "in ciò classico" was ambiguous and could mean that Della Porta's *commedie erudite* were a standard source for *commedia dell'arte* plots, but not that Della Porta himself ever wrote *scenari*. The *scenari* of the Correr Collection obviously represent the repertory of a theatrical company and were written down in the first half of the seventeenth century. Rossi analyzed one of them, *L'astrologo del Porta*, showing that the *scenario* depends upon anterior knowledge of the complete *Astrologo* and that some parts of the action are carelessly transposed in the *scenario*, all of which leads inescapably to the conclusion that the comedy antedated the *scenario*.[15] Scherillo was unable to answer Rossi's arguments but still maintained that Della Porta had written some *scenari*.[16]

The matter rested there for a time, but Milano touched on it again a few years later, admitting that other scholars had cast strong doubt on the possibility, but declaring himself inclined to believe in it, basing his belief on Fabrizio de Fornaris' statement that he wrote *Angelica* on a *scenario* given him by a Neapolitan gentleman,[17] and perhaps also on Francesco Bartoli's unsupported assertions that Fornaris constructed the play on a mere sketch.[18]

[14] "Gli scenari di Basilio Locatelli," *Nuova rassegna*, II (Roma, 1894, 15 settembre), 441–56.

[15] "Una commedia di G. B. della Porta ed uno nuovo scenario," *Rendiconti del R. Istituto Lombardo*, Serie II, XXIX, fasc. 16 (1896), 881–95.

[16] Review of "V. Rossi. Una commedia di G. B. della Porta . . . ," *Rassegna critica di letteratura italiana*, I (1896), 140–43.

[17] "Le commedie di Givanbattista della Porta," *Studi di letteratura italiana*, II, fasc. 2 (Napoli, 1900), 319.

[18] *Notizie istoriche de' comici italiani che fiorirono intorno all anno MDL fino a' giorni presenti: opera ricercata raccolta ed estesa da Francesco Bartoli* . . . (Padova, 1781), I, 230, quoted in A. L. Stiefel, "Tristan L'Hermites *Le Parasite* und seine Quelle," *Archiv für das Studium der neueren Sprachen und Literaturen*, LXXXVI (1891), 50, note 11.

No one contradicted Milano, but someone should have done so, for his argument collapses when Fornaris' actual words are examined:

> . . . essendo in Venetia gl' anni adietro mi fu da un gentil-homo Napolitano virtuosissimo spirto, donata questa comedia, laquale essendo da me vista, & in qualche parte imbellita, ò fiorita, per quanto con la Comica prattica sapevo introducendo il Capitano Coccodrillo cō alcune sue rodamōtate; me disposi cō questa dico comparirle davante.[19]

Moreover, *Angelica* is much too close a paraphrase of *Olimpia* for Fornaris to have worked from anything less than the complete comedy.

Despite Milano, "Carletta" and Rossi had fairly triumphed. Their arguments were convincing and later discoveries of still more *scenari* offered further support. Croce turned up 183 Neapolitan *scenari* in 1897 and De Simone-Brouwer another 48 in 1901; both surrendered their former opinions and agreed that Della Porta probably did not write scenari.[20]

The final word belonged to Tina Beltrame, who developed Rossi's theory in a pair of definitive articles. Studying the various collections of *scenari* brought to light by her predecessors, she counted five different reductions of Della Porta's *Trappolaria*: Perrucci's, Locatelli's, one in the Correr Mss., and two in Croce's *Zibaldone napoletano*. Among other things, she ascertained that *Olimpia* was adapted as *Il finto schiavo* [21] and that *La furiosa* and *La finta sorella* of the Correr Mss. are *scenari* of Della Porta's *Furiosa* and *Sorella*, respectively, the latter joined with the resolution from Groto's *Emilia*.[22] Although he himself wrote no

---

[19] *Angelica* (Paris, 1585), dedication (being in Venice a few years ago, this comedy was given me by a most gifted Neapolitan gentleman, and when I had seen it and here and there, embellished or adorned it, inasmuch as my stage experience enabled me, introducing Captain Coccodrillo with some of his rodamontades; with this I was disposed to appear before you).

[20] Croce, "Una nuova raccolta di scenarii," *Giornale storico della letteratura italiana*, XXIX, fasc. 85 (1897), 211–15; De Simone-Brouwer, "Ancora una raccolta di scenari," *Rendiconti della R. Accademia dei Lincei. Classe di scienze morali* . . . Serie 5, X, fasc. 11–12 (1901), 391–407.

[21] "Giovanni Battista Della Porta e la *commedia dell'arte*," *Giornale storico della letteratura italiana*, CI, fasc. 3 (1933), 278.

[22] Gli scenari del Museo Correr," *Giornale storico della letteratura italiana*, LXXXXVII, fasc. 1–2 (1931), 1–48.

scenari, Della Porta was apparently a treasure trove for those who did. Possibly all of his comedies were played in this form on the popular stage. Professor Beltrame's general conclusion is that Della Porta was exceptionally popular with the *comici dell'arte*. She offers no explanation, but one is near at hand. The *mestieranti* had their characters ready made, but they needed plots, and Della Porta's were beautiful pieces of machinery. Moreover, he had himself borrowed something of the *commedia dell'arte* masks to add humor to the stock characters he inherited from Latin and earlier Renaissance comedy; the results were made to order for *comici*. The broadest but perhaps most cogent reason for Della Porta's appeal was that his comedies were dependably good theater—to the professionals, this is the *summum bonum*.

Translations of Long Passages

TURCA (180–83)

DERGUT. Wretched me, for I have to die.

BOJA. Brother, whom have you seen who doesn't have to die? He who doesn't want to die shouldn't bother to be born: death is common to all.

DERGUT. I shall die before my time.

BOJA. Nobody dies before his time, or after, but each in his own time; and for each there is a determined time, which can't be avoided: and if this weren't your time, you would not be dying.

DERGUT. I mean to say that I am dying young.

BOJA. Who told you that you were supposed to die old? Haven't you seen children die before they were born, and others at birth, and others in youth; and despite the long time you've lived, when it comes to dying, it seems to you that you've lived only a short while.

DERGUT. I am dying against my will.

BOJA. In this you're not alone, for everyone dies against his will, because nobody would want to die; and even if you had lived five hundred years, when it came time to die, you would still die against your will.

DERGUT. I say that I am dying by force.

BOJA. In this case there's a remedy: die willingly, for thus you will not die by force. You know certainly that you must die and won't be able to escape: if you die by force, you'll feel two pains, one of dying, the other of dying by force; therefore, in order to have less pain, die willingly, for anything, no matter how difficult, always becomes easy, if done willingly.

DERGUT. And the worst of it is that I die infamous and dishonored.

BOJA. Man feels honor and infamy while he lives: but after you're dead, no one will come to the other world to reproach you for being hanged.

DERGUT. How harsh and bitter it is to die by hanging!

BOJA. Tell me, have you been hanged before?

DERGUT. Not I.

BOJA. Then how do you know that it's harsh and bitter to die by hanging? or perhaps some hanged man has risen from the dead and told you so? With your imagination you are making death more horrible and frightening to yourself. Don't you know about that German who had himself hanged for conversation's sake? I promise to let you feel little or no pain in dying. I'll make you die before you know it; in fact, you'll be dead and it will seem as if you were still alive: and when I've hanged you, if it isn't like that, I want you to hang me. Under your noose I'll put a little cord which, being very thin, makes a tight knot and will strangle you without your feeling it: it will seem like a flea biting your neck: I'll jump on your shoulders as lightly as a deer: you may be sure that as you are rich and deserving of it, I shall give you many caresses.

DERGUT. A hangman's caresses; oh, what a loving executioner!

BOJA. If, after death, you remain with your eyes open, bulging, and squinting: if your tongue hangs out, and if one eye looks at heaven and the other at earth, I'll close them for you and I'll shut your mouth; if you drool, I'll dry you, and I'll make you look the most beautiful hanged corpse that ever was.

DERGUT. I die at the hands of the basest man on earth.

BOJA. On the contrary, of the greatest man on earth. I kill lords, princes, and kings, without being punished; moreover, I'm paid for doing it: I have free dominion over all: I am allowed to lower the proudest heads on earth, and to tread on the necks of the greatest men: I have yoked the Romans, who have put under their yoke all the nations of the universe: I am allowed to spur on, using as stirrups the shoulders of valorous men: I dispense crowns, and like a counselor, I am master of the wheel [*ruota* referred also to a special tribunal]; and when I seat myself in that tribunal, I am terrifying to all. I ride in triumph on the tumbrils, and in my triumph, the public, with enormous din and in great numbers, lines my path: along the route, I have soldiers and policemen about me to make way for me: on the tumbril are naked men chained around me, and I with regal majesty and hangman-ish dignity, cut off hands, saw arms, and with hot pincers burn whichever limbs I choose: and if other lords have jurisdiction over the property of their vassals, I am master of their bodies and limbs, for I cut, break, hang, and quarter as I please. Do these privileges of mine seem slight to you?

DERGUT. Oh, what strange consolations!

BOJA. Brother, the thought of death is more painful than death itself: the least painful death is a quick one; and therefore, so that you'll feel little pain, have yourself hanged right away. One should accept the moment when it is offered: since you have this opportunity to be hanged, take advantage of it quickly, and to do you a favor, I'll finish you off immediately.

FRATELLI RIVALI (209–11)

MARTEBELLONIO. I'm going to tell you about the battle I had with Death. . . . Know that Death was alive at first, and it was her job to kill people with a scythe: happening to be in Mauritania, I was on close terms with Atlas, who, being oppressed by the weight of the world, was ill-treated by her: because I can't stand to see unfair advantage taken, I transferred the world from his shoulders to mine . . . finally I put it on these three fingers and supported it like a melon.

LECCARDO. When you supported the world, where were you —out of the world or in it?

MARTEBELLONIO. In the world.

LECCARDO. And if you were in it, how did you hold it from outside?

MARTEBELLONIO. I meant to say I was outside it.

LECCARDO. And if you were outside, were you in another world, and not in this one?

MARTEBELLONIO. Oh, wretch, I was where Atlas was when he held the world.

LECCARDO. All right, all right, continue with the fight.

MARTEBELLONIO. Milady Death, feeling affronted because I had aided her enemy, glared at me with a rather lowering and harsh expression, and mocked me with scornful words. I challenged her to mortal combat: she accepted the invitation, and because she had the choice of arms, she wanted to play ball for our lives. . . . For our playing field we designated the whole world: she went to the orient, I to the occident.

LECCARDO. You chose the worse place, for the sun was in your eyes: and besides, that word occident is a bad omen that you would be killed.

MARTEBELLONIO. Your job is the kitchen, and you can hardly tell when the meat is well boiled; what do I fear the Sun? . . . The ball was the Mountain of Mauritania: I had the first turn: I struck that mountain so furiously that it went so high it reached the sphere of Mars, who didn't let it fall back to earth, as a sign of his son's valor.

LECCARDO. Thus you deprived the world of that mountain. But the one that is there now—what mountain is that?

MARTEBELLONIO. Oh, you are irritating! Listen, if you want; if not, go and hang yourself.

LECCARDO. I'll listen.

MARTEBELLONIO. She said she had won the game, since the ball was swallowed up; I took her by the throat with two fingers, and I killed her like a quail, so that she is no longer alive, and I am left in her job. . . .

LECCARDO. But I'm going to tell you about a battle I had with Hunger. . . . Hunger was a live person, lean and thin, who barely had bones and skin; and she used to go about with famine, plague, and war, and she killed more people than the swords did. We challenged each other: the field was a lake of fat broth, in which swam capons, chickens, suckling pigs, calves, and whole beeves: into this we plunged to fight with our teeth: before she ate one calf, I gulped down two beeves, and everything which remained; and because I was still hungry and had nothing left to eat, I ate her; thus there was no more hunger in the world and I am her lieutenant, and have two hungers in me, hers and mine. Now let's eat immediately, or I'll eat you whole. God save you from my maw.

MARTEBELLONIO. You're a big liar.

MORO (217–18)

ORIANA. I shall weep, I shall pray, I shall throw myself at his feet, I shall forget myself, I shall suffer any indignity, provided that I remain Pirro's wife. And what worse thing could happen to me in my life than not to be Pirro's wife? Oh, what a cruel battle—should I obey my father or my husband? I stand between two deaths and do not know which to choose. If I obey my father, I shall marry the Governor's son, but that will be against my wishes and my love, which forces me, threatens me, and wants me to be wife to Pirro, who is my eyes and my heart. Shall I therefore obey my father? Oh, treacherous wife. Shall I obey my husband? Oh, unloving daughter: whom, then, must I obey, wife and daughter? Alas, Pirro, unhappy husband of an unhappy wife. Obeying my father, I shall bind myself to a man I hate and shall hate all my life; and love terrifies me with threats of horrible hatreds and cruel deaths. Obeying love, I fail in duty to my father, whom I should obey more than any man on earth: I shall be called an unloving and indiscreet daughter, I shall earn his hatred and that of my relatives and everyone else. I shall be pointed out among a thousand other women: what then must I do. If I flee one death, I run into another. Which of the two shall I choose. It is better to disobey my father, and obey love: dying, I shall feel less pain: I shall at least die satisfied with my love, nor shall I be the first, or the second who has sacrificed all for love; I shall have many companions. Alas, foolish wish, alas empty choice. Then, to follow a disordered appetite for love, I must disobey my father? that my evil may be preserved as a justifying precedent among the dishonorable and unchaste examples of other women? There is no excuse for a freely chosen sin. Therefore, one must die and obey one's father. Dying, I shall at least have the satisfaction of having obeyed my father: I shall be praised as an honorable daughter of good repute. Alas, if I do that, how am I acting toward Pirro, who has loved me so affectionately and for me now suffers long exile, far from the comforts of his home, and perhaps in wretched slavery; and should a man of such worth and valor be so little esteemed? Is this the reward of his love? of his valor? of his exile? Alas, one should rather die and keep faith with him; if we poor women cannot rival men in arms and strength, let us at least vie with them in constancy and faith.

BALIA. Be still, here comes your father.

ORIANA. This man, my father! This is my worst enemy: He seeks to take me from my husband, and give me to another. But in what words can I answer him that will not be rage and despair: for I can speak nothing but rage and despair, being myself all rage and despair . . .

Bibliography

This bibliography is limited to those works which have contributed to this study, have been mentioned in it, or are not to be found in other bibliographies. For additional material toward a general Della Porta bibliography, and for descriptions of Della Porta manuscripts, authentic and doubtful, see Gabrieli, "Bibliografia lincea," and Ferguson, *Bibliotheca chemica*, listed below in the general bibliography.

I. DELLA PORTA'S PUBLISHED WORKS

A. First editions of Della Porta's nondramatic works in chronological order.

Magiae naturalis sive de miraculis rerum naturalium libri IV. Jo. Baptista Porta Neapolitano auctore. Neapoli, 1558.

De furtivis literarum notis, vulgo de ziferis libri IIII. J. B. P. Neap. autore. Neapoli, 1563.

L'arte del ricordare, del signor Gio. Battista Della Porta Napolitano. Napoli, 1566.

Phytognomonica Jo. Baptistae Portae Neap. octo libris contenta. In quibus nove, facillimaque affertus methodus, qua plantarum, animalum, metallorum, rerum denique omnium ex prima extimae faciei inspectione quivis abditas vires assequatur. Accedunt ad haec confirmanda infinita propemodum selectiora secreta, summo labore, temporis dispendio, et impensarum iactura vestigata, explorataque. Neapoli, 1588. (The first edition appeared in 1583.)

Jo. Baptistae Portae Neapol. suae Villae Pomarium. Neapoli, 1583.

Baptistae Portae Neap., suae Villae Olivetum sive liber sextus. Neapoli, 1584.

Jo. Baptistae Portae Neapolitani De humana physiognomonia libri IIII. Vici Aequensis, 1586.

Jo. Bapt. Portae Neapolitani Magiae naturalis libri XX, ab ipso authore expurgati, et superaucti, in quibus scientiarum naturalium divitiae, et delitiae demonstrantur. Neapoli, 1589.

Villae Jo. B. P. Neapolitani libri XII: 1, Domus; 2, Sylva caedua; 3, Sylva glandaria; 4, Cultus et insitio; 5, Pomarium; 6, Olivetum; 7, Vinea; 8, Arbustum; 9, Hortus cornarius; 10, Hortus olitorius; 11, Seges; 12, Pratum. Francofurti, 1592.

Bibliography

J. B. P. Neap. De refractione, optices parte, libri novem. Neapoli, 1593.

Coelestis physiognomoniae libri sex Joan. Baptistae Portae Neapolitani. Unde quis facile ex humani vultus extima inspectione, poterit ex coniectura futura praesagire. In quibus etiam astrologia refellitur, et inanis et imaginaria demonstratur. Neapoli, 1603. (The first edition appeared in 1601.)

Jo. Bapt. Portae Neapol. Pneumaticorum libri tres. Quibus accesserunt curvilineorum elementarum libri duo. Neapoli, 1601.

Claudi Ptolomaei magnae constructionis liber primus. Cum Theonis Alexandrini commentariis. Jo. Baptista Porta Neap. interprete. Neapoli, 1605.

Jo. Ba. Portae Neap. De munitione libri III. Neapoli, 1608.

Jo. Bap. Portae Neapolitani De distillatione libri IX. Quibus certamethodo, multiplicique artificio, penitioribus naturae arcanis detectis, cuiuslibet mixti in propria elementa resolutio perfecte docetur. Romae, 1608.

Jo. Baptistae Portae Napolitani Elementorum curvilineorum libri tres. In quibus altera geometriae parte restituta, agitur de circuli quadratura. Romae, 1610.

Jo. Baptistae Portae Neapolitani De aëris transmutationibus libri IV. In quo opere diligenter pertractur de ijs, quae, vel ex aëre, vel in aëre oriuntur. Romae, 1610.

Della chirofisonomia overo di quella parte della humana fisonomia, che si appartiene alla mano libri due del signor Gio: Battista Della Porta Napolitano tradotti da un manoscritto latino dal signor Pompeo Sarnelli doctor dell'una, e l'altra legge, Contro i chiromanti impostori, che con vane osservationi havevano sporcato questa scienza, la quale si mostra fondata sopra naturali congetture. Napoli, 1677.

Paparelli, Gioacchino (ed.). "Giovanbattista della Porta. i) *Della Taumatologia.* ii) *Liber medicus*," *Rivista di storia delle scienze mediche e naturali,* XLVII (Firenze, 1956), 2–47. (The first ten pages are Paparelli's introduction; the rest is from the Della Porta Ms. 169 of the Montpellier Medical School Library.)

Ronchi, Vasco, and Maria Amalia Naldoni (eds.). *De telescopio.* Firenze, 1962. (An edition with introduction of the treatise discovered in Linceo Ms. 14, also published in installments in *Atti della Fondazione Giorgio Ronchi,* 1961, 297, 316, 324, 431, 574.)

Bibliography

B. All reported editions of Della Porta's dramatic works in alphabetical order.

(An asterisk indicates an edition which I have examined; a question mark indicates a doubtful edition.)

SELECTED WORKS

* *Comedie . . . La Trappolaria, L'Olimpia, e La fantesca.* Vinegia, 1597. (Reprintings of the first editions with a new title-page added.)
* Muzio, Gennaro (ed.). *Delle commedie di Giovanbattista de la Porta Napolitano.* 4 vols. Napoli, 1726. (All fourteen comedies.)
* Spampanato, Vincenzo (ed.). *Giambattista Della Porta. Le commedie.* 2 vols. Bari, 1910–1911. (*La sorella, La carbonaria, La fantesca, La tabernaria, L'Olimpia, La Cintia, I due fratelli rivali, L'astrologo.*)

INDIVIDUAL WORKS

L'astrologo, commedia. Venetia, 1606 *; D'Amico, Silvio (ed.). *Teatro italiano. II — dal dramma pastorale al 'settecento* (Milano, 1955).

La carbonaria, commedia. Venezia, 1601 *; Venezia, 1606; Venezia, 1628.*

La Cintia, commedia. Venetia, 1601 *; Venetia, 1606 *; Venetia, 1616 ?; Venetia, 1626 *; Venetia, 1628 * ". . . in 9 quadri in 3 atti . . . Riduzione di Anton Giulio Bragaglia. Rappresentata al Teatro delle Arti di Roma," *Il dramma*, xvii, No. 35 (1941), 11–28.*

La Chiappinaria, commedia. Roma, 1609 *; Napoli, 1615; Napoli, 1626.

I due fratelli rivali, commedia. (In early eds. *Gli duoi fratelli rivali*) Venetia, 1601 *; Vinegia, 1606 *; "Riduzione in tre atti di Gerardo Guerrieri," *Il dramma*, xix, No. 408–9 (1943), 31–49.*

I due fratelli simili, commedia. Napoli, 1604 ? ; Napoli, 1614.*

La fantesca, commedia. Venezia, 1592 *; Venezia, 1596; Vinegia, 1597 * (with *Olimpia* and *Trappolaria*); Vinegia, 1610 *; Bragaglia, A. F. (ed.). *Commedie giocose del cinquecento*, iii (Milano, 1947). Apollonio, Mario (ed.). *Commedia italiana.*

Bibliography

Raccolta di commedie da Cielo d'Alcamo a Goldoni. Milano, 1947.*

La furiosa, commedia. Napoli, 1609 *; Napoli, 1618.*

Il Georgio, tragedia. Napoli, 1611 *; Act IV, Scene 4–De Simone-Brouwer, Francesco (ed.). *Una scena di sponsali; edizione di 500 esemplari per nozze Sogliano-Mari*. Napoli, 1893. (Scene extracted from the Naples Biblioteca Nazionale Ms. XIII.E.8.)*

Il moro, commedia. Viterbo, 1607 *; Viterbo, 1609.

L'Olimpia, commedia. Napoli, 1589; Vinegia, 1597 * (with *Fantesca* and *Trappolaria*); Siena, 1613.

La Penelope, tragicommedia. Napoli, 1591 *; Roma, 1620 ? ; Roma, 1628 ?

La sorella, commedia. Napoli, 1604 *; Venezia, 1607 *; Borlenghi, Aldo (ed.). *Commedie del Cinquecento*, II (Milano, 1959).*

La tabernaria, commedia. Ronciglione, 1612 ? ; Ronciglione, 1616 *; ". . . Riduzione in Tre Atti di Camillo Bonanni," *Sipario*, Anno nono, No. 100–1 (Agosto-Sett. 1954), 17–31. Trevisani, Giulio (ed.). *Teatro napoletano dalle origini a Edoardo Scarpetta*, II (Parma, 1957. Excerpt).

La trappolaria, commedia. Bergamo, 1596 *; Vinegia, 1597 * (with *Fantesca* and *Olimpia*); Napoli, 1613; Ferrara, 1615 *; Venezia, 1626; Venezia, 1628.*

La turca, commedia. Venezia, 1606.*

L'Ulisse, tragedia. Napoli, 1614.*

II. GENERAL BIBLIOGRAPHY

A. Unpublished Material.

Brooke, Samuel. "Scyros and Adelphe, two Latin plays, reproduced in facsimile from Ms.R.3.9 in the Library of Trinity College, Cambridge." (Negative rotograph copy in Library of Congress Manuscript Division, MLA 01000.)

Della Porta, G. B. "Il Georgio, tragedia." (Naples Biblioteca Nazionale Ms.XIII.E.8. Corrections indicate that this manuscript was the final revision of *Georgio*, as sent to the printer.)

———. Archivio dell'Accademia Nazionale dei Lincei, Roma. Codice IX. (In addition to a miscellany of scientific material, this manuscript contains the twenty-five *imprese* composed for various occasions and published by Gabrieli in "Spigolature Dellaportiane . . .")

Bibliography

———. Archivio dell'Accademia Nazionale dei Lincei, Roma. Codice xiv. (At the end of this scientific miscellany, which includes the manuscript of *De telescopio*, appear ten smaller pages written in a different hand and with different ink. These contain notes on a number of superstitious practices and three acts of a Latin comedy in which a character named Theophila is conspicuous and which ends with the reunion of a long-separated family. These pages, numbered 148–158, have never been published, and their connection with Della Porta is uncertain.)

[Hawkesworth, Walter]. "Labarinthus [*sic*]," *Ms.* i.8, Library of St. John's College, Cambridge. (Bound with this is a manuscript of "Leander," dated Jan. 7, 1599.)

———. ("Hauksworth"). "Labyrinthus," Ms. R.3.9, Library of Trinity College, Cambridge. (Hawkesworth is identified as the author and is listed in the cast. Bound with this is a manuscript of "Leander," marked "Acta est secundo A.D. 1602.")

———. "Labyrinthus," Ms. Ee.5.16, Cambridge University Library, Cambridge. (Probably another stage-copy of the Trinity College manuscript listed above.)

Orr, David. "The Influence of Learned Italian Drama of the Sixteenth Century on English Drama Before 1623." Library of Congress Microfilm 60–4853. Abstract in *Dissertation Abstracts* xxi (1961), 2705. (Unpublished Doctoral Dissertation, University of North Carolina, 1960.)

B. Articles.

Accademia Nazionale dei Lincei. "Il carteggio linceo della vecchia accademia di Federico Cesi (1603–1630)," *Atti e memori dell'Accademia Nazionale dei Lincei. Classe di scienze morali, storiche e filologiche*, Ser. 6, vii (Roma, 1938), fasc. 1.

Alessandrini, Ada. "Cimeli lincei in mostra nella Biblioteca Accademica," extracted from *Rendiconti della R. Accademia Nazionale dei Lincei. Classe di scienze morali, storiche e filologiche*, Ser. 8, xi (Roma, 1956), fasc. 7–10.

Beltrame, Tina. "Giovanni Battista Della Porta e la commedia dell'arte," *Giornale storico della letteratura italiana*, ci (1933), fasc. 3, 277–289.

———. "Gli scenari del Museo Correr," *Giornale storico della letteratura italiana*, xcvii, fasc. 1–2 (1931), 1–48.

Bibliography

Boughner, Daniel Cliness. "Traditional Elements in Falstaff," *Journal of English and Germanic Philology*, XLIII (1944), 417–28.

Bruers, A. "Giambattista Della Porta," *Luce e Ombra*, XIII (Roma, 1913), 406–10.

Bruschini, Nino. "Giambattista della Porta," *Roma della Domenica*, 16 aprile, 1939. 8.

Burian, Orhan. "Drama in the Universities," *English Miscellany*, 4 (Rome, 1953), 45–65.

Caprin, Giulio. "Il commediografo del secentismo," *Marzocco*, 9 ottobre 1910, 3–4.

Cecchini, Lionello. "Giovanni Della Porta e la 'Cintia,'" *Meridiano di Roma*, 15 dicembre 1940, viii.

Cerreta, Florindo V. "Clarifications concerning the Real Authorship of the Renaissance Comedy *Ortensio*," *Renaissance News*, X (1957), 63–69.

Churchill, George B., and Keller, Wolfgang. "Die lateinischen Universitäts-Dramen Englands in der Zeit der Königin Elisabeth . . . mit Vorwort von A. Brandl," *Jahrbuch der Deutschen Shakespeare-Gesellschaft*, XXXIV (Weimar, 1898), 221–325.

Corrigan, Beatrice M. H. "Sforza Oddi and his Comedies," *Publications of the Modern Language Association of America*, XLIX (1934), 719–42.

Corsano, Antonio. "Per la storia del pensiero del tardo rinascimento. G. B. Della Porta," *Giornale critico della filosofia italiana*, Ser. 3, Anno XXXVIII (1959), fasc. 1, 76–97.

Crinò, Anna Maria. "Virtuose di canto e poeti a Roma e a Firenze nella prima metà del seicento," *Studi secenteschi*, I (Firenze, 1960), 175–93.

Croce, Benedetto. "Il 'Georgio' di Giambattista Della Porta," *Giornale storico della letteratura italiana*, XXII (1893), fasc. 64–65, 421.

——. "Una nuova raccolta di scenarii," *Giornale storico della letteratura italiana*, XXIX (1897), fasc. 85, 214.

De Simone-Brouwer, Francesco. "Ancora una raccolta di scenari," *Rendiconti della R. Accademia dei Lincei. Classe di scienze morali, storiche e filologiche*, Ser. 5, X (1901), 11–12, 391–407.

———. "Due scenari inediti del secolo xvii," *Giornale storico della letteratura italiana*, xviii (1891), fasc. 3, 277–90.

Dèttore, Ugo. Articles in *Dizionario letterario Bompiani delle opere e dei personaggi di tutti i tempi e di tutte le letterature*. 9 vols. Milano, 1947–1950: "*Astrologo, Lo*," i, 294; "*Chiappinaria, La*," ii, 218; "*Cintia, La*," ii, 262; "*Due fratelli rivali, I*," ii, 867; "*Furiosa, La*," iii, 534; "*Moro, Il*," iv, 815; "*Olimpia, L'*," v, 197.

Dick, Hugh G. "The Lover in a Cask: a Tale of a Tub," *Italica*, xviii (1941), 12–13.

Dictionary of National Biography. Edited by Leslie Stephen and Sidney Lee. IX. London, 1908. Article, "Hawkesworth, Walter," 205.

Di Giacomo, S. "La villa del Porta a Vico Equense," *L'Illustrazione italiana*, xxvii, No. 47 (Milano, 25 novembre 1900), 357–58.

Eccles, Mark. "Middleton's Birth and Education," reprinted from *Review of English Studies*, vii, No. 28 (October, 1931).

Favaro, Antonio. "Antichi e moderni detrattori di Galileo," *La rassegna nazionale*, cliii (16 febbraio 1907), 577–600.

Firpo, Luigi. "Appunti campanelliani, xxv, storia d'un furto," *Giornale critico della filosofia italiana*, Anno xxxv (1956), fasc. 4, 541–49.

Gabrieli, Giuseppe. "Bibliografia lincea. I. Giambattista Della Porta.–Notizia bibliografica dei suoi mss. e libri edizioni, ecc. con documenti inediti," *Rendiconti della R. Accademia Nazionale dei Lincei. Classe di scienza morali, storiche e filologiche*, Ser. 6, viii (Roma, 1932), 206–77.

———. "Il carteggio scientifico ed accademico tra i primi Lincei," *Memorie della R. Accademia Nazionale dei Lincei. Classe di scienze morali, storiche e filologiche*, Ser. 6, i (1925), fasc. 2, 137–219.

———. "Giovan Battista Della Porta Linceo. Da documenti per gran parte inediti," *Giornale critico della filosofia italiana*, Anno viii (1927), fasc. 1, 360–97, 423–31.

———. "Indice cronologico e topografico del carteggio linceo," *Memorie della R. Accademia Nazionale dei Lincei*, Ser. 6, iii (1930), fasc. 2, 127–208.

———. "Le ricerche e le carte di A. Statuti sulla storia dei primi

Bibliography

Lincei (per gli anni 1603–1630)," *Memorie della Pontificale Accademia dei Nuovi Lincei,* Ser. 2, VIII (1925), 401–54.

——. "Spigolature Dellaportiane," *Rendiconti della R. Accademia Nazionale dei Lincei,* Ser. 6, XI (1936), fasc. 7–10, 491–517.

——. "Verbali delle adunanze e cronaca della prima Accademia lincea (1603–1630)," *Memorie della R. Accademia Nazionale dei Lincei. Classe di scienze morali, storiche e filologiche,* Ser. 6, II (1927), fasc. 6, 463–512.

Gilbert, Allan H. "The Duel in Italian Cinquecento Drama and Its Relation to Tragicomedy," *Italica,* XXVI (1949), 7–14.

Gliozzi, Mario. "L'invenzione della camera oscura," *Archeion,* XIV (Roma, 1932), 221–29.

Goggio, Emilio. "Dramatic theories in the prologues to the *commedie erudite* of the sixteenth century," *Publications of the Modern Language Association of America,* LVIII (1943), 322–36.

——. "The Prologue in the *commedie erudite* of the sixteenth century," *Italica,* XVIII (1941), 124–32.

Gordon, D. J. "Middleton's *No wit no help like a woman's,* and della Porta's *La sorella,*" *Review of English Studies,* XVII (1941), 400–14.

——. "*Much Ado About Nothing:* a Possible Source for the Hero-Claudio Plot," *Studies in Philology,* XXXIX (1942), 279–90.

Grazzini, Giovanni. "Della Porta," *Enciclopedia dello spettacolo,* IV (Roma, 1957), 403.

Holm, Theodore. "Joan [*sic*] Baptista Porta," *American Naturalist,* LII (Lancaster, Pa., 1918), 455–61.

Jourdan, A. J. L. "Porta, J. B.," *Dictionaire des sciences médicales. Biographie médicale,* VI (Paris, 1824), 475–79.

Kaufman, Helen, "The Influence of Italian Drama on pre-Restoration English Comedy," *Italica,* XXXI (1954), 8–23.

Lebègue, Raymond. "La comédie italienne en France au XVIe siècle," *Revue du littérature comparée,* XXIV (Paris, 1950), 5–24.

Lester, John A. "Italian Actors in Scotland," *Modern Language Notes,* XXIII (1908), 240–42.

Lothian, John M. "Sforza d'Oddi's 'Erofilomachia'–the Source of Hawkesworth's 'Leander,'" *Modern Language Review,* XXV (1930), 338–41.

Magrini, Silvio. "Il 'de magnete' del Gilbert," *Archeion*, VIII (Roma, 1927), 17–39.

Mander, G. P. "Thomas Tomkis," *Times Literary Supplement*, 31 March 1945, 151.

Milano, Francesco. "Le commedie di Giovanbattista della Porta," *Studi di letteratura italiana*, II (Napoli, 1900), fasc. 2, 311–411.

Minieri-Riccio, Camillo. "Cenno storico delle accademie fiorite in Napoli," *Archivio storico per le province napoletane pubblicato a cura della società di storia patria*, IV (Napoli, 1879), fasc. 1, 161–78, fasc. 2, 379–94, fasc. 3, 516–36; V (1880), fasc. 1, 131–57, fasc. 2, 349–73, fasc. 3, 578–612.

Naldoni, Maria Amalia. "Un manoscritto inedito di G. B. della Porta," *Atti della Fondazione Giorgio Ronchi*, I (1946), Nos. 1–2, 48, Nos. 5–6, 180; VII (1952), No. 1, 54; 1961, 316.

Nicolini, Fausto. "Della Porta," *Enciclopedia italiana di scienza, lettere ed arti*, XII ([Milano], 1940), 548-f.

Nicolson, Marjorie H. "The Telescope and Imagination," *Modern Philology*, XXXII (1935), 233–60.

Ortiz, Maria. "La cultura del Goldoni," *Giornale storico della letteratura italiana*, XLVIII, fasc. 1–2, 76.

Paparelli, Gioacchino. "La data di nascita di Giambattista Della Porta," *Vita italiana*, IV (Buenos Aires, 1955), No. 38, 14–15. (Reprinted in *Filologia romanza*, III (1956), No. 9, 87–89.)

——. "Della Porta," *Dizionario letterario Bompiano degli autori di tutti tempi e di tutte le letterature*, I (Milano, 1956), 620–21.

——. "La 'Taumatologia' di Giovanbattista della Porta," *Filologia romanza*, II (1955), fasc. 4, No. 8, 418–29.

Perman, R. C. D. "The Influence of the *commedia dell'arte* on the French Theatre before 1640," *French Studies*, IX (1955), No. 4, 293–303.

Pullini, Giorgio. "Stile di transizione nel teatro di Giambattista Della Porta," *Lettere italiane*, VIII (Padova, 1956), 299–310.

Retrospective Review, XII (London, 1825), Part 1, 1–42. Article, "The Latin plays acted before the University of Cambridge."

Ronchi, Vasco. "Du *De refractione* au *De telescopio* de G. B. Della Porta," *Revue d'histoire des sciences et de leurs applications*, VII (1954), No. 1, 34–59.

——. "Il *De Refractione* di G. B. Della Porta," *Bolletino dell'Associazione dell'Ottica Italiana*, XVI (1942), No. 2, 75.

Bibliography

Restori, A. "Appunti teatrali spagnuoli," *Studj di filologia romanza*, VII (Roma, 1898), fasc. 20, 426–30.

Rossi, Vittorio. "Una commedia di G. B. della Porta ed uno nuovo scenario," *Rendiconti del R. Istituto Lombardo*, Ser. 2, XXIX (1896), fasc. 16, 881–95.

Scherillo, Michele. "V. Rossi. Una commedia di G. B. della Porta ed uno nuovo scenario," *Rassegna critica di letteratura italiana*, I (Napoli, 1896), 140–43. (A response to Rossi's article. See above.)

Sergio, Giovanni Antonio. "Elogio di Gio. Battista Porta," *Novelle letterarie pubblicate in Firenze*, XIX (1758), 694–704, 714–20.

Spampanato, Vincenzo. "I Della Porta ne' *Duoi fratelli rivali*," *Anomalo* [giugno, 1918], 199–201.

——. "Somiglianze tra due commediografi napoletani," *Rassegna critica di letteratura italiana*, XI (Napoli, 1906), 145–67.

Spector, Norman B. "Odet de Turnèbe's *Les contens* and the Italian Comedy," *French Studies*, XIII (1959), No. 4, 304–13.

Stevenson, Hazel Allison. "The Major Elizabethan Poets and the Doctrine of Signatures," *Florida State University Studies*, No. 5 (1952), 11–31.

Stiefel, Arthur Ludwig. "Tristan L'Hermites *Le Parasite* und seine Quelle," *Archiv für das Studium der neueren Sprachen und Literaturen*, LXXXVI (1891), 47–80.

——. "Unbekannte italienische Quellen Jean de Rotrou's," *Zeitschrift für französische Sprache und Literatur*, Supplement No. 5 (1891).

Teagarden, Lucetta J. "The Dekker-Middleton Problem in *Michaelmas Term*," *Studies in English*, Austin, Texas, 1947, 49–58.

Toldo, Pietro. "La comédie française de la Renaissance," *Revue d'histoire littéraire de la France*, IV (1897), 366–400; V (1898), 220–64; VI (1899), 571–608; VII (1900), 263–83.

——. "Les morts qui mangent," *Bulletin italien*, V (Bordeaux, 1905), No. 3, 291–97.

——. "Tre commedie francesi inedite di Carlo Goldoni," *Giornale storico della letteratura italiana*, XXIX (1897), fasc. 2–3, 377–91.

Ukas, Michael. "Didactic Purpose in the *Commedia Erudita*," *Italica*, XXXVI (1959), No. 3, 198–205.

Bibliography

Valeri, A. ("Carletta"). "Gli scenari di Basilio Locatelli," *Nuova rassegna*, II (Roma, 15 settembre 1894), 441–56.

Vianey, Joseph. "Deux sources inconnues de Rotrou," *Archives historiques, artistiques et littéraires*, II (Paris, 1890–1891), 241–50.

Weiss. "Porta, Jean-Baptiste," *Biographie universelle*, XXXV (Paris, 1823), 442–46.

Wolff, Max J. "Molière und Della Porta," *Archiv für das Studium der neueren Sprachen und Literaturen*, CXXXIV (1916), 148.

Wood, Casey A. "Johannes Baptista Porta (1540–1615), Neapolitan oculist and natural philosopher," *Charaka Club Proceedings*, VIII (New York, 1935), 118–34.

Zuccarelli, Angelo, *et al.* "Cronaca della erezione del busto a G. B. Della Porta e della inaugurazione rimandata dal 9 giugno al nuovo anno scolastico 1918–1919," *Anomalo* [giugno, 1818], 222–225. (In this special issue of the departmental journal of the University of Naples Gabinetto-Scuola di Antropologia Criminale "Giambattista Della Porta" are a number of tributes to Della Porta by the director, Professor Zuccarelli, and his associates. The only article of real scholarly interest is that of Spampanato. See above.)

C. Books

Each of the following entries contains whatever is part of the title proper, but repetitions of authors' and editors' names and of honorary titles etc. have been omitted. The omissions are signified by three spaced dots.

Ademollo, Alessandro. *I teatri di Roma nel secolo decimosettimo*. Roma, 1888.

Allacci, Lione (comp.). *Drammaturgia di . . . Accresciuta e continuata fino all'anno MDCCLV*. Venezia, 1755.

Altamura, Antonio. *Dizionario dialettale napoletano con introduzione storico-linguistica e note etimologiche*. Napoli, 1956.

Amabile, Luigi. *Fra Tommaso Campanella, la sua congiura, i suoi processi e la sua pazzia*. 3 vols. Napoli, 1882.

———. *Fra Tommaso Campanella ne' castelli di Napoli, in Roma ed in Parigi*. Vol. I. Napoli, 1887.

Bibliography

Amabile, Luigi. *Il. S. Officio della Inquisizione in Napoli.* 2 vols. Città di Castello, 1892.

Amico, Silvio d', *et al. Storia del teatro italiano, a cura di . . . , con introduzione di Luigi Pirandello e 10 capitoli di Paolo Toschi, Giuseppe Toffanin, Silvio d'Amico, Fausto Torrefranca, Cesare Padovani, Emilio Bodrero, Mario Ferrigni, Cipriano Giachetti, Goffredo Bellonci, Corrado Pavolini.* Milano, 1936.

Andreini, Francesco. *Le brauure del Capitano Spavento, diuise in molti ragionamenti in forma di dialogo; di Francesco Andreini da Pistoia Comico Geloso. Et in questa terza impressione dal proprio autore ricorrette; aggiuntoui molti nuoui ragionamenti diletteuoli, e curiosi non più stampati.* Venetia, 1615.

Angelita, Giovanni Francesco. *I pomi d'oro di . . . Dove si contengeno due lettioni de' fichi l'una, e de' melloni l'altra. Nelle quali non solo si scorgano le lor lodi, e le loro eccellenze, ma si scoprono molti segreti per usarli, e per cultivarli. E si notaui molti errori di diuersi grand' huomini intorno al loro sentimento. Aggiuntaui una lettione della lumaca dove si pruoua, ch'ella sia maestra della vita humana. Opra non meno ripiena di dottrina, che piacere.* Ricanato, 1607.

Atanagi, Dionigi. *Delle lettere facete, et piacevoli, di diversi grandi huomini, et chiari ingegni, raccolte per M. Francesco Turchi.* Libro Secondo. Venetia, 1575.

Antonini, G. *I precursori di C [esare] Lombroso.* Torino, 1900.

Apollonio, Mario. *Storia del teatro italiano.* 2d ed. 3 vols. Firenze, 1943–1951.

Arber, Agnes. *Herbals, their origin and evolution. A chapter in the history of botany, 1470–1670.* 2d ed. rewritten and enlarged. Cambridge University Press, 1953.

Aristotle. *The poetics. "Longinus": On the sublime. Demetrius: On style.* Translated by W. H. Fyfe. The Loeb Classical Library. London, 1932.

Ayrer, Jacob. *Comoedia von der Schönen Phaenicia und Graf Tymbri von Golison auss Arragonien, wie es ihnen in ihrer Erlichen Lieb gangen, biss sie Ehelich zusammen komen. Mit 17 Personen und hat 6 Actus.* Abridged version from Ayrer's *Opus Theatricum* (Nuremberg, 1618) printed in Cohn, *Shakespeare in Germany.*

Bibliography

Baldwin, Charles Sears. *Renaissance Literary Theory and Practice. Classicism in the Rhetoric and Poetic of Italy, France, and England 1400–1600.* Edited by Donald Lemen Clark. New York, 1939.

Bandello, Matteo. *Le novelle.* Edited by Giochino Brognoligo. 2d ed. 3 vols. Bari, 1928.

Barbieri, Matteo. *Notizie istoriche dei mattematici e filosofi del regno di Napoli.* Napoli, 1778.

Baretti, Giuseppe. *The Italian Library. Containing an Account of the Lives and Works of the Most Valuable Authors of Italy. With a Preface, Exhibiting the Changes of the Tuscan Language, from the barbarous Ages to the present Time.* London, 1757.

Barker, Richard H. *Thomas Middleton.* New York, 1958.

Barrera y Leirado, Cayetano Alberto de la. *Catálogo bibliográfico y biográfico del teatro antiguo español.* Madrid, 1860.

Baschet, Armand. *Les comédiens italiens à la cour de France sous Charles IX, Henri III, Henri IV et Louis XIII d'après les lettres royales, la correspondance originale des comédiens, les registres de la "Trésorerie de l'Epargne" et autres documents.* Paris, 1882.

[Basile, Giovanni Battista]. *Le muse napolitane. Egloghe di Gian Alesio Abbattutis.* Napoli, 1635.

——. *Osservationi intorno alle rime del Bembo e del Casa. Con le tavola delle desinenze delle rime, & con la varietà de testi nelle rime del Bembo.* Napoli, 1618.

Belloni, Antonio. *Il seicento.* Storia letteraria d'Italia. Milano, [1898–1899].

Bentley, Gerald Eades. *The Jacobean and Caroline Stage.* 5 vols. Oxford, 1941–1956.

Bertana, Emilio. *La tragedia.* Storia dei generi italiani. Milano, [1905].

Biancale, Michele. *La tragedia italiana nel cinquecento.* Roma, 1901.

Bianchi, Giovanni (J. Plancus). *Fabii Columnae Lyncei . . . vita.* Prefixed to Fabio Colonna's *Phytobasanos.* Florentia, 1744.

Boas, Frederick S. *An Introduction to Stuart Drama.* Oxford, 1946.

——. *University Drama in the Tudor Age.* Oxford, 1914.

Bibliography

Bodin, Jean. *De magorum demonomania libri IV*. Basileae, 1581.

Bond, Richard Warwick (ed.). *Early Plays from the Italian*. Edited with essay, introductions and notes. Oxford, 1911.

Botero, Giovanni. *The Reason of State*. Translated by P. J. and D. P. Waley. With an introduction by D. P. Waley, and The Greatness of Cities. Translated by Robert Peterson, 1606. New Haven, 1956.

Boughner, Daniel Cliness. *The Braggart in Renaissance Comedy. A Study in Comparative Drama from Aristophanes to Shakespeare*. Minneapolis, 1954.

Brathwait, Richard. *The Honest Ghost, or a Voice from the Vault* . . . London, 1658.

Brooke, Samuel. *Melanthe, a Latin pastoral play of the early seventeenth century*. Edited, with a biographical introduction, by Joseph S. G. Bolton. New Haven, 1928.

[Brunet, Charles]. *Bibliothèque dramatique de Monsieur de Soleinne. Catalogue rédigé par P. L. Jacob, bibliophile* [pseud.] . . . 5 vols. Paris, 1843–1844.

Bulifon, Antonio. *Giornali di Napoli dal MDXLVII al MDCCVI*. A cura di Nino Cortese. Vol. I, 1547–1691. Società Napoletana di Storia Patria. Cronache e documenti per la storia dell'Italia meridionale dei secoli XVI e XVII. Vol. IV. Napoli, 1932.

Camerini, Eugenio. *I precursori del Goldoni. Saggi di* . . . Milano, 1872.

Campanella, Tommaso. *Medicinalium juxta propria principia*. Lugduni, 1635.

Campori, Giuseppe (ed.). *Gio. Battista della Porta e il cardinale Luigi d'Este, notizie e documenti per cura di* . . . Modena, 1872.

Capaccio, Giulio Cesare. *Delle imprese trattato di* . . . *in tre libri diviso*. Napoli, 1592.

Caputi, Ottavio (comp.). *La pompa funerale fatta in Napoli nell' essequie del Catholico Re Filippo II di Austria* . . . Napoli, 1599.

———. *Relatione della pompa funerale che si celebrò in Napoli, nella morte della Serenissima Reina Margherita d'Austria* . . . Napoli, 1612.

Carutti, Domenico. *Breve storia della Accademia dei Lincei*. Roma, 1883.

Bibliography

Castro y Bellvis, Giullen de. *Obras*. Biblioteca selecta de clásicos españoles. 2d Series. 3 vols. Madrid, 1921–1927.

Celano, Carlo. *Notizie del bello, dell'antico e del curioso della città di Napoli, per i signori forastieri . . . divise in dieci giornate*. 4 vols. Napoli, 1692.

Chambers, Edmund K. *The Elizabethan Stage*. 4 vols. Oxford, 1923.

Charbonnel, J. Roger. *La pensée italienne au XVI siècle et le courant libertin*. Paris, 1919.

Chasles, Émile. *La comédie en France au seizième siècle*. Paris, 1862.

Cherpack, Clifton. *The Call of Blood in French Classical Tragedy*. Baltimore, 1958.

Chioccarelli, Bartolomeo. *De illustribus scriptoribus qui in civitate et regno Neapolis ab orbe condito ad annum usque MDCXXXXVI floruerunt*. Neapoli, 1780.

Cohn, Albert. *Shakespeare in Germany in the Sixteenth and Seventeenth Centuries*. London, 1865.

[Colangelo, Francesci, sacerdote dell'Oratorio]. *F.C.S.D.O. Racconto istorico della vita di Giovanni Battista Della Porta filosofo napolitano con un'analisi delle sue opere stampate*. Napoli, 1813.

Colomb de Batines, Paul. *Bibliografia delle antiche rappresentazioni italiane sacre e profane stampate nei secoli XV e XVI*. Firenze, 1852.

Crasso, Lorenzo. *Elogii di huomini letterati*. Venetia, 1666.

Croce, Benedetto. *Nuovi saggi sulla letteratura italiana del seicento*. Bari, 1931.

——. *Saggi sulla letteratura italiana del Seicento*. 3d ed. revised. Bari, 1948.

——. *La Spagna nella vita italiana durante la Rinascenza*. 4d ed. revised and enlarged. Bari, 1949.

——. *Storia della età barocca in Italia. Pensiero—poesia e letteratura—vita morale*. 2d ed. revised. Bari, 1946.

——. *I teatri di Napoli: secolo XV–XVIII*. Napoli, 1891.

D'Ambra, Raffaele. *Vocabolario napolitano-toscano domestico di arti e mestieri*. Napoli, 1873.

D'Ancona, Alessandro. *Origini del teatro italiano*. 2 vols. Torino, 1891.

De Job, Charles. *De l'influence du Concile de Trente sur la littérature et les beaux-arts chez les peuples catholiques.* Paris, 1884.

Domenichi, Lodovico. *Della scelta de motti, burle facetie di diversi signori, et d'altre persone private. Libri sei. Raccolto da . . . & da lui ultimamente riformate.* Fiorenza, 1566.

Doria, Gino. *Le strade di Napoli.* Napoli, 1943.

[Duchesne, Henri Gabriel]. *Notice historique sur la vie et les ouvrages de J. B. Porta, gentilhomme napolitain, par D.* Paris, [1801].

Duckworth, George E. *The Nature of Roman Comedy. A Study in Popular Entertainment.* Princeton, 1952.

Dyer, George. *An English Prologue and Epilogue to the Latin Comedy of Ignoramus.* London, 1797.

Farinelli, Arturo. *Italia e Spagna.* Torino, 1929.

Ferguson, John. *Bibliotheca Chemica; a bibliography of books on alchemy, chemistry, and pharmaceutics.* 2 vols. 2d ed. London, 1954.

Ferro, Giovanni. *Teatro d'imprese.* Venetia, 1623.

Fiorentino, Francesco. *Bernardino Telesio, ossia studi storici sull'idea della natura nel Risorgimento italiano.* 2 vols. Firenze, 1872–1874.

———. *Studi e ritratti della Rinascenza. A cura della figlia Luisa.* Bari, 1911. Chapter V, "Giovan Battista de la Porta" is composed of material originally published in *Nuova Antologia,* xxi (Roma, maggio, 1880), 251–284, and in *Giornale napoletano di filosofia e lettere, scienze morali e politiche,* Nuova serie, Anno ii, Vol. iii, fasc. 7 (Napoli, marzo, 1880), 92–118 and 329–43.

Flamini, Francesco. *Il cinquecento.* Storia letteraria d'Italia. Milano, [1898–1902].

Fleay, Frederick Gard. *A Biographical Chronicle of the English Drama 1559–1642.* 2 vols. London, 1891.

Fletcher, Jefferson Butler. *Literature of the Italian Renaissance.* New York, 1934.

Fornari, Cesare. *Di G. B. della Porta e delle sue scoperte.* Napoli, 1871.

Freeburg, Victor Oscar. *Disguise plots in Elizabethan Drama. A study in stage tradition.* New York, 1915.

Galilei, Galileo. *Le opere di . . . Ristampa della Edizione Na-*

zionale. Edited by Antonio Favaro, et al. 20 vols. Firenze, 1929–1939.

Garin, Eugenio. *L'umanesimo italiano. Filosofia e vita civile nel Rinascimento.* Bari, 1952.

Gaspary, Adolf. *Geschichte der italienischen literatur; von . . .* Vol. II. Berlin, 1888.

Gassendi, Pierre. *The Mirrour of True Nobility & Gentility. Being the Life of the Renowned Nicolaus Claudius Fabricius, Lord of Peiresk, Senator of the Parliament at Aix . . .* Englished by W. Rand. London, 1657.

Genta, Felice. *Dopo la denigrazione di G. B. della Porta.* Napoli, 1928.

Ghilini, Girolamo. *Teatro d'huomini letterati.* Venetia, 1647.

Ghirardelli, G. B. Filippo. *Il Costantino, tragedia . . . con la Difesa della medesima.* 2d ed. Roma, 1660.

Giannone, Pietro. *Istoria civile del regno di Napoli.* Vol. IV. 5th Italian ed. Napoli, 1770.

Giraldi Cinthio, Giovanni Battista. *Discorsi di . . . intorno al comporre de i romanzi, della comedie, e delle tragedie, e di altre maniere di poesie.* Vinegia, 1554.

Gosson, Stephen. *Playes Confuted in Five Actions . . .* London, [1582].

Grazzini, Antonfrancesco (il Lasca). *La cena di . . . Ove si raccontano dieci bellissime, e piacevolissime novelle non mai più stampate.* Stambul, Dell'Egira 122 [Firenze, 1743].

Greg, Walter Wilson. *A Bibliography of the English Printed Drama to the Restoration.* 3 vols. London, 1939–1957.

Guacci-Nobile, M. G. *Giambattista Della Porta; stanze . . .* [no date or place]. (Twenty octaves in the nineteenth-century style.)

Guarini, Giovanni Battista. *Compendio della poesia tragicomica, tratto dai duo verati . . .* Venetia, 1601.

[——]. *Il verrato ovvero difesa di quanto ha scritto M. Giason Denores contra le tragicomedie, et le pastorali, in un suo discorso di poesia . . .* Ferrare, 1588.

Guibert, Nicolas. *De interitu alchymiae metallorum transmutatoriae tractatus aliquot. Adjuncta est Apologia in Sophistam Libavium . . .* Tulli, 1614.

Guiscardi, Roberto. *MDCXV(?)* [no place, 1885?].

Bibliography

Harbage, Alfred. *Annals of English Drama 975–1700*. Philadelphia, 1940.

Hawkesworth, Walter. *Labyrinthus: Comoedia habita coram Sereniss. Rege Iacobo in Academia Cantabrigiensi*. Londini, 1636.

Herrick, Marvin Theodore. *Italian Comedy in the Renaissance*. Urbana, 1960.

———. Tragicomedy. *Its Origin and Development in Italy, France, and England*. Urbana, 1955.

Homer, *The Odyssey of* . . . Translated by S. H. Butcher and A. Lang; with introduction, notes and illustrations. New York, 1909.

Imperiali, Giovanni. *Musaeum historicum et physicum*. Venetiis, 1640.

Ingegneri, Angelo. *Della poesia rappresentativa & del modo di rappresentare le favole sceniche. Discorsi di* . . . Ferrara, 1598.

Kennard, Joseph Spencer. *The Italian Theatre from its beginning to the close of the seventeenth century*. New York, 1932.

Kepler, Johannes. *Dissertatio cum nuncio sidereo*. In Galilei, *Opere*, Vol. III. Firenze, 1930.

Klein, Julius Leopold. *Geschichte des Drama*. 7 vols. Leipzig, 1856–1876.

Lancaster, Henry Carrington. *A History of French Dramatic Literature in the Seventeenth Century. Part II. The Period of Corneille 1635–1651*. 2 vols., and Part. III. *The Period of Molière 1652–1672*. 2 vols. Baltimore, 1932 and 1936.

Lea, Kathleen M. *Italian popular comedy. A study in the Commedia dell'Arte 1560–1620 with special reference to the English stage*. 2 vols. Oxford, 1934.

Lettere d'uomini illustri, che fiorirono nel principio del secolo decimosettimo, non più stampate. Venezia, 1744.

Libri, Guillaume. *Histoire des sciences mathématiques en Italie, depuis la Renaissance des lettres jusqu'à la fin du dix-septième siècle*. Vol. IV. Paris, 1841.

Lisoni, Alberto. *Imitatori del teatro spagnuolo in Italia*. Parma, 1895.

Marino, Giovanni Battista. *La Galeria del* . . . *Distinta in pitture, e sculture*. Napoli [1620].

Massinger, Philip. *The Parliament of Love*. Malone Society Reprints 1928. London, 1929.

Bibliography

Maylender, Michele. *Storia delle accademie d'Italia.* 5 vols. Bologna, 1930.

Mazzamuto, Pietro. *Rassegna bibliografico-critica della letteratura italiana.* 3d ed. enlarged. Firenze, 1956.

Menander. *Dyskolos, or The Man who didn't like people.* Translated into English prose by W. G. Arnott. London, 1960.

Meozzi, Antero. *La drammatica della Rinascita italiana in Europe. Secolo XVI–XVII.* Pisa, 1940.

Middleton, Thomas. *The Works of . . . Now first collected, with some account of the author, and notes, by the reverend Alexander Dyce.* 5 vols. London, 1840.

——, and Rowley, William. *The Changeling.* Edited by N. W. Bawcutt. London, 1958.

Milton, John. *The Minor Poems, and Samson Agonistes.* Edited by Merritt Y. Hughes. New York, 1937.

——. *Prose Selections.* Edited by Merritt Y. Hughes. 2d ed. New York, 1947.

Minieri-Riccio, Camillo. *Memorie storiche degli scrittori nati nel Regno di Napoli.* Napoli, 1844.

Miotto, Antonio. *Galleria di medici strani: Gian Battista Della Porta, Franz Anton Mesmer.* Como, [1956].

Molière, Jean-Baptiste Poquelin. *Oeuvres de . . . nouvelle édition revue sur les plus anciennes impressions et augmentée de variantes, de notices, de notes, d'un lexique des mots et locutions remarquables, d'un portrait, de fac-simile, etc. par MM Eugène Despois et Paul Mesnard.* Vols. VI and VIII. Paris, 1881 and 1883.

Momigliano, Attilio. *Storia della letteratura italiana dalle origini ai nostri giorni.* 8th ed. completely revised. 10th reprinting. Milano, 1960.

Montucla, Jean Etienne. *Histoire des mathématiques. Dans laquelle on rend compte de leurs progrès depuis leur origine jusqu'à nos jours . . .* 2d ed. Vol. 1. Paris [1799].

Napoli-Signorelli, Pietro. *Storia critica de' teatri antichi e moderni.* Vol. VI. Napoli, 1813.

——. *Vicende della cultura nelle Due Sicilie.* 2d Neapolitan ed. Vols. IV–VI. Napoli, 1810–1811.

Neri, Ferdinando. *Storia e poesia.* Torino, 1944.

——. *La tragedia italiana del cinquecento.* Firenze, 1904.

Niceron, Jean Pierre. *Mémoires pour servir à l'histoire des hom-*

mes illustres dans la République des lettres avec un catalogue raisonné de leurs ouvrages. Vol. XLIII. Paris, 1745. The bibliographical sketch of Della Porta in this volume was written by Michaut de Dijon.

Nicodemi, Lionardo. *Addizioni copiose de . . . alla Biblioteca Napoletana del Dr. Niccolò Toppi.* Napoli, 1683.

Nicoll, Allardyce. *A History of Restoration Drama 1660–1700.* 2d ed. Cambridge University Press, 1928.

Odescalchi, Baldassare. *Memorie istorico-critiche dell'Accademia de' Lincei . . .* Roma, 1806.

Orlando, Francesco. *Rotrou dalla tragicommedia alla tragedia.* Università di Pisa Studi di Filologia Moderna. Nuova Serie IV. Torino, 1963.

Ornstein, Martha. *The Role of Scientific Societies in the Seventeenth Century.* 3d ed. Chicago, 1938.

Palmieri, Giovanni. *Tentativo d'una biografia di G. B. Della Porta e d'una esposizione della sua Magia naturale.* Salerno, 1871.

Parascandalo, Gaetano. *Notizie autentiche sulla famiglia e sulla patria di G. B. della Porta con appendice delle famiglie e degli uomini illustri di Vico Equense.* Napoli, 1903.

Pausanius. *Description of Greece with an English translation by W. H. S. Jones.* Vol. III. The Loeb Classical Library. London, 1933.

Perrucci, Andrea. *Dell'arte rappresentativa premeditata, e all'improviso.* Napoli, 1699.

Petit de Julleville, Louis. *Le théâtre en France, histoire de la littérature dramatique depuis ses origines jusqu'à nos jours.* Paris, 1901.

Plautus, Titus Maccius. *Plautus with an English translation by Paul Nixon.* 5 vols. The Loeb Classical Library. London, 1930–1938.

Price, Derek J. Introduction to *Natural Magick by John Baptista Porta.* The Collector's series in Science. Edited by . . . New York, 1957. (Facsimile edition of the anonymous English translation of 1658.)

Prince, Frank Templeton. *The Italian Element in Milton's Verse.* Oxford, 1954.

Prouty, Charles Tyler. *The Sources of Much Ado about Noth-*

ing: a Critical Study, together with the Text of Peter Bever-ley's Ariodanto and Ieneura. New Haven, 1950.

Quadrio, Francesco Saverio. *Della storia, e della ragione d'ogni poesia.* Vol. III, Parts 1 and 2. Milano, 1743 and 1744.

Ravenscroft, Edward. *The English Lawyer; a comedy acted at the Royal Theatre* . . . London, 1678.

Reinhardstoettner, Karl von. *Plautus. Spätere Bearbeitungen plautinischer Lustspiele. Ein Beitrag zur vergleichenden Litteraturgeschichte.* Leipzig, 1886.

Riccoboni, Louis. *Histoire du théâtre italien depuis la decadence de la comédie latine; avec un catalogue des tragédies et comédies italiennes imprimées depuis l'an 1500 jusqu'a l'an 1660. Et une dissertation sur la tragédie moderne.* Paris, 1728.

Rigal, Eugène. *De Jodelle à Molière.* Paris, 1911. Chapter entitled "*L'Étourdi* de Molière et *Le Parasite* de Tristan L'Hermite" is reprinted from *Revue Universitaire,* 15 février, 1893.

——. *Le théâtre français avant la période classique (fin du XVIe et commencement du XVIIe siècle)* . . . Paris, 1901.

Rigillo, M. *La dominazione spagnuola a Napoli.* Piacenza, 1926.

——. *Il seicento e i pregiudizi sul seicentismo.* Cagliari, 1907.

Romei, Annibale. *Ferrara e la corte estense nella seconda metà del secolo decimosesto. I discorsi di* . . . Edited by Angelo Solerti. Città di Castello, 1891.

Ronchi, Vasco. *Il cannocchiale di Galileo e la scienza del seicento.* Torino, 1958. (2d ed. augmented of *Galileo e il cannocchiale*).

Rosen, Edward. *The Naming of the Telescope.* New York, 1947.

Rossi, Giuseppe. *Giovan Battista Della Porta e la filosofia naturale del suo tempo.* Roma, 1883.

Rota, Bernardino. *Delle poesie di* . . . *colle annotazioni di Scipione Ammirato sopra alcuni sonetti.* Napoli, 1737.

Rotrou, Jean. *Oeuvres de* . . . Vol. IV. Paris, 1820.

Rowley, William. . . . *his All's Lost by Lust, and a Shoemaker, a Gentleman with an Introduction on Rowley's Place in the Drama* . . . Edited by Charles Wharton Stork. Philadelphia, 1910.

[Ruggle, George]. *Ignoramus, comoedia coram Regia Maiestate Iacobi Regis Angliae etc.* Londini, 1630.

Bibliography

[Ruggle, George]. *Ignoramus: a comedy . . . translated into English by R[obert] C[odrington]*. London, 1662.

——. *Ignoramus, comoedia; . . . nunc denuo in lucem edita cum notis historicis vita auctoris, et subjicitur glossarium vocabula forensia dilucide exponens: accurante Johanne Sidneio Hawkins*. Londini, 1787.

Saitta, Giuseppe. *Il pensiero italiano nell'umanesimo e nel rinascimento*. Vols. II and III. Bologna, 1950 and 1951.

Sanesi, Ireneo. *La commedia*. 2 vols. 2d ed. revised and enlarged. Storia dei generi letterari italiani. Milano, 1954.

Sarnelli, Pompeo. *Vita di Giovanni Battista Della Porta*, prefixed to Sarnelli's translation of Della Porta's *Della chirofisonomia* . . . Napoli, 1677.

Sarton, George. *Six Wings: Men of Science in the Renaissance*. Bloomington, 1957.

Schelling, Felix E. *Elizabethan Drama, 1558–1642. A History of the Drama in England from the Accession of Queen Elizabeth to the Closing of the Theaters, to which is prefixed a Résumé of the Earlier Drama from its Beginnings*. 2 vols. Boston, 1908.

——. *Foreign influences in Elizabethan Plays*. New York, 1923.

Scherillo, Michele. *La commedia dell'arte in Italia, studi e profili*. Torino, 1884.

Schlegel, August Wilhelm. *Corso di letteratura drammatica*. Translated by Giovanni Gherardini. Milano, 1844.

Scott, Mary Augusta. *Elizabethan Translations from the Italian*. Boston, 1916.

Settembrini, Luigi. *Lezioni di letteratura italiana*. 3 vols. Napoli, 1869–1881.

Shakespeare, William. *The complete works of* . . . Edited by George Lyman Kittredge. Boston, 1936.

Smith, G. C. Moore. *College Plays Performed in the University of Cambridge*. Cambridge University Press, 1923.

Smith, Winifred. *The Commedia dell'Arte. A Study in Italian Popular Comedy*. New York, 1912.

Soldati, Benedetto. *Il Collegio Mamertino e le origini del teatro gesuitico con l'aggiunta di notizie inedite sulla drammatica conventuale messinese nei secoli XVI, XVII, XVIII, e con la pubblicazione della Giuditta del P. Tuccio*. Torino, 1908.

Bibliography

Solerti, Angelo. *Vita di Torquato Tasso* . . . 3 vols. Torino, 1895.

Spampanato, Vincenzo. *Quattro filosofi napoletani nel carteggio di Galileo.* Napoli, 1907.

———. *Vita di Giordano Bruno con documenti editi e inediti.* Messina, 1921.

Spingarn, Joel Elias. *Critical Essays of the Seventeenth Century.* 3 vols. Oxford, 1908.

Summonte, Giovanni Antonio. *Historia della città e regno di Napoli.* 2d ed. Napoli, 1675.

Tafuri, Giovanni Bernardino. *Istoria degli scrittori nati nel Regno di Napoli.* Vol. III. Napoli, 1754.

Tallarigo, Carlo M., and Imbriani, Vittorio. *Nuova crestomazia italiana per le scuole secondarie.* Vol. III. Napoli, 1884.

Tasso, Torquato. *Discorsi di . . . dell'arte poetica; et in particolare del poema heroica . . . Venezia,* 1587.

———. *Discorsi del poema heroico* . . . Napoli, 1594.

———. *La Gerusalemme liberata.* Preface by Rosolino Guastalla. Classici italiani e stranieri. Firenze, 1927.

———. *Il mondo creato.* Critically edited with introduction and notes by Giorgio Petrocchi. Firenze, 1951.

Terentius Afer, Publius. *Terence; with an English translation by John Sargeaunt* . . . 2 vols. The Loeb Classical Library. London, 1912.

Thorn-Drury, G. (Ed.). *Covent Garden Drollery. A Miscellany of 1672.* London, 1928.

Thorndike, Lynn. *A History of Magic and Experimental Science.* 8 vols. New York, 1923–1958.

Tiraboschi, Girolamo. *Storia della letteratura italiana* . . . 2d Modenese ed. revised and enlarged. 9 vols. Modena, 1787–1794.

Tomkis, Thomas. *Albumazar: a Comedy (1615).* Edited by Hugh G. Dick. Berkeley and Los Angeles, 1944.

Tonelli, Luigi. *Il teatro italiano dalle origini ai giorni nostri.* Milano, 1924.

Toppi, Niccolò. *Biblioteca napoletana.* Napoli, 1678.

Toscanella, Oratio. *Precetti necessarie, et altre cose utilissime, parte ridotti in capii parte in alberi sopra diverse cose pertinenti alla grammatica, poetica, retorica, historia, topica, loica, et ad altre facoltà.* Venetia, 1562.

Bibliography

Toscanò, Giovanni Matteo. *Peplus Italiae . . . In quo illustres viri grammatici, oratores, historici, poëtae, mathematici, philosophi, medici, iurisconsulti (quotquot trecentis ab hinc annis tota Italia floruerunt) eorumque patriae, professiones, & litterarum monumenta tum carmine tum soluta oratione recensentur.* Lutetiae, 1578.

Tristan L'Hermite, François. *Le parasite, comédie.* Edited with notes by Jacques Madeleine. Paris, 1934.

Turnèbe, Odet de. *Les contens.* In Fournier, Edouard (ed.). *Le théatre français au XVIe et au XVIIe siècle . . .* Paris [1871?].

Van Gundy, Justin Loomis. *"Ignoramus," comoedia coram Regia Maiestate Jacobi regis Angliae. An examination of its sources and literary influence with special reference to its relation to Butler's "Hudibras."* Lancaster, Pa., 1906.

Ward, Sir Adolphus William. *A History of English Dramatic Literature to the death of Queen Anne.* Vol. III. London, 1899.

Weinberg, Bernard. *A History of Literary Criticism in the Italian Renaissance.* 2 vols. Chicago, 1961.

Wiese, Bertoldo, and Pèrcopo, Erasmo. *Storia della letteratura italiana dalle origini ai giorni nostri.* Torino, 1904.

Wiley, W. L. *The Early Public Theatre in France.* Cambridge, Mass., 1960.

Wilkins, Ernest Hatch. *A History of Italian Literature.* Cambridge, Mass., 1954.

Zannetti, Bartolomeo. *Bartholomaeus Zannettus amico lectori . . .* [Romae, 1611]. (A second edition, slightly augmented, of the list of Della Porta's works appended to his *Elementorum curvilineorum,* 1610.)

III. ITALIAN PLAYS

The following are short titles of Italian plays, exclusive of Della Porta's which have been consulted directly for this study. In the text I have given in parentheses the earliest date associated with each play (that of its composition, dedication, first performance or first edition). The dates on this list, however, are of the editions available to me.

Alamanni, Luigi. *La Flora, comedia . . . con gl'intermedii di Andrea Lori.* Fiorenza, 1556.

Bibliography

Andreini, Giovanni Battista. *L'Adamo, sacra rapresentatione.* Milano, 1613.

Anguillara, Giovanni Andrea dell'. *Edippo, tragedia.* Vinegia, 1565.

Aretino, Pietro. *Commedie* [i.e. *La cortigiana, Il filosofo, Lo ipocrito, Il marescalco, La Talanta*] . . . *aggiuntavi L'Orazia, tragedia.* Milano, 1875.

Ariosto, Lodovico. *Commedie* . . . *La cassaria, I suppositi, La Lena, La scolastica, commedie in versi. La cassaria, I suppositi, commedie in prosa.* Firenze, 1856.

Bargagli, Girolamo. *La pellegrina, commedia.* Siena, 1589.

Benedetti, Pietro. *Il magico legato, tragicomedia pastorale.* Venezia, 1607.

Bonarelli della Rovere, Prospero. *Il Solimano, tragedia.* Roma, 1632.

Borghini, Raffaello. *L'amante furioso, comedia.* Fiorenza, 1583.

——. *La donna costante, comedia.* Fiorenza, 1582.

Bozza, Francesco. *Fedra, tragedia.* Vinegia, 1578.

Bracciolini, Francesco. *L'Evandro, tragedia.* Fiorenza, 1613.

——. *L'Harpalice, tragedia.* Fiorenza, 1613.

——. *La Pentesilea, tragedia.* Fiorenza, 1614.

Brunetto, Pier Giovanni. *David sconsolato, tragedia spirituale.* Fiorenza, 1586.

Bruno, Giordano. *Candelaio, comedia.* Pariggi, 1582.

Caetani, Filippo. *Le tre comedie famose* . . . *La schiava, L'Ortensio, Li due vecchi.* Napoli, 1644.

Campeggi, Ridolfo. *Il Tancredi, tragedia.* Bologna, 1614.

Capelletti, Giovanmaria. *Clesebia, overo scorta alla religione, comedia spirituale.* Siena, 1616.

Castelletti, Cristoforo. *Il furbo, comedia.* Vinegia, 1597.

——. *Le stravaganze d'amore, comedia.* Venetia, 1613.

——. *I torti amorosi, comedia.* Venetia, 1591.

Cecchi, Giovanni Maria. *Comedie* . . . *Il corredo, Il donzelo, La dote, Gli incantesimi, Lo spirto, La moglie, La stiava.* Venetia, 1585.

Cenati, Bernardino. *La Silvia errante, arcicomedia capriciosa morale.* Venezia, 1608.

Cigogna, Strozzi. *Delia, tragedia de pastori.* Vicenza, 1593.

Cini, Giovanni Battista. *La vedova, commedia. Con introduzione di Benedetto Croce*. Napoli, 1953.

Contile, Luca. *La comedia . . . chiamata la pescara*. Milano, 1550.

Cortone, Giacomo. *Alvida, tragedia*. Padoa, 1615.

D'Ambra, Francesco. *Commedie [i.e. Il furto, I Bernardi, La cofanaria]*. Trieste, 1858.

Decio, Antonio. *L'Acripanda, tragedia*. Firenze, 1592.

Della Valle, Federigo. *Adelonda di Frigia, tragicommedia; Iudit, tragedia; La reina di Scozia, tragedia*. In Fassò, Luigi (ed.). *Teatro del seicento*. Milano, 1956.

D'Isa, Francesco. *L'Alvida, comedia*. Napoli, 1616.

——. *La Flaminia, comedia*. Viterbo, 1622.

——. *La Fortunia, comedia*. Napoli, 1621.

——. *La Ginevra, comedia*. Napoli, 1645.

——. *Il malmaritato, comedia*. Napoli, 1628.

Dolce, Lodovico. *La Fabritia, comedia*. [Vinegia], 1549.

——. *Ifigenia, tragedia*. Venetia, 1566.

——. *La Marianna, tragedia*. Vinegia, 1565.

——. *Il Marito, comedia*. Venetia, 1586.

Dottori, Carlo de'. *L'Aristodemo, tragedia*. Padova, 1692.

Dovizi, Bernardo, cardinal Bibbiena. *La Calandria, commedia*. In Borlenghi, Aldo (ed.). *Commedie del cinquecento*, I. Milano, 1959.

Epicuro, Marc'Antonio. *Cecaria, tragicomedia*. Venezia, 1538.

Ercolani, Ercolano. *Eliodoro, commedia spirituale*. Siena, 1605.

Errico, Scipione. *Le rivolte di Parnaso, comedia*. Venezia, 1625.

Fornaris, Fabrizio de. *Angelica, comedia*. Paris, 1585.

Giraldi Cinthio, Giovanni Battista. *Le tragedie . . . Orbecche, L'Altile, Didone, Gl'Antivalomeni*. 2 vols. Venetia, 1583.

Glorizio, Ottavio. *L'impresa d'amore, comedia*. Venezia, 1607.

Gratarolo, Bongianni. *L'Astianatte, tragedia*. Vinegia, 1589.

Grazzini, Antonfrancesco (il Lasca). *Comedie . . . [i.e. La gelosia, La spiritata, La strega, La sibilla, La pinzochera, I parentadi]*. Venetia, 1582.

Groto, Luigi. *La Dalida, tragedia*. Venetia, 1572.

——. *La Emilia, comedia*. Venetia, 1583.

——. *La Hadriana, tragedia*. Venetia, 1583.

Gualterotti, Raffaelle. *La Verginia, rappresentazione amorosa*. Fiorenza, 1584.

Bibliography

Guarini, Giovanni Battista. *Il pastor fido, tragicommedia*. In Fassò, Luigi (ed.). *Teatro del seicento*. Milano, 1956.

Guazzoni, Diomisso. *L'Andromeda, tragicommedia boscareccia*. Venezia, 1587.

——. *La Quintilia, tragicomedia*. Mantova, 1579.

Guidotti, Lorenzo. *L'imbriachezza d'amore, commedia*. Roma, 1625.

Iacobilli, Vincenzo. *L'Hippolito, tragedia*. Roma, 1601.

Intronati, Sienese academy. *Comedia del sacrificio. (Gl'ingannati)*. [no place], 1537.

[——.] *L'Hortensio, comedia*. Siena, 1571.

Lanci, Cornelio. *Mestola, comedia*. Fiorenza, 1583.

Leoni, Giovanni Battista (Lauro Settizonio). *Antiloco, tragicomedia*. Ferrara, 1594.

[——.] *Roselmina, favola tragisatiricomica*. Venetia, 1595.

Liviera, Giovanni Battista. *Giustina vergine, e martire santissima, hierotragedia*. Padova [1593].

Lottini, Giovanni Angelo. *Sacra rappresentazione di S. Agnesa*. Firenze, 1592.

——. *Sacra rappresentazione di S. Lorenzo*. Firenze, 1592.

Machiavelli, Niccolò. *La mandragola, comedia*. Firenze, 1548.

Malavolti, Ubaldino. *L'amor disperato, comedia*. Siena, 1612.

——. *La menzogna, comedia*. Siena, 1614.

——. *I servi nobili, comedia*. Siena, 1604.

Marotta, Fabrizio. *Il ratto, comedia*. Napoli, 1603.

Medici, Lorenzino di Pier Francesco de'. *L'aridosia, commedia*. Trieste, 1858.

Morone, Bonaventura. *La Giustina, tragedia spirituale*. Venetia, 1617.

——. *Il mortorio di Christo, tragedia spirituale*. Cremona, 1612.

Noci, Carlo. *La Cinthia, favola pastorale*. Napoli, 1594.

Oddi, Sforza degli. *Comedie . . . Il duello d'amore et d'amicitia [Erofilomachia]. Li morti vivi. La prigione d'amore*. Vinegia, 1597.

Parabosco, Girolamo. *Comedie . . . La notte, Il viluppo, I contenti, L'hermafrodito, Il pellegrino, Il marinaio*. Vinegia, 1560.

Piccolomini, Alessandro. *L'Alessandro, comedia*. Venetia, 1554.

——. *L'amor costante, comedia*. Venetia, 1540.

Ploti, Giovanni Andrea. *Giuditta, rappresentata*. Piacenza, 1589.

Poggi, Beltrame. *La Cangenia, tragicomedia.* Fiorenza, 1561.

Razzi, Girolamo. *La balia, comedia.* Firenze, 1564.

——. *La Gostanza, comedia.* Firenze, 1565.

Salviati, Lionardo. *La Spina e il Granchio, commedie.* Trieste, 1858.

Secchi, Niccolò. *Gl'inganni, comedia.* Fiorenza, 1562.

——. *L'interesse, comedia.* Venetia, 1581.

Speroni degli Alvarotti, Sperone. *Canace, tragedia.* Vinegia, 1562.

Spezzani, Antonio. *Rappresentazione di Santa Catherina.* Bologna, 1587.

Tasso, Torquato (?). *Intrichi d'amore, comedia.* Viterbo, 1603.

——. *Il Re Torrismondo, tragedia.* Bergamo, 1587.

Torelli, Giulio Cesare. *L'anchora, comedia.* Napoli, 1604.

Torelli, Pomponio. *Merope, tragedia.* Parma, 1589.

——. *Il Polidoro, tragedia.* Parma, 1605.

——. *Il Tancredi, tragedia.* Parma, 1597.

——. *La Vittoria, tragedia.* Parma, 1605.

Trissino, Giovanni Giorgio. *La Sophonisba, tragedia.* Vicenza, 1529.

Varchi, Benedetto. *La suocera, commedia.* Trieste, 1858.

Villifranchi, Giovanni. *La greca schiava, comedia.* Firenze, 1618.

Zinano, Gabriele. *L'Almerigo, tragedia.* Reggio, 1590.

Index

Index

Index

Index

Index

Index

Index

Index

Index

Index

Index

Index

Index